King Edward VI and the Pope by unknown artist, oil on panel, circa 1570, National Portrait Gallery, London (NPG 4165)

Thomas Cranmer among friends and foes: the Archbishop's programme of reform was shaped largely by his devotion to the monarchy as the head of the Church and by his antipathy to the Papacy. The nature and pace of reform often depended on his relations with other members of the Council. Cranmer himself is seen here growing his beard on the death of Henry VIII, possibly as a sign of mourning but also clerical beards were badges of affiliation to anti-Catholic reform. (See D. MacCulloch, *Thomas Cranmer: A Life*, p. 361.) The changes in Cranmer's theology signified by this new appearance form the greater part of this book.

Signs of God's Promise

Signs of God's Promise

Thomas Cranmer's
Sacramental Theology
and the Book of Common Prayer

GORDON P. JEANES

t&t clark

Published by T&T Clark

A Continuum imprint

The Tower Building, 11 York Road, London SE1 7NX

80 Maiden Lane, Suite 704, New York, NY 10038

www.continuumbooks.com

British Library Cataloguing-in-Publication Data
A catalogue record for this book is available from the British Library

ISBN-13: 978-0-567-03188-4 (Hardback)
ISBN-13: 978-0-567-03189-6 (Paperback)

Typeset by Free Range Book Design *&* Production Limited
Printed and bound in Great Britain by Athenaeum Press Ltd, Gateshead, Tyne and Wear

In memory of Edward Yarnold SJ
liturgist and ecumenist

CONTENTS

PREFACE

This study of Cranmer was meant to have been only one chapter, or even the introduction, of a work on baptism in the Anglican tradition. But almost immediately it became obvious how vast the potential is in this field, and I remained with the first Archbishop of the Church of England. There is something attractive in the study of an individual, and I have often mused on (but not ventured to share) the 'compare and contrast' between this Reformation scholar and the equally learned and pastoral (but otherwise very different) subject of my earlier study, the fourth-century Zeno of Verona.

It would be nice to say that this is the study of a living rite, but it would not be true. I myself would have been baptized according to the baptism service of 1662 – or its successor of 1928 – and certainly I remember its use in the baptism of my younger brother. I do not remember ever baptizing anyone using the Prayer Book rite, but I have often celebrated the eucharist in that form. But 1662 is not 1552, let alone 1549, and this study is historical and ignores the later and modern perceptions and use of the altered rite. It remains with the liturgist, his times and his creation.

I manage always to take an extremely long time over my writing, and fear that I ought to be thanking people whom in my ingratitude I have forgotten, and who have forgotten me in my delays. In Durham where I began this study as a staff PhD I was foisted on the unfortunate David Brown, who gamely took up the role of supervising a strange area, and together we tyros had many an enjoyable hour. A move to Cardiff took me out of the reach of Durham, but within range of Lampeter where I could sit at the feet of David Selwyn who shared his immense knowledge of Cranmer and his period. To both, this work owes more than I can say. Also I must give my thanks to the many people who helped in various ways: among others, to Paul Ayris, Peter Macardle, Diarmaid MacCulloch, Bridget Nichols, Ashley Null, Bryan Spinks, and to all those librarians whose patience and enthusiasm are boundless despite the number and weight of ancient tomes. Paul Bradshaw and the late David Wright were kind examiners of my doctoral thesis who encouraged me to publish it, but it is thanks to Tom Kraft that I finally dedicated enough time from the parish to revise the work. My colleagues and students in the universities of Durham and Cardiff must have been weary of Cranmer, my parishioners and fellow clergy in Wandsworth must wonder what insanity obsesses their vicar, and my children, Emily, Catherine and Christopher, have no idea of life without the company of a dead Archbishop. I thank them all for their patience and encouragement.

Gordon Jeanes

TRANSCRIPTION PRACTICES

When transcribing texts from manuscripts or works which have no modern edition, the practice has been to expand abbreviations. In transcribing the letters v–u I have followed modern spelling, but left other letters as found in the text. Where manuscript underlining is reproduced, in either a manuscript or printed book, it is represented by underlining in this text. It is impossible to place manuscript marginal comments more than approximately in the right place relative to the text reproduced.

Usually where a passage has been copied from a commonplace, no attempt has been made to compare it with the presumed edition of the published original or correct it against the original. The relation of the commonplace material to the various books in Cranmer's library has yet to be fully established, and to attempt this would go far beyond the limitations of this study. The ascriptions in the commonplaces are not always accurate or complete, and so, in the more substantial passages at least, the ascription given in Migne's *Patrologia* is normally added.

ABBREVIATIONS

BL	British Library
CCCC	Corpus Christi College, Cambridge, Library
CR	Corpus Reformatorum
DNB	*Dictionary of National Biography*
DRS	*De re sacramentaria*
HBS	Henry Bradshaw Society
JEH	*Journal of Ecclesiastical History*
JTS	*Journal of Theological Studies*
LW	*Luther's Works*
PL	*Patrologia Latina*, ed. Migne
PS	Parker Society (the volume is that of the writer unless otherwise specified)
SJT	*Scottish Journal of Theology*
WA	*D. Martin Luthers Werke*

INTRODUCTION

There is an ambivalence in the study of Cranmer. As the main architect of the liturgy of the Anglican Church for some 400 years, he has obviously been a major figure, perhaps even the most important individual in the formation of Anglicanism. But there we see one major ambivalence, in that there is no such thing as Anglicanism, if we mean a school of thought or a Church with a specific and particular identifying set of beliefs. Where we can point to theological markers, such as the Book of Common Prayer or the Thirty-Nine Articles, neither remain unchanged since Cranmer's day, and the changes include significant rejections of his thought.[1] But the character and temper of the greater part of his work remained unchanged up to this century. His own scheme for a reformed Church of England remained incomplete; in particular his plans for a revised canon law were never put into effect. The incomplete reform as it was left at the death of Edward became, in many ways, the Church of England as defended by Elizabeth. This ambivalence in his theology and policy also partly produced and partly reflected the ambivalence of the man. Two decades as Archbishop of Canterbury had involved him necessarily in the tortuous policies of Henry VIII, the political subjugation of the Church and the stripping of its assets under that king and the Council of his successor, and in the humiliation of his trials and examinations under Mary. When he died he held out a hand to be burnt because it had offended, but he passed on no clear beacon to his successors. Perhaps he should appeal more to our age, which is suspicious of strong heroes, than to any other.

Most studies of Cranmer concentrate on his eucharistic theology. This reflects both the most controversial issue in his own day and the subject of greatest interest since. This work tries to examine both the

---

1   The third para. of Article 28 rejects Cranmer's opinions in the 42 Articles. C. Richardson, *Zwingli and Cranmer on the Eucharist: Cranmer Dixit et Contradixit* (Evanston, IL: Seabury–Weston Theological Seminary, 1949), p. 1. The theology of the eucharist in 1662 is different from that of 1552: see for example C.O. Buchanan, *What did Cranmer Think he was Doing?* Grove Liturgical Study, 7 (Bramcote: Grove Books, 1982; 2nd edn), pp. 30–1.

dominical sacraments together. In part this is because it began as a study in Cranmer's baptismal liturgy, and detailed examination of the baptism service is offered here while often it is simpler to refer the reader to other works on the eucharist; but also this approach provides a useful perspective on the progress of his thought, and it will be seen below that the Archbishop's sacramental theology with regard to baptism shifted towards his mature position some years in advance of his thoughts about the eucharist.

Cranmer changed his theological position at least once in important respects, in all probability more than once (leaving aside his abjurations under Mary). Following this difficult spiritual odyssey is not made any easier by the nature of the evidence. Whatever the quality of his liturgical prose, his major theological writings in defence of his eucharistic theology (*A Defence of the True and Catholic Doctrine of the Sacrament* of 1550 and *An Answer unto a Crafty and Sophistical Cavillation devised by Stephen Gardiner* of 1551) are not only polemical and negative in tone, but obscure and equivocal. They provide infinite difficulties for the sympathetic reader, and innumerable traps for the unwary. Despite the publication of much material in two volumes of the Parker Society, and in the appendices of Strype's *Memorials of Thomas Cranmer*, important sources are still unpublished, in particular the commonplace books preserved in the British Library, now often called the Great Commonplaces, and the commonplaces on eucharistic theology entitled *De re sacramentaria* in the Parker Library in Corpus Christi College, Cambridge.[2] As a prelude to this study, I have found it necessary to edit and comment on one document since it is related to the early stages of Cranmer's career.[3] Only when all the commonplaces are published (and also their actual relation to Cranmer himself established) will we have a proper picture of their potential for understanding the progress of his thought.

But recent years have been favourable for Cranmer studies. In particular two collections of essays emanated from the 500th anniversary of his birth,[4] and Diarmaid MacCulloch's magisterial biography has brought up to date the previous work by Jasper Ridley and also painted a worthy portrait of the Archbishop of the English Reformation.[5] David Selwyn's

---

2   CCCC, MS 102, pp. 151–93.

3   G.P. Jeanes, 'A Reformation Treatise on the Sacraments', *JTS*, n.s. 46 (1995), pp. 149–90.

4   P. Ayris and D.G. Selwyn (eds), *Thomas Cranmer: Churchman and Scholar* (Woodbridge: Boydell Press, 1993); M. Johnson (ed.), *Thomas Cranmer: Essays in Commemoration of the 500th Anniversary of his Birth* (Durham: Turnstone, 1990).

5   D. MacCulloch, *Thomas Cranmer: A Life* (New Haven, CT, and London: Yale University Press, 1996); J. Ridley, *Thomas Cranmer* (Oxford: Clarendon Press, 1962).

work on Cranmer's library, providing an inventory of the identified surviving volumes and assessing the overall scope of the collection, will stand as a necessary tool for Cranmer studies for generations to come.[6] In terms of Cranmer's own theology, Ashley Null's work places the question of justification at the very heart of Cranmer's theology and his programme of reform.[7] This present work on Cranmer's sacramental theology seeks to build on these significant recent achievements.

The recent years have also seen a radical change in the scholarly approach to the English Reformation in general. A.G. Dickens's *English Reformation* told the story of the Reformation as experienced and appreciated by ordinary people, the new evangelicals.[8] It fell to other scholars to tell the same story as it was experienced but not appreciated by other ordinary people, those labelled as the traditionalists.[9] But I warm to Felicity Heal's questioning of the approach which she calls 'the "it all depended on what happened in Much Snoring" mentality'. The international perspective was also important but, most importantly, Heal says,

> Does it in fact matter as much as our protagonists have suggested that something did, or did not, happen in Much Snoring? How far were Tudor monarchs and their religious counsellors responsive to the concerns and needs of the populace? . . . There is an awareness that a more subtle and complex narrative is needed in the face of the last thirty years, that the interaction between leading reformers, crown, court, government and gentry requires more reflection, and perhaps different methodological approaches.[10]

Her words have echoed in my mind as I have tried to bring together my study of one man's sacramental theology. MacCulloch's Cranmer the Archbishop is one who is involved in politics and administration, who is so busy fighting his corner, as it were, that it is a tribute to his

---

6   D. Selwyn, *The Library of Thomas Cranmer* (Oxford: Oxford Bibliographical Society, 1996).

7   Ashley Null, *Thomas Cranmer's Doctrine of Repentance* (Oxford: Oxford University Press, 2000).

8   A.G. Dickens, *The English Reformation* (London: Batsford, 1989; 2nd edn).

9   E.g. J.J. Scarisbrick, *The Reformation and the English People* (Oxford: Basil Blackwell, 1984); C. Haigh, *English Reformations: Religion, Politics and Society under the Tudors* (Oxford: Clarendon Press, 1993); E. Duffy, *The Stripping of the Altars: Traditional Religion in England 1400–1580* (New Haven, CT, and London: Yale University Press, 1992); idem, *The Voices of Morebath: Reformation and Rebellion in an English Village* (New Haven, CT, and London: Yale University Press, 2001).

10   F. Heal, 'The English Reformation Revisited', *Ecclesiastical Law Journal*, 4 (1996), pp. 450–1.

energy and determination that he achieved as much as he did. Null's Cranmer the theologian is one who evolves his understanding of justification not in solitary study or in sympathetic company, but in debate and competition with theologians of a very different outlook, each battling for the ear of Henry VIII. I hope to complement these with a picture of Cranmer the liturgist, widely read in traditional and new forms of liturgy, anxious to apply his theological principles to liturgical reform but also engaged in a continual dilemma: how far to try to carry consensus with him, and where to stand boldly on principle. In this respect others come into the story, both fellow reformers and also others less sympathetic to his endeavour, sometimes known to us by name, sometimes anonymous.

In the past it has seemed difficult for people to believe that Cranmer was his own master. Even in his own day, contemporary reformers gossiped about him as though he were going to be won over by the latest guest to stay in Lambeth Palace. 'Bucer has very great influence with him.'[11] 'That Thomas [Cranmer] himself . . . by the goodness of God and the instrumentality of that most upright and judicious man, master John à Lasco, is in a great measure recovered from his dangerous lethargy.'[12] 'Ye [Cranmer] have gotten nothing by this your reasoning, my lord, but only declared thereby your ignorance, as ye do, when you following your great God, Peter Martyr, deny that these words, this is my body, are the words of consecration.'[13]

At the beginning of this century, many, especially those of the Anglo-Catholic wing of the Anglican Church, believed that the first Prayer Book of 1549 represented his true preference, but he was influenced by the more extreme reformers who in the second Prayer Book pushed him further than he wanted to go. Thus for example Procter and Frere's *New History of the Book of Common Prayer* has an entire section with the title, 'Influence of Foreigners', summarizing the activities of some of these characters. That work describes how they had been allowed to interfere with the process of revision, something which had not been allowed in the case of the first Prayer Book, and the whole sorry tale reaches its climax with the words, 'Thus against the Archbishop's will

---

11   John Hooper to Bullinger, 31 May 1549, in *Original Letters relative to the English Reformation*, ed. H. Robinson, PS, 2 vols (PS) (Cambridge: Cambridge University Press, 1846–47), Vol. 1, p. 64.

12   John ab Ulmis to Bullinger, 27 November 1548, PS, *Original Letters*, Vol. 2, p. 383.

13   Richard Smith, *A Confutation of a certain Book, called a Defence of the True and Catholic Doctrine of the Sacrament etc. set forth of late in the name of Thomas Archbishop of Canterbury* (Paris: Chaudière, 1550), fols 50ᵛ–1; quoted by P.M.J. McNair, 'Peter Martyr in England', in J.C. McLelland (ed.), *Peter Martyr Vermigli and Italian Reform* (Waterloo, Ontario: Wilfred Laurier University Press, 1980), pp. 85–105 (91).

and without the consent of the Church, English religion reached its low water mark and the ill-starred book of 1552 began its brief career.'[14]

A period of important publications in Cranmer studies over two decades from 1945 to 1965 began with Dom Gregory Dix's *Shape of the Liturgy*. He changed the agenda of the debate when he proposed that Cranmer's eucharistic theology from 1547 onwards was that of Zwingli.[15] This proposal was a momentous one. It could be said with very little exaggeration that it ended one false trail in Cranmer studies but started another. The trail which ended was that just described as typified by Procter and Frere. Since Dix's work, even Anglo-Catholics were forced to contemplate the fact that Cranmer himself sincerely held and promoted the theology of the 1552 communion service, and indeed had held that very position in 1549. But the Archbishop still had not been emancipated from foreign influences. The false trail begun was the debate over whether Cranmer was indeed a Zwinglian, or a Calvinist, or a Bucerian, or by whom else he may have been influenced (Ridley? Hooper? Martyr? Laski? Osiander?).[16] Every possibility seems to have been attempted except the hypothesis that he knew his own mind and reached his own opinions. Even G.W. Bromiley, the only person to write an entire (brief) book on Cranmer's theology as a whole, and the only person I have found from this period who could speak of him influencing others as well as being influenced by others, spoke of him as more the pure scholar than the independent thinker: 'His primary impulse was to amass knowledge rather than to state or discuss it.'[17] And apart

---

14 *New History of the Book of Common Prayer* (London: Macmillan, 1905; 2nd edn, 3rd corr. imp.), pp. 66–90, esp. p. 85.

15 *The Shape of the Liturgy* (Westminster: Dacre Press, 1945), pp. 646, 656.

16 As a selection of imputations of influence, in addition to those discussed in this study, there are, *inter alios*:

For Osiander, P. Wilson-Kastner, 'Andreas Osiander's Probable Influence on Thomas Cranmer's Eucharistic Theology', *Sixteenth Century Journal*, 14 (1983), pp. 411–25; cf. P. Collinson, 'Thomas Cranmer', in G. Rowell (ed.), *The English Religious Tradition and the Genius of Anglicanism* (Wantage: Ikon Productions, 1992), pp. 79–104 (97–8).

For Martyr, J.C. McLelland, and G.E. Duffield (eds), *The Life, Early Letters and Eucharistic Writings of Peter Martyr*, Courtenay Library of Reformation Classics, 5 (Abingdon: Sutton Courtenay Press, 1989), pp. 116–17; M. Anderson, 'Rhetoric and Reality: Peter Martyr and the English Reformation', *Sixteenth Century Journal*, 19 (1988), pp. 451–69.

S. Leuenberger cites the 'powerful influence' of Martyr, Bucer and Hooper in *Archbishop Cranmer's Immortal Bequest* (Grand Rapids, MI: Eerdmans, 1990), p. 88. W. Nijenhuis, 'Traces of a Lutheran eucharistic doctrine in Thomas Cranmer' in *Ecclesia Reformata: Studies on the Reformation* (Leiden: Brill, 1972), pp. 1–22, says he was 'subject to manifold influences' (p. 3) and, in addition to Lutheran sources, cites Ridley (p. 19), Martyr and Laski (p. 21).

17 *Thomas Cranmer, Theologian* (London: Lutterworth Press, 1956), pp. 3–4, 7.

from Bromiley, nearly all of the literature on Cranmer's thought focuses entirely on his understanding of the eucharist. Other sacraments, and other issues in theology, are rarely mentioned. We must now follow some of the mileposts along this sorry path.

To begin with Dix: in a lengthy discussion of Cranmer's eucharistic theology he includes three issues we need to concentrate on for consideration of his general sacramental theology. On the question of the eucharistic presence of Christ, Dix understands the Archbishop as saying that 'spiritually eating the Body and drinking the Blood of Christ' means *'thinking with faith that Christ died for my sins on Calvary'*. On the question of the sacrament conferring or only signifying grace, we are told that the right use of the Lord's Supper is as a testimony to confirm the faith of the communicant. And on the relation of the elements and action to the grace, he says that for Cranmer consecration is the setting apart of a common thing to a spiritual use, so that it represents the spiritual but undergoes no change.[18]

The reply to Dix was led by George Timms, who among other points questioned Dix's understanding of Cranmer's use of 'faith' as being 'mere mental remembrance'. Rather it was, he said, an 'unconditional self-commitment to the Saviour which results in mystic union with him'.[19] Timms has a sound grasp of Cranmer's concerns in his eucharistic theology, though he falls into a curious description of it with his 'dynamic receptionism'. He sees the ways in which Cranmer is more guarded in speaking about the eucharist than baptism, but like other writers links him with Bucer and Calvin.[20]

Cyril Richardson contributed two important works to the debate. In his first, a lecture, *Zwingli and Cranmer on the Eucharist: Cranmer Dixit et Contradixit*, he picks up the question of whether Cranmer should be classed as Zwinglian and in what ways. Richardson sets out a summary of Zwingli's teaching and points out the essential features underlying it, denying that the Christian can participate in the substance of the body of Christ and also that the consecrated elements bear an essential relation to this substance; and affirming that participation in the substance of the body of Christ is irrelevant: 'the flesh profiteth nothing' (Jn 6.63); and that the holy cannot be mediated by physical objects.[21] For Zwingli the sacraments cannot convey grace.[22] Cranmer uses many of the same

---

18   *Shape of the Liturgy*, pp. 648–56.

19   'Dixit Cranmer', Part 1 *CQR* 143 (January–March 1947), pp. 217–34, and Part 2 Vol. 144 (April–June 1947), pp. 33–51; also published separately (London: A.R. Mowbray, 1947).

20   'Dixit Cranmer', Part 2, pp. 37, 39.

21   *Cranmer Dixit et Contradixit*, pp. 11–12.

22   *Cranmer Dixit et Contradixit*, p. 12.

scriptural verses as Zwingli, and like him, but unlike Calvin and Bucer, affirms Christ's presence by his divinity, not by his humanity in the substance of his flesh. Richardson says the issue is not *whether* Christ is present, but *how* he is present.[23] There are, however, differences between Cranmer and Zwingli. In particular Cranmer believes that God acts in the sacrament, whereas for Zwingli the sacrament is a token of God's previous action.[24] Richardson also analyses Cranmer's language of union with Christ and claims that it is based on a traditional realist notion of the incarnation, but is not related to the sacramental action because of Cranmer's nominalist views. Why such a contradictory approach? Richardson attributes this to an exaggerated reaction by Cranmer against the medieval practice of the Mass; however he had simply accepted the traditional view of the incarnation and had failed to apply the logic of one issue to the other.[25] Richardson finishes his article with a note on the shift in Cranmer's theology around 1548 and a brief consideration of his baptismal theology (which we shall consider below), bringing out the difference between Zwingli and Cranmer in that the latter affirms strongly the sacrament as an instrument of God's grace. The outstanding feature of Richardson's approach is that he tries to identify landmarks to distinguish between these theologians as well as simply noting points in common. One of great importance, which we shall use as an important landmark throughout this study, is the analogy of the sun used by the reformers to explain their various notions of the eucharistic presence of the humanity of Christ.[26] Such an approach might seem self-evident, but as we shall see it has rarely if ever been followed. Perhaps it is a pity that in the light of this approach Richardson could ask again in his conclusion, 'Was Cranmer a Zwinglian?' His reply is qualified: Cranmer's 'Eucharistic thought moved within the basic framework of Zwingli's opinions. Yet he is distinguished from the Zurich reformer in esteeming the Lord's Supper more highly and in emphasizing that faithful observance is accompanied by the operation of God's grace.'[27] Here Richardson might fairly have included other reformers' names (earlier he notes points in common with Bucer), but to this extent at least the debate remains set in the path mapped out by Dix.[28]

In *The Mass and the English Reformers*, C.W. Dugmore argued that Cranmer espoused a patristic and early medieval rather than Reformed

23 *Cranmer Dixit et Contradixit*, for Cranmer, pp. 20–3; for Zwingli, p. 16.
24 *Cranmer Dixit et Contradixit*, pp. 33–5.
25 *Cranmer Dixit et Contradixit*, p. 47.
26 *Cranmer Dixit et Contradixit*, pp. 23–6.
27 *Cranmer Dixit et Contradixit*, p. 48.
28 Cf. J.R. Porter, review of Richardson, *Cranmer Dixit et Contradixit*, *JTS*, n.s. 4 (1953), pp. 62–3.

doctrine of the eucharist, though he has enjoyed little following.[29] Indeed it could be said that the patristic doctrine of the eucharist was (next to that of scripture) precisely the point under dispute. Peter Brooks in his study, *Thomas Cranmer's Doctrine of the Eucharist*, was as eager to deny Zwinglianism as Dix was to support it. Brooks gave the classic description of the 'three-stage' theory of Cranmer's theological development, namely that he was, by turn, a traditional Catholic, then a Lutheran, then a Reformed. He used the commonplaces and *De re sacramentaria* in search of material for the two later stages.[30] However, he gave less evidence for the details of Cranmer's final doctrinal position than he did for his 'Lutheran' phase. Brooks maintained that Zwinglianism was a thing of the past by the 1540s and 1550s and that Cranmer should be seen as fully in the same camp as the major Reformed theologians, Bucer and Calvin (among others).[31] He dubbed the theological position of this group after the *Consensus Tigurinus* as that of the 'True' Presence of Christ in the Eucharist, and applied this title to Cranmer's own view.[32] Brooks was circumspect in identifying Cranmer wholeheartedly with any one theologian, and maintained that he was not a 'blind disciple' of Oecolampadius, but that Bucer 'approved of what he took to be Cranmer's basic position'.[33] He maintained this line more on the basis of the *Consensus Tigurinus* than on any close comparison of theological positions. He mentioned, but failed to discuss, Richardson's point about the analogy of the sun.

Richardson returned to the debate again in his second work, the review article in which he criticized Dugmore's *The Mass and the English Reformers*, and set out a summary of Cranmer's eucharistic theology.[34] This is a most useful and judicious overview of publications on Cranmer in the previous few years, and it is perhaps due to the subsequent dearth of Cranmer studies that Richardson's contribution has been neglected. After a discussion of his philosophical position and a brief discussion of Brooks and Dugmore, Richardson restated his earlier position by setting out things that are clear in Cranmer and things that are unclear. In the first category he cited the following:

---

29   *The Mass and the English Reformers* (London: Macmillan, 1958), reviewed by T.M. Parker, *JTS*, n.s. 19 (1961), pp. 132–46.

30   But see my comments in 'Reformation Treatise', pp. 165–7.

31   Brooks understands Richardson as reaffirming and strengthening Dix's basic position, though he quotes only the first half of Richardson's balanced conclusion cited above, and omits the ways in which Cranmer is 'distinguished from the Zurich reformer'. *Thomas Cranmer's Doctrine of the Eucharist* (London: Macmillan, 1992; 2nd edn), p. 58, and n. 4.

32   *Cranmer's Doctrine of the Eucharist*, pp. 61–71.

33   *Cranmer's Doctrine of the Eucharist*, pp. 91, 76 and n. 1.

34   'Cranmer and the Analysis of Eucharistic Doctrine', *JTS*, n.s.16 (1965), pp. 421–37.

1. The body of Christ is an empirical object located in a definite and circumscribed space in heaven.
2. Christ is present by his divinity and not by his humanity.
3. The bread and wine remain bread and wine. They cannot receive sanctification or holiness. Nature cannot participate in the holy.
4. The patriarchs spiritually fed on Christ just as Christians do. The sacrament is the same thing as what goes on in preaching and meditation.

In the category of the unclear Richardson repeated his claim that there is a clash between a nominalist view of sacramental theology and an understanding of the incarnation based on realist notions, so that the mutual indwelling of Christ and the believer based on the incarnation seems to contradict Cranmer's affirmation of the absence of Christ's body from the eucharist.

Richardson made a strong point in claiming that Cranmer was a 'Nominalist' but only in a popular and unsophisticated manner. Things are self-enclosed objects: when a wafer is broken its substance is likewise broken; the sun's rays do not participate in its substance.[35] Richardson's article in many ways closed the two decades of study opened by Dix. It may well be that it is Brooks's work which has been more often read, but that has been to the detriment of Cranmer studies which have forgotten much important work.

It was in 1993 that Basil Hall offered the most detailed and stringent critique of Brooks's work in an excursus to his own study, 'Cranmer, the Eucharist and the Foreign Divines'. Among other things he objected to Brooks's use of the term 'True Presence' to describe the Archbishop's mature theology, to a confusion of Bucer and Calvin with the 'Swiss', and to his suggestion that the *Consensus Tigurinus* represented a real agreement between Calvin and the Berne pastors.[36] However, on the most important point Hall was at one with Brooks,

---

35   'Cranmer and the Analysis of Eucharistic Doctrine', pp. 421–2, reviewing articles by E.K. McGee 'Cranmer and Nominalism', *Harvard Theological Review*, 57 (1964), pp. 189–216, and W.J. Courtenay, 'Cranmer as a Nominalist, *Sed contra*', *Harvard Theological Review*, 57 (1964), pp. 367–80. McGee responded with a restatement of his position in 'Cranmer's Nominalism Reaffirmed', *Harvard Theological Review*, 59 (1966), pp. 192–6'. However, against this approach, the consistent and important treatment which we shall see Cranmer adopted of baptism and the eucharist as two members of the same species, as it were, is hardly Nominalist thinking. The 'universal', the sacrament, is determinative for Cranmer's understanding of baptism and the eucharist as it was for many of his fellow reformers, though he appeals to the principle as often as any of them.
36   'Cranmer, the Eucharist and the Foreign Divines', in Ayris and Selwyn, *Thomas Cranmer, Churchman and Scholar*, pp. 217–58 (51–8).

for he enthusiastically made a case for the thesis that Cranmer was a Bucerian.[36] Yet there is very little detailed discussion of his theological or liturgical writings. The main bulk of this article is an identity parade of the various suspect theologians, and the evidence considered is largely circumstantial. For example, Laski is said to have had no theological influence on Cranmer, largely because Hall could detect no influence on the English liturgy.[38] Likewise Martyr's influence on the liturgy is played down – the differences between his draft for the Communion exhortation and the English translation, very small in my own view, are stressed.[39] On the other hand, Bucer's liturgical influence is emphasized, though the extent to which, for example, his *Censura* is followed or ignored by Cranmer is not discussed in any meaningful detail.[40] Nor are the differences between Bucer and Cranmer such as are outlined by Richardson discussed or explained by Hall.

Moving away from the question of eucharistic theology, Cranmer's understanding of baptism has received scant attention from scholars. Cyril Richardson devoted to the sacrament an Appendix in his *Cranmer Dixit et Contradixit*, mainly in order to establish the difference between the Cranmerian and the Zwinglian views of the sacrament. For Zwingli, baptism is a sign of something that has taken place. For Cranmer, it is 'a means through which much the same thing takes place'. The distinction between the sign and the reality makes the connection somewhat difficult to maintain, but, as Richardson says, for Cranmer, 'God works *with* his sacraments, but not *in* them.'[41] As well as various references in his general work on baptism in the Anglican Reformation,[42] Bromiley devoted a chapter to the subject in his study of *Thomas Cranmer, Theologian*.[43] This work is mainly a survey of the material to be found in the Parker Society volumes. As MacCulloch says, the absence of the theme of predestination creates a strange picture of the Archbishop, which makes the portrait as a whole a flawed one.[44] But Bromiley gave an accurate description of the distinction between the spiritual presence and action of Christ in the faithful (or elect) recipient, and the sacramental action of the sign itself; also the essential similarity of the two sacraments of baptism and the eucharist. These and other themes will be examined in detail below.

---

37   'Cranmer, the Eucharist and the Foreign Divines', pp. 217–51.
38   'Cranmer, the Eucharist and the Foreign Divines', pp. 224–5, 243.
39   'Cranmer, the Eucharist and the Foreign Divines', pp. 227–34.
40   'Cranmer, the Eucharist and the Foreign Divines', pp. 225–6, 235–7.
41   *Cranmer Dixit et Contradixit*, pp. 52–4.
42   *Baptism and the Anglican Reformers* (London: Lutterworth Press, 1953).
43   *Cranmer, Theologian*, pp. 57–68.
44   MacCulloch, *Cranmer*, p. 211.

Between 1965 and the publications marking the quincentenary of Cranmer's birth, the more important publications have been in the liturgical world. Geoffrey Cuming's *History of Anglican Liturgy* was published in 1969 and a second edition appeared in 1982. This gives a good general introduction to the period. His *Godly Order*, which appeared in 1983, as well as looking at other aspects of the history of the Anglican Prayer Book, enquires more closely into aspects of Cranmer's work. Colin Buchanan's examination of the eucharist of 1549 and 1552, *What did Cranmer Think he was Doing?* is one of the most accurate and imaginative exercises in liturgical exegesis. Generally the liturgists are the ones most likely to acknowledge the independence of Cranmer. This is not just a matter of sentiment. It is one of the outstanding features of the Edwardine Prayer Books that they possess a remarkable coherence which seems to reflect the guiding hand of a single author. Committees existed and conducted their business, as we shall see. We know of occasional contributions from other writers, of which the most obvious was Martyr's contribution of an exhortation in the eucharist.[45] But, hard as it is to conceive of one man composing the entire Prayer Book (much of it radically revised after only a few years), it is also hard to see the work or influence of others. No doubt chaplains and secretaries contributed, but it is probable that the Archbishop closely supervised whatever he himself did not compose.

However, it would be a mistake to suppose that Cranmer's liturgies, any more than his theology, were composed in the carefree company of likeminded friends. As well as seeking to discover the appropriate liturgical expression of his theological principles (and the spirit of the age was such that dogmatic theology was seen as the mistress of liturgy), he had to take into account not only the pastoral situation of a people content with their worship and unreceptive to reform, but also the doctrinal definitions arrived at by the state and the opinions of theologians (both fellow-travellers and opponents) whom he needed to mollify or refute.

This work attempts to set Cranmer the liturgist in this context. He was a man who knew his own mind, and who had worked hard over the years to discover his own theological views. To that extent we can regard Cranmer as free from the 'influence' of his colleagues and seek to understand and take seriously his theological position. And as the picture is revealed, it will be seen that his liturgical work is both consistent with his theology and also expresses it to a high degree of exactitude and sophistication. There is no need to see liturgy as a rough

---

45 A. Beesley, 'An Unpublished Source of the Book of Common Prayer: Peter Martyr Vermigli's *Adhortatio ad Coenam Domini Mysticam*', *JEH*, 19 (1968), pp. 83–8.

and ready version of theology, lacking its precision. While it will be seen that some parts of the liturgy are ambiguous, indeed often deliberately so, in other respects the liturgy will be an essential part of our attempts to understand Cranmer's theological position.

So much for Cranmer the individual. But the views of other people of his time will need to be considered, first in order to establish by way of comparison and contrast the Archbishop's own position, secondly in order to see ways in which he may have needed to take others' views into account. This is the portrayal of the liturgist as pastor and politician, the one who strives for consensus or who needs to stand on principle.

In order to build up the portrait, first we shall examine the practice and, as far as we know it, the contemporary perception of baptism and the eucharist just before the Reformation. Then we shall follow the basic story of the reforms under Henry VIII and Edward VI and trace the development of Cranmer's thought with it. The first years of Edward's reign and the first Prayer Book of 1549 will have to be examined in great detail, since it was at this point that the Archbishop experienced a radical change in his theology, reflected in the liturgy of the Prayer Book. The second Prayer Book of 1552 is, by comparison, simple to understand; and it comes at the end of the story as a monument to the theologian who had achieved a new and consistent understanding of the sacraments. Ironically that Prayer Book lasted for only the remaining months of Edward's life, and its subsequent history (which lies beyond this present study) reveals the influence of a different theology from that of Thomas Cranmer.

Chapter 1

THE TRADITIONAL RITES:
PRACTICE AND PERCEPTIONS

1 BAPTISM

a. Sources

In England and Wales the traditional rite of baptism followed the medieval forms. Cranmer and his colleagues had no practical experience of any other. The Sarum *Manual* was most commonly followed.[1] Of course we know very little of how it was actually used. There is always the customary use as well as the actual text. Both are influential, but for the most part we have no more than a few clues of the former, and are forced to rely on the latter.

The absolute necessity of baptism for salvation was widely agreed, though Lollards had long disputed it and attacked the sacrament.[2] Tyndale mocks the common concern over whether a child has been properly baptized:

Ask the people what they understand by their baptism or washing. And thou shalt see, that they believe how that the very plunging into the water saveth them; of the promises they know not, nor what is signified thereby . . . Behold how narrowly the people look on the ceremony. If aught be left out, or if the child be not altogether dipt in the water, or if, because the child is sick, the priest dare not plunge him into the water, but pour water on his head,

---

1   G.J. Cuming, *A History of Anglican Liturgy* (London: Macmillan, 1982; 2nd edn), p. 14, compares the 13 printed editions of the Sarum *Manual* with the two of the York *Manual* between 1475 and 1549. For a modern critical edition of the *Manual*, we use *Manuale ad Usum Percelebris Ecclesiae Sarisburiensis*, ed. A.J. Collins; Henry Bradshaw Society, 91 (Chichester: Moore & Tillyer, 1958). No manuals for the other 'uses' of England and Wales were printed. W. Maskell, *Monumenta Ritualia Ecclesiae Anglicanae*, 3 vols (London: William Pickering, 1846), Vol. 1, pp. 3–32, notes the differences of the York *Manual* text from the baptismal rite of the Sarum *Manual*. None are of particular interest for our study of Cranmer.

2   Margaret Aston, *Faith and Fire* (London and Rio Grande: Hambledon Press, 1993), pp. 256–7, gives examples of Lollard attacks on baptism from the fifteenth and early sixteenth centuries.

how tremble they! How quake they! 'How say ye, Sir John', say they, 'is this child christened enough? Hath it his full christendom?' They believe verily that the child is not christened . . .[3]

The necessity of baptism was assumed, not argued, by Mirk's *Instructions for Parish Priests*, in which is provided a detailed description of the right administration of baptism, in particular the right pronunciation of the baptismal formula. Midwives are given explicit advice on how to baptize a child in the case of difficult childbirth: it is important that water should come in contact with the child.[4] Maskell quotes an account from the consistorial acts of the diocese of Rochester in 1523, of a baptism delivered by a midwife in which she affirms,

I the aforesaid Elizabeth [Gaynesforde] seeing the child of Thomas Everey late born in jeopardy of life, by the authority of mine office, then being midwife, did christen the same child under this manner, 'In the name of the Father, the Son and the Holy Ghost, I christen thee Denys; effundend' meram aquam super caput infantul.'

The child was subsequently successfully delivered, taken to church where the priest 'gave to it that christendom that lacked, and the child is yet alive'.[5] In respect of midwife baptism, here we certainly have a case in which the text of the *Manual* is to be read with caution, since a note at the end of the service says that lay people may not baptize except in case of necessity, and then a man should, all things being equal, baptize rather than a woman.[6] In whatever circumstances this applied, it ignored the reality of the situation in which the midwife was the person at hand in the vast majority of cases when baptism was urgently required and, as seen in the case above, carried the authority to baptize by virtue of her office. Bishop Rowland Lee's Injunctions for the Diocese of Lichfield and Coventry in 1537 carried the following requirement which seems to have been entirely conventional:

Ye shall teach and instruct your parishioners, at least twelve times in the year, the spiritual manner and form of Christenings in English; and that the midwife may use it in time of necessity;

---

3   *Obedience of a Christian Man*, in *Works*, ed. H. Walter, PS, 3 vols (Cambridge: Cambridge University Press, 1848–50), Vol. 1, pp. 276–7.

4   John Mirk, *Instructions for Parish Priests*, ed. G. Kristensson, Lund Studies in English, 49 (Lund: Gleerup, 1974), pp. 96–102.

5   Maskell, *Monumenta Ritualia*, Vol. 1, pp. ccix–ccx.

6   Sarum *Manual*, p. 41.

commanding the women when the time of birth draweth near, to have at all seasons a vessel of clean water for the same purpose.[7]

The Sarum *Manual* carried the basic instructions for valid baptism,[8] as fulfilled by Elizabeth Gaynesforde. For further details one could look to Mirk.

As for the actual performance of the rite in church, rather than taking the text of the *Manual* at face value, as it were, it might be better to approach it through the perceptions of contemporary writers who were seeking to address the ordinary people of the time. We shall therefore not look at the text of the service in any detail until we consider Cranmer's revision of it. Suffice it here to summarize the contents of the rite.[9]

The rite begins at the church door. According to the introductory title in the *Manual*, the first part is engaged with making the infant into a catechumen. The child receives the sign of the cross on the forehead and breast. Some prayers are recited; then salt is exorcized and placed in the child's mouth. There follow a series of exorcisms; different forms are given for boys and girls. The gospel of Jesus receiving and blessing the children is read from the gospel according to Matthew, and then the priest spits into his left hand and with the spittle touches the right ear, the nostrils and the left ear; the accompanying formula repeats Christ's saying over the deaf-mute – *effeta* – and speaks of opening the candidate to the odour of sweetness and to the devil taking flight. The priest and godparents recite the Lord's Prayer, Hail Mary and Apostles' Creed, the priest makes a sign of the cross on the child's right hand, blesses it, and then the party proceeds to the font. The *Manual* then details the blessing of the font. Some instructions to the godparents are inserted here in English: they are to recite the Lord's Prayer, Hail Mary and the Apostles' Creed (this time presumably in the vernacular) for the fruitful ministration of the sacrament, and they are charged to take good care of the child and teach it these formulas and see that it be confirmed. The blessing of the font would not have happened at most baptisms, and so the priest would have turned directly to the section marked, 'De baptismo'. The godparents in the child's name renounce the devil; the child is anointed on its breast and back. Then they affirm belief in God, Father, Son and Holy Spirit, and the child is baptized with a threefold

---

7   W.H. Frere (ed.), *Visitation Articles And Injunctions Of The Period Of The Reformation*, Alcuin Club Collections, 14, 3 vols (London: Longmans, Green, 1910), Vol. 2, p. 23. (Lee for York [pp. 49–50] and Shaxton for Salisbury have similar injunctions in 1538 [p. 58] but the index then gives nothing until Bonner in 1554 [p. 335].)
8   Sarum *Manual*, pp. 38–9.
9   Text in the Sarum *Manual*, pp. 25–38. See trans. in E.C. Whitaker, *Documents of the Baptismal Liturgy*, ed. M.E. Johnson (London: SPCK, 2003; 3rd edn), pp. 284–307.

immersion. Finally the *Manual* describes how the child is to be anointed on the head, dressed in a white garment and given a lighted candle. If a bishop is present, the child is straightaway confirmed, and then, if old enough (hardly likely in late medieval England), receives communion. The instructions to the godparents are given again in the text, only this time in Latin, and Mk 9.16–28 is read (a defence against epilepsy) and then Jn 1.1–14.

Such is the shape of the rite as given in the *Manual*. We have a number of texts which can help us to learn something of how the rite was perceived and understood.

Thordynary of crysten men, a work first published in 1504 and the adaptation of a French work, was frequently reprinted in the early sixteenth century and was no doubt influential. It gives a large amount of space to the consideration of baptism. The correct performance of emergency baptism is described (it is of course a Christian duty).[10] The 'vertue and theffecte' of baptism is set out in a list of 'goodnesses' to the soul, of which the first four are signified by the properties of the water of the sacrament: the soul is cleansed from sin; the corruption of fallen human nature is cooled; the soul is refreshed; and finally it bears spiritual fruits. Then we are told that in baptism the soul receives the livery, the token and character of the sacrament which distinguishes the Christian from pagans; it receives grace and knowledge and is incorporated into the Church, the mystical body of Christ; it is freed from 'the oblygacion in that every person not baptysed is bounden'; and finally by baptism the gate of heaven is opened to the soul.[11] The full text of the rite is given in the *Ordynary*, and it is also translated and a detailed commentary added.

A description of the rite of baptism in church, as experienced in 1537, is given to us by *A Declaracion of the Seremonies a nexid to the Sacrament of Baptyme*.[12] This document is larded with heavy criticism of the clergy and a deep scepticism concerning the efficacy of water baptism, and in both respects might seem to be allied with old or new dissent (though criticism of the clergy was unremarkable). The author was probably Thomas Gibson, who printed a number of books between 1535 and 1539. He seems to have been trained in medicine at Cambridge, and had links and sympathies with the reforming theologians from that university. Hugh Latimer describes

---

10   *Thordynary of crysten men* (London: Wynken de Worde, 1506), sig. A5ᵛ. The French original of the rite is *L'Ordinaire des chrétiens* (Paris: Iehan Petit, 1502), sig. A6–C4.

11   *Ordynary of crysten men*, sig. D2–D2ᵛ.

12   T. Gibson, *Declaracion of the Seremonies a nexid to the Sacrament of Baptyme, what they Sygnyffie and how we owght to understande them* (London: James Nicholson? 1537).

him sympathetically in a letter to Cromwell, in which he introduces him as an associate of Edward Crome and a possible printer for the Bishops' Book: 'He is an honest poor man and will set it forth in a good letter, and set it good cheap, whereas other do sell too dear, which doth let many to buy.' Gibson himself generally wrote the books he published, and the present work certainly shows more enthusiasm than learning.[13]

The author of the *Declaracion* makes no attempt to attack the rite as such. The problem is that the clergy and people are not living up to it. The account therefore probably gives us a good picture of the rite of baptism as experienced on the eve of the Reformation. More scholarly and of unimpeachable orthodoxy, the draft so-called *Rationale of Ceremonial* will be seen to support the approach of the *Declaracion* in identifying what was of interest to those who experienced the rite and how it might have been understood at least by the more learned participants. The *Rationale* was drafted by a committee set up in April 1540, but unlike its sister committee which in 1543 produced the King's Book, it failed to get its work authorized. Two manuscript versions survive: that in the Cotton manuscripts of the British Library, Cleopatra E V, seems to have a more Catholic version, while that in Lambeth Palace Library, MS 1107, is of a more Protestant flavour. MacCulloch and Duffy see the gaps in the *Rationale*, for example no discussion of the eucharistic sacrifice, as showing the lack of agreement between the various parties, but Duffy recognizes that overall the *Rationale* presents a 'decisive reaffirmation of the value of the traditional ceremonies'.[14]

None of the documents is anything like a perfect witness of the traditional perception of the service. The English works are infected, in one way or another, with Reformation sympathies, and all reflect the concerns of the intelligentsia rather than of the great majority of churchgoers. But they are addressed, in one way or another, to the ordinary churchgoer and might be supposed to take into account such a readership or audience.

---

13 For Thomas Gibson see the *DNB* and E.G. Duff, *A Century of the English Book Trade* (London: Bibliographical Society, 1948), p. 55. J. McConica, *English Humanists and Reformation Politics* (Oxford: Clarendon Press, 1968), p. 172, says that this publication had official status, but this may be overrating the piece.
14 *Rationale of Ceremonial*, ed. C.S. Cobb, Alcuin Club collections, 18 (London: Longmans, Green, 1910); MacCulloch, *Cranmer*, p. 276; Duffy, *Stripping of the Altars*, p. 428. It is not altogether clear how the two manuscripts relate to one another. MacCulloch believes the Lambeth version to be based on the British Library version; Cobb (pp. lxv–lxix) says the Lambeth version is the earlier one.

In addition we have a number of anecdotal references to baptism services, and some idea of the pomp of aristocratic baptisms from contemporary rules governing the royal household of Henry VII (dated 1494) and the household of the Earl of Huntingdon (drawn up in 1525).[15] These are obviously exceptional, but we shall also see connections with very modest occasions.

In the absence of any other guide to the whole service, we shall follow the three theological commentaries and include other evidence where it exists. Since the *Declaracion* does not enjoy a modern edition, and since it is the more simple description of the commentaries, its text is given in full below and will shape our approach to the baptism service.

b. Preparations

The service begins in the porch. The ordinances for the royal and earl's household go to considerable lengths describing the decoration of the church with various hangings of silk and arras, and the latter makes much of decorating the porch, no doubt because of its liturgical importance. The aristocrats expect a bishop to be present with attendant clergy, and many guests and retainers with all their finery and elegance. They also bring to the church some of the objects used in the ceremony of baptism. The royal ordinances detail that

> ITEM that the servant of the pantry, either of the King or Queen's, to be ready with a little salt cellar of gold and salt therein ready, and take the assay before it be hallowed with a towel of raynes about his neck, and the treasurer of the household to go before him with his staff, and present the assay.[16]

Also the chrisom cloth is brought in by the baptism party, pinned to the shoulders of a lady. The earl's household ordinances also have brought in the candle and a pair of basins for the godparents to wash their hands in after the service, and a font is set up in the middle of the church, with a 'hollow basin of silver'.[17] The bringing of salt was not just an aristocratic custom: in an account of a modest baptism in Marian

---

15 'Articles Ordained by King Henry VII for the Regulation of his Household', 1494, in *A Collection of Ordinances and Regulations for the government of the Royal Household, made in Divers Reigns from King Edward III to King William and Queen Mary, also Receipts in Ancient Cookery* (London: Society of Antiquaries, 1790), pp. 103–33; 'Orders and Regulations for an Earl's House', Bodleian Library, MS Eng. Hist. b.208, fols 15–22.
16 'Articles Ordained by King Henry VII', p. 126.
17 'Regulations for an Earl's House', fols 15–18.

times, the salt was provided by the family of the child. A Protestant mother, disliking the ceremonies of popish baptism, put sugar instead of salt in the handkerchief that was to be given to the priest.[18]

c. The signing

> [*Declaracion*, sig. Aii] Whan a christen mannis chylde is bornn into this worlde it is brought to churche and iii witnesses comyth with hym, that is Godfader and godmother, and whan they be a greed what name shalbe to the chyld than the prest makyth a signe of the crosse in the forhed of the chyld and seyth thus, 'A token of the holy crosse of our lorde Jesu Christ I set in thy forhed', and so at the breste in lyk manere, and than the prest seith many orisons over the chylde commaundynge the devel to knolech hys sentense and gyve worshipe to the lyvyng god and trewe and to Jesu christ and to the Holy Ghost and departe from this servaunt of god.

The author of the *Declaracion* pays no attention whatever to the *Manual*'s divisions of the rite into the Order for Making a Catechumen, the Blessing of the Font (which is not mentioned at all) and the baptism service proper. These distinctions had been lost with the end of adult initiation as a common practice. The writer is more concerned, in true didactic style, with the main symbolic actions of the rite and with the replies to be made by godparents. Here at the beginning of the rite the business of naming the child and the sign of the cross on the forehead and breast are described in good detail, but the long series of exorcisms are passed over with minimal comment.

The *Ordynary* likewise ignores the divisions in the rite and, even though it gives and translates the text of the *Manual*, tends to concentrate on the symbolic actions and objects for its commentary. As a translation of a French work it begins with an element found in some continental rites but not in Sarum: the priest breathes on the child and says: 'Come out of him, unclean spirit, and give place to the coming of the Holy Spirit, the Paraclete.' Then the signing on the forehead and breast is described. In the commentary it is explained that the child is addressed as the devil because it is in the devil's power and not yet a servant of Christ. The cross made on the forehead signifies grace to resist the devil openly, and that on the breast signifies the same in the

---

18   D. Cressy, *Birth, Marriage and Death: Ritual, Religion and the Life-Cycle in Tudor and Stuart England* (Oxford: Oxford University Press, 1997), p. 135.

'secretnes of conscyence'.[19] The *Ordynary* also discusses the opening
prayer (*Omnipotens sempiterne Deus . . . respicere dignare super nunc
famulum tuum . . .*) and presents it as the prayer of the Church for the
infant being baptized. It invokes Christ's promise (Jn 16.23) that God
will answer prayer in Christ's name.

The *Rationale* acknowledges the historical origin of the 'catechism'
as relating to the time of adult initiation, but makes no attempt to relate
this to infant baptism, referring instead to the exhortation to godparents
to teach the child in due course. Then it proceeds (in a manner similar
to the *Ordynary*) to explain the sign of the cross on the forehead, 'in
tokening that he is come to be professed and totally to be dedicated to
Christ crucified, whom he will never be ashamed openly before men to
confess and knowledge'. Then the cross on the breast is taken to refer to
inward belief in the heart. The content of the first prayer is summarized,
that God will take away the blindness of heart of the candidate and
make him 'apt to receive grace given in baptism'.[20]

d. The salt and exorcisms

> [*Declaracion*, sig. Aii] And than he puttyth salt in the mouth of the
> chyld and seith thus, 'Take Thou [sig. Aii b] salt of wysdom that
> god be mercyfull to the in to everlastyng lyfe. Amen.' This salt of
> wysdom understande goddes word whiche shulde be lerned in the
> mouth of the chylde whanne it begynneth to speke, as the Apostle
> seith, 'Be our word savord with salt evermore in grace' . . .

The administration of salt comes within the flow of exorcistic formulas
and belongs to them. But the explanation in the *Declaracion* bears no
relation to this context. A simple moral is drawn from the ceremony.
The *Ordynary* gives a very lengthy discussion of the properties of salt
and how they may be understood spiritually in symbolizing wisdom and
discretion in discerning right from wrong: salt dries the earth so that it
cannot grow vegetation, and the candidate puts spiritual good before
worldly goods; salt gives savour to food, and the Christian puts reason
and discretion in his thoughts, words and deeds, so that they 'be swete of
savoure and pleasaunt unto God and unto his neyghbours'; salt preserves
food from rotting, and the Christian avoids following bad examples but
gives a good example to others; salt is made from sea water by the heat
of fire, and the 'salte of dyscrecyon is made of the water of devocyon

---

19   *Ordynary*, sig. Bii–Biii.
20   *Rationale*, pp. 6–7.

and of fyre of true dyleccyon'; finally God told Moses to put salt in all his sacrifices, and the Christian cannot please God without the salt of discretion in fasting, almsgiving and prayer.[21]

The *Ordynary* gives the text of the lengthy exorcisms and translates them in full, but makes no comment on them at all! It is as though the writer can find nothing to say about them.

The *Rationale* takes a similar but more succinct approach to the salt, looking for the removal of 'the filthy savour of stinking sin' and the hope that the child may be a 'more apt vessel to continue in the moisture of wholesome and godly wisdom'. The *Rationale* goes on to comment on the sign of the cross on the child's forehead as an exorcistic formula, with a brief translation of the exorcistic address to the devil, but proceeds straightaway to note the reading of the gospel reading from Mt. 19, taken to justify the baptism of children.[22] Curiously, the *Declaracion* and the *Ordynary* both omit any discussion of the gospel reading. The question of exorcisms was a delicate one in the *Rationale*. The Lambeth MS carries a proposal to omit 'all such exorcisms and prayers which attribute remission of sins, redemption, propitiation, salvation or other like to any other creature than to Christ'.[23] Presumably this must have carried some implications for the baptismal ceremonies. However evidently there was no agreement over the matter. As for the popular view, Eamon Duffy believes that the exorcisms 'provided the laity with paradigms for countless "magical" charms and invocations'.[24] While this may well have been the case for such prayers, these contemporary accounts of baptismal exorcisms suggest that they were not always taken very seriously, and the godparents' eyes may well have glazed over as the priest dutifully proceeded through a long series of incomprehensible formulas.

e. Effeta *and exorcisms*

> [*Declaracion*, sig. Aii b] . . . Than the prest weetyth his thombe in spotil and touchith the chyldes ear and seith, 'Be thou openyd', that is, understande in alle thy fyve wittys to here and speke the word of god with love and drede and holy devocion. For the Judgement of god shall touche in whiche we shulde yelde account of every ydel word. Also the prest toucheth the nose thrylles of the chyld for it shuld smyll the odour of swetnes of hevenly thyngis more than every eartly thynges . . .

---

21 *Ordynary*, sig. Cii–Cii[v].
22 *Rationale*, pp. 7–8.
23 *Rationale*, p. 42.
24 Duffy, *Stripping of the Altars*, p. 473.

The *effeta* rite again carries an exorcistic overtone with the final formula, which is said when the priest touches the left ear: 'But flee, Satan, for the judgement of God draws close.' This is omitted by the writer of the *Declaracion* who concentrates on the formulas for the right ear and the nose, and a moral understanding of them. The *Ordynary* gives a very full explanation:

> By the ryght ere to us may betoken that wylfully we sholde here good doctryne, the whiche unto us is sygnefyed by the spitel of the preest. By the spetell put into the nosethrylle the whiche recyveth good odour by the whiche the brayne is comforted unto us, is sygnyfyed the swetnes and pleasure that a good spyryt ought to take in holy doctryne, by the whiche he fortefyeth hym ayenst all temptacyons. By the conjuracyon the whiche is made unto the left ere is understande that he ought to put out of us all evyll thoughtes and evyll operacyons to shewe all occasyon the whiche myght stere us unto yll.[25]

The *Rationale*, noting the gospel story of the deaf and dumb man, says that this signifies the 'grace and godly influence descending from heaven which by the operation of the Holy Ghost openeth our nose to take the sweet odour and savour of the knowledge of Christ and our ears to hear his words and commandments'.[26]

f. Lord's Prayer, Hail Mary, Creed

> [*Declaracion*, sig. Aii b] Sone after this the prest biddith alle the peple that ther be to seye a *Pater* [sig. Aiii] *noster* and an *Ave* and a *Credo* bysekyng God that the child may rightfully take his christendom, and well kepe it to the endyng of his lyfe. And thanne the prest takyth the chyld by the right hande and callyth his name and seyth, 'Come thou in to the temple of God that thou may have everlastyng lyfe and lyve in to worlde of worldis. Amen.'

The *Declaracion* concludes the section of the service held in the porch with mention of the Lord's Prayer, Hail Mary and the Creed which are recited. This is explained as the child taking his 'christendom'. The *Rationale* includes also the signing of the cross on the right hand of the child, which is explained as admonishing us to resist the devil.[27]

---

25 *Ordynary*, sig. Cvii^v.
26 *Rationale*, p. 8..
27 *Rationale*, p. 9.

g. *Coming to the font: declaration of faith*

Thanne the chylde is brought to the fonte and the prest callyth it
by name and seyth, 'Abranuncio Satane et omnibus operibus eius et
omnibus pompis eius', that is, I for sake Satanas, that is the devyl,
and alle his werkis and alle his pompis or prydes, and the godsibbis
sayth, 'Abranuncio', that is, I for sake. Therfore wher he is not a
fals Christen man that kepith not the covenaunt of these wordis
but after ward wrappyth him in the fendis [sig. Aiii b] pryde in hert
and in clothyng and in wycked worckynge, for yf this covenaunt
shold be trewly kept, all the tokenes of pryde in man must be don a
way, seyng eche token of pryde is a pompe of the fende. After seyth
the prest to the chylde, 'Belevest thou in God the Fader almyghty,
maker of hevene and erth?' The chyld is domb and may not speke
but and yt were of age and myght speke, it shuld answere for it
self, therfore the godsibbis answere seyng, 'Credo', that, I beleve.
Efte axith the prest, 'And belevest thou in Jesu Christ his only Sone
our Lord, born and sufferd?' and they saye, 'I beleve'. The thride
tyme axeth the prest, 'And belevest thou in the Holy Ghost, in holy
Church, fayth in communion of saintes, for gevenes of synnes, the
rysyng of fleshe and after the ever lastyng lyfe?' And they saye [sig.
Aiv] 'I beleve'. Than sayth the prest, 'Quid petis?' what axist thou?
They sey, 'Baptim'. 'Wold thou be baptized?' seyth the prest, and
they say, 'Volo', I wole.

The blessing of the font, a large part of the text in the *Manual*, is omitted
in all three commentaries, since it would not have been used for most
baptisms. Bonner's Articles of Enquiry for the diocese of London in 1554
refer to a monthly renewal of the baptismal water as being 'according to
the old custom of the Church', but we are not told whether the blessing
of the water was carried out in the course of a baptism (following the
text of the *Manual*) or in readiness for it.[28] The renunciation of Satan
and the articles of belief in God are described in great detail. The actual
formula is conflated somewhat, but the evident concern here is that the
godparents should know exactly what is demanded of them (a concern
which will emerge towards the end of the *Declaracion* when the author
launches into a tirade against the ignorant clergy who oppress those
who seek to fulfil God's will). Likewise the *Rationale* has a marginal
note in one version of the text suggesting that the questions and answers
ought to be administered in English.[29] An anointing of the child on the

---

28 *Visitation Articles*, Vol. 2, p. 346.
29 *Rationale*, p. 10.

breast and back is passed over in silence by the *Declaracion*, but linked
by the *Rationale* to the yoke of Christ, and by the *Ordynary* to the love
of Christ and to obedience to the ten commandments. After the credal
questions and affirmations, the *Declaracion* and the *Rationale* describe
the additional questions and answers exactly as they are to be found in
the *Manual*. The etymology of 'volowing', a popular term for baptizing,
as being derived from '*volo*', no doubt underlies the commentary in the
Declaracion. Tyndale refers to the notion, which was evidently a popular
one at the time, though it is possibly incorrect.[30] The *Ordynary* includes
a spiritual understanding of the font as representing the Passion and
Cross which provide the fountain of life for the world, and refers to
blood and water flowing from Christ's side. There is meaning derived
from the number of times the child is asked if he or she wants to be
baptized, and also from the threefold immersion and the number of
times the sign of the cross is made on the child.[31]

h. Immersion

[*Declaracion*, sig. Aiv] Than the prest takyth the chyld and sayth,
'I baptise the in the name of the Father and of the Sone and of
the Holy Ghost. Amen.' And so he plungyth it in the water and
commaundyth the gossipis to ley hond on the chyldes heed for
they ben wytnesses of his baptim and receve the charge to teach
it and the trewthe of his beleve, that is the commaundementis
and the domes of God, and to flee the pompis and prydes of the
fend, for the comon peple and all men shuld knowe and kepe the
commaundementis of God. And prestis his holy counseyles, and
lordis his just domes, and yf they do not this, they be wrongfully
called Christen men. And thus blinde prestis bear [sig. Aiv b] fals
wytnesses of yong chyldren christened, that afterwarde serve the
devel whome they forsooke, seying, 'Abronuncio'.

The plunging of the child into the water, total immersion, was still
common in Britain, though it had been replaced in some other countries
by the custom of pouring water over the head. The *Ordynary*, perhaps
following its French original, speaks of water being poured over the

---

30 Tyndale, *Obedience of a Christian Man*, PS, Vol. 1, p. 276: 'Baptism is called volowing
in many places of England, because the priest saith, "*Volo* say ye".' C.S. Cobb discusses
the possible derivations of the word in *Rationale*, p. 9, n. 2, and suggests a connection with
fullere, an Anglo-Saxon word for a bleacher, and the verb *fullian*, to make white.
31 *Ordynary*, sigs Cviii^v, Di^v, Diii.

child.[32] We have already seen Tyndale's remarks about the care over this part of the service and the concern that some felt if the weakness of the child led the priest simply to pour water over it. The *Manual* gives detailed directions for the threefold immersion, the first time with the child facing north, the second time facing south and, finally, facing downwards.[33] The *Rationale* is somewhat pedantic in outlining the various modes of administration of the sacrament. The Lambeth manuscript says that the immersion signifies the death and resurrection of Christ and our own daily mortification of our evil desires and corrupt affections, and the requirement to live a godly life. The Cotton manuscript carefully inserts a mention of the remission of sins by the operation of the Holy Spirit.[34] The *Ordynary* describes the cleansing from sin, 'be it mortall, actuall or venyall', and in the baptism is a figure of the baptism of Christ at which the Trinity was revealed. And the writer goes on to describe the baptismal 'character':

> And theris tonge ne ymagynacyon that may say, thynke or declare that beaute of a soule after the baptym and to hym is gyven a spyrytuell token that these theologyens cal caractere, that maye never be defaced be he saved or dampned after that he hath been baptysed, the whiche token shall be to the grete honoure and glory of those that be blyssed, as shall be temporall the lyveray of a grete lord gyven lyberally unto a man of lowe condycyon.[35]

The command to the godparents to lay their hand on the child's head is an addition to the text of the *Manual*, which speaks only of them taking the child out of the font. It is reasonable to trust the *Declaracion* as evidence both for the practice and its understanding at this time. We shall see that Cranmer's Prayer Book seems to continue the custom.

i. Post-baptismal ceremonies

> [*Declaracion*, sig. Aiv b] After these thyngis the prest a noyntyth the chylde wyth oyl and lappyd in his chrisome and takith yt a candell brinnynng in his hond and seyth, 'Accipe lampadem ardentem

---

32 Bromiley, *Baptism and the English Reformers*, p. 140, n. 5, cites a passage in Erasmus as evidence of the distinctive English custom. Unfortunately I have not been able to confirm his citation which he gives as *Tert. disput.*, p. 145, n. 2.

33 *Manual*, p. 36.

34 *Rationale*, pp. 11–12.

35 *Ordynary*, sig. Dii.

irreprehensibilem. Custodi baptismum tuum, serva mandata ut cum
venit dominus ad nuptias possis occurrere ei una cum sanctis in
aula celesti ut habeas vitam eternam et vivas in secula seculorum.
Amen', that is to sey, 'Have thou a brennynge lampe unreprovable.
Kepe thou thy baptym and kepe thou the commaundementis
that whan the Lorde cometh to the weddyngis thou mayst renne
agenst hym as one wyth seyntis in the hevenly halle that thou have
everlastyng lyfe and lyve in to the world [sig. Av] of worldes. Amen'.
Here endith the reulys of baptim.

The three ceremonial actions of anointing with chrism, the dressing in
the chrisom cloth and the delivery of the candle are somewhat conflated
in the *Declaracion*. The author is interested only in drawing out the
moral of the third action, and it is quite possible that his particular
interests lead him to pass over what was of interest to others. For Duffy
paints a picture of an altogether different approach to this part of the
service:

> The blessed water in the font was kept under lock and key to
> prevent its removal and use in magical rites . . . The priest was
> strictly charged to prevent anyone except the child from even
> touching the baptismal water. The chrisom or cloth tied over the
> anointed spot on the child's forehead was to be returned to the
> priest by the mother when she came for her churching, and he was
> to burn it, or keep it for 'the uses of the church'. The godparents
> were required to wash their hands before they left the church in
> case any of the holy oils remained from contact with the child. The
> service ended with the priest reading over the child the Gospel,
> 'Respondens unus de turba', from St Mark, describing the casting
> out of a demon by Jesus because 'according to the greatest scholars
> it was good for the falling sickness'. This reading was followed
> immediately by the prologue of St John's Gospel, a text which, as
> we have already seen, was regularly used in exorcism, healing, and
> against thunder and storms.[36]

---

36 *Stripping of the Altars*, pp. 280–81. Duffy's listing of the fate of the chrisom cloth
seems somewhat dramatic, when the rubric in the *Manual* simply forbids its use for
secular purposes and requires its return to the church for church use. No doubt it was used
repeatedly until worn out. But it was a common custom that infants who died soon after
baptism (before the cloth was returned by the mother at her churching) would be buried
in their chrisom, hence the frequent 'chrisom brasses'. Cf. J. Litten, *The English Way of
Death: The Common Funeral since 1450* (London: Robert Hale, 1991), p. 61.

Duffy paints a picture almost the opposite to that given by the *Declaracion*. Even allowing for the reformist agenda of the latter, it is hard to believe without some qualification Duffy's portrait of a people interested only in spells and talismans. For the writer of the *Declaracion* must have had some sort of readership who, he believed, would be interested in what he was trying to say.

The *Rationale* gives more equal treatment to each of the three ceremonies. The anointing signifies that the infant 'is made an Christian man by Christ the head of his congregation; and that he is anointed with the spiritual unction of the Holy Ghost, that by his assistance and grace he may attain everlasting life'. The white vesture is a token of his manumission from slavery to the devil, and Christian purity and innocency. The candle signifies the need to show 'a light of good example and godly works'. The eschatological element of all three is included. There is an element of promise in the *Rationale* as well as of exhortation.[37]

In the *Ordynary* the cross on the head at the post-baptismal anointing is discussed:

Al faythful Chrysten men ought to receyve the token of the crosse for honourre, for tryumphe, for it is the shelde and defence ayenst all our adversarys. That is to knowe the world the devyl and our sensualyte or pryde covetous and lechery. Wherfore in the mystery of baptim the newe knyght entrynge into the batayl of Chrystente ayenst these thre adversarys aforesayd taketh and receyveth the soules [*sic*: ? viz. wages; cf. *L'Ordinaire*: soulz] and the lyveray of blissed Jhesu Cryst chefe duke and captayne of all them that ben chosen . . .

By the chresome is sygnyfyed the beaute and the innocencye of the soule the whiche is annorned and ennobled with all vertues as the noble spouse of Jhesu Cryst. And by that is sygnyfyed the beaute and the dowares of the body after the resurreccyon . . . By the lyght the whiche ought to be in the hande and not in the mouthe or between the fete is sygnyfyed the example of good werkes by the whiche werke every good Cristen man ought to be lyght before the worlde.[38]

Again we have a somewhat didactic and moralizing element. The interest in the sign of the cross suggests that Cranmer's 1552 version

---

37   *Rationale*, p. 12.
38   *Ordynary*, sig. D3^V, D4^V.

might well have enjoyed wide support, not least from the many readers of this popular devotional work.

The order given in the *Manual* and the two commentaries is of the anointing first and the dressing in the chrism cloth second. However, as we shall see below, Cranmer's rite and also another rite composed in Reformation England invert the order. The fact that two writers do this suggests the possibility that this reflects in some way actual practice, at any rate clothing the child before it is anointed and the chrisom cloth arranged over the forehead.[39]

The giving of the lighted candle to the infant was the signal for great ceremonial embellishment in the royal and noble families. For the earl's household, 50 yeomen enter the church and their torches are lit when the taper is put into the child's hand. They stand on either side of the way to the chancel, and the godmother carries the child between the torches up to the high altar. Two hundred torches are used in the royal baptism.[40] At the high altar, the gospel is read over the child, as specified in the Sarum *Manual*, and both sets of regulations provide for it to be confirmed. (The Princess Elizabeth was confirmed immediately after her baptism by Cranmer.)[41] The regulations for the earl's household go on to mention 'an anthem to be sung of our Lady or of St George in the choir'. And in both the royal and noble households, everyone partakes of spice and wine.[42] In the light of this considerable ceremonial at the altar, we might consider the custom criticized by Puritans in 1641, among the 'innovations in discipline' of 'carrying children from the baptism to the altar so called, there to offer them up to God'.[43] Was this indeed an innovation, or a preservation or restoration of earlier practice?

The chrisom cloth was to be returned by the mother at the time of her churching. Cranmer's 1549 Prayer Book retains this and a reference to the 'accustomed offerings'. David Cressy describes the later sixteenth-century practice in Salisbury (which was no doubt a continuation of the medieval one), that an offering of 1d to 4d was paid at the churching. In addition, the chrisom cloth was offered, or its cash equivalent (usually in the region of 4d to 6d). The variations reflected the wealth of the family. The offerings could accumulate to be a useful sum in church accounts.[44]

---

39 The *Ordynary*, sig. Aiii, has a woodcut of a naked baby receiving the candle, which may or may not contradict this theory.
40 'Regulations for an Earl's House', fol. 19; 'Articles Ordained by King Henry VII for the Regulation of his Household', p. 126.
41 MacCulloch, *Cranmer*, p. 98.
42 'Regulations for an Earl's House', fols 20–1; 'Articles Ordained by King Henry VII for the Regulation of his Household', p. 126.
43 E. Cardwell, *History of Conferences* (Oxford: Oxford University Press, 1849; 3rd edn), p. 273.
44 Cressy, *Birth, Marriage and Death*, p. 211.

According to John Bale, James Tregennow, the curate of St Ives in Cornwall, admitted 'that in one daye he had beget ii fisher mens wyves of the paryshe there wyth child only to up hold the churches profyts in chrisyms and offerings'.[45]

The *Declaracion* thus completes its commentary on the baptism rite. But it goes on with two discussions of baptism, the first summarizing the teaching of baptism through four symbolic actions, and the second distinguishing between the baptism of water and that of the Holy Spirit. The first discussion effectively repeats and emphasizes the moralistic content of the commentary:

[Sig. Av] But alle Christen folk shulde besily lerne to know the gretnes of charge whiche they receve in ther baptym. For wyth iiii thyngis we be chargyd in our baptym, although blinde prestis knowe yt not, whan they geve to us iiii elementis in tokenyng of them, that is salt and water and oyle and fier. The fyrst charge is that we take salt of wysdom of Goddes word and rewle our lyfe therafter and salt our soules that they stynk not in sinne. For and thys hevenly salt fayl fro men they shulde be cast out as Christ techyth in the gospel. The ii charge is, that our eeris be openyd ever more redy to here Chrystes gospel and understande yt. For Christ seyth, 'He that hath eerys of heryng, let him here', and, 'He that redyth, let him understande'. The [sig. Av biii] charge is this, that we kepe our baptym, that is the covenaunt of our baptym and trew beleve in the Father and the Sone and the Holy Ghost as the prest apposith us when we saye, 'Credo'. The iiii charge is this, that we kepe the commaundementis of God as the prest commaundith us at the font puttyng a candel brennynge in our hand, for as a candille brennynge is wastyd by fyer, so synnes in our soule shulde be wastyd and destroyed wyth kepyng of the commaundementis of God, havyng devout love to hym and to our even Christen.

It is only in the last section that we have a strong suggestion of heterodox teaching, following either earlier Lollard sympathies or the example of Tyndale or Frith. But the following does not adopt any reformed theology of justification; rather it rejects sacramental efficacy in so far as it is negated by sin. The unorthodox nature of the passage is in the strong 'sacramentarian' distinction between the two baptisms rather than in any different theology of salvation. But the charge that priests

---

45 *A declaration of Edmonde Bonners articles concerning the cleargye of London dyocese* (London: Jhon Tysdall, for Frauncys Coldocke, 1561), fol. 19ᵛ.

are pursuing those who are trying to observe the commandments sounds like the voice of a persecuted minority.

[The *Declaracion* continues:] And this is the seconde baptym that saynt John techyth whan he sayth, 'I baptyse in water but a nother shall come after me strongir than I, and he shall baptyse you in the Holy Ghost and fyer', and wyth out this seconde [sig. Avi] baptym may no man be saved as Christ seyde to Nichodeme, 'Truly I saye to the, but a man be born agen of water and of the Holy Ghost, he may not enter into the kyngdom of God.' Also Paul techyth that the fyrst baptym in water only maketh us not saef, but the axinge of a good conscience in God and fayth not fayned yet beleve that workyth by charite, for Christ sayth, 'He that belevyth in me, flodis of quyk water shulde flow fro hys wombe', that is the Holy Ghost that Chryst callyth the comfortour, whyche flowyth ever in to the hertis of meke men that make them redy to die, for that man that shall dwelle byfore the blessed face of God in hevene shall receve the ernest of the Holy Ghost here in erthe. And this is the second baptym that fleshely prestis and swynysh peple knowyth not, for [sig. Avi b] ther hertis be stoppyd wyth fleshly lust that the flodis of the Holy Ghost may not entre in to them, and there fore prestis be in perel that teach not the secounde baptym. For yt sufficyth not to salvacion of man to wayshe his body in water of baptym and suffre his soule to stynk in syn thorow brekyng of the commaundementis of God, for thus prestis reade in the holy Psalm, 'Increpasti superbos, maledicti qui declinant a mandatis tuis', that is to seye, Thou blamest the proude, they be a cursyd that bow a wey from thyn hestis. And thus God shall blame proud prestis for they pursew powre men for the lernynge of the commaundementis, the whyche they charge them to kepe in the our of ther baptym, and all that bere the name of Chrysten men shulde crie agenst this errour. [Sig. Avii] For what errour is more vyle in the syght of God than to byende men to a lawe and afterwarde pursue them for the same lawe and thus for drede of evel prestis men dar not kepe Chrystis heestis, and the ghostly byrth of our mother holy Churche is despysed of proude men that knowe not the bond of ther baptym. Amen. FINIS.

Thus finishes the *Declaracion*. But while its author seems indifferent to the issues of ceremonial, others already probably took another view. For in later evangelical polemic the ceremonial details of the baptism ceremony became symbols of all that was wrong in popish rites: 'crossing and conjuring, begreasing and bespewing of the poor infants';

'blowing, censing, salting, spitting, oil and cream'. The 1552 Prayer Book 'alloweth neither spattle nor salt, cream nor yet stinking oil, with other pilled peltries of the Pope'.[46]

We are left with two pictures of baptism. The concentration of teaching around the ceremonies even by those of Reforming sympathies suggests that many people believed them to be actually or potentially helpful in appropriating the meaning and even the grace of the sacrament. On the other hand there are those who, at least in later years, believed these same ceremonies to be the very horns of the popish devil. Some features of the rites clearly conveyed the purpose and importance of the sacrament. Though made little of by the commentaries, the lighting of the torches at the noble baptisms must have been dramatic occasions. The sign of the cross was of very great significance in both negative (exorcistic) and positive terms. The questions and answers are important enough to be translated and explained in detail, and even for a suggestion to be made that they be administered in English. But the texts of the prayers are rarely even summarized (except in the *Ordynary* which sets out to give such a full account), and one gains the impression that if a reviser were to abbreviate the rite (omitting much of the repetitious material) and translate it into the vernacular, it would have been a popular and welcome move.

2. THE EUCHARIST

a. Sources

The medieval Mass is a vast subject in its historical significance, in its theological understanding and in the literature devoted to it; and a brief description is by its very nature inadequate. But some attempt must be made to sketch the way in which people understood the service which was the cornerstone of their religious experience, indeed a service which many would attend daily, and which must therefore have largely embodied their understanding of God and the Christian gospel.

As in the case of the baptism service, an attempt will be made to view the entire service and so the survey will be shaped by commentaries of the time. We have already met the *Rationale of Ceremonial* in its discussion of the baptism service, and we will also consider two other commentaries: *Meditations in the Time of Mass*, written by B.

---

46   D. Cressy, *Birth, Marriage and Death*, p. 136: John Calfhill, *Answer to John Martiall's Treatise of the Cross*, ed. R. Gibbings, PS (Cambridge: Cambridge University Press, 1846), p. 215; James Pilkington, *Works*, ed. J. Scholefield, PS (Cambridge: Cambridge University Press, 1842), p. 541; John Bale, *Declaration*, fol. 150ᵛ.

Langforde, a priest, in the fifteenth or possible early sixteenth century;[47] and *The interpretacyon and sygnyfycacyon of the masse . . . composed and ordeyned by frere Gararde frere mynoure of the ordre of the Observauntes.*[48] These commentaries share a common and ancient tradition of allegorizing the service to represent the life and ministry of Christ. Since at least the fifth century this had influenced understanding of the eucharist, and in the Middle Ages Amalarius of Metz and Durandus of Mende were immensely influential in Western Christendom. Durandus's *Rationale divinorum officiorum* enjoyed more printed editions before the Reformation than any book other than the Bible and liturgical texts.[49] Allegory offered attractive possibilities for making sense of every detail of the liturgy, no matter how obscure or whatever its historical origins. However, it suffered from the tendency to be arbitrary; to focus on comparatively trivial ritual detail to the detriment of the text and the shape of the service as a whole, breaking down the one eucharistic mystery into countless trivial mysteries; and to rely on an essentially Platonist detachment from the liturgical action. It did not survive the Reformation in either Protestant or Roman Catholic circles, though it is still influential in Eastern Orthodoxy.[50]

The three commentaries used here reflect the arbitrary nature of the genre, with agreement as well as disagreement about what individual parts of the service signified. We shall follow the text of *The interpretacyon and sygnyfycacyon* since it lacks a modern edition, and includes features from the other commentaries and from other descriptions of the rite.

The Mass was the main Sunday service, following on after Matins and the procession. Laity would attend all these devotions, but the larger congregation was present for the Mass.[51] On weekdays churches would if possible provide several Masses each morning so that people could attend a service, however briefly.[52] The Sunday parish Mass would involve considerable singing and ceremonial, while the daily Mass could be a starkly simple and intimate affair with clergy and laity together in a tiny chapel; but the basic structure and significance remained the same.

---

47   B. Langforde, 'Meditations in the Time of the Mass', in J. Wickham Legg, *Tracts on the Mass*, Henry Bradshaw Society no. 27 (London: Harrison & Sons, 1904), pp. 17–29.
48   Fr Gararde (Gherit van der Goude), *The interpretacyon and sygnyfycacyon of the Masse . . . composed and ordeyned by frere Gararde frere mynoure of the ordre of the Observauntes* (London: Ro. Wyer, 1532).
49   P. Rorem, *The Medieval Development of Liturgical Symbolism*, Grove Liturgical Study 47 (Bramcote: Grove Books, 1986), p. 29.
50   Rorem, *Liturgical Symbolism*, pp. 30–3.
51   M. Bucer, *Censura*, ed. E.C. Whitaker, *Martin Bucer and the Book of Common Prayer*, Alcuin Club Collection, 55 (Great Wakering: Mayhew–McCrimmon, 1974), p. 84.
52   Duffy, *Stripping of the Altars*, pp. 98–100.

b. Introductory rites

The interpretacyon and sygnyfycacyon begins its commentary in the 'Second book of the mass' with a Prologue in which it sets out a way of understanding the Mass as representing the whole of Christ's life and ministry:

> [Sig. Kii] [The second book is divided into three parts, as is our Lord's life and the mass, in 33 articles]
> The fyrste tyme is from his humanyte unto his passyon and that doeth sygnyfye the begynnynge of the masse: unto the Canon or Sanctus. The seconde tyme from his passyon unto his resurreccyon and that doth sygnyfye from Sanctus unto that the preest have receyved the sacrament. The thyrde tyme from that unto the fynysshynge of the masse and that doth sygnyfye after his resurreccyon unto that tyme that our lorde dyd ascende in to heven. [Sig. Kiii] The fyrste Artycle of the masse
> Howe the preest doth make hym redy in the vestry to say masse and the deacon and subdeacon do helpe hym, but the preest alone doth take and caste upon hym the chesuble: which doth sygnyfie how chryste hath taken upon hym the nature of man, and was conceyved in the vestry of the blyssed body of our lady, wherein the father and the holy ghost have gyven ayde & helpe. The mynyster or he that doth helpe to serve at the masse, doth sygnyfye the aungell Gabryell. [Each article is followed by a Pater and Ave and a prayer]

The robing of the clergy, in itself a practical exercise of putting on the traditional robes, takes place either in the vestry or (at any rate in small churches or at weekday services) at the altar itself. Gararde, in his *Interpretacyon*, is setting the scene with a Sunday parish Mass in a church which enjoyed both a vestry as a separate room and the ministry of a deacon and subdeacon. It will be seen later that these ministers disappear from the commentary: the important character is the priest who represents the figure of Christ in the drama.

In the *Interpretacyon* the robing is described very simply as representing the incarnation of Christ in the womb of the Blessed Virgin Mary. Other commentaries, including the *Rationale*, give a meaning for each of the vestments 'partly representing the mysteries that were done in the time of the passion, partly representing the virtues that he himself ought to have that celebrates the mass'. Thus, for example, 'The girdle as touching the mystery signifyeth the whip or scourge wherewith Christ was whipped, and as touching the minister it signifyeth the continent and chaste living or else the close mind which he ought to have in prayer when he celebrates.' In this scheme the chasuble (whatever its colour!) represents the purple mantle that Pilate's soldiers put on Christ. The vestry, however, as in the *Interpretacyon*, represents the womb of the Virgin Mary and the incarnation.[53]

The Mass begins with the priest's prayers of preparation, originally a private devotion, but there was no way to distinguish it from the Mass proper.

> [*Interpretacyon*, sig. Kiii^v] The ii Artycle of the masse
> Howe the preest doth go out of the vestry towardes the aulter with the deacon and subdeacon: where he doth tary a lytel space betwene them with scylence the whiche doth sygnyfye how Jhesus was borne betwene Joseph and our lady and layde betwene an Oxe and an Asse.
> The thyrde Artycle of the masse
> How the preest beynge betwene them sayth with great devocyon Confiteor, and doth confesse hym selfe as a [sig. Kiiii] synner, albeit that he hath confessed hym selfe afore all of his deedly synnes: whiche doth sygnyfye that the innocent chylde Jhesus dyd suffre hym selfe to be cyrcumcysed as a pure & a clene myrour without any spotte.

The *Rationale* here shows a reflection of the Reformation in its comments on the priest's confession:

> And albeit that that sacrifice [of Christ] be a sufficient price and redemption for all the world, yet it is not efficient or effectual but only to them which knowledgeth themselves with penance to be sinners whom he came to justify as he saith himself. Non veni vocare justos sed peccatores. Therefore the minister in the beginning teacheth all men by his confession to humiliate and knowledge themselves sinners and to ask remission to the intent they may be the more apt to be participant of this high mystery. Nam justus in principio accusator est sui.[54]

The Mass proceeds with the singing of the Kyries and on Sundays (except in Lent and Advent) the Gloria. Since these were sung by the choir, the *Interpretacyon* does not refer to them, only to the priest's ritual actions:

---

53 *Rationale*, pp. 16–18.
54 *Rationale*, p. 18.

[*Interpretacyon*] The fourth Artycle of the masse
Howe the preest after Confiteor gothe to the aulter with great
reverence & lowly inclynyng hym selfe doth worshyppe god
almyghty, which doth sygnyfye unto us howe the thre kynges with
(Kiiiiᵛ) great reverence and devocyon have worshypped the swete
chylde Jhesu, and have humbly gyven hym theyr offrynges.
The fyfth Artycle of the masse
How the preest after that with great reverence doth begynne the
masse, betwene deacon and subdeacon at the one syde of the
aulter: which doth sygnyfie that Jhesus was presented in the temple
upon the aulter of the soveraygne preest, with great devocyon and
reverence betwene [sig. Li] Joseph & Mary, and his other frendes.

Langforde's *Meditations* relates the angelic hymn of *Gloria in excelsis*
to the nativity. The *Rationale*, while referring to the 'angels' hymn'
moralizes the liturgy: 'we be learned not only to know that we receive
all our benefits of God being bound to give him thanks therefore, but
also the means whereby we receive them which is by the mediation of
Christ, that is both God and man, by whom the Father is pleased, man
reconciled, and angels and men agreed'.[55]

c. Collect and Readings

The collect is passed over in silence by the *Interpretacyon*. Langforde
interprets it as representing the continual prayers of Christ to the Father,
and the *Rationale* as declaring that we can only be heard by Christ and
without him our prayer is of no value.[56] The epistle and gospel follow,
and in these two writers they signify the preaching of the gospel by
Christ. The *Rationale* mentions how 'the church with light and other
ceremonies of gladness and peace, readeth it to the people standing up
diligently to hear the same, declaring thereby their prompt and ready
minds that they have to the doctrine of the gospel'.[57] However the
Interpretacyon is still involved with the childhood of the Saviour and the
career of the Holy Family:

The vi Artycle of the masse
How the preest, the deacon and subdeacon do go from the aulter,
& the preest and the deacon do sytte them downe, and the

---

55 *Rationale*, p. 19.
56 *Meditations*, p. 31; *Rationale*, p. 19.
57 *Rationale*, p. 20.

subdeacon doth synge the epystell. This doth sygnyfie unto us how Jhesus Mary and Joseph fled out of theyre countre from the face of Herode where they dyd dwell in to Egypte, where Joseph laboured for them.

[Sig. Li^v] The vii Artycle of the masse

Howe the preest dothe come agayne to the aulter, where dylygently he doth rede the gospell. This sygnyfyeth howe Jhesus Mary and Joseph have retourned from Egypte in to theyr countre from whens they fled by the commaundment of the holy aungell.

[Sig. Lii] The viii Artycle of the masse

Howe the preest after that he hath red and herde the gospel: he goth to the myddes of the aulter and doth synge with a hygh voyce Credo in unum deum. This doth sygnyfye that mary with great ioye and gladnesse hath founde her dere sone Jhesus in the temple amonges the doctours, and dyd go with her to Nazareth.

While the *Interpretacyon* relates the Creed (usually omitted on weekdays) to the 12-year-old Jesus being lost in the Temple, it is presented by both Langforde and the *Rationale* rather more sensibly as our response to the teaching of the gospel.

d. Offertory

On Sundays the Bidding of the Beads would follow after the Creed. These prayers, recited in the vernacular, were lengthy but are not mentioned in any of the commentaries we have been examining. In part they would presumably not need any explanation; also it is likely that they would not share the same mystery and aura as the Latin formulas.[58] And so the commentaries move to the next part of the Latin Mass, the Offertory. The bread and wine are prepared on the altar, and there are lengthy silent prayers of offering by the priest. The *Interpretacyon* leaps forward in time to Jesus's adulthood and the beginnings of his ministry:

[Sig. Lii^v] The viiii Artycle of the masse

Howe the preest with scylence doth make redy, prepare and offre the sacryfyce: and afterwarde goth to the ende of the aulter & doth wasshe his handes. This sygnyfyeth unto us that chryste from the xii yeres of his age unto xxx yeres dyd nothynge openly that a man can fynde in wrytynge. Yet nevertheless he was not Idle, but at the

---

58   For the Bidding of the Beads see F.E. Brightman, *The English Rite*, 2 vols (London: Rivington, 1915), Vol. 2, pp. 1020–45.

xxx yeres of his age he went towardes Jordan for to be baptysed of saynt Johnn Baptyste.

[Sig. Liii] The x Artycle of the masse

Howe the preest doth go to the myddes of the aulter prayeng al those that be *in* heven to pray for hym: and than he doth tourne hym towardes the people desyrying them also to pray for hym. This doth sygnyfye that chryste dyd pray for us in the deserte or wyldernes, whan he dyd fast xl dayes and xl nyghtes, and after was tempted of the evyll spyryte and enemy of hell.

[Sig. Liiiᵛ] The xi Artycle of the masse

Howe the preest beynge in the myddes of the aulter begynneth to synge with a hygh voyce the preface, Per omnia secula seculorum. This doth sygnyfye that oure lorde hath preched at his xxx yeres to the people: the holy catholyke fayth confyrmynge the same by mervaylous myracles: to the honour of his father celestyall.

Langforde and the *Rationale* both seek to involve the reader more in what is happening. In the former, the reader is exhorted to remember how Christ 'most willingly offered himself to his eternal Father to be the sacrifice and oblation for man's redemption, and offer yourself to him again both body and soul which he so dearly bought'.[59] The *Rationale* says that by the Offertory 'we be learned to prepare ourselves to the intent we may be partakers of the blessed sacrifice, which Christ offered for us upon the cross'. The silent prayers,

> which is called the secret of the mass . . . signifyeth Christ's secret and privy conversation, which he kept with his disciples a little before his passion, for after the determinate sentence of death conspired by Caiaphas and the Jews against him he walked no more amongst them openly but amongst his disciples secretly.[60]

Langforde gives a similar interpretation for the secret.

e. *Eucharistic Prayer: Preface and Sanctus*

Now we begin to see all three commentaries moving into a very similar interpretative scheme as we approach the eucharistic prayer. The Sursum corda and Preface were seen as a separate prayer from the Canon, the eucharistic prayer proper. Not that such niceties would come to the fore

---

59 *Meditations*, p. 23.
60 *Rationale*, pp. 22–3.

in an allegorical commentary! The *Benedictus qui venit*, coming after the Sanctus, links this part of the liturgy to Christ's entry into Jerusalem:

> *Interpretacyon* The xii Artycle of the masse
> [Sig. Liiii] Howe after that the preest hath songe the preface they do synge Sanctus Sanctus Sanctus benedictus qui venit in nomine domini. This doth sygnyfye how the humble Jhesus on Palme Sonday dyd humbly come in to Jerusalem syttynge upon an Asse: where the Jewes dyd receyve hym with great reverence: the chyldren dyd synge: benedictus qui venit osanna in excelsis.

The *Rationale* curiously does not make this link, but picks up another thread which we shall see was dear to the hearts of reformers: the Sursum corda was meant to take our minds not into the past, but to heaven:

> preparing the minds of the faithful people to the reverence of [Christ's body and blood], and moving them to erect their hearts to Almighty God, giving him thanks for inestimable benefits with desire that their voice joined with the company of angels in one consent of laud and praise, proceeding as well from the church triumphant as militant unite and knit together, may without end sing this seraphical hymn and song, Sanctus, Sanctus, Sanctus.[61]

f. Eucharistic Prayer: the Canon

The Canon of the Mass was the most sacred part of the liturgy and perhaps the most significant moment of a medieval Christian's devotional life, when Christ was made present for all to see and worship under the appearance of bread and wine. The *Interpretacyon* marks the beginning of the Canon by moving to the 'second part of the Mass' in its interpretative framework: 'The seconde parte of the masse: in the which is declared the passyon of our lorde Jhesu christe: & ye shal rede these prayers & shall have xl vi yeres of pardon . . .'

But the three commentaries handle the Canon in slightly different ways. Because the *Rationale* comments most closely upon the text, it might be useful to begin with that commentary displayed next to a translation of the Canon.[62] The *Rationale* first explains that the Canon is said silently, not out of necessity but so that priest and people may be the more devout in their prayers.

---

61 *Rationale*, p. 23.
62 *Rationale*, pp. 23–6; (translation of the Canon is my own).

Therefore, most merciful Father, we humbly pray and beseech you through Jesus Christ your Son our Lord that you will accept and bless these gifts, these offerings, these holy and unblemished sacrifices which we offer to you above all for your holy catholic Church, that you will deign to grant it peace, protection, unity and guidance throughout the world, together with your servant our Pope N. and our bishop N. and our King N and all right believers and worshippers of the catholic and apostolic faith.

Remember, O Lord, your servants and handmaids and all here present, whose faith is known and devotion recognized by you, who offer to you this sacrifice of praise for themselves and for all their own, for the redemption of their souls, for the hope of salvation and protection from harm, and who pay their vows to you, the eternal, living and true God. In fellowship with (a special commemoration of the day may be added here) and venerating above all the memory of the glorious ever-virgin Mary, mother of our God and Lord Jesus

Then the priest beginning to represent in his sacrifice of the mass, the most painful and bloody sacrifice, once offered for our salvation upon the cross, and prayeth the Father to accept these gifts prepared for the consecration, and inclining his body maketh a cross upon the altar and kisseth it, signifying thereby, the humble inclining and willing obedience of Christ to his Father's will to suffer upon the cross for our salvation.

And then, following the example of Christ, the high bishop, which, approaching the time of his passion, gave himself to prayer, and also according to the apostle's doctrine to Timothy, the minister giveth himself to prayer; First in general for the universal church, of which he desireth peace and preservation, second for princes and rulers, that govern the same, third, for all Christian and faithful people, remembering especially in his memento such as charity most bindeth him and time sufficeth him to do,

making an honourable mention also of the saints which be departed, and first of our Lady, the XII apostles and as many martyrs which either by their bodily presence preaching or their

Christ, and also of your blessed apostles and martyrs Peter, Paul, Andrew, James, John, Thomas, James, Philip, Bartholemew, Matthew, Simon and Thaddeus, Linus, Cletus, Clement, Xystus, Cornelius, Cyprian, Laurence, Chrysogonus, John and Paul, Cosmas and Damian, and all your saints; by their merits and prayers grant that we may be defended in all things by the help of your protection; through Christ our Lord.

blood shedding in their life time did bear witness and testimony to Christ's Passion joining them as it were both in one communion and participation of Christ's death and merits which hath deserved as well grace to the one as glory to the other desiring God by their prayers to protect and defend the whole congregation of all Christians;

We therefore beseech you, O Lord, that you will graciously accept this offering of the duty that we and all your household owe you; that you will order our days in your peace; and that you will bid us be rescued from eternal damnation and be numbered in the flock of your elect; through Christ our Lord.

and after certain prayers and petitions made for the people

O God, we beseech you graciously to make this offering wholly blessed, approved, ratified, spiritual, and acceptable, that it may become for us the body and blood of your most beloved Son our Lord and God Jesus Christ.

and also that the oblation may be acceptable unto God,

Who on the day before he suffered, took bread in his holy and blessed hands, lifted his eyes to heaven to you, God his almighty Father, he gave you thanks, blessed, broke, gave it to his disciples, saying, 'Take and eat from this, all of you, for this is my body.'

In the same way after supper, taking also this glorious cup in his holy and blessed hands, again

he proceedeth with all reverence to the consecration first of the bread, taking it in his hands and giving thanks following the example of Christ by virtue and power of whose words the substance of bread is turned to the substance of the body of Christ and likewise the substance of wine into his precious blood which he lifteth up both that the people with all reverence and honour may worship

he gave you thanks, blessed, gave it to his disciples, saying, 'Take and drink from it, all of you; for this is the cup of my blood of the new and eternal covenant, the mystery of faith, which will be shed for you and for many for the forgiveness of sins. As often as you do this, you will do it for my remembrance.'

Therefore, O Lord, we your servants and also your holy people remember the blessed passion of your Son Christ our Lord God, and also his resurrection from the dead, and his glorious ascension into heaven, and we offer to your excellent majesty from your gifts and bounty a pure victim, a holy victim, a spotless victim, the holy bread of eternal life and the cup of everlasting salvation. Graciously look upon them with a favourable and kindly countenance, and accept them as you graciously accepted the offerings of your righteous servant Abel, and the sacrifice of our patriarch Abraham, and that which your high priest Melchizedek offered to you, a holy sacrifice, a spotless victim. We humbly pray you, almighty God, bid these things be brought by the hands of your angel to your altar on high, in the sight of your divine majesty, that as many of us as receive the most holy body and blood of your Son by partaking at this altar may be

the same and also to signify thereby partly Christ's Exaltation upon the cross for our redemption which was figured by the serpent set up by Moses in the desert and partly signifying that triumphant advancement and exaltation that God the father because of his passion hath exalted him above all creatures bidding the people to have it in remembrance as oft as they shall do the same.

After the which the priest extendeth and stretcheth abroad his arms in form of a cross declaring thereby, that according to Christ's commandment, both he and the people not only have the fresh remembrance of the passion, but also of his resurrection and glorious ascension.

filled with every heavenly blessing and grace; through Christ our Lord.

Remember also, O Lord, your servants and handmaids N and N who have gone before us with the sign of faith, and sleep in the sleep of peace. We pray that you will bestow upon them and all who rest in Christ a place of refreshment, light and peace; through Christ our Lord.

Graciously grant to us sinners also, your servants who trust in the multitude of your mercies, some part and fellowship with your holy apostles and martyrs, with holy Stephen, Matthias, Barnabas, Ignatius, Alexander, Marcellinus, Peter, Felicity, Perpetua, Agatha, Lucy, Agnes, Cecilia, Anastasia, and all your saints. Admit us into their company, we beseech you, not weighing our merit but freely granting forgiveness; through Christ our Lord.

Through him, O Lord, you ever create, sanctify, quicken, bless all these good things, and grant them to us. Through him and with him and in him all honour and glory are yours, O God the Father almighty, in the unity of the Holy Spirit, for ever and ever. Amen.

And so proceedeth to the second memento in which he prayeth for them that be dead in the faith of Christ and sleep in peace that it might please god to grant them a place of refreshing, light and quietness.

Then he joineth himself with the people knocking upon his breast, teaching thereby them that he and they both be sinners, and have need of mercy and grace purchased by Christ's passion and desireth Almighty God to given them a society with the holy apostles and martyrs, not as an esteemer of their merits, but as a merciful grantor of remission, and that by Christ, by whom he worketh and granteth all these benefits

wherefore all honour and glory is to be rendered to him by Christ and with Christ the Holy Ghost being knit in unity to them, and then expressing with a loud voice how long his honour and glory is due to God he saith per omnia secula seculorum, that is to say, perpetually, the church answering Amen, so be it.

The *Interpretacyon* uses the Canon for a lengthy meditation on the Passion, as follows:

[Sig. Mi.] The xiii Artycle of the masse
Howe after Sanctus the preest begynneth with scylence secretly the Canon havynge the curteynes drawen: to the entent that he be not troubled, and doth inclyne hym selfe very lowe. This doth sygnyfye howe our lorde Jhesus with the dore closed hath eaten the pascall lamb with his dyscyples | [sig. Miᵛ] and afterwarde he hath inclyned hym selfe downe to the grounde, wasshynge the fete of his apostelles.
The xiiii Artycle of the masse
Howe the preest after the fyrste Memento, maketh the crosses upon the chalyce, sayenge secrete wordes. This doth sygnyfie & showe unto us that our lorde hath prayed to his father almyghty in the garthen, thre tymes secretly in the nyght.
[Sig. Mii] The xv Artycle of the masse
Howe the preest is in his fyrste Memento, and than he prayeth for all his frendes lyvynge yt god may gyve them grace and mayntayne them in all goodnes. This doth sygnyfye & showe howe oure lorde Jhesus was taken in the garthen at the most secrete tyme of the nyght, prayenge the Jewes to spare his dyscyples & to do them no hurte.
[Sig. Miiᵛ] The xvi Artycle of the masse
Howe the preest doth make fyve crosses upon the hoste afore that he do consecrate it in sacrament. This doth sygnyfye that the thre fyrst crosses do sygnyfye that there was thre pryncypall Juges examynynge our lorde to deth, as Annas, Cayphas, and Pylate. The other two crosses sygnyfye the two pryncypall effusyons of blode as whan our lorde was scourged & crowned.
[Sig. Miii] The xvii Artycle of the masse
Howe the preest maketh clene his handes upon the aulter as puryfyenge them. This doth sygnyfye how Pylate hath wasshed his handes afore the Jewes as knowlegynge hym selfe not culpable of the deth of the innocent Jhesus, to the whiche the Jewes dyd seduce hym, for fere of leasynge of his offyce, & not to be loved of the Emperoure.
[Sig. Miiiᵛ] The xviii Artycle of the masse
How the preest taketh the hoste in his handes and doth mynyster it: lyftynge the chesuble upon his sholdres, & doth make hym redy to consecrate and offre the holy sacrament and body of oure lorde. This sygnyfyeth how after the sentence of Pylate, our lorde made hym redy to dye takynge the hevye crosse upon his blyssed sholdres, and went therwith towardes the mount of Calverye.

[Sig. Miiii] The xix Artycle of the masse

Howe the preest whan he hath consecrate the holy sacrament he doth lyfte the body of our lorde on high afore all the people betwene his two handes as a medyatoure betwene god the father & man. This doth sygnyfye howe the son of god was lyfte up of the Jewes, nayled upon the crosse betwene two theves and of two sortes of people mocked as of the Jewes and infydelles.

[Sig. Miiii^v] The xx Artycle of the masse

Howe the preest after that he hathe lyfte the blyssed body of oure lorde, he doth lyfte the chalyce with the precyous blode of god. This doth sygnyfye how our lorde beynge lyfte up with the crosse, the Jewes dyd lette it fall so rudely with the body in to the mortays: that all his woundes and specyally the fyve woundes did renne downe with blode abundauntly as a fountayne upon the erth.

[Sig. Ni.] The xxi Artycle of the masse

How the preest after the elevacyon doth stand upryght with his armes spred abrode prayenge for the people. This doth sygnyfye howe our lorde hangynge on the crosse was mocked of the Jewes and paynyms which did not knowe hym. Yet nevertheles he dyd praye for them, which dyd kyll and crucyfye hym, as for symple folkes and infydelles whiche dyde not knowe what they dyd.

[Sig. Ni^v] The xxii Artycle of the masse

How the preest after this dothe make vii crosses upon the sacrament. This sygnyfyeth howe God hangynge on the crosse dyd speke these vii wordes in great sorowe and anguysshe of his herte. The fyrste worde, Father forgyve them, for they can not tell what they do. The ii. thou shall be with me this daye in paradyse. The iii. mother se here thy sone, and to his dyscyple, se here thy mother. The iiii. O my god, why hast thou forsaken me. The v. I am a thrust. The vi all is accomplysshed and ended. The vii. father I betake or commende my soule in to thy handes.

[Sig. Nii] The xxiii Artycle of the masse

Howe the preest beynge in his seconde Memento prayeth for the soules that be departed beynge in purgatorye. This doth sygnyfie the great darkenes and scylence that was throughout the worlde, whyles that god dyd speke on the crosse afore that he dyed for our synnes.

Langforde in the first part of the Canon concentrates on the Last Supper, then when he comes to the words of institution, seen as words of consecration, gives directions for prayers to be said at the elevation:

Honour this blessed sacrament to the profit of your own soul, your friends and all Christian souls, both quick and dead, and if it like

you, ye may say with due reverence to the blessed body of our
Lord, in the first elevation, this little orison following; it is taken of
the Church, wherefore is it of more authority.
Salve lux mundi Rex regum gloria celi
Ultro qui mortis pro nobis Iura subisti
Salve nostra salus, pax vera redemptio virtus. Qui.
And likewise to the blessed blood of our Lord. In the second
elevation at your pleasure you may say thus,
Ave precium redemptoris nostri
Ave pignus hereditatis eterne
Benedictus sit dominus deus meus
Iesus xpus de cuius latere
Effusus es pro redemptione mundi. Amen.[63]

This moment, of the consecration of the bread and wine to be the
body and blood of Christ, was the emotional and spiritual as well as
the theological high-point of the Mass. Cranmer himself provides one
of the most vivid and oft-quoted descriptions of this moment:

For else what made the people to run from their seats to the altar,
and from altar to altar, and from sacring (as they called it) to
sacring, peeping, tooting, and gazing at that thing which the priest
held up in his hands, if they thought not to honour that thing which
they saw? What moved the priests to lift up the sacrament so high
over their heads; or the people to cry to the priest, 'Hold up! Hold
up!' and one man to say to another, 'Stoop down before;' or to say,
'This day have I seen my Maker;' and, 'I cannot be quiet, except I
see my Maker once a-day?' What was the cause of all these, and
that as well the priest as the people so devoutly did knock and kneel
at every sight of the sacrament, but that they worshipped that visible
thing which they saw with their eyes, and took it for very God?[64]

The remainder of the Canon is covered by Langforde with
a long description of the trial, mockery and passion of Christ. He
also emphasizes the same ritual as we saw in the *Rationale* and
Interpretacyon: the priest 'immediately after the sacring spreads and
splays his arms abroad in the manner of a cross, signifying the press of
the Passion of Christ'.[65]

---

63 *Meditations*, p. 24.
64 Cranmer, *Defence*, 4, in T. Crammer, *Works*, ed. J.E. Cox, PS, 2 vols (Cambridge:
Cambridge University Press, 1844, 46), Vol. I, p. 229.
65 *Meditations*, p. 25.

The end of the Canon makes no break in the allegorical sequence for either the *Interpretacyon* or for Langforde. For the latter, the Lord's Prayer which follows directly after the Canon, with its seven petitions, evokes mention of the seven last words of Christ on the cross; and the embolism 'Grant us peace . . .' leads the reader to remember peace between God and humanity, peace in each person's heart and peace between individuals. At the doxology of the Lord's Prayer Langforde comments:

> Never forget this most tender loving Pelican which of his mere mercy would vouchsafe not only to die for to save his birds but over that he hath ordained and disposed his most glorious and blessed flesh and blood to be our daily food, ministered and consecrate in the masse in that most gracious sacrament of the Altar signifying the blessed oblation and sacrifice of the most precious death and passion of our merciful redeemer.

Christ is then described as a lamb among lions and wolves, which leads the writer to discuss the Agnus Dei.[66]

g. Lord's Prayer, communion devotions

The *Interpretacyon* continues to explain the Lord's Prayer and communion devotions as follows:

> The xxiiii Artycle of the masse
> [Sig. Nii^v]How the preest after the Memento with a hygh voyce dothe synge to the father celestyall: Pater noster qui es in celis. This doth sygnyfye that our lorde preparynge hym selfe on the crosse to dye hath cryed with a hygh voyce, the heed inclyned, the iyes closed, the vysage pale, the voyce sorowynge agaynst nature, o father celestyall in to thy handes I do yelde my soule.
> The xxv Artycle of the masse
> [Sig. Niii] Howe the preest doth breke the holy sacrament in thre partyes and sayth thre tymes Agnus dei qui tollis peccata mundi miserere nobis. This doth sygnyfye howe god hangynge on the crosse hath converted and hath had mercy of thre maner of folkes. That is to say, of the thefe at his ryght hande: of Longinus whiche dyde perce the herte of oure lorde with a spere, and of many other of the common people which were there present.

---

66 *Meditations*, pp. 25–7.

The xxvi Artycle of the masse
[Sig. Niii^v] Howe the preest brekynge the sacrament doth let one peace fall in to the chalyce. This doth sygnyfye that whan the herte of our lorde was braste on the crosse he descended in to hell brekynge the same and delyvered from thens the patryarches, prophetes, and the auncyent fathers there beynge prysoners.

Langforde also used the placing of a piece of the host in the chalice to represent the burial of Christ and the descent to hell.[67]

The xxvii Artycle of the masse
Howe the preest dothe take the paxe holdynge the sacrament a lytell space in his handes, and after doth lay it downe upon the aulter. This doth sygnyfye | [sig. Niiii] how chryste a lytel whyle after his deth was taken downe from the crosse, & layed before the lappe of our lady his blyssed mother there present & very pensyve & dolent.
The xxviii Artycle of the masse
How the preest doth take the blyssed sacrament with both his handes reverently receyvyng it. This dothe sygnyfye howe god was reverently put in the sepulchre betwene the handes of Joseph and Nycodemus: after moche hevynes and | [sig. Niiii^v] sorowe whiche our lady & other his frendes there had showed and made afore that they dyd let hym departe from them.

Communion here completes the allegory of the Passion of Christ. This section is missing in Langforde's commentary, but a summary gives his overall scheme:

From the beginning of the mass unto the sacring you may have meditation of our Lord's blessed Incarnation and preaching. And from the sacring unto the using be done, you may remember the Maundy, the torments, the passion and death of our Saviour, and, after the post Communion you may consider the joyful state of the resurrection, and in the time of *Ite Missa est* his glorious ascension as it appeareth in the next Meditation following.[68]

So both Langforde and Gararde take a similar scheme in this section of the Mass, in that they both take the priest's communion (communion by the laity was infrequent and ignored in these commentaries which

---

67 *Meditations*, p. 27.
68 *Meditations*, p. 28.

evidently were intended to support the worshipper's usual attendance at Mass) to conclude the Passion, death and burial of Christ; and in so doing they ignore the structure of the prayers, basing themselves instead on the landmarks of the consecration and the communion.

The *Rationale* works more closely to the text of the Mass, and so opts for a different approach after the Canon. The Lord's Prayer is said by the priest as a preparation for communion; the breaking of the bread symbolizes the distribution at the Last Supper as well as the breaking of Christ's body in his Passion; and the Peace picks up Christ's words at the Last Supper: 'Peace I give to you.' The threefold Agnus Dei represents

> three effects of Christ's passion, wherefore the first is deliverance from the misery of sin, the second is from pain of everlasting damnation wherefore he saith twice 'miserere nobis', that is to say, have mercy upon us: and the third effect is giving of everlasting peace consisting in the glorious fruition of God, wherefore he saith 'dona nobis pacem', that is to say, give us peace.

The placing of the bread in the chalice, unlike the commentaries above, is said to represent 'the joining together of [Christ's] body and soul in the resurrection, which before were severed at the time of his passion'.[69]

The sharing of the Peace was an important feature of the parish Mass on Sundays and holy days. The ceremony was performed by each person kissing a tablet called the paxbred, beginning with the priest, and with due sensitivity to peace but also social status in the community.[70]

The *Rationale* acknowledges that the priest is usually the only one to receive communion, but tries to incorporate the congregation by saying that its purpose is 'an exciting or a moving to the people to laud and praise God'; also it reminds the reader that in earlier days general communion was common. So at the post-communion prayer the priest gives thanks for the congregation's 'spiritual refection'.[71]

h. Post-communion

> Here begynneth the thyrde parte of the masse, of the glorious resurreccyon of our lorde Jhesu chryste . . .
> [Sig. Oi^v] The xxix Artycle of the masse

---

69 *Rationale*, pp. 26–7.
70 Duffy, *Stripping of the Altars*, pp. 125–7.
71 *Rationale*, p. 27.

Howe the preest doth take all that is within the chalyce and dothe emptye it and leve it open. This doth sygnyfye how our lorde on the thyrde day dyd ryse from deth and left the sepulchre emptye and open, and dyd fyrste appere to his hevy mother: & than afterwarde to his other frendes.

[Sig. Oii] The xxx Artycle of the masse

How the preest cometh with the chalyce towardes the end of the aulter takynge wyne for the percepcyon. This doth sygnyfye how our lorde after that he was rysen from deth dyd appere to his dyscyples eatynge with them fysshes rosted: the which they had taken by the commaundment of god.

The xxxi Artycle of the masse

Howe the preest in the myddes of the aulter doth tourne hym in dysioynynge and takynge his handes a sondre sayth Dominus vobiscum. This doth [sig. Oiiᵛ] sygnyfye howe our lorde after that he was rysen from deth, dyd appere & showe hym selfe amonges his dyscyples sayenge Pax vobis, that is to saye, peace be with you, showynge his handes & fete persed through.

The xxxii Artycle of the masse

How the preest doth tourne hym sayeng Ite missa est, that is to saye in a maner, go ye the mysterye of the masse is done. This sygnyfyeth how god afore that he dyd ascende in to heven he commaunded to his dyscyples, to go preche sayenge, | [sig. Oiii] Go through all the worlde and preche the holy gospell to all creatures, and he that doth byleve and is baptysed, he shall be saved.

The xxxiii Artycle of the masse

Howe the preest, whan he hath sayd and red all: he gyveth the benedyccion upon all those that be there present & than he dothe tourne hym from the people retournynge thyther from whens he came. This doth sygnyfie that after that the sone of god had accomplysshed all thynge after the wyll | (Oiiiᵛ) of god his father, he gave his benedyccyon to all those that were upon the Mount of Olyvete, & dyd ascende in to heven where he doth syt on the ryght hande of god his father.

Here endeth the seconde boke of the masse.

The final blessing and dismissal in all three commentaries takes us to the Ascension. The allegorical cycle is thus complete. In none of these three commentaries is the descent of the Holy Spirit at Pentecost included at this point. The historical narration is bounded in time; the individual worshipper and the congregation are not bidden to include themselves as Christ's Church within the narration, but approach it, as it were, from outside through the Mass.

The end of the parish Mass was marked by a final important ceremony: the distribution of blessed bread. (A similar custom is observed today in the Eastern Orthodox Churches.)[72]

i. The limitation of the commentaries

In the light of Reformation controversy, it is worth considering the way in which these commentaries handle the theme of the eucharist as sacrifice. It has been observed that the *Rationale* keeps almost total silence on the issue, and it has been suggested that this betrays the lack of agreement between conservatives and evangelicals on the drafting committee.[73] Certainly it is remarkable that when the commentary is set out beside the text of the Canon (above) the sacrificial elements of the prayer are passed over in silence, and this does carry some significance in a commentary which pays very close attention to the text. However, it must be said that in the genre of commentaries on the eucharist, the theme of eucharistic sacrifice is remarkable for its absence. Josef Jungmann comments on this very point when he considers the allegories through the whole of the Middle Ages and observes:

> The Mass is viewed almost exclusively as an action of God. In the liturgical unfolding of the celebration of Mass, the action of the Church, its prayer of thanks, and its gift-offerings are no longer perceived as in former ages; only the work, the redeeming work of God. The priest alone is active. The faithful, viewing what he is performing, are like spectators looking on at a mystery-filled drama of our Lord's Way of the Cross . . . The *eucharistia* has become an *epiphania*, an advent of God who appears amongst men and dispenses his graces. To gain a share in these graces, we are gathered before the altar, in an attitude of wondering contemplation that bespeaks our longing to take part in the Mass as often as possible.[74]

But more can be said from comparing the *Rationale* with the other commentaries. In them the communion devotions form the focus of Christ's death, and it is then that Langforde speaks most explicitly of sacrifice: 'signifying the blessed oblation and sacrifice of the most precious death and passion of our merciful redeemer'. Likewise in

---

72   Duffy, *Stripping of the Altars*, p. 125.
73   MacCulloch, *Cranmer*, p. 276.
74   J.A. Jungmann, *The Mass of the Roman Rite*, trans. F.A. Brunner, 2 vols (New York: Benzinger Bros, 1951), Vol. 1, p. 117.

the explanation by the *Rationale* it is in the communion devotions rather than in the Canon that we do have one example of traditional eucharistic piety: the priest says the Lord's Prayer 'to the intent he may the more worthily receive the holy and blessed body and blood of Christ both to the comfort and strength, as well of him self as of them that be present'.[75] This issue, whether one person could receive communion to the benefit of someone else, depended on the theology of eucharistic sacrifice and would be closely debated in the preparations for the English Prayer Book.[76]

In conclusion, contemporary records reveal the Mass to have been regarded as the cornerstone of popular faith and practice. To see and adore the consecrated host, daily if possible, was important for very large numbers of people. The Sunday parish Mass was adorned with considerable ceremony and represented a considerable financial investment by communities both great and small. For those who had the leisure and education, devotional aids such as primers and commentaries enabled an intelligent and prayerful attendance at frequent, even daily, Masses and equipped the worshipper to engage in the entire service even in its smallest ceremonial detail.

On the deficit side, while there was no significant theological controversy (except from Lollards) before the Reformation, there was a distance created by the intricacies of a service conducted in Latin, much of it in silence, and overlaid by ceremonial. The role of these commentaries was to enable the worshipper to engage in these intricacies, and where they did not intrude (such as the Bidding of the Bedes and the elevation of the Host) the commentaries fell silent. The allegorical approach would probably have been known more widely than just by the readers of the commentaries at least in its more salient features, and one might suppose that the majority of worshippers would have understood that the clergy coming out of the vestry represented the incarnation, the readings signified his life and ministry; that the consecration linked them to the Last Supper and after that the priest stretching out his arms presented to them the sacrifice of Calvary. Then the Peace, whether or not shared ceremonially as on a Sunday, was that peace bought by Christ on the cross, and the final blessing was that given by the ascended Lord.

It might be unfair to suggest that the consecration of the bread and wine as the Body and Blood of Christ to be seen and worshipped

---

75 *Rationale*, p. 26. Cobb's edition notes some small differences in this passage between the two manuscripts, but they are not theologically significant.
76 See 'Questions put concerning some abuses of the Mass' with Cranmer's Answers, PS, II, p. 150.

was somehow intruded into this cognitive framework, and there is no suggestion that it was consciously perceived in this way; but this moment was seen as a thing apart from the rest of the Mass, and the way in which Langforde breaks off from his explanation to include particular prayers is no doubt a clue as to how the consecration was experienced. The *Interpretacyon* does not include any particular prayers to mark the elevation, and we may be confident that many a reader would have used other prayers at that point gleaned from primers or childhood memory.

It is no wonder that under the spotlight of reform and renewal, and of theological controversy, this approach to the eucharist could not survive. The greatest of all the Western allegorical commentators, Durandus, was the most published human author in the late fifteenth century with 44 separate editions before 1501, but with virtually no editions after 1614.[77] Even the *Rationale*, whose Reformist agenda was broadly conservative, was attempting to bring the worshipper's attention more closely to the text. Whatever the popularity of the Mass in the early 1500s, the ways in which its appropriation was detached from its textual and liturgical core made it all the more vulnerable to the storms of the Reformation.

As for other forms of liturgical practice, the sharing of the Pax and blessed bread enabled regular active participation and spared all but the clergy and the very pious the considerable discipline of frequent confession and communion. We shall see in the response to the 1549 Prayer Book that the reform which provoked most hostile comments was the pressure on ordinary churchgoers to receive frequent communion; and while Tudor obedience impelled most ordinary people to abandon the old religion with little or no comment it was another matter to persuade them to take up new patterns of devotion.

---

77   Rorem, *Liturgical Symbolism*, p. 29.

Chapter 2

REFORM DURING THE REIGN OF HENRY VIII

1 CRANMER'S THEOLOGY OF JUSTIFICATION

The Edwardian Prayer Books represent only the very end of a long and tortuous process of attempts at liturgical revision. Throughout that time Cranmer's theology also underwent considerable development. His notebooks, questions and answers in questionnaires, speeches and published works, letters and various remarks enable us to build up a fragmentary but reasonably consistent picture of how his sacramental theology developed over nearly two decades. But we cannot study this development in isolation. First, his sacramental theology evolved in the context of his understanding of justification. Secondly, Cranmer's theology was worked out among other theologies, the religious background of traditional Catholicism and the various official statements of faith which served as signposts of Henry VIII's religious policies.

When we reach the House of Lords debate on the eucharist in December 1548 we enter a period in which there is much more material for understanding the mature Cranmer's thoughts. But even before that date, it will be evident that there was significant development in Cranmer's thought. Sir John Cheke claimed that his eucharistic doctrine reached its maturity in 1546, though in the old-style dating this could mean any time up to March 1547, by which time it was safe to think other than Henry did.[1] However, it will become clear below that Cranmer's sacramental theology had changed significantly in around 1543, and perhaps even earlier, while his eucharistic theology was still developing through the middle of 1548. In effect there was a period of some years in which he tried to straddle two different approaches to the sacraments. The change in sacramental theology is closely linked to the evolution of his understanding of justification, and depends upon it.

Ashley Null's *Thomas Cranmer's Doctrine of Repentance* is one of the most important studies of the Archbishop's theology in recent years. Null outlines a picture of the development of Cranmer's understanding of

---

1   MacCulloch, *Cranmer*, pp. 354–5.

forgiveness and justification beginning with his early days in Cambridge when he would seem to have been a Scotist. Then in all likelihood there was a long period in which the new Archbishop looked to the Lutherans as, at least broadly, a model for the Church in England.[2] Null suggests that from the time of his visit to Nuremberg he adopted the interpretation of Paul through Augustine rather than, as formerly, through Erasmus, and espoused the view that justification precedes good works rather than vice versa. Justification was extrinsic, by imputation, and the accompanying renewal of the will was intrinsic.[3]

Cranmer's views on justification matured in the 1540s, largely in reaction to his conservative opponents whose views were to be enshrined in the King's Book of 1543. This conflict provides the context for understanding the development of Cranmer's sacramental and baptismal theology. Null summarizes Cranmer's progress to his mature doctrine thus:

> In response to his conservative opponents, Cranmer engaged in a massive research project to prove that justification *sola fide et gratia ex praedestinatione ante praevisa merita* was the true Augustinian soteriology. Crucial to Cranmer's argument was the renovation of the will and its affections which justification by imputation effected. In the moment of justification God granted both faith and love. The believer's faith laid hold of the extrinsic righteousness of Christ on which basis his sins were pardoned. At the same time the Holy Spirit indwelt the believer, stirring in him a love for God out of gratitude for the assurance of salvation.[4]

The renovation of the will was a central aspect of Cranmer's theology. Works cannot justify, since before the moment of justification no work, lacking love, can be acceptable to God. Good works after justification are a response to it. Repentance is part of being 'right-willed' and evidence of election to eternal salvation. 'To protect the utter gratuity of this saving faith Cranmer appealed to Augustine's teaching on the unconditional predestination of the elect to eternal life.'[5]

We shall see that this emphasis on election and on the moment of justification pre-empting any human initiative forced a split in Cranmer's theology between the sacrament of baptism and the grace which it signifies. In an age of infant initiation, ironically it was the theology of

---

2   MacCulloch outlines evidence for Cranmer's early resistance to Luther: see *Cranmer*, pp. 26–30.
3   Null, *Repentance*, pp. 72, 103–5.
4   Null, *Repentance*, pp. 251–2.
5   Null, *Repentance*, p. 252.

adult baptism which brought most pressure to bear, but the baptism of infants too presented its difficulty in the case of the faith of the child, and long before the Archbishop was ready to apply the logic to the eucharist, he had accepted in some way the principle that the sacrament of baptism signifies but cannot be identified unequivocally with the grace.

2 THE BEGINNINGS OF REFORM

a. *Cranmer's earliest interests in liturgical reform*

There is some evidence that Cranmer was seriously considering a reformed English liturgy as early as the mid 1530s. The Book of Common Prayer of 1549 represents Cranmer's mature theological position as he presented it in the House of Lords debate of 1548; however, it probably also contains much material drafted in earlier periods of his work and thought. Good texts drafted earlier are more likely to be retained and adapted than simply discarded. Therefore as we approach the Prayer Book liturgy it is necessary to explore the various times when liturgical change might have been considered, and might have provided material which would find its way into the later published liturgies.

Cranmer's interest in liturgical details is first attested by a colleague, Sir Thomas Elyot, whom Cranmer accompanied on an embassy to the Holy Roman Emperor. They arrived at Nuremberg in 1532, where they witnessed Lutheran worship for the first time. Elyot reported:

> The priest, in vestments after our manner, singeth everything in Latin, as we use, omitting suffrages. The Epistle he readeth in Latin. In the meantime the subdeacon goeth into the pulpit and readeth to the people the Epistle in their vulgar; after, they peruse other things as our priests do. Then the priest readeth softly the Gospel in Latin. In the mean space the deacon goeth into the pulpit and readeth aloud the Gospel in the Almain tongue. Mr Cranmer saith it was showed to him that in the Epistles and Gospels they kept not the order that we do, but do peruse every day one chapter of the New Testament. After, the priest and the choir do sing the Creed as we do; the Secrets and Preface they omit, and the priest singeth with a high voice the Words of the Consecration; and after the elevation the deacon turneth to the people, telling to them in the Almain tongue a long process how they should prepare themselves to the communion of the flesh and blood of Christ; and then may every man come that listeth, without going to any confession . . . [6]

---

6   Cuming, *History*, p. 279, quoting *Original Letters*, PS, pp. 11, 191.

It was at Nuremberg that Cranmer married Osiander's niece; thereby his visit to this city demonstrated for the first time his positive attitude to the Reformation as well as his continued affection for matrimony. However, when he returned to England in the next year, now as Archbishop elect, he had to be discreet about both his marriage and his theological leanings.

b. The movement in the theology of penance among the Henrician theologians

The traditional Western view was that sacramental penance for sins after baptism was effective *ex opere operato*. Erasmus discouraged this view in his *Exomologesis sive modus confitendi* of 1524, but still believed that confession had many benefits. He took an *ex opere operantis* position, in which the sacrament encouraged and helped the penitent's growth in love and trust. The penitent's disposition was all-important.[7]

The Henrician theologians conducting the anti-papal campaign connected the idea of *ex opere operato* sacramental penance with the papal authority. Whereas Henry's *Assertio septem sacramentorum* of 1521 had affirmed the traditional theology on the basis of Mt. 16.19,[8] the *Collectanea satis copiosa*, attacking clerical authority, noted Jerome's comments on the same verse from scripture, that one is neither bound nor loosed by the priest's sentence, but only by one's own innocence or guilt. And it asserted that the pope has no greater authority in this matter than any ordinary priest.[9] Null traces from this time, if indeed not earlier under the influence of Erasmus, Cranmer's own move in his theology of penance from an *ex opere operato* position.[10]

The Henrician consensus continued with the principle that sacramental confession operated *ex opere operantis* and was not obligatory by divine command. According to a contemporary treatise, auricular confession was required only by 'the law of man'.[11] A similar view was suggested by a questionnaire of c. 1537.[12]

---

7   Null, *Repentance*, pp. 89–93.

8   Henry VIII, *Assertio septem sacramentorum* (London: in aedibus Pynsonianis, 1521), sig. B2[v]; Null, *Repentance*, p. 97.

9   'Hieronimus ergo existimat reum sacerdotis sententia nec solvi nec alligari, sed sola sua ipsius vel innocentia vel culpa. Item non maiorem esse hac in re pontificis auctoritatem quam cuiusque sacerdotis', *Collectanea satis copiosa*, BL, Cotton MS Cleop. EVI, fol. 69[v]; Null, *Repentance*, p. 97.

10   Null, *Repentance*, p. 103.

11   A. Aless, *A treatise concernynge generalle councilles, the bisshopes of Rome and the clergy* (London: Berthelet, 1538).

12   PS, *Cranmer*, II, pp. 465–6 where it is attributed to Cranmer. But Null (*Repentance*, pp. 119–20), attributes it to Simon Haynes, Dean of Exeter.

c. First steps in reform

The first reformed liturgical publication in England was *A Primer in English*, edited by William Marshall, in 1534. Like medieval primers, designed to be used by lay people in their private or household prayers, it contained versions of Matins, Evening Prayer with prayers during the day based on the monastic hours. In addition to devotional and didactic material from Luther, Marshall used an earlier banned work, the *Hortulus animae* of George Joye which had used material from Bucer, Luther and Tyndale's Bible translation. A later edition included material omitted out of Reformist sensibilities: a Litany (based on Luther's but with saints now included) and the Office of the Dead. Marshall's *Primer* and other similar publications enjoyed a semi-official status, and in effect provided experimental translations of prayers and canticles which would be drawn on in time for the Prayer Book.[13] But more radical change was being considered.

> Last of all, how think you of matrimony? Is all well here? What of baptism? Shall we evermore in ministering of it speak Latin, and not in English rather, that the people may know what is said and done? What think ye of these mass-priests, and of the masses themselves? What say ye? Be all things here so without abuses, that nothing ought to be amended? Your forefathers saw somewhat, which made this constitution against the venality and sale of masses, that, under pain of suspending, no priest should sell his saying of tricennials or annals.[14]

This was no soapbox orator speaking, but the Bishop of Worcester preaching to the Convocation of Clergy in 1536, and his sermon, delivered in Latin, was published in English for general distribution. Bishop Hugh Latimer outlined two separate issues which, he believed, called for reform: in liturgy an English language form of the two occasional offices of baptism and marriage; and in canon law the suppression of fees for Masses.

When Henry VIII broke with Rome there were at first no implications for the liturgical life of England beyond the removal of the name of the pope from the liturgy. But Henry's attempts to forge an alliance with the Lutherans against the papacy were soon to raise the spectre of a

---

13 Cuming, *History*, pp. 30–2; idem, *The Godly Order*, Alcuin Club Collection, 65 (London: SPCK, 1983), pp. 26–55.
14 Sermon before the Convocation of the Clergy, 9 June 1536; the Second Sermon; in *Sermons*, ed. G.E. Corrie, Parker Society (Cambridge: Cambridge University Press, 1844), pp. 55–6.

much more radical change in ceremonies. MacCulloch quotes Chapuys as linking the return from Saxony of Bishop Foxe of Hereford on 4 July (possibly bearing a copy of the Wittenberg Articles) with a motion in parliament 'for the reformation of the state and ceremonies of the Church in imitation of what has been accomplished in that country'. However, a statute going through parliament extinguishing the papal authority ended up with a clause affirming that the statute did not affect traditional ceremonies used in the Church.[15]

d. The Ten Articles (1536) and the Bishops' Book (1537)

The period from 1536 to 1538 saw intense activity in the formation of a series of statements of faith, all looking in various ways in the Lutheran direction. Two sets, the Wittenberg Articles of 1536 and the Thirteen Articles of 1538, were the results of discussions directly with Lutheran representatives. The Ten Articles, published in 1536, and the *Institution of a Christian Man* (the Bishops' Book) of 1537 were primarily 'domestic' productions and not always sympathetic to Lutheranism, but they and the two sets of Articles belong together as part of the same process of English reform.

The Ten Articles discussed both issues of faith and the ceremonies of the Church. With regard to the former, there is a very close link to the Wittenberg Articles which were not published at the time but seem to have been brought back to England by the delegates just in time to be used in the process of drafting.[16] With regard to the sacraments, the Ten Articles, like those of Wittenberg, covered only baptism, eucharist and penance. Silence covered those sacraments not accepted by the Lutherans.

When dealing with baptism, the Ten Articles followed the 'ecumenical' agreement very closely, tending mainly to expand the earlier work with scriptural references. The sacrament was instituted by Christ as necessary for the attainment of everlasting life (quoting Jn 3.5), and for forgiveness of sins and the grace and favour of God (quoting Mk 16.16). The article includes much material against the Anabaptists (greatly expanding the Wittenberg version), and affirms the rightness of baptizing infants. They, as much as adults, receive the remission of sins by baptism. It is affirmed that children are born in original sin, which is remitted by baptism and not otherwise, and adults

---

15 MacCulloch, *Cranmer*, p. 165.
16 MacCulloch, *Cranmer*, pp. 161–6.

coming to be baptized receive forgiveness of all their sins, though the condition of penitence and faith in the case of adults is carefully and fully spelt out. Baptism is not to be repeated.[17]

One phrase in this Article, that concluding the section on the necessity of baptism for infants, has drawn much comment in later writers: 'Inasmuch as infants and children dying in their infancy shall undoubtedly be saved thereby, *and else not*.'[18] This affirms the traditional doctrine of the necessity of baptism for the salvation of children who die in their infancy. The final three words seem to lay inordinate stress on this particular item. However, it may be that this is accidental. For the draft version of the Article preserved in the Cotton Manuscripts and published by Lloyd has the same phrase, 'or else not' concluding this section and that on the necessity of baptism for adults and those who have the use of reason.[19] In the second instance the phrase can only be understood as qualifying the entire section, namely that baptism, repentance and faith are all necessary for grace and remission of sins for adults. The qualifying phrase disappeared from this section before publication of the Articles, and so it may have been a mere scribal error. However, it is hard to avoid at least the possibility that the paired qualifications were originally deliberate, and that, in the light of this, the qualification on infant baptism should be read as referring to the entire section, not just to the case of infant mortality.

Some material from the Wittenberg Article on baptism did not find its way into the Ten Articles. Details of the continuation of concupiscence are omitted, and also the Wittenberg version includes extra scriptural verses on the necessity of faith for baptism.[20] The softening of both might be the result of an attempt by the drafters in England to draw a veil over the battle between English and Lutheran orthodoxies.

The description of the sacrament of penance is wholeheartedly traditionalist, maintaining that it was instituted by Christ and necessary for salvation for the forgiveness of sins committed after baptism.[21]

The article on the eucharist contented itself with a firm restatement of the Real Presence of Christ 'under the form and figure of bread and

---

17   C. Lloyd (ed.), *Formularies of Faith put forth by Authority during the Reign of Henry VIII* (Oxford: Clarendon Press, 1825), pp. xviii–xx.

18   Lloyd, *Formularies of Faith*, p. xix (my italics). For later discussions, see e.g. J.D.C. Fisher, *Christian Initiation, the Reformation Period*, Alcuin Club Collection, 51 (London: SPCK, 1970), pp. 74–5.

19   Lloyd, *Formularies of Faith*, p. 7.

20   Wittenberg Article III: N.S. Tjernagel, *Henry VIII and the Lutherans: A Study in Anglo-Lutheran Relations from 1521 to 1547* (St Louis, MO: Concordia, 1965), p. 257.

21   Lloyd, *Formularies of Faith*, pp. xx–xxi.

wine'. Transubstantiation is neither affirmed nor denied by name, but only the term itself is absent from a wholly traditional statement.[22]

The Ten Articles were incorporated with minimal changes in the *Institution of a Christian Man*, published in 1537 under the authority of the bishops, and known as the Bishops' Book (though the bishops themselves asked the king for licence to publish the book).[23] The Book when published affirmed that there are seven sacraments, but that while matrimony, confirmation, orders and unction were rightly called sacraments, they were inferior to baptism, penance and eucharist which were instituted by Christ as 'instruments or remedies necessary for our salvation'; they are commanded by Christ to be administered; and they concern grace for the remission of sins and our renewal and sanctification as members of Christ's body.[24] Articles were added on these four sacraments.

The section on confirmation in the Bishops' Book also affirms the importance of the sacrament of baptism, that by its virtue and efficacy the candidates are 'perfectly regenerated in Christ, perfectly incorporated and made the very members of his body, and had received full remission of their sins, and were replenished with abundance and plentifulness of the graces and gifts of the Holy Ghost'. Nevertheless it is conceded that the apostles, while recognizing all this, gave the Holy Ghost by the laying-on of hands and prayer. This is explained by saying that many who had received the gifts of the Holy Spirit by baptism lost them by temptation. Therefore it was expedient for all to be confirmed by the bishop:

> that is to say, they should receive such gifts of the Holy Ghost, as whereby they should not only be so corroborated and established in the gifts and graces before received in baptism, that they should not lightly fall again from the same but should constantly retain them, and persevere therein, and should also be made strong and hardy, as well to confess boldly and manfully their faith before all the persecutors of the same, and to resist and fight against their ghostly enemies, the world, the Devil and the flesh, as also to bear the cross of Christ, that is, to suffer and sustain patiently all the afflictions and adversities of this world; but also that they should attain increase and abundance of the other virtues and graces of the Holy Ghost.

Finally it is stated that salvation is assured by baptism, and confirmation is not necessary.[25]

---

22   Lloyd, *Formularies of Faith*, pp. xxv–xxvi.
23   Lloyd, *Formularies of Faith*, pp. 92–4; Fisher, *Christian Initiation*, pp. 73–5.
24   Bishops' Book, appendix to Article on Extreme Unction, Lloyd, *Formularies of Faith*, pp. 128–9.
25   Lloyd, *Formularies of Faith*, pp. 94–6; Fisher, *Christian Initiation*, pp. 221–2.

This section is of interest because we see first how confirmation is already presented as a recapitulation of baptism rather than a sacrament giving a separate grace. The language of renunciation of the world, the Devil and the flesh is obviously reminiscent of the later baptismal rite and the mention of the cross of Christ points in particular to the formula of signing the forehead.

A full analysis of the Ten Articles and the Bishops' Book is beyond the scope of this work. With regard to the former, MacCulloch mentions how unsatisfactory the article on penance would have seemed to the Lutherans and indeed to Cranmer himself.[26] It is hard to see what in the article on baptism would require a Lutheran interpretation.[27] The Bishops' Book continued to sit on the same fence; the other sacraments are included but in a second league: the article on confirmation exploits the difficulties of the silence of scripture but all could sign it because nothing was actually denied. For a more clear picture of Cranmer's own views, we have to look elsewhere.

e. Questions and answers concerning confirmation, 1537

Cranmer's personal views on confirmation at about this time are to be found in his 'Answers to Queries concerning Confirmation'. Cranmer denies that confirmation is a sacrament instituted by Christ, saying that there is no record of any institution but that it was a special gift given to the apostles for the confirmation of God's word at that time, but that it did not continue to later generations; that scripture makes no mention of any exterior sign in confirmation but the Church has used chrism; and that the efficacy of the sacrament is 'of such value as is the prayer of the bishop made in the name of the church'. This last answer seems, in one way, to be somewhat disingenuous, for Cranmer sets himself to answer the question of the efficacy of confirmation, but the other returns from bishops and divines deal with the question of what promise be made of the grace of the sacrament.[28] Did Cranmer avoid discussing the promise

---

26 MacCulloch, *Cranmer*, pp. 161, 164.

27 Richard Rex, *Henry VIII and the English Reformation* (London: Macmillan, 1993), pp. 145–8, portrays the Ten Articles as essentially conservative.

28 Cranmer's own answers are to be found in PS, II, p. 80. Fisher, *Christian Initiation*, pp. 208–20, gives the replies of other bishops and divines with an accurate summary of the questions. J. Strype, *Ecclesiastical Memorials*, 3 vols (Oxford: Clarendon Press, 1822), Appendix no. 88 (Vol. 1/2, pp. 340–63) gives a transcript of the individual questions as well as the answers in the manuscript. Fisher and also D. Selwyn, 'Cranmer's Writings: a Bibliographical Survey', in Ayris and Selwyn, *Cranmer: Churchman and Scholar*, pp. 281–302 (p. 290), date the queries and replies to c. 1537.

deliberately? For certainly if there was no institution of the sacrament or command to administer it, then there could be no promise. But more than the question of logic, it is fair to see here a contrast in Cranmer's mind between the efficacy of 'the prayer of the bishop made in the name of the church', no doubt of great value in itself, and the sacrament, instituted and commanded by Christ with promises of grace. But besides the difference over the institution of the sacrament, Cranmer's answer about what it achieves is conventional in that it looks to growth after baptism – 'strength and constancy with other spiritual gifts'. There is no mention here of the confession of faith which, in the Bishops' Book, harks back to baptism.[29]

So there is a difference of emphasis between Cranmer's own statement and that of the Bishops' Book, but no contradiction. The Book describes the origins of confirmation as the apostolic practice rather than an explicit institution by Christ, and distinguishes between apostolic practice and later church practice. The use of chrism is attributed to ecclesiastical rather than apostolic authority. All these features are strongly reminiscent of both Cranmer's own views and the Lutheran approach to confirmation, but are different from the consensus of the other English divines shown in the responses to the questionnaire.[30]

f. Cranmer's method: questionnaires

In the questionnaire we see the Archbishop's method of proposing solutions to problems which he continued to use throughout his career. Questionnaires were very much the order of the day, with the bishops being asked to submit their views on whatever was the contentious issue of the time. (Henry VIII's annotations on the Bishops' Book were also circulated for comment among a small group, so the method was not unique to the Archbishop.) We have questionnaires and answers right up to the late 1540s, and it could be said that Bucer's comments on the 1549 Prayer Book belong to this type of material, though there is no set of questions as such, in that they were submitted along with other

---

29 In the Answer of Hilsey, Bishop of Rochester, to the 'Questions concerning Confirmation' (Fisher, *Christian Initiation*, p. 210) there is reference to a book by Edward Foxe, Bishop of Hereford, which described how 'this holy and godly ceremony began by holy fathers, to examine the faith of them that were baptized infants, when that they should come to years of discretion . . . and then, through the word and prayer and imposition of hands, confirmed that faith which they did confess with their mouths'. This may be the origin of the passage in the Bishops' Book.

30 Cf. Fisher's remarks, *Christian Initiation*, p. 220. It is a great pity that we do not have Foxe's reply.

people's observations to a committee looking at further reform. Cranmer himself would answer the questionnaires, even on the occasions when it is very probable, from surviving draft sets of questions, that he himself had been their author. It is not certain what was done with the replies to these questionnaires. No doubt on occasion the aim was to conciliate; at other times he would have sought to overrule the opposition. In either case the replies gave Cranmer the information he needed to formulate his policies. The management of the various groups and interests was a most difficult part of his search for reform, and it will be suggested below that many features of the Prayer Books were in response to the views set out in these questionnaires, whether or not Cranmer sympathized with them.

g. Cranmer's speech to the bishops

In early 1537 there was a debate among the bishops on the number of sacraments as part of the preparations for the Bishops' Book. Cranmer himself, in the version of his speech preserved, questioned whether confirmation, orders and unction should rank with baptism and the Lord's Supper since they cannot be proved to have been instituted by Christ. There seems to have been no mention of penance and matrimony in his speech. Evidently he was keeping his counsel on those more difficult subjects.[31]

h. Cranmer's annotations to Henry VIII's corrections of the Bishops' Book

There was soon talk of revising the Bishops' Book, and Henry himself suggested various emendations. He sent his draft to Cranmer, and we possess his text and the Archbishop's comments, made in January 1538, and mostly unflattering. Theologically they are of interest in that they provide the first concrete evidence of Cranmer's understanding of justification, which he defends against Henry's traditionalist position. Thus where the king wishes to see a balance between the works done by the penitent and the merits of Christ, the latter being 'chiefly' the cause, Cranmer will have none of it:

---

31   PS, II, p. 79. For the date of the debate, Null (*Repentance*, p. 133, n. 52) reviews Ridley's and Rupp's preferred dates (May and February respectively) and argues for the debate occurring in the first week of Lent (18–25 February). MacCulloch (*Cranmer*, pp. 187–8), follows Null's dating and gives a description of the whole meeting as reported by Alexander Aless, *Of the auctorite of the word of God agaynst the bisshop of London* (Leipzig?, 1537?).

Certain it is, that our election cometh only and wholly of the benefit and grace of God, for the merits of Christ's passion, and for no part of our merits and good works: as St Paul disputeth and proveth at length in the epistle to the Romans and Galatians, and divers other places, saying, *Si ex operibus, non ex gratia; si ex gratia, non ex operibus.*[32]

And he opposes an assertion by Henry about 'having assured hope and confidence in Christ's mercy, willing to enter into the perfect faith'; Cranmer maintains rather that 'he that hath assured hope and confidence in Christ's mercy, hath already entered into a perfect faith'. He puts works firmly in their place:

These works only which follow our justification, do please God; forsomuch as they proceed from an heart endued with pure faith and love to God. But the works which we do before our justification, be not allowed and accepted before God, although they appear never so good and glorious in the sight of man. For after our justification only begin we to work as the law of God [requireth. Then we shall do all good works willingly, although not so exactly as the law] requireth, by mean of infirmity of the flesh. Nevertheless, by the merit and benefit of Christ, we being sorry that we cannot do all things no more exquisitely and duly, all our works shall be accepted and taken of God, as most exquisite, pure and perfect.

Cranmer proceeds to attack any idea of justification by one's own actions; one can look only to the righteousness of Christ 'by whom only all the saints in heaven, and all other that have been saved, have been reputed righteous and justified'.[33] Null identifies this with Melanchthon's doctrine of justification by *reputatio iustitiae Christi alienae.*[34]

The division of the sacraments into the three major and the four minor ones has to be defended by Cranmer, at any rate in preventing the addition of matrimony to the former category. The Archbishop reminds the king that matrimony does not fit the definition applied to the other three in the Bishops' Book, that it be instituted by Christ, that it be necessary to salvation, and that it be the means of regeneration and justification.[35] MacCulloch presents a splendid picture of the promotion of this sacrament

---

32 Annotations on Henry VIII's 'Corrections of the Institution of a Christian Man', PS, II, p. 95.
33 Annotations, PS, II, pp. 113–14.
34 Null, *Repentance*, p. 122.
35 Annotations, PS, II, pp. 99–100.

having been suggested by Henry in his 'almost neurotic reverence for marriage',[36] but we should not forget that it is described as a *sacramentum magnum* in scripture (Eph. 5.32), and Cranmer himself in his speech to the bishops on the sacraments had passed over its status in silence.

A different problem about the sacraments may be seen in another annotation. Henry proposes that priests be described as having the power 'to consecrate sacraments, and to administer the same'. Cranmer comments: 'Consecration is called only of the sacrament of the altar: therefore it is more plain to say thus: "to consecrate the body of Christ, and to minister the sacraments".'[37] His use of the word 'consecrate', as referring only to the eucharist, is very different from how he will apply it in years to come.

i. Preparations for reform of services

Liturgical reform was still on the agenda. A document published in 1538, *A treatise concernynge generalle councilles*, attributed to Alexander Aless (a confidant of Cranmer), argued for the right and responsibility of kings (not the pope, or even councils) to order the liturgy in their own realms: *cuius regio, illius ceremonia*! It was presupposed that the independence of the Church of England included the right, and in certain situations the duty, to reform the liturgy. Thus far a revision of the liturgy entailed only a Catholic revision, a pruning rather than a radical rejection of traditional forms. It was a further step to introduce Lutheran or Reformed doctrines into the revised liturgy. Parliament had evidently feared that Bishop Foxe's alliance with the Lutherans suggested a strong move in that direction. Later events were to prove that Henry himself was by no means committed to such a move; perhaps he was happy to let the various factions jockey for influence. But it is hard to imagine that he would have renounced indefinitely the right to govern the liturgical life of the Church of which he was supreme head.

The right of the monarch to order worship independently of pope or council may well underlie Cranmer's interest in traditional, especially non-Roman liturgical models, which became evident in the 1549 Prayer Book. (We may also note Cuming's suggestion that Cranmer's revision of the eucharistic prayer began with a translation of the Canon as found in the Sarum Missal and then proceeded to make his own alterations.)[38] What may seem to many as simply the arcane and obscure, the Eastern

---

36   MacCulloch, *Thomas Cranmer*, p. 212.
37   Annotations, PS, II, p. 97.
38   *Godly Order*, pp. 91–8.

eucharistic liturgies, Mozarabic blessings of the font, quotations from the Fathers, contemporary Spanish draft revisions of the office, can be seen equally as attempts by the king's servant to make good his master's claim to be lord in his own realm. What good is it to be free of Rome, and still to have to use Roman forms? At whatever date he wrote it, no doubt it was with satisfaction that Cranmer, when he read in his text of Ambrose's *De sacramentis* the Latin Father's comments on the footwashing, inserted a comment by the text: 'Ambrose did not follow the Church of Rome in everything.'[39]

Liturgical reform proceeded piecemeal. The suppression of shrines and certain holy days affected public life, though often the days continued to be observed.[40] Cromwell was encouraging outbursts of iconoclasm.[41] What we see of a positive direction in change reveals a concern for provision of the vernacular, as we have already noted in Latimer's sermon in 1536. In 1537 Edward Lee, Archbishop of York, required readings in English at Mass, and in 1538 it was stipulated that a Bible should be placed in every church, that the Creed, Lord's Prayer and Ten Commandments should be recited in English, and that no one be admitted to communion without having learnt them. In 1539 the Great Bible was published, and in 1540 reissued with a preface by Cranmer in which he promoted the benefits of reading scripture.[42] Editions of the Sarum Primer appeared with these English texts.[43] Privately, Cranmer seems to have been engaged in composing draft forms of the daily office around this time, based largely on the work of the Spanish Cardinal Quiñones but also with an eye to Lutheran examples. Although the form of service was in Latin, the emphasis on the people being instructed by the readings suggests that at least a vernacular scripture reading was envisaged.[44] It was possibly the daily office that we hear of in April 1538 when Cranmer wrote to Cromwell about the latter's chaplain whom the Archbishop had left behind in Ford 'occupied in the affairs of our church service, and now at the writing up of so much as he had to do'.[45] Apparently he had taken the labour in good part, but it was to bear no

39 'Non in omnibus secutus est Ambrosius ecclesiam Romanam', Ambrosius *Opera omnia*, 3 vols (Basle: A. Petri, 1516); BL, press mark 1355.k.9, fol. 234[r].
40 MacCulloch, *Cranmer*, p. 198.
41 MacCulloch, *Cranmer*, p. 214; S. Brigden, *London and the Reformation* (Oxford and New York: Clarendon Press, 1989), pp. 288–93.
42 MacCulloch, *Cranmer*, pp. 238–40, 258–60.
43 Cuming, *History*, p. 31.
44 Cuming, 'The Reform of the Daily Office', in *The Godly Order*, pp. 1–23: J. Wickham Legg (ed.), *Cranmer's Liturgical Projects*, Henry Bradshaw Society, 50 (London: Harrison & Sons, 1915).
45 Letter to Cromwell, 11 April 1538; PS, II, pp. 366–7.

fruit. In March 1539 it was reported to Conrad Pellikan in Zurich that Cranmer was composing prayers in English.[46] MacCulloch is led to guess that he was at work at this time on the baptism and marriage services as well as the daily office.[47]

What evidence we have of these early proposals seems to amount to mere straws in the wind. But the consistent emphasis on the vernacular makes it very likely that if indeed Cranmer was working on the baptism service at so early a date, it would from the beginning have been largely or entirely in English.

j. The commonplaces and De sacramentis

i. Reading the commonplace collections

It is from about this time that we have a more detailed view of Cranmer's understanding of the sacraments through extensive quotations in his Commonplace Books and, more particularly, an essay, *De sacramentis*, which can be read almost as a key to sections of his commonplaces.

Several sets of Cranmer's commonplaces survive. The 'Collections of Law', 'Notes on Justification' and the collection *De re sacramentaria* all carry their own title and seem to have been the work of individual projects; the otherwise untitled Commonplace Books (sometimes called the 'Great Commonplaces' if only in recognition of their physical size) are a collection covering a wide range of subjects, bound together in two volumes.[48] A full study of the collection is urgently needed, but there is some consensus about aspects of it. Warner and Gilson divide it into three sections, the first covering arguments against the authority of the Church apart from scripture, which was later to be used by the writer of the *Confutation of Unwritten Verities*; the second section covering questions of sacraments and other issues; and the third section being a collection of quotations on justification, purgatory and connected items.[49] It is difficult to date the various sections. The Archbishop's own hand is not seen, even in marginal notes or underlinings, and it is likely that much or all of the two volumes represents a fair copy of earlier

---

46 *Epistolae Tigurinae*, ed. H. Robinson, Parker Society (Cambridge: Cambridge University Press, 1847), p. 406. MacCulloch, *Cranmer*, p. 224, adopts the translation 'prayers' rather than 'discourses' for *orationes*.

47 MacCulloch, *Cranmer*, p. 226.

48 BL, MSS Royal 7B XI, 7B XII.

49 G.F. Warner and J.P. Gilson, *Catalogue of the Western Manuscripts in the Old Royal and King's Collections in the British Museum*, 4 vols (Oxford: Oxford University Press, 1921), Vol. 1, pp. 172–3: section 1: 7B XI, fols 6–49; section 2: 7B XI, fols 50–end, 7B XII, fols 3–81, 298–end; section 3: 7B XII, fols 82–297.

drafts.[50] While exact dating is impossible, the present consensus is that Section 2 was compiled c. 1536–38, and Section 3 c. 1542–44.[51] Peter Brooks has examined much of the material on eucharistic theology in Section 2 and attributed it to the 1530s, and he has been followed by Ashley Null and myself, who both independently connect the material on sacraments with the essay *De sacramentis*, which can be dated to around 1537–38.[52] Null has also examined the material on justification in Section 3 and related it to the debates connected with the publication of the King's Book in 1543. Since we are following Cranmer's path in a chronological order, we shall refer to the relevant passages in Section 2 first, together with the essay *De sacramentis*, and come to Section 3 when we reach the 1540s.

ii. *De sacramentis*: what is a sacrament?

This essay, as I have shown in an earlier work, seems to depend on related material in the Commonplace Books for much of its material. I have argued that it was written by Cranmer, probably in connection with the Lutheran embassy of 1538.[53] While the material in *De sacramentis* and in the commonplaces is related, there is a significant difference in that we have an essay with particular views (rather than a series of quotations and notes, in which it is difficult and perilous to say what were the opinions of the collector).

If we leave aside for one moment the first folio of the essay, which seems to have been added as a preamble to the document, the second folio begins with the bold declaration that 'The Sacraments of the

---

50   The work of comparing the marginalia and underlinings in the commonplaces with those in Cranmer's books is an important task, but a very complicated one. Cranmer often owned multiple copies, and not all have survived. I have followed the consensus in attributing these annotations to the Archbishop, but it is more an assumption than an established fact.

51   Warner and Gilson, *Catalogue*, pp. 172–3; Ayris and Selwyn, 'Cranmer's Commonplace Books', in *Cranmer, Churchman and Scholar*, pp. 312–15; Null, *Repentance*, pp. 254–69.

52   Null, *Repentance*, pp. 269–76; Jeanes, 'Reformation Treatise'.

53   Lambeth MS 1107, fols 84–93[v]: Jeanes, 'Reformation Treatise'. Null (*Repentance*, pp. 269–76) who believes the work was close to, but not written by, Cranmer himself, sees it as part of the discussions leading up to the Bishops' Book, since it includes the four sacraments covered by that work but not discussed with the Lutherans in 1538. I prefer to link it with the Lutherans because of the international reference in the first folio. (Null believes this to belong to a totally separate work.) Also relevant is the fact that it is written in Latin, while documents of a domestic nature were composed in English, and the sacraments are discussed in the order found in the King's Book, not the Bishops' Book, so it would seem that if there is any link with domestic publications it would be with the ill-starred revision of the Bishops' Book which we have already discussed.

New Testament are the visible signs of an invisible justifying grace, or ceremonies instituted in the Gospel to signify the remission of sins.' Quite succinctly two definitions are combined, one from Peter Lombard and the other from Melanchthon.[54] The latter source is then seen to be the one which determines the shape of the discussion, for it is declared that a proper sacrament is one which is instituted and commanded in the New Testament for the forgiveness of sins. (Melanchthon does not include the command.) And, again following Melanchthon, only three of the traditional seven are deemed to pass the test: baptism, the eucharist and sacramental absolution. The last, however, undergoes a stringent critique, and it is affirmed that obligatory auricular confession is an invention of Innocent III.

Returning to the discussion of the sacraments in general, the preamble added a number of definitions, concluding in the statement, 'By the agreement of all a sacrament consists of two things, that is the word and the element, and the word is indeed that of God himself, not the voice of the Law which ordains only the performance of a ceremony, but of the Gospel which in the ceremony promises to us the remission of sins.'

The sacrament is conceived as an instrument of God's grace. It is not only a sign of the invisible grace, but the vehicle of the word of God. In the light of this and the shape of Cranmer's thought which we have seen so far, when the preamble to *De sacramentis* states that the schoolmen declare that there are seven sacraments and grace is conferred *ex opere operato*, but that others 'affirm that only three are necessary and that these are to be received by faith', we may confidently presume that Cranmer would ally himself with the second group. Faith, as a gift of God, is what determines the graceful reception of the sacrament.

iii. *De sacramentis* and baptism

The section in the commonplaces which covers baptism does not reveal anything helpful about Cranmer's thought, nor (unlike the section on the sacraments) are there significant quotations taken up by *De sacramentis*. Many passages follow the course of the rite of

---

54 'Sacramenta Novi Testamenti sunt visibilia signa invisibilis gratiae iustificantis, vel ceremoniae institutae in Evangelio ut significent remissionem peccatorum, quia hoc proprie in Novo Testamento promittitur.' Cf. Sentences IV.i.2, 'Sacramentum est sacrae rei signum . . . Item sacramentum est invisibilis gratiae visibilis forma', and Melanchthon's *Loci Communes*, in *Opera quae supersunt omnia*, ed. C.G. Bretschneider and H.E. Bindseil, Corpus Reformatorum (CR), Vols 1–28 (Berlin, Brunswick, 1834–), Vol. 21, pp. 470–71: 'Itaque si sacramenta vocamus ceremonias seu ritus in Evangelio institutos et proprie pertinentes ad hanc praecipuam promissionem et Evangelii propriam, scilicet de remissione peccatorum' (MS Royal 7B XI, fols 62, 64).

baptism in Ps. Dionysius and Ambrose. Fols 75ᵛ–6 contain a series of texts from St Augustine supporting the baptism of infants. The arguments cover the authority of the consensus of the Church, Jesus's command to let the children come to him, the analogy of circumcision and the requirement of baptism in Jn 3.5.

In the section of *De sacramentis* on baptism the essayist says that the sacrament was instituted by Christ (Mk 16.15–16). The remainder of the section is concerned with justifying the baptism of infants. First its necessity for salvation is stated, with regard to both adults and children alike. Scripture (Jn 3.5) is quoted, and patristic writers. Like Melanchthon,[55] but going beyond what we have seen in the Commonplace Books, the author states that circumcision in the Old Testament gave access to the people of God, and baptism in the New Testament allows entry into the kingdom of heaven, which is the Church. John 3.5 succeeds Gen. 17.14.

The necessity of baptism to counter original sin is affirmed, again with the testimony of both scripture and the Fathers, and the essayist uses the Lutheran treatment of John the Baptist to affirm that children can have faith (again going beyond what we find in the Commonplace Books). He denies (against the Anabaptists who rely on Rom. 10.17) that the gospel must be preached and received before accepting the sacrament, and asserts instead the story of Christ blessing the children. The actions in the story are set out as a list and subsequently numbered in the manuscript. After ordering the children to be brought to him, Jesus first took them into his arms, then laid his hands on them, then blessed them. By saying that thus he sanctified them, forgiving their sins and imparting the Holy Spirit, the essayist makes the intimate connection with baptism complete. We have here the basic principle which will underlie the liturgical use of the story in 1549 and 1552.[56] But the key to understanding Cranmer's approach is his presumption of the efficacy of the sacrament:

> Christ through his sacrament and because of the promise added to the sacrament can be as efficacious through the Holy Spirit in infants as he was in the Baptist by means of his mother's voice. Faith indeed is a gift of God, and, just as it is not acquired by

---

55 Cf. Melanchthon, *Loci Communes*, col. 474:

Quod vero non sit extra Ecclesiam salus, constat quia Ecclesia est regnum Christi . . . Testatur idem locus in Genesi [17.14] de circumcisione. Masculus, cuius praeputii caro non fuerit circumcisa, delebitur anima illa de populo, quia pactum meum irritum facit. Hic clare pronuntiat eum, qui signum non habet, reiici a Deo. Fuit autem et Circumcisio signum Ecclesiae Dei, sicut nunc Baptismus.

56 *De sacramentis*, fols 84ᵛ–6ᵛ; Jeanes, 'Reformation Treatise', pp. 170–1, 161–2.

everyone who hears preaching, so also is it foolhardy to say it is not given to infants through the sacrament without preaching.

Several themes are woven together here:

First, the efficacy of the sacrament is affirmed as Christ acting 'through his sacrament' because of the promise added to it.

Secondly, we are invited to see the power of Christ as the word of God, in the Lutheran antecedents of the image of John the Baptist; also because of the preamble to *De sacramentis* which speaks of the word of God added to the element, the word of God being that of the gospel 'which in the ceremony promises to us the remission of sins'; and then because of the comparison with the preached word, by which some, but not all, receive faith.

Thirdly, the importance of faith is affirmed, but it is a gift of God, and so presumably can be his gift to an infant as much as to an adult (as we see in the case of the unborn John the Baptist).

iv. *De sacramentis* and confirmation and penance

We may glance briefly at what *De sacramentis* has to say about confirmation and penance and how they relate to baptism. Confirmation is stated not to be a sacrament instituted by Christ. The gifts of strength and the imparting of the Holy Spirit are effected by it, but not the remission of sins which belongs to baptism. But the advantage of keeping confirmation is that suggested by Melanchthon in his *Loci communes*, namely that it could be used to affirm for oneself one's faith which had been affirmed by the godparents at baptism. *De sacramentis* adds that this would be a good refutation of the Anabaptists.[57] The theme of confirmation as a recapitulation of baptism is important here. We have seen it in the Bishops' Book, and now it is adopted by Cranmer.

Penance is described as a sacrament instituted by Christ with the promise of the forgiveness of sins. However, confession is a matter of confession to God, and, apart from the discipline of excommunication, the requirement of private confession to a priest, annually and listing all one's sins, is an innovation of the Church. Private confession is expedient but not obligatory.[58]

---

57 *De sacramentis*, fols 92–92^V; Jeanes, 'Reformation Treatise', p. 179.
58 *De sacramentis*, fols 86^V–8^V; Jeanes, 'Reformation Treatise', pp. 171–4.

v. *De sacramentis* and the eucharist

After an affirmation of Christ's institution of the sacrament and his command to 'do this', the essay proceeds to discuss two controversial issues: the question of the presence of Christ in the eucharist, and the question in what way it may be understood as a sacrifice. The latter point can be discussed briefly. It is acknowledged that the recipient of the sacrament receives forgiveness of sins, but it is denied that the eucharist is a propitiatory sacrifice (appeal is made to the one sacrifice of Heb. 7.27, etc.) or that priests are able to apply it to some particular individuals: Christ offers it to all and it is received by each person by their own faith. Here the essay follows Melanchthon in appealing to the Greek Orthodox liturgy and its description of the eucharist as a liturgy of thanksgiving – λειτουργία εὐχαριστικός – for the living and the departed, and a spiritual sacrifice – λογικὴ λατρεία– an unbloody offering.[59] The Orthodox approach allows the use of the language of sacrifice while avoiding the scholastic developments.

The question of the eucharistic presence is more vexed, at least in the way in which it is handled in the essay. At first sight the essayist affirms categorically the Real Presence of Christ in the bread and wine of the eucharist: that is what Jesus said. Inability to perceive this by faith renders the communicant to be guilty of the body and blood of the Lord. There is then a rather long discussion of tropological language which seems to lose conviction as it proceeds. Other places in scripture do use tropes, but that does not apply to this case. It is acknowledged that circumcision is called both the covenant and the sign of the covenant. Christ was indeed the spiritual rock as described in 1 Corinthians, John the Baptist was indeed Elijah. But the ambiguity of calling the cup of the Last Supper the New Covenant does not undermine the clear statements by Matthew and Mark concerning the blood of Christ. Evidently the essayist has been thinking long and hard about tropological language. Appeal then is made to the Fathers, and here there is no clear answer. It is acknowledged that Tertullian and Augustine do indeed use figurative language about the eucharistic presence, and for a clear affirmation of the Real Presence appeal is made to Cyril of Alexandria and Theophylact (an eleventh/twelfth-century archbishop of Ochrid). The essayist is forced to conclude that when the Fathers disagree, their testimony is weak, 'and nowhere weaker than in this sacrament'.[60]

---

59 Cf. Melanchthon, *Apologia Confessionis Augustanae*, 1531, CR 27, cols 625–6; Jeanes, 'Reformation Treatise', pp. 176–7. No section of the surviving commonplaces is devoted to this issue of the sacrifice of the Mass, though no doubt Cranmer would have made many notes in his time.

60 Jeanes, 'Reformation Treatise', pp. 175–6.

There are many links between the essay *De sacramentis* and the attested works of Cranmer. This particular passage on the eucharist would seem to cast doubt on its ascription to the Archbishop. For at about the same time (around June 1537) Cranmer wrote to the Swiss reformer Vadianus, making clear his rejection of the teachings of Oecolampadius and Zwingli and affirming his belief in the Real Presence, holding fast to the clear teaching of scripture and the Fathers. In this letter Cranmer was willing to say that 'everything of everyone's writings must be read with discrimination', applying that dictum to his contemporaries and quoting Jerome's cautious reception of Origen, but he concluded:

Since this Catholic faith which we hold respecting the true presence has been declared to the Church from the beginning by so open and manifest passages of scripture, and subsequently the same has also so clearly and devotedly been commended to the ears of the faithful by the first ecclesiastical writers; do not, I pray, persist to me in wishing any longer to weaken or undermine a doctrine so well rooted and supported.[61]

Both the attested letter and the ascribed essay have been compared with the private collection of quotations and marginalia in Cranmer's commonplaces. Peter Brooks, who quotes the letter to Vadianus, also devotes much of his book to Cranmer's quotations from the polemic between Luther and his sacramentarian opponents and his annotations in which he takes Luther's side.[62] According to this line of thought, Cranmer the writer to Vadianus is one with Cranmer the collector and annotator of the commonplaces. However, closer examination of the commonplaces reveals a more complicated story. The section on the eucharist can be divided as follows:

a. scriptural references (fols 78–9)
b. patristic quotations (fols 79–101^v)
c. scriptural quotations which support the sacramentarians (fol. 102)
d. extracts from Brenz's *Syngramma Suevicum* (fols 103–10)
e. Lutherans vs Reformed (fols 110^v–20)
f. patristic quotations (fols 120–3^v)

---

61 Cranmer to Vadianus (following trans. in MacCulloch, *Cranmer*, p. 180), Cranmer II, PS, pp. 342–4.
62 Brooks, *Cranmer's Doctrine of the Eucharist*, pp. 21–34.

Brooks's evidence is taken from sections b and e. Most of the other sections are entirely unremarkable for our present purpose, and no more than one might expect from a careful theologian. However, section f seems to have been collected from a different standpoint than that which underlies b. It is no coincidence that the Fathers cited in favour of the Real Presence, Cyril and Theophylact are to be found in section b, and passages from Augustine and Tertullian suggesting a tropological approach are all grouped in section f. In that section there are no marginal comments, but all the underlining would support a tropological understanding of the eucharistic presence.[63]

This intimate relationship between the essay and the commonplaces is, for me at least, strong evidence for the ascription of the former to Cranmer himself. By reading the former our attention is drawn to nuances in the latter.[64] But the essay and the letter to Vadianus are not necessarily so far apart anyway. The Archbishop of Canterbury is not going to wear his heart on his sleeve when writing to a foreign churchman, nor is he going to go against government policy in such a letter. And as MacCulloch points out (in a note where admittedly he doubts my ascription of *De sacramentis* to Cranmer), there is a certain scepticism about the Fathers in the letter as well as in the essay.[65] What I suggest that we see here is two sides of the same person, not contradictory but rather one of the public image, expressing government policy with an aura of confidence and certainty and the other more open and willing to express doubt and enquiry.

The essayist shows us a person who sees the force of the tropological argument in eucharistic theology even if he has not consented to it. The discussion ends somewhat inconclusively, with a dissatisfied comment about the ambiguity of the Fathers. It is not enough to undermine – yet – a theological position which is broadly Lutheran, but it represents the first steps of Cranmer's journey that took him on a new understanding of the scriptures and the Fathers; that he would build a new consensus around the tropological approach which at this stage he has rejected.[66]

---

63   More details can be found in my article, 'Reformation Treatise', esp. ns 34–40, pp. 175–6.

64   Null (*Repentance*, p. 275) suggests that a research assistant 'familiar enough with Cranmer's views as well as the political situation and with access to Cranmer's library' might have composed the essay. That is indeed true, and could equally be true for every word, liturgical and polemical, ever ascribed to Cranmer. In this case at least such a ghost writer must have known the commonplaces and his master's mind extraordinarily well.

65   MacCulloch, *Cranmer*, n. 19, p. 181.

66   Peter Brooks acknowledges the problem when he says that any detailed acceptance of the Lutheran position would have made it much more difficult for Cranmer to have moved to the Reformed position. *Cranmer's Doctrine of the Eucharist*, p. 36, n. 1.

Liturgically we have seen the principles enunciated which will eventually underlie the use of the gospel in the baptism service. It is no coincidence that the 1549 Prayer Book baptism service is based on Luther's second *Taufbüchlein* and adopts the Lutheran reading of Jesus and the children from Mark's gospel (rather than the Matthean version of Sarum); and that this reading alone in the Prayer Book is not taken from the Great Bible but is an independent translation, as if neither the Great Bible nor Coverdale were yet available when the service was drafted. Although this predates some relevant sources it is quite likely that a first draft of the baptism service dates from around this time.[67]

k. The Thirteen Articles

The Lutheran embassy to London in the summer of 1538 returned without any final agreement. However, discussions had advanced far enough for a set of Thirteen Articles to be drawn up, covering the sacraments of baptism, penance and the eucharist. The Articles are very close to the Wittenberg Articles. That on baptism affirmed its necessity for salvation, that adults and infants receive remission of sins and grace. The Holy Spirit is said to be *efficax* in infants, and Pelagians and Anabaptists are condemned.[68]

The brief article on the eucharist affirms the presence of the body and blood of Christ in the bread and wine, and their reception by all who communicate 'whether they be good or evil'.[69]

The Article on penance is notable for Cranmer's attempts to correct the drafts so that confession is said to be fitting (*commoda*) rather than necessary. However, he is only partly successful: not all his emendations were accepted and confession was still said to be *summe necessaria*.[70]

An article on the use of the sacraments affirms that they are not just signs of grace but are efficacious, that by them God pours his grace into us and our faith is stirred up and strengthened by them. It is denied that they confer grace *ex opere operato*; faith is required on the part of the recipient, but that in the case of infant baptism the Holy Spirit is efficacious in the child.[71]

---

67 See commentary in Ch. 6. For possible work on the marriage service at this period, see Jeanes, 'Reformation Treatise', p. 159.
68 Thirteen Articles, Cranmer, PS, II, pp. 474–5.
69 Thirteen Articles, Cranmer, PS, II, p. 475.
70 Thirteen Articles, Cranmer, PS, II, pp. 475–7.
71 Thirteen Articles, Cranmer, PS, II, p. 477.

3 REFORM TAKES A NEW DIRECTION

a. *The Six Articles*

The publication of the Great Bible in April 1539 must have represented
a milestone for the evangelical reform agenda. Ironically, within a couple
of months that same agenda seemed to have been completely halted by
the passing of the Six Articles which upheld transubstantiation in all
but name, communion in one kind, clerical celibacy, vows of chastity,
private Masses and auricular confession (though in one concession it
was acknowledged that confession was a matter of church discipline
rather than scriptural command). Modern opinion interprets the impact
of these Articles and the course of the last years of Henry's reign in
different ways. Christopher Haigh could describe the period 1538–47
as 'Reformation Reversed'.[72] At the other extreme G.W. Bernard could
argue for a complete consistency of policy throughout the reign.[73] A
proper analysis lies beyond this study, though the Articles were certainly
regarded as a significant disappointment both by English evangelicals
and continental observers. Even if nothing was in theory changed and the
status quo merely affirmed, perhaps the adage about modern politics can
be applied to the sixteenth century, that momentum is everything; and
the hopes of those who looked for a Lutheran alliance and reformation
were dashed. Not that that ruled out any reformation, but nor was
the future course plain. As Felicity Heal points out, whatever Henry's
own views were, they remained unclear even to senior members of the
regime.[74] The question now was not just whether reform was possible,
but what sort of reform, and that was now to be decided. In 1540,
just before the fall of Cromwell, the commissions were launched which
would eventually produce *A Necessary Doctrine and Erudition for any
Christian Man*, known as the King's Book, in 1543, and the *Rationale
of Ceremonial*, which was never promulgated and was published only in
1910. The King's Book would be the definitive guide to late Henrician
religion.

b. *Questions and answers on the sacraments (1540)*

The 'Questions and Answers concerning the Sacraments and the
Appointment and Power of Bishops and Priests' is another example of

---

72 *English Reformations*, p. 152.
73 *The King's Reformation: Henry VII and the Remaking of the English Church* (New
Haven, CT, and London: Yale University Press, 2005). In particular, Bernard rejects the idea
that the Six Articles are in any important sense a reversal of royal policy (see pp. 499–500).
74 *Reformation in Britain and Ireland* (Oxford: Oxford University Press, 2003), p. 134.

the questionnaire approach to establishing some sort of agreement. They were circulated during the last three months of 1540, and seem to have been the first moves in the revision of the Bishops' Book.[75] Draft forms of the questions exist in Cranmer's hand, and the coincidence of question and answer (for example question 8, on confirmation, or question 9, on the power of the apostles 'lacking a higher power, as in not having a Christian king among them') serves to bolster this view that he was their author, in whole or part.[76]

Leaving aside the items concerning the clergy, the questions and the answers about the sacraments are intriguing: by asking separately about the nature and number of sacraments in scripture and in the 'ancient authors', a distinction between them is invited. And if they are different, then one cannot appeal to the ancient authors. K.J. Walsh comments how Cranmer's description of patristic writers as 'authors' rather than 'Fathers' or 'doctors' in the *Defence* reflects the usage of the schools, where *auctor* carried the connotation of *auctoritas*.[77] That may well be the case, and these writers continued to carry authority with him. But their authority in these questions is radically qualified by being set over against that of scripture.

In scripture *sacramentum* is said by Cranmer (in his answers) to be the translation of *mysterium*, and thereby to describe the incarnation, matrimony and the *'mysterium iniquitatis'* or *mysterium meretricis magnae et bestiae'*. The authors called the sacrament the sign of a holy thing, a visible word, a symbol and an agreement by which we are bound; as to their number, Cranmer could produce a veritable arsenal of 23 sacred rites and objects called sacraments, besides the parables of Christ and the prophecies of the Apocalypse. As for the seven sacraments, not even the old authors ever knew such a group, let alone scripture.

The questionnaire asks for what is found in scripture of what is commonly called the seven sacraments, and Cranmer answers:

> I find not in the scripture the matter, nature, and effect of all those which we call the seven sacraments, but only of certain of them: as of baptism, in which we be regenerated and pardoned of our sin by the blood of Christ.
>
> Of *eucharistia*, in which we be concorporated unto Christ, and made lively members of his body, nourished and fed to the

---

75　See MacCulloch, *Cranmer*, pp. 277–80.

76　Cranmer, PS, II, p. 115.

77　'Cranmer and the Fathers, especially in the *Defence*', *Journal of Religious History*, 11 (1980), pp. 227–47 (237).

everlasting life, if we receive it as we ought to do; and else it is to us rather death than life.

Of penance also I find in the scripture, whereby sinners after baptism, returning wholly unto God, be accepted again unto his favour and mercy. But the scripture speaketh not of penance, as we call it a sacrament, consisting in three parts, contrition, confession and satisfaction; but the scripture taketh penance for a pure conversion of a sinner in heart and mind from his sins unto God, making no mention of private confession of all deadly sins to a priest, nor of ecclesiastical satisfaction to be enjoined by him.

Of matrimony also I find very much in scripture . . . it is a mean whereby God doth use the infirmity of our concupiscence to the setting forth of his glory, and the increase of the world . . . and in this matrimony is also a promise of salvation, if the parents bring up their children in the faith, love, and fear of God.

Of the matter, nature and effect of the other three, that is to say, confirmation, order, and extreme unction, I read nothing in the scripture, as they be taken for sacraments.[78]

The appeal to a scriptural treatment of the sacraments sets them in a new light. It is as though Cranmer has tried to free himself not only from the Scholastic seven but also from the Lutheran categories of the three which were 'ceremonies instituted in the Gospel to signify the remission of sins'.[79] The minimalist definitions from patristic writers fit in with this approach, and the treatment of penance and matrimony is, compared with discussions in the 1530s, original and creative.

How are we to understand Cranmer here? Null believes that he is moving from a Lutheran line on penance to one influenced by Calvin, freeing justification from sacramental penance, and adopting the position that there are two sacraments of the gospel, not three.[80] This in itself makes good sense, in that baptism and the eucharist are both discussed as sacraments 'in which' the grace is received, whereas penance and matrimony are described using the term 'whereby'. The distinction is unlikely to be accidental. However, we also have the lengthy and entirely positive description of marriage, even to the extent that it is said that 'in this matrimony is a promise of salvation'. This is very different from Calvin's approach, in which he says that 'marriage is a good and holy ordinance of God; and farming, building, cobbling, and barbering are

---

78 PS, II, pp. 115–16.
79 *De sacramentis*, fol. 85, quoting Melanchthon, *Loci Communes*, col. 470: Jeanes, 'Reformation Treatise', p. 169.
80 Null, *Repentance*, pp. 127–8.

lawful ordinances of God, and yet are not sacraments'.[81] And Cranmer's curt dismissal of confirmation, order and unction, even when he could have said something about them in scripture though not as sacraments, suggests strongly that he is here trying to redefine what the first four are as scriptural sacraments. In this light, what is distinctive about Cranmer's redefinition of penance is not so much its status, for, as Null shows, repentance and conversion after baptism are very much a feature of his mature theology, as the further removal of ecclesiastical power. In *De sacramentis* the requirement of confession to a priest was qualified and curtailed, and even in the Six Articles Cranmer had successfully campaigned against the notion that it was 'necessary according to the law of God', but is merely 'expedient and necessary to be retained'.[82] In the Questions and Answers, as in the earlier documents, Cranmer says that confession to a priest is not required by scripture,[83] But penance is far too important in Cranmer's mind to be left in such a position, and he reclaims scriptural authority for it by releasing it from what he regards as its ecclesiastical baggage.

It is perhaps no coincidence that we see in the same document the radical demotion of the clergy and indeed the whole spiritual realm. Question 9 contemplates the unhappy situation of the apostles, 'lacking a higher power, as in not having a Christian king among them'. And the appointment of clergy is said to be just the same as that of lay officials. Ordination adds nothing. In every respect, the work of the Church is subject to the office of the Christian prince.[84]

It would be gross anachronism to call this secularization. In one sense, Cranmer's Christian king is modelled on the Old Testament reforming monarchy,[85] and it would be more true to say that the monarchy was sacralized rather than the Church secularized. However, the removal of the separate and independent role of the Church in ordering people's lives left no other public arena than that of the state. What was not subject to the monarch was removed to the hidden world of the private conscience.

---

81 *Institutes of the Christian Religion, 1536 edition*, trans. F.L. Battles (Grand Rapids, MI: Eerdmans, 1975), p. 173.

82 MacCulloch, *Cranmer*, p. 252.

83 'Questions and Answers on the Sacraments', Answer 15: 'A man is not bound by the authority of this scripture, "*Quorum remiseritis*", and such like, to confess his secret deadly sins to a priest, although he may have him' (PS, II, p. 117).

84 'Questions and Answers on the Sacraments', PS, II, pp. 116–17.

85 Henry seems to have thought of himself in the light of the reforming king Josiah. See G.W. Bernard, 'The Making of Religious Policy, 1533–1546: Henry VIII and the Search for the Middle Way', *Historical Journal*, 41.2 (June 1998), pp. 321–49 (330).

'Thomas Cantuariensis' set his signature to his Answers, but added
that he did not 'temerariously define' his opinion. In part that was simple
prudence, but it may also be the case that he was genuinely seeking a
new definition of the Christian life, and was not in a position to make
more categorical statements.

c. The Act for Advancement of True Religion: the King's Book

In 1542, in a piece of Tudor standardization, the Use of Sarum was
made the standard liturgy throughout the realm (the first instance
when this realm should 'have one use'). In February 1543 Convocation
ordered that on every Sunday and holy day there should be a reading of
a chapter from the Bible in English, without exposition.[86] The restriction
on exposition was as significant as the order for the public reading:
this was followed up by the Act for the Advancement of True Religion
which restricted the reading of the Bible to the upper classes and banned
all books (as well as ballads, plays, rhymes and songs) which differed
from the teaching set forth by the king's authority.[87] This benchmark
of orthodoxy was contained in the revision of the Bishop's Book, *A
Necessary Doctrine and Erudition for any Christian Man*, known as the
King's Book and published at the same time as the Act, and it remained
as such until the Act was repealed in November 1547. The importance of
the King's Book will therefore be seen later, when it appears as a shadow
lying behind the Prayer Book of 1549.

i. The King's Book

Cranmer was on the commission which produced the King's Book,
and it was an uncomfortable time for him, with the traditionalists
in the ascendancy. Among many other defeats, Fisher's doctrine of
justification was adopted through the labours of Redman and others,
and all seven sacraments were asserted against the Lutheran three. It
is hard to say what part Cranmer had in the composition of the King's
Book. MacCulloch believes that his distaste for the doctrine in it must
suggest that his 'main contribution was probably to tidy up the literary
style'.[88] However, Glyn Redworth points out that while other bishops
and divines were involved in much of the drafting, the early history of

---

86 Cuming, *History*, p. 34; S.E Lehmberg, *The Later Parliaments of Henry VIII, 1536–
1547* (Cambridge: Cambridge University Press, 1977), p.184.
87 Haigh, *English Reformations*, p. 161.
88 MacCulloch, *Cranmer*, p. 309.

the book lies in the long discussions between Henry VIII and Cranmer over emendations of the Bishops' Book.[89] Also it is hard to imagine that defeat over particular issues would have led Cranmer to give up trying to contribute what he could to other matters.

In the King's Book justification is said to be achieved by the grace of God helping the individual. Free will, though corrupted and weakened by sin and unable of itself to achieve righteousness, is important: 'It pleaseth the high wisdom of God, that man, prevented by his grace (which being offered, man may if he will refuse or receive) shall be also a worker by his free consent and obedience to the same, in the attaining of his own justification, and by God's grace and help shall walk in such works as be requisite to his justification.'[90] Adult converts are baptized, having first faith and repentance, and trusting in the merits of Christ. 'As for infants, it is to be believed that their justification is wrought by the secret operation of the Holy Ghost in their baptism, they being offered in the faith of the church.'[91]

The Article of Good Works in the King's Book sets out a view of grace which sees works to be 'of two sorts'. The first are those done by the already justified, performed in the faith of Christ and accepted by God as the fruits of righteousness. The second are of a lesser kind, performed by those in deadly sin (the unbaptized or those who have fallen from grace after baptism). These works are enabled by grace, 'yet this man is not to be accounted a justified man, but . . . by these means doth enter into justification'.[92] Null identifies these two forms of grace with those proposed by the traditionalist theologians, depending on John Fisher's ideas of justification, with the omission of his Scholastic terminology.[93]

ii. Justification and the sacraments: John Fisher

St John Fisher, vice-chancellor then chancellor of the University of Cambridge and bishop of Rochester, executed by Henry VIII in 1535, was the foremost English exponent of the traditionalist theology of the early sixteenth century. Schooled in both Scholastic and humanist theology, he was a Scotist and also deeply influenced by Augustinianism.

Fisher adapted the traditional Scotist understanding of salvation, by which God has first elected those who are to be saved, then, as a

---

89 *In Defence of the Church Catholic: The Life of Stephen Gardiner* (Oxford: Basil Blackwell, 1990), pp. 167–8.
90 Article of Justification, in Lloyd (ed.), *Formularies of Faith*, p. 365.
91 Lloyd (ed.), *Formularies of Faith*, p. 366.
92 Article of Good Works, *Formularies of Faith*, p. 371.
93 *Repentance*, p. 158.

means of their salvation *de potentia Dei ordinata*, establishes charity as the basis of justification, with its meritorious value being accepted *ex pacto divino*. Even with the doctrine of election and the divine initiative of acceptance, the activity of the human will still leaves such an understanding open to the charge of Pelagianism. And so Fisher, who was firmly opposed to any form of Pelagianism, affirmed the necessity of grace freely given for the individual even to engage in this initial activity.[94] Having established the principle of prevenient grace, Fisher used the two ways in Scotist understanding in which a sinner may be restored: the initial 'unformed' sorrow – *attritio informata* – (which is itself the result of grace: Fisher rejected the Scholastic notion that this could be achieved by our own efforts)[95] is perfected to be perfect contrition – *contritio* or *attritio formata* – either directly by an infusion of God's grace or by receiving the sacraments. In either case the sinner is made intrinsically righteous by grace: *gratia gratum faciens*.[96]

Fisher presented a rationale of sacramental efficacy in the first article of his *Assertionis Lutheranae Confutatio*. In it he referred to Henry VIII's *Assertio septem sacramentorum* for a defence of the efficacy of the sacraments, but repeated Henry's main points in the course of his discussion. The command of Christ to baptize can hardly be redundant; the consensus of sacrament and faith complement one another and both are necessary; the sacrament bolsters the weakness of faith. In addition Fisher developed his argument in the light of his theology of justification. The role of the sacraments (in particular that of penance) was seen as an alternative to *contritio* which is both hard and uncertain.[97] With regard to baptism, he acknowledged that one can achieve the fullness of saving faith without the aid of sacramental grace (and the case of Cornelius was cited as an example),[98] but this is extremely rare, and one would not be justified if one refused baptism.[99] For the vast majority of people, 'where faith is more remiss, grace is offered through the sacrament',[100] a fact

---

94 Null, *Repentance*, p. 77.

95 See R. Rex, *The Theology of John Fisher* (Cambridge: Cambridge University Press, 1991), pp. 39, 125 and Null, *Repentance*, p. 79, for a discussion of the precise way in which Fisher eschewed the scholastic doctrine of attrition, either by avoiding the language (Rex) or effectively by redefining it (Null).

96 Null, *Repentance*, pp. 80–1.

97 'Quoniam igitur via contritionis seu attritionis formatae, non minus est dura quam incerta peccatoribus, idcirco viam hanc alteram per sacramentorum susceptionem multo mitiorem et securiorem docent utpote ob quam nihil exigitur nisi ut non ponatur obex' (*Assertionis Lutheranae Confutatio* [Antwerp: Hillenius, 1523], fol. 35).

98 *Confutatio*, fol. 26v.

99 *Confutatio*, fol. 27v.

100 'Ceterum ubi fides remissior fuit, iam per sacramentum praestatur gratia' (*Confutatio*, fol. 26v).

which is very convenient in the battle against Luther's concentration on the role of faith. In a passage dealing with this very issue, Fisher set out the two alternatives:

> On this point, one must admit one or other of these possibilities: either that anyone before they come to the washing of baptism has such faith that they are justified before they are washed; or that what faith they have (if anything is lacking in it) receives from God ample additional *iustum* in the very washing when they receive baptism. If you state the first alternative, the scriptures will cry out against you, for they testify that most have faith, but not sufficient for justification. If you allow the second, it has fully proved our case . . . The boundless kindness of Christ willed it that, since no one can be certain of their own justification by faith alone, what may have been lacking in the adequacy of faith is now augmented through the sacraments.[101]

It was this theology of grace and of the sacraments that Cranmer firmly opposed.

iii. The King's Book: baptism

The section on baptism in the King's Book was considerably longer than its counterpart in the Bishops' Book and was thoroughly redrafted.[102] It now begins with the institution of the sacrament in Mt. 28.19, and defines the sacrament's effect as the forgiveness of sins and the grace of the Holy Spirit, quoting Acts 2.38, Mk 16.16 (with a caveat about those who sin after baptism, based on Henry VIII's correction to the Bishops' Book), Rom. 5.12 and only then Jn 3.5, and mention of attaining salvation and everlasting life. Adults are forgiven both original and actual sin when they are baptized, and infants are forgiven original sin, and so need to be baptized.

---

101 *Confutatio*, fol. 33.

Ad haec, alterum horum necesse est confiteare, aut quod ante baptismatis lavacrum quisquis accedens tantam habeat fidem ut priusquam abluatur iustus fiat, aut quod fidei (si quis in ea defectus fuerit) per susceptionem sacramenti sub ipso lavacro iustum augmentum a deo suppeditetur. Si primum dixeris reclamabunt tibi scripturae, quae plerosque testantur fidem habuisse, sed citra mensuram iustificationis. Sin posterius concesseris, hoc pro nobis abunde facit . . . Voluit immensa Christi benignitas, ut quoniam nemo per solam fidem de sua iustificatione poterit certus esse, iam per sacramenta supplerentur, quidquid fidei sufficientiae defuerit.

102 Lloyd (ed.), *Formularies of Faith*, pp. 253–7; Fisher, *Christian Initiation*, pp. 76–9.

The fate of the unbaptized has been said to be less clear, in that there is a change from the statement in the Bishops' Book that 'Inasmuch as infants and children dying in their infancy shall undoubtedly be saved thereby, and else not'. The King's Book omits the last three words of this sentence, and J.D.C. Fisher sees the change as significant.[103] However, the necessity of baptism is elsewhere stated nearly as strongly: 'Wherefore seeing that out of the church neither infants nor no man else can be saved, they must needs be christened and cleansed by baptism, and so incorporated into the church.' And we have seen above that it is possible that 'and else not' in the Bishops' Book was not significant in this respect anyway. All in all, it is likely that the change in the King's Book was stylistic, and that the drafters did not believe that they were allowing a more evangelical understanding of baptism.

There is a long explanation of the pervasiveness of original sin. Baptism is also said to give help to the baptized in their struggle against concupiscence, or inclination to sin. These paragraphs seem entirely traditional, but we need not presume that Cranmer would have disagreed; rather, as we shall see below, there are passages in the Great Commonplaces which might underlie the discussion here.

The refutation of Anabaptists demanded an enlarged defence of infant baptism: the universal consent of the Church; the example of the Apostles; the necessity of baptism summarized in Eph. 5.26 and Jn 3.5; the analogy of circumcision. Re-baptism is denounced, and the Anabaptists and Pelagians condemned.

The sacrament is said to be efficacious regardless of the unworthiness of the minister, because the efficacy is of the word of God 'which by his Holy Spirit worketh all the graces . . . to all those that worthily receive' the sacraments, and is 'nothing diminished or hurted neither in infants, nor yet in them which being endued with the use of reason come thereunto truly contrite and penitent of all their sins done before, believing and confessing all the articles of the creed, and having a sure faith and trust in the promises of God'. This wording seems to tread a path which includes both the Catholics (for whom it is sufficient that the recipient does not put up an obstacle – *obex*) and the evangelicals who would look for a stronger emphasis on faith and less on the efficacy of the sacrament to confer grace. (This formula, and the precise wording of the relation of the work of the Holy Spirit to the sacramental administration, will be looked at in more detail when we consider the theology of consecration in Chapter 5.)

Finally we have a summary of the meaning of baptism: baptism is described as a covenant between God and us; God testifies that he

---

103 Fisher, *Christian Initiation*, p. 77, n. 1.

justifies us for Christ's sake, and forgives our sins, and gives us grace and everlasting life, and on our part we 'ought most diligently to remember and keep the promise that we in baptism have made to almighty God'. Then Romans 6 is cited, and said to mean that we 'have professed and bound ourselves in baptism to die from sin, and utterly to abstain from the corruption of our old sinful life, and to walk and proceed in a new life of grace and the Spirit'. And, being baptized into the mystical Body of Christ, we are bound to die to sin and walk according to grace and the Holy Spirit.[104]

iv. The King's Book: eucharist

The section on the eucharist is much longer than its counterpart in the Bishops' Book, but its main purpose is similar: to affirm traditional teaching and practice. Although the word 'transubstantiation' is never used, it is declared that 'the creatures which be taken to the use thereof, as bread and wine, do not remain still in their own substance, but by the virtue of Christ's word in the consecration be changed and turned to the very substance of the body and blood of our Saviour Jesu Christ'. Trust in Christ's words is recommended rather than vain speculation. The sacrament was instituted (in words foreshadowing the later Prayer Book?) for a remembrance of Christ's death and passion and for spiritual nourishment. We should remember Christ and his passion 'in the using, receiving and beholding of this sacrament' – the reader is warned against unworthy reception. Reception in one kind is approved and the spiritual life-giving nature of the body of Christ affirmed. The unity of all who receive the sacrament in the mystical body of the Church is described, based on 1 Cor. 10; and fasting communion and reverent behaviour during Mass is commended.[105]

d. The King's Book and Cranmer's commonplaces

So much is written of Cranmer's opposition to the King's Book that it is tempting to try to read his commonplaces as always presenting a case against the contents of the Book. But the defence of infant baptism against the Anabaptists is not out of keeping with Cranmer's notes made in all likelihood in the 1530s, as seen above,[106] or the substantial

---

104 This passage has many reminiscences of the final exhortation and the prayer of thanksgiving in the Prayer Book baptism service, and will be discussed in more detail below.
105 *Formularies of Faith*, pp. 262–9.
106 MS Royal 7B XI, fols 75ᵛ–6.

quotations from St Augustine devoted to the issue of original sin, a doctrine essentially unchallenged by the reformers.[107] Therefore, while Cranmer was justifiably aggrieved at much in the Book, it is possible that he still contributed significantly to it, and politically some of it might be read more as a tactical withdrawal than an outright defeat.[108]

i. Cranmer's response to the King's Book: the Commonplace Books: salvation

Null follows Warner and Gilson in attributing to the 1540s the material in fols 82–297 of the second volume of the commonplaces (Royal MS 7B XII). The dating is made in the first instance on the basis of books quoted in this section, and Null's own reading of the commonplaces makes excellent sense in the light of events surrounding the publication of the King's Book in 1543.[109] It is difficult to know how much of the material was assembled as part of the preparations, and how much in response to Cranmer's defeat in debate and the publication of a traditionalist statement of faith. Null seems inclined to place much material in the second category (certainly some must date later because of the inclusion of quotations of the *Antididagma*, published in 1544).[110]

Against the King's Book's position, upholding the traditional view of salvation and the twofold understanding of justifying grace, Null sees Cranmer's own view in a note in the commonplaces: 'according to the writer Augustine, Scripture speaks only of justifying grace which is spread in our hearts through the Holy Spirit'.[111] This basic observation is the foundation of Cranmer's mature theology of justification which has been outlined at the beginning of this chapter. Justification is the

---

107 MS Royal 7B XII, fols 311–14, with quotations e.g. from *Contra duas epistulas Pelagianorum* 1.26–8 (= *PL* 44: cols 562–4); *De nuptiis et concupiscentia* 1.25–9 (= *PL* 44: cols 428–30); *De spiritu et littera*, 64–5 (= *PL* 44: cols 243–5). These folios are connected with the material collected in the 1530s ('Section 2').

108 MacCulloch (*Cranmer*, p. 309) stresses Cranmer's opposition to the Book, but Cuming (*Godly Order*, pp. 97–109), and B.D. Spinks ('Treasures Old and New: A Look at Some of Thomas Cranmer's Methods of Liturgical Compilation', in Ayris and Selwyn, *Churchman and Scholar*, pp. 175–88 [182–3]) set out parallels between the King's Book and the later Prayer Book which hint at a more positive relationship.

109 Null, *Repentance*, pp. 257–8: this section includes quotations from the *Antididagma* of 1544 and a homily of Chrysostom edited by Cheke in 1543 (Warner and Gilson, *Catalogue*, p. 172).

110 Null, *Repentance*, p. 268.

111 Null, *Repentance*, p. 159: Royal MS 7B XII, 225ᵛ, 'Scriptura, authore Augustino, loquitur dumtaxat de gratia iustificante quae diffusa est in corda nostra per Spiritum sanctum.'

initiative of God alone. And it is in response to this position that he begins to work out a new sacramental theology. As it happens, it is in the context of baptism that this theology evolves, for it is in response to the questions over justification that he has to confront the relation of sacramental efficacy to saving grace.

ii. The commonplaces and baptism

Null points to the importance of a series of entries in the commonplaces where Cranmer collected authorities for the principle that baptism is the beginning of renewal in the Christian life. Under the heading, *'Incipit'*, Cranmer recorded a number of patristic quotations, including:

'Baptism takes away whatever sins there be, at which point the regeneration of man <u>begins</u> in which every guilt, both original and actual, is forgiven'; '<u>love begun therefore is righteousness begun</u>'; 'The new man . . . is born from the old, since spiritual regeneration <u>begins</u> by a change of the old and worldly life'; 'We believe in him, when <u>we begin</u> to enter into a good life.'[112]

Null sees in this Cranmer's doctrine that 'justification imparted in this life only the beginnings of a personal righteousness . . . For Cranmer, justification made the ungodly "right-willed", not inherently righteous.'[113] However, this raises not only the question of the time when justification is fulfilled but also the point when that process is begun, and that raises a problem for his sacramental theology. If right will is the result of grace, and Cranmer has rejected the two distinct forms of grace and righteousness proposed by Fisher and the Catholic camp as enshrined in the King's Book, then what difference does the sacrament of baptism make to one who is already beginning to show the fruits of grace in repentance, belief and seeking baptism?

Some passages in this section need to be examined more closely. A passage of Augustine, *De peccatorum meritis et remissione* 2.7. is

---

112 7B XII, heading: *Incipit* fol. 204; 'Baptismus quaecumque peccata tollit, unde <u>incipit</u> hominis renovatio in qua solvitur omnis reatus et ingeneratus et additus', Augustine *Encheiridion*, 64 (ibid.); <u>Caritas ergo incohata, incohata iustitia est</u>', Augustine, *De natura et gratia,* 70 (ibid., fol. 205); 'Novus . . . homo ex veteri nascitur, quoniam spiritualis regeneratio mutatione vitae veteranae [sic] atque secularis, <u>incohatur</u>', Augustine, *In psalmum 8* (ibid., fol. 206[V]); 'Illi credimus, quando <u>incipimus</u> vitam bonam ingredi', Augustine, *In psalmum 13* (ibid., fol. 207). Null's reading and translation, *Repentance*, pp. 182–3.
113 Null, *Repentance*, pp. 182, 184.

linked with an *incipit*, not of baptism but of the forgiveness of sins. The underlining and the marginal note make it clear that the point is not lost on the Archbishop:

> They become the children of God from the time when they begin to live in the newness of the Spirit and to be renewed in the inner person, according to the image of the one who created them. For it is not from the hour someone is baptized that all his old infirmity is destroyed, but renovation begins with the remission of all his sins. [And Cranmer adds in the margin:] Adoption begins from renewal, renewal from the forgiveness of sins.[114]

Lest we may imagine that Cranmer has missed the devaluation of the administration of baptism in this quotation, there are two passages where the marginal notes place a particular slant on the text:

> In every good work we do not begin and then are helped through the mercy of God, but he himself, without any good works being done first, begins by inspiring us with faith and love for him, so that we faithfully seek the sacraments of baptism and after baptism we are able, with the help of the Spirit, to fulfil those things which are pleasing to him. [marg.:] God begins every good thing in us whether before baptism or afterwards.[115]

> In every good work, we do not begin and then afterwards are helped through the mercy of God, but he himself first inspires us, so that we may with faith ask for the rites of baptism and after baptism are able with his help to fulfil what is pleasing to him.

---

114 Idem, *De peccatorum meritis et remissione*, li.2 ca.7. Eo quique fiunt filii dei, quo esse incipiunt in novitate spiritus et renovare in interiorem hominem, secundum imaginem eius qui creavit eos. Non enim ex qua hora quisque baptizatur, omnis vetus infirmitas eius absumitur, sed renovatio incipit a remissione peccatorum. [marg.:] Adoptio incipit a renovatione, renovatio a remissione peccatorum. (Royal MS 7B XII, fol. 207^V [= PL 44: col. 156]). There is similar underlining of this passage in Cranmer's copy of the works of St Augustine, Vol. 7 (BL C.79.c.1).

115 Idem, *De ecclesiasticis dogmat*, ca. 51:

> In omni opere bono non nos incipimus postea per Dei misericordiam adiuvamur, sed ipse nullis praecedentibus bonis meritis et fidem et amorem sui prius inspirat et ut baptismi sacramenta fideliter requiramus et post baptismum, cum spiritus adiutorio, ea quae sibi sunt placita implere possimus. [marg.:] Incipit in nobis deus omne bonum sive ante baptismum sive post. (Royal MS 7B XII, 237^V [= Gennadius, PL 58: col. 993])

[marg.:] God helps our will in every good work, both before baptism and afterwards.[116]

'Before baptism or afterwards'; 'before baptism and afterwards': Cranmer has made an important step away from the principle of the instrumentality of baptism in salvation. If God's work of salvation can be begun in us before or after the administration of the sacrament, then what role is left to the sacrament? When God's grace begins beforehand, one can conceive of the sacrament as a seal (as we shall see Peter Martyr did, for example), but when the work of salvation is begun only afterwards, then even this role for baptism is redundant.

The problem of the centurion Cornelius is a case in point. The acceptance by God of the man's prayers before he heard the gospel from Peter and was baptized was an issue between the proponents of the various understandings of faith and grace. But also it raised the question of sacramental efficacy. In a series of lengthy quotations from Augustine, Cranmer picked out some important principles which demonstrate his way of thinking:

> So even as in Abraham the righteousness of faith came first, and circumcision came after as a seal of righteousness, so in Cornelius the spiritual sanctification came first in the gift of the Holy Spirit and the sacrament of regeneration came after in the washing of baptism.
>
> By this it is shown that the sacrament of baptism is one thing, and the confession of the heart is another . . . The conversion of the heart can be present even when baptism is not received, but it cannot be present when baptism is spurned.
>
> Before he was baptized he received the Holy Spirit itself as signs made abundantly clear . . . he made no delay in receiving the most holy seals (of which the reality came first in him) for the perfection of his knowledge of the truth.[117]

---

116 [Re. PS, Augustine, *De Eccles. dogmat.* 51]:

In omni opere bono, non nos incipimus et postea per Dei misericordiam adiuvamur, sed ipse primus inspirat, ut et baptismi sacram fideliter requiramus et post baptismum cum ipsius adiutorio ea quae sibi sunt placita implere possumus. [marg.:] In omni opere bono, et ante baptismum et post, Deus praevenit nostram voluntatem. (7B XII, 278)

117 Idem, *De baptismo contra donatistas* (li.1 ca.8 and li.4 ca. 21, 22, 24.

Sicut Cornelius etiam dono spiritus sancti ditatus est, etc. Sicut ergo in Abraham praecessit fidei iustitia, et accessit circumcisio signaculum iustitiae, ita in Cornelio praecessit sanctificatio spiritualis in dono spiritus sancti et accessit sacramentum regenerationis in lavacro baptismi. ET MOX ca. 25 Quibus rebus ostenditur aliud

In Abraham justification precedes the external seal. Cornelius's faith, and his salvation, is seen in his seeking baptism; whereas had he spurned it, that would have been evidence that his faith was not right and he had not received saving grace. The neglect of baptism, not its absence, is a fault. The underlining of 'the reality (*res*) came first' suggests that Cranmer is already alive to a distinction between the sacrament and the reality which it signifies. Already there is more a feeling of the distance rather than the relationship between the two.

Very often the underlinings and marginal comments in Cranmer's copies of the Fathers add little to our understanding which is not equivocal. But the volume of St Augustine preserved in the British Museum (C.79 c.1) contains interesting annotations to the text of *De baptismo contra donatistas* (4.21–5) which correspond to and amplify the selection of texts and the marginalia in the commonplaces. The quotation from 4.24 given above continues in the text with the following underlinings:

> And just as the seal of the righteousness of faith came first in Isaac, who was circumcised on the eighth day from his birth, and just as he imitated his father's faith and righteousness itself followed in the child as he grew up though its seal had been already in the infant, so in baptized infants the sacrament of regeneration comes first.[118]

While Cranmer did not take into his commonplaces the notion spelt out by Augustine, that in adults the grace precedes the sacrament and in infants the sacrament precedes the grace, he at least showed an interest in it.

It is presumably in the light of this problem of the relation of the sacrament of baptism to the moment of justification that Cranmer

---

esse sacramentum baptismi, aliud confessionem cordis, sed salutem hominis ex utroque compleri, nec si unum horum defuerit, ideo putare debemus ut et alterum desit, quia et illud sine isto potuit esse in infante, et hoc sine illo in latrone, complente deo, sive in illo sive in isto, quod non ex voluntate defuisset. Conversio cordis potest inesse non percepto baptismo, sed contempto baptismo non potest. Lege totum. ca. 21, 22, 23, 24 and 25. [= *PL* 43: cols 174–6].

. . . Idem in Epistulam ad Rom. Cornelius centurio voluntatem Dei utique Apostolo Petro docente, cognovit, et ipsum spiritum sanctum manifestissimis coattestantibus signis, antequam baptizaretur accepit. Quamquam non ideao sacramento illa contempserit, sed multo certius baptizatus sit, ut etiam ipsam sacrosancta signacula (quorum res in eo praecessit) ad perficiendam scientiam veritatis, percipere nullo modo moraretur. ([= *PL* 35: col. 2101] Royal MS 7B XII, fol. 209)

118 Augustine, *Opera*, Vol. 7, fol. 88ᵛ: *De baptismo contra donatistas*, 4.24: 'Et sicut in Isaac, qui octavo nativitatis die circumcisus est, praecessit signaculum iustitiae fidei, et quoniam patris fidem imitatus est, secuta est in crescente ipsa iustitia cuius signaculum in infante praecesserat, ita et in baptizatis infantibus precedit regenerationis sacramentum.'

went on to muster a series of quotations on the baptism of infants with extensive and useful underlining and marginalia. What concern was exercising Cranmer's mind here? We do not have here what we find in the first volume of the commonplaces, where he collected a series of justifications of infant baptism. The question now is not whether infants are suitable candidates for baptism, but how baptism is seen to work. If the grace of justification begins elsewhere, what happens to the notions of salvation and the forgiveness of sin effected in baptism, to the role of faith, to the principle of the indispensability of baptism?

First, we find a series of extracts of Sermon *de Verbis Apostoli* 14 (Sermon 294). In the first and second extracts Augustine defends the unity of baptismal grace against the Pelagians: there is no salvation separate from the kingdom of heaven and so both are granted together. The basic principle of infant baptism is not at issue. (Cranmer underlines this, no doubt with satisfaction.) But Augustine's attack on those who say that baptism has nothing to do with salvation or eternal life, but only with the kingdom of heaven, could have contemporary bearings.[119] What does this say for those who see baptism simply as initiation into the Church or congregation of those who are already held to be justified by God?

The other extracts of particular note cover the question of the faith of the infant and of original sin. In the first case, that of the faith of infants, Cranmer notes Augustine's desire to number the infant baptized among those who believe. (Augustine plays on the use of the word *fidelis* for a baptized Christian.)[120] A further quotation explains the same point.

---

119 Concedunt parvulos baptizari oportere. <u>Non ergo quaestio est inter nos et ipsos utrum parvuli baptizandi sunt, sed de causa quaeritur quare baptizandi sunt . . . illi autem dicunt non propter salutem, non propter vitam aeternam, sed propter regnum coelorum.</u> Quid sit hoc, dum exponimus ut possumus, parumper attendite. Parvulus, inquiunt, etsi non baptizaretur, merito innocentiae, eo quod nullum habeat omnino, proprium, nec originale peccatum, nec ex se, nec de Adam tractum, necesse est, aiunt, ut habeat salutem et vitam aeternam, etiamsi non baptizetur; sed propterea baptizandus est, ut intret etiam regnum Dei, hoc est, in regnum coelorum. ET MOX <u>Ergo est vita aeterna extra regnum coelorum?</u> Primus hic error aversandus ab auribus, exstirpandus a mentibus. Hoc novum in Ecclesia, prius inauditum est, esse vitam aeternam praeter regnum coelorum, esse salutem aeternam praeter regnum Dei. ([= *PL*, 38: cols 1335–48] MS Royal 7B XII, fol. 293ᵛ)

120 Ubi ponis parvulos baptizatos? Profecto in numero credentium. Nam ideo et consuetudine Ecclesiae antiqua, canonica, fundatissima, parvuli baptizati fideles vocantur. Et sic de his quaerimus: Iste infans christianus est? Respondetur: Christianus. Catechumenus, an fidelis? Fidelis; utique a fide, fides a credendo. Inter credentes igitur baptizatos parvulos numerabis: nec judicare ullo modo aliter audebis, si non vis esse apertus haereticus. Ergo ideo habent vitam aeternam: quia 'qui credit in Filium, habet vitam aeternam'. Noli eis sine ista fide, et sine isto sacramento huius fidei, promittere vitam aeternam. (Ibid.)

Cranmer adds the marginal note: 'Infants have faith' to the words: 'Far be it from me to say that infants do not have faith. For I have argued above, that he who sinned in another believes in another. And it is said, He believes, and he prospers and he is numbered among the baptized faithful.'[121] Then Cranmer quotes a further short section: 'And infants have faith. How do they have faith? In what way do they have faith? By the faith of their parents.'[122] This is an important series of quotations. We have moved a long way from the Cranmer of *De sacramentis* in which the efficacious working of the Holy Spirit produces the response of faith in the infant. The profession of faith is made vicariously (Augustine says by the parents), and infants have the status of the faithful by virtue of their baptism and this vicarious faith.

Cranmer's use of another quotation of Augustine throws down the gauntlet to the traditional notion of sacramental efficacy in baptism. The salvation of the just thief was always the exception, indeed the exception who proved the rule of the ordinary necessity of baptism (for the Reformers) or the absolute necessity of baptism, excepted only by martyrdom, for Augustine and traditional Christianity. Here however Cranmer turns the idea on its head. When Augustine praises the witness of the thief: 'Therefore it is to be believed without doubt, that what occurred to that thief for the commending of his faith happened for our hope and our advantage', Cranmer underlines the sentence and adds in the margin, 'We are saved in the same way as was the thief.'[123] Augustine did not say that.

In these entries in the commonplaces we can see Cranmer taking an important step in his sacramental theology. In order to achieve consistency in his theology of justification, he is forced logically to break the strict link between the sacrament of baptism and the salvation which it signifies. We are not told to what extent the link is broken: is this an exception or the rule? But the principle has been established in his mind, and it will gradually work its way through his whole theological understanding.

---

121 '[marg: Credunt infantes] Absit ut ego dicam non credentes infantes. Iam superius disputavi, credit in altero, qui peccavit in altero: dicitur, Credit; et valet; et inter fideles baptizatos computantur' (ibid., fol. 294ᵛ).

122 'Credunt et infantes. Unde credunt? Quomodo credunt? Fide parentum' (ibid.).

123 IDEM de tempore seria 3a post do. palm. Serm. 1, 'Quare indubitanter credendum est, ut quod latroni illi ad commendationem fidei suae venerat etiam causa spei nostrae et utilitatis accesserit [marg: Nos eodem modo salvamur quo et latro]' (= Ps. Augustine, Appendix, Sermon 154.2: *PL*, 39: col. 2044), MS Royal 7B XII, fol. 295ᵛ).

e. The Litany in English

The year 1544 saw the publication of the first service in English: the Litany. Processions were a major feature of worship on Sundays and holy days, and it was also customary for the government to order special processions of intercession in times of emergency. These were based on the Rogation processions which had a penitential flavour: the Litany was sung and the seven penitential psalms as time permitted. The 1544 injunction was connected with an invasion of France. But on this occasion Cranmer provided a translation and simplification of the Latin form of procession. The psalms were omitted and much else was simplified, and many of the petitions of the Litany were conflated, in particular the long list of saints whose prayers were invoked. Later, Cranmer attempted an English version of the procession for festivals, but this came to nothing. In October 1545 the Litany was ordered to be used at all processions. (From August 1547 the procession itself was discontinued, leaving the Litany to be sung kneeling in church.) The second scheme for a revised breviary, more conservative than the first but like it doomed to failure, is usually dated to this period.[124]

f. Cranmer peruses books of service

In January 1546 Cranmer headed a committee to 'peruse certain books of service'. The result was a proposal to Henry to suppress certain ceremonies because they were not in accordance with the King's Book.[125] There is a particular importance here in that it shows the way in which that Book, enshrined by law as the standard of doctrine in England, could actually be invoked as a justification of reform.

---

124 Cuming, *History*, pp. 34–8; MacCulloch, *Cranmer*, pp. 328–33; Wickham Legg, *Cranmer's Liturgical Projects*. Roger Bowers, 'The Vernacular Litany of 1544 during the Reign of Henry VIII', in G.W. Bernard and S.J. Gunn (eds), *Authority and Consent in Tudor England* (Aldershot: Ashgate, 2002), pp. 151–78, astutely observes that Cranmer was asked by Henry to compose an English version of the Processional for festivals, not for Sundays (letter of Cranmer to Henry, PS, II, p. 412, dated 7 October and usually ascribed to 1544 but by Bowers to 1545). However, I think he is wrong in believing that the injunction of 15 October 1545 prescribed the use of the Litany in addition to the Processional rather than in its place – despite quoting Wriothesley's Chronicle which says that the English version 'be song in everie parish church throughout England everie Soundaie and festivall daie, and non other'.
125 MacCulloch, *Cranmer*, pp. 334, 351–2.

g. Cranmer asked to pen the communion service

In August 1546 Henry astonished Cranmer by proposing to agree with
Francis I of France 'to have changed the Mass in both the realms into
a communion'. Cranmer was directed 'to pen a form thereof to be sent
to the French king to consider of'.[126] However, the enterprise never got
any further, owing to the death of both monarchs shortly after. Cranmer
deeply regretted the lost opportunity, since even when reform did move
forward in Edward's reign it lacked the authority of the boy's father
who would have carried all before him. But if Cranmer had managed to
draft anything before Henry's death, it would have been subject to the
theological benchmark of the King's Book.

h. An early version of 1549

We can see the role of the King's Book when at different times both
sides in the theological debate appealed to it as backing their cause:
Cranmer, as we have seen, in 1546 with proposals for the suppression
of idolatrous practices, and Gardiner in the summer of 1547 when he
resisted the authorization of the new *Book of Homilies*.[127] Of course
the legislation enshrining the Book was doomed from the time that the
boy-king's Council had determined its religious policy at the beginning
of that year, and it was indeed repealed in November. But the shadow
of 1543 now can be seen to draw very close to 1549. While Cranmer
had the space of nearly two years between the death of Henry and the
authorization of the 1549 Prayer Book, this period would be perilously
short even for someone engaged full-time on the liturgical revision. It
would not be suprising if we had in the first Prayer Book material which
had been written earlier; indeed it has been suggested that significant
parts of the baptism service, among other rites, go back to the 1530s.
Any material written between 1543 and 1547 would have to be in line
with the position of the King's Book. (We might consider the possibility
of a communion service penned by Cranmer in response to Henry's
request in August 1546.) This may partly provide the reason behind the
fact that many passages have been identified in the Prayer Book of 1549
with links to the King's Book.[128] Whatever Cranmer's own view of the

---

126 The account of this was told to Morice by Cranmer in Edward's reign, as reported
in J. Foxe, *Acts and Monuments*, ed. J. Pratt and J. Stoughton, 8 vols (London: Religious
Tract Society, n.d.; 4th edn), pp. 563–4; quoted also in Cranmer, PS, II, pp. 415–16.
127 MacCulloch, *Cranmer*, pp. 351–2; Redworth, *In Defence of the Church Catholic*,
pp. 258–65.
128 Cf. Cuming, *Godly Order*, pp. 97, 108–9; B.D. Spinks, 'Treasures Old and New',
pp. 182–3.

theology of the services, he would have needed to justify them *vis-à-vis* the authoritative doctrinal standard of the day. Even after the repeal of the Act, the King's Book still represented the views of an influential group who could not be ignored. In either case we need not be surprised to find allusions to the King's Book in the Prayer Book liturgy. To some extent this picture is hypothetical: we do not, for example, have any evidence that Cranmer managed to draft his communion service as ordered. But the very reasonableness of the hypothesis should lead us to look out for the King's Book as a possible rationale for doctrinally sensitive material in the first Prayer Book. Likewise we shall find that the *Rationale of Ceremonial*, although it never achieved the authoritative status enjoyed by the King's Book, probably influenced elements of the baptism service in the 1549 Prayer Book, presumably since it represented the interests of a particular group.

But while Cranmer was sensitive to the interests of powerful colleagues, his own theology has moved significantly. In the late 1530s, while espousing a theology that was broadly Lutheran, he had at least noted the figurative approach to the sacraments. In the mid 1540s his thoughts on the sacrament of baptism had led him away from the idea that the Holy Spirit endows the infant with faith towards a theology in which the grace is not tied to the administration of the sacrament. There is no reason to suppose that he has yet drawn any conclusions from this for his eucharistic theology; but the death of Henry and the accession of Edward VI will present both opportunities for liturgical reform and challenges for Cranmer's understanding of the eucharist.

The evangelical view of the true Church with the two dominical sacraments seen together and the word of God preached. From John Foxe, *Acts and Monuments*.

Chapter 3

THE BEGINNINGS OF REFORM
UNDER EDWARD VI: 1547–48

1 Reform under the new Council

a. The Coronation of Edward VI

The accession of King Edward VI on 28 January 1547 brought the first breeze of change almost at once, with the coronation on 20 February featuring a pageant of a boy representing Truth, who condemned heathen rites and detestable idolatry.[1] The coronation itself was traditional in all respects, but Cranmer's speech afterwards (which we shall examine below, Chapter 4) reveals a decidedly untraditional understanding of it. The ascendancy of the reformers on the Council was assured by the fall of the traditionalist Wriothesley and the appointment of Somerset as Lord Protector on 12 March. MacCulloch sees the Edwardian years as a period in which one group held continuous power and a coherent programme of reform:

> This evangelical establishment grouping knew from the start in 1547 exactly what Reformation it wanted: whatever hesitations occurred were primarily attributable to the need to disarm conservative opposition. Despite the superficial break in Edwardian politics caused by the overthrow of Somerset and his replacement by the ascendancy of John Dudley in 1549, there was an essential continuity of purpose in a graduated series of religious changes over seven years. These changes were designed to destroy one Church and build another, in a religious revolution of ruthless thoroughness. Thomas Cranmer was the one man who guaranteed the continuity of the changes, and he was chiefly responsible for planning them as they occurred, although more practical secular politicians decided the pace at which they should be put into effect.[2]

---

1   MacCulloch, *Cranmer*, p. 364.
2   MacCulloch, *Cranmer*, pp. 365–6.

MacCulloch is, of course, not unaware of the different ways in which the various players viewed this reformation. It is hard to imagine some members of the Council sympathizing with every twist and turn of the Archbishop's eucharistic theology. And Cranmer showed his unhappiness with financial aspects of the suppression of the chantries by going to the lengths of voting against the legislation at one point.[3] But the main agenda of reform was driven on by common consent at great speed. The *Book of Homilies* was published in July (despite Gardiner's appeal to the King's Book, the theology of which they contradicted).

b. The homily of Salvation

The *Book of Homilies* of July 1547 publicly ushered in the religious teaching of the reign of Edward VI. The gestation of these homilies had been a long one; Cranmer had proposed their drafting as long ago as 1542. The collection lacked a treatise on the eucharist: that needed cautious delay. But the homilies on Salvation, on Faith and on Good Works annexed to Faith were composed by the Archbishop himself and set out his mature theology of justification in no uncertain terms. Technical theological terms were avoided, as befits a publication aimed at the ordinary congregation; only predestination remained 'the doctrine that dared not speak its name', though it underlay the principles of the homilies throughout.[4]

In the homily of Salvation, the place of baptism is discussed:

Insomuch that infants, being baptized, and dying in their infancy, are by this sacrifice washed from their sins, brought to God's favour, and made his children, and inheritors of his kingdom of heaven. And they which actually do sin after their baptism, when they convert and turn again to God unfeignedly, they are likewise washed by this sacrifice from their sins, in such sort, that there remaineth not any spot of sin that shall be imputed to their damnation.[5]

While the language of the homily in itself could be read as supporting a traditional theology of the sacrament being efficacious, instilling inherent righteousness *ex opere operato*, the equally valid reading, that the washing from sin refers to a forensic forgiveness imputed by God to the child, would reflect Cranmer's theology more closely.

---

3   MacCulloch, *Cranmer*, p. 377.
4   MacCulloch, *Cranmer*, pp. 371–5.
5   Homily of Salvation, Cranmer, PS, II, p. 128.

c. Ceremonies banned: draft vernacular services

In August a set of injunctions required the readings at the eucharist to be in English, not in Latin, the Litany to be sung kneeling, not in procession, the offices to be curtailed to make room for Bible reading and sermons; and images before which lights were burnt were to be removed.[6] In January 1548 traditional ceremonies on Candlemas, Ash Wednesday, Palm Sunday and Good Friday were forbidden. The injunction was interpreted more or less strictly; in many places all the ceremonies of Holy Week and Easter were omitted, including the solemn blessing of the font at the Easter vigil.[7]

As well as the new Order of the Communion (to be considered below), translations of the offices, Mass and other services were being aired in 1548. On 12 May at Westminster 'the masse song all in English, with the consecration of the sacrament also spoken in English, the priest leaving out all the canon after the creede, save the "Pater Noster", and then ministering the communion after the Kinges book'. On 4 September the Protector wrote to the Vice-Chancellor of Cambridge University instructing them to use 'one uniform order, ryte, and ceremonyes in the masse, matens and evensonge, and all other dyvine service in the same to be said or songe, such as is presentlie used in the King's majestie's chapel, and none other. The which, for the more plain information we have by this berer sent unto you.'[8] Sadly, all trace of these forms of service have disappeared, but we may presume that they looked forward to that of the new Prayer Book.

2 THE ORDER OF THE COMMUNION

a. An inconsistent theology

As we shall see in the next chapter, Cranmer's mature sacramental theology is not in any significant doubt. That theology is set out clearly

---

6   Duffy, *Stripping of the Altars*, pp. 450–4.

7   Cranmer's Articles for Canterbury Diocese 1548: 58. 'Item, Whether they upon Easter-even last past hallowed the font, fire, or paschal, or had any paschal set up, or burning in their churches': Frere, *Visitation Articles*, Vol. 2, pp. 183–4. Duffy, *Stripping of the Altars*, pp. 461–2, records a similar complete removal of ceremonies in Robert Parkyn's Adwick le Street near Doncaster, but the observance of what did not offend the letter of the law was maintained in Worcester and Winchester.

8   J.T. Tomlinson, *The Great Parliamentary Debate in 1548 on the Lord's Supper* (London: J.F. Shaw, n.d.; 2nd edn), pp. 6–7, quoting Wriothesley's Chronicle, *A Chronicle of England during the reign of the Tudors from AD 1485–1559 by Charles Wriothesley, Windsor Herald*, ed. W.D. Hamilton, 2 vols (London: Camden Society, 1875, 1877), Vol 2, p. 2, and CCCC, MS 106, p. 493. Cuming, *History*, pp. 39–40.

in the Prayer Book of 1552 and, with some ambiguity, in that of 1549. However, as well as some ambiguities, some features of the first Prayer Book are inconsistent with Cranmer's mature theology. It could be the case that he was simply allowing pastoral sensitivity or the needs of political consensus to outweigh theological exactitude. However, a close examination of other documents from around 1547 to the middle of 1548 reveal that there was movement in his theology. At the end of 1547 an outside observer might have been confident that the new regime was in favour of the doctrine of the Real Presence. A royal proclamation of 27 December affirmed the 'verity' of the presence and encouraged simple trust in Christ's words rather than useless speculation. Ridley preached a sermon supporting the same teaching, and Gardiner later claimed that at that time he and Cranmer were in agreement on that point.[9]

b. The Cologne reformation

Before we trace the progress of Cranmer's thought through this period, one attempted reformation on the Continent, that at Cologne, deserves our attention here. Archbishop Hermann had enlisted the help of notable Reformers, and Bucer in particular was both extremely active and of special note for our story. While the reform came to nothing through the opposition of the Cathedral Chapter to its evangelical direction, the literature that emanated from the debates was widely read. In 1545 the *Simplex ac pia deliberatio*[10] was published, a Latin translation of the German *Einfältiges Bedencken* of 1543. This in turn was translated into English as the *Simple and Religious Consultation* and published by John Day in 1547, with a revised edition in the following year. The work, probably in the Latin version, was used by Cranmer at many points in his liturgical writings.

Meanwhile, Bucer's opponents in Cologne had been prompt in getting a Latin version of their criticisms into circulation, publishing the *Antididagma* in 1544,[11] the same year as appeared its German original, the *Christlische und katholische Gegenberichtung*. Occasional references to the *Antididagma* are found in Cranmer's commonplaces; furthermore,

---

9   MacCulloch, *Cranmer*, pp. 378–9; D.G. Selwyn, 'A New Version of a Mid-Sixteenth Century Vernacular Tract on the Eucharist: A Document of the Early Edwardian Reformation?', *JEH*, 39 (1988), pp. 217–29 (220).

10   *Nostra Hermanni, Archiepiscopi Colon. et Principis Electoris, etc., Simplex ac Pia Deliberatio, qua ratione Christiana et in verbo Dei fundata Reformatio . . . instituenda sit* (Bonn: L. Mylius, 1545).

11   Cologne Cathedral Chapter, *Antididagma, seu Christianae et Catholicae religionis per reverendos Canonicos metropolitanae Ecclesiae Coloniensis Propugnatio* (Louvain: S. Zassenus, 1544).

it will be suggested below that the replies to a questionnaire addressed to conservative theologians in the late 1540s show interest in the *Antididagma's* criticisms of evangelical liturgy. In 1545 Bucer published a reply to the *Antididagma*, called the *Bestendige Verantwortung*. One Latin translation, entitled the *Constans defensio*, was made in 1550 by Martin Brem, Bucer's amanuensis, and dedicated to Matthew Parker, the future archbishop but already a prominent reformer in Cambridge. This translation circulated in manuscript form and was finally published in 1613.[12] A different manuscript translation has been found interleaved in the 1549 edition of the *Antididagma* owned by Thomas Sampson, a Reformer who became dean of Chichester, went into exile under Mary and returned to become dean of Christ Church, Oxford. Bucer's reply to the *Antididagma* was influential in English circles in that it was also used by one Richard Bonner in a treatise in 1548.[13] Bonner also corresponded with Bucer, before the latter's arrival in England, on the use of the words of institution in the celebration of the eucharist. We possess Bucer's reply which we will consider below.[14]

This considerable amount of literature shows that the debate in Cologne influenced not only individual writers but also the theological debate in England, and thereby had its effect on the liturgy of 1549. This will be seen as we examine in particular Cranmer's theology of consecration below.

Another English version of the baptism service of the *Pia Deliberatio* was made by a certain Richard Ryce.[15] Ryce, in his preface, declares

---

12   *Constans Defensio ex sacra Scriptura . . . Deliberationis de Christiana Reformatione, quam Reverend. Hermannus Archiep. Colon. iam ante publicavit* (Geneva: P. and I. Chouët, 1613).

13   *A Treatyse of the ryght honourynge and wourshyppyng of our Saviour Jesus Christe in the sacrament of breade and wyne . . .* (London: W. Lynne, 1548). MacCulloch, *Cranmer*, pp. 399–403. C. Hope suggests that Cranmer may have been induced to insert a prayer of consecration into his 1549 Prayer Book under the influence of the *Antididagma*, and that Bonner wrote his treatise in order to familiarize the Archbishop with Bucer's riposte: 'An English Version of Parts of Bucer's Reply to the Cologne *Antididagma* of 1544', *JTS*, n.s. 11 (1960), pp. 94–110; but this approach does not stand. On Cranmer's use of Hermann, see Cuming, 'Cologne and Canterbury', *Godly Order*, pp. 68–90.

14   The identity of Richard Bonner is problematic. The dedication to Cranmer in his *Treatyse* suggests that he was a priest in the Canterbury diocese. MacCulloch, *Cranmer*, pp. 399–403, has suggested that he never existed but the name was used as a fictional front-man for dealing with difficult issues. However Paul Ayris has found a reference to a Richard Bonner in Cranmer's register, instituted as rector of St Tricat, Calais, on 16 June 1541. I am very grateful to Dr Ayris for supplying me with this information.

15   *The Right Institucion of baptisme sett forth by the Revd Father in Christ Herman Archbishop of Coleyne, translated by the unproffytable Servant of Christ Richard Ryce* (Ipswich: A. Scoloker, 1548). For the identity of Ryce see MacCulloch, *Cranmer*, p. 393, n. 143.

that the purpose of the work is to educate the godparents, which is, he says, a widely felt need. In this respect the extensive exhortations and the detailed questions of the *Deliberatio* would be very appropriate. But even a brief perusal reveals that Ryce's work is more like a proposal for a Reformed rite of baptism than an educative aid, with considerable variations from Hermann's rite and interpolations of some traditional ceremonies which might make the service acceptable to English parishioners. The rubrics are more clear than in Hermann, again making the book seem to have been written for use rather than study.

The contents of Ryce's liturgy need not detain us long. Theologically it is not a remarkable work. Its main concern seems to be for the moral and covenantal aspects of baptism. It seems to be innocent of Anabaptist issues, and in the changes it makes it unravels the intricate motifs woven by Hermann and his colleagues, and puts nothing in their place. The sacramental theology is close to that of Zwingli: baptism is a sign of God's grace rather than an instrument of it. But this may reflect a weakness of thought on Ryce's part rather than a well-argued position. Its importance is as an example of popular moves towards reform and, liturgically, a willing acceptance of traditional ceremonial if it can be used to communicate the message of the gospel. There is no evidence that Cranmer knew of this publication, and it is unlikely that he would have been impressed by it. So it is interesting to note that Ryce retains the post-baptismal ceremonies in the order of the vesting, the candle and the formula of anointing (the last emended to be a general blessing; the anointing itself seems to have been omitted). This change of order from the traditional pattern as found in the *Manual* is also to be seen in Cranmer's 1549 service, and this coincidence may reflect actual use – getting the naked baby dressed as quickly as possible – rather than some dependence of Cranmer on Ryce.

c. The principle of consecration

i. The Middle Ages

When Cranmer published his 1549 Prayer Book, he was extraordinarily conservative by Reformation standards in that he included what looked like a prayer of consecration both at the eucharist and the baptism service. In 1552 neither of their equivalent replacements is a prayer of consecration of the elements, but an invocation over the recipients. But the purpose of the prayers in both books is that the grace of the sacrament should be applied to the recipients. The concerns embodied in the prayers, though altered, essentially remain: how is the grace of God applied to the contemporary instance? Whether we are dealing with the relationship of the physical objects of bread, wine or water to the sacramental grace, or with administering the grace to the recipient, some model of application is necessary. In the ancient and medieval rites a request for God's grace was conventional, in the Roman Mass performed above all by the *Quam oblationem*: 'O God, we beseech you graciously to make this offering wholly blessed, approved, ratified, spiritual, and acceptable, that it may become for us the body and blood of your most dearly beloved Son our Lord and God Jesus Christ, who, on the day before he suffered . . .' Other rites, especially Eastern ones, included an epiclesis of the Holy Spirit, and this could apply to baptism as well as to the eucharist. However, the popular tradition in the West, following from Ambrose and enshrined by Thomas Aquinas, was that the words of institution in the eucharist were words of consecration.[16] In the final notes of the Sarum *Missal* there was provision for the accident in which the priest realizes after the Canon that there was no wine in the chalice: in this case he places wine and water in it and recites the appropriate words of institution as a form of consecration.[17] Cranmer used this method for *additional* consecration (a new concept) in the 1548 *Order of the Communion*, where the small size of the medieval chalice (made to accommodate only clerical communion) and the general lack of experience of lay communion in both kinds made such provision highly desirable.[18]

ii. The continental Reformers

In the Reformation rites, a theological model of applying the grace was still required. In the eucharist the notion that the words of institution were themselves words of consecration lessened the importance of other models, and we find in the early Lutheran rites the words of institution standing alone. With Luther's own word theology, this presented no problem. Not only did the word of Christ effect the Real Presence in the sacrament, it took precedence, as it were, in every respect.

> . . . in every promise of God there are two things which one must consider, the word and the sign. As in baptism there are the words of the baptizer and the dipping in water, so in the mass there are the words and the bread and wine. The words are the divine vow, promise and testament. The signs are the sacraments, that is, sacred

---

16   Cf. R.F. Buxton, *Eucharist and Institution Narrative*, Alcuin Club Collection 58 (Great Wakering: Mayhew–McCrimmon, 1976), p. 42.
17   *Eucharist and Institution Narrative*, pp. 46–9.
18   Cuming, *History of Anglican Liturgy*, p. 43; Buxton, *Eucharist and Institution Narrative*, pp. 63–4.

signs. Now as the testament is much more important than the
sacrament, so the words are much more important than the signs
. . . We see then that the best and greatest of all sacraments and
of the mass is the words and promise of God, without which the
sacraments are dead and are nothing at all.[19]

Similarly Luther's baptismal rite lacked any blessing of the water.
The scriptural words contained in the administration of the sacrament
fulfilled all that was necessary. His Flood prayer included a reference to
the blessing of all waters for baptism by the baptism of Christ by John,
but this is very different from the notion of a liturgical consecration of
the font. In 1540 Luther attacked the idea that to 'add the word to the
water' implied a blessing of the element. There was no command from
God for such a practice. Rather we have simply:

> God's word beside and with the water, which is not something we
> have invented or dreamed up, but is rather the Word of Christ, who
> said, 'Go into all the world and baptize them in the name of the
> Father and of the Son and of the Holy Spirit.' When these words
> are added to the water, then it is no longer simple water like other
> water, but a holy, divine, blessed water. For when the word of God,
> by which he created heaven and earth and all things, is present,
> there God himself is present with his power and might.[20]

Spinks comments, 'Thus to add the word to water is to obey God and
baptize in water in the name of God . . . To bless the water would be to
imply that God's own word was insufficient.'[21]

In 1533 Osiander's Brandenburg–Nuremberg rite declared that a
consecration was unhelpful: 'the blessing of the font is rather a hindrance
than a furtherance of baptism, and serves only for superstition'. Likewise
Bucer in 1524, in his *Grund und Ursach*, rejected the consecration of the
water.[22] Farel's French Evangelical Service Book of 1533 took a similar
line.[23]

---

19 *Treatise on the New Testament*, 17, *Luther's Works*, ed. J. Pelikan and Helmut
Lehmann, 55 vols (Philadelphia, PA: Muhlenberg Press, 1955–), Vol. 35, p. 91.
20 Sermon on Mt. 3.13-17 at the Baptism of Bernhard von Anhalt (1540), quoted by B.D.
Spinks, 'Luther's *Taufbüchlein*', *Liturgical Review* (part 1), 5 (1975), pp. 17–20; (part 2), 6
(1976), pp. 13–21: part 2, p. 17.
21 Spinks, 'Luther's *Taufbüchlein*' (part 2), p. 17.
22 H.O. Old, *The Shaping of the Reformed Baptismal Rite in the Sixteenth Century*
(Grand Rapids, MI: Eerdmans, 1992), p. 55.
23 Neuchâtel French Evangelical Service Book of 1533, quoted by Old, *Reformed
Baptismal Rite*, p. 160.

The wrong attitude to the consecration of water was one of popular superstition rather than of medieval theology. The Reformers knew full well that the Scholastic theologians had not taught there was a particular grace in blessed water or that there was any kind of transubstantiation of the water.[24] Old shows how Jud, Zwingli and their followers adapted the Flood prayer into an invocation over the recipients of the sacrament, removing at the same time all mention of even the generalized concept of the consecration of water. By and large the baptismal invocations were derived in form from preliminary prayers in the services, and not from the consecration prayers. The natural contrast was between the blessing of objects and that of people.[25]

iii. The Cologne debate

Thus far we may suppose that the rejection of a prayer of consecration was total and absolute. However, we find around 1543 a consciousness of the question and even a softening of attitudes on the part of both Bucer and Osiander, the former in his defence of Hermann's *Consultation* against the *Antididagma*, and the latter in his liturgical writing. First let us look at the dispute over the *Consultation*, which, needless to say, had no consecration of the water or, as far as its opponents were concerned, of the bread and wine. Of the consecration of the bread and wine in the eucharist, the *Antididagma* attacked Hermann's use of the words of institution alone:

> Here we must state that it is total madness that some people reckon they can consecrate the Sacrament without the catholic prayer which we call the Canon, and without any invocation of the divine name over the gifts which are set forth, but simply with a recitation or reading of the words of Paul in 1 Corinthians 11, 'The Lord Jesus on the night in which he was betrayed etc.' For the Apostle is only giving an historical account there of what Christ did, and is not seeking to hand down some form of consecration which the priestly minister of the Church can use with an invocation of the divine name to bless and sanctify the gifts set forth, albeit not with his own words but the all powerful words of our Lord Jesus Christ.[26]

---

24 Old, *Reformed Baptismal Rite*, p. 261.
25 Old, *Reformed Baptismal Rite*, pp. 227–34.
26 *Antididagma*, fol. 112 (author's trans.).

The writer continues by citing the *Quam oblationem* in the Canon, Psuedo-Dionysius (the Areopagite) and John Chrysostom, then proceeds to give the testimony of the Greek liturgy:

> The Greek liturgy directs the bishop to stand upright and to sign the offering (no doubt with the sign of the cross) and to say: Make, O Lord, this bread the precious Body of thy Christ. Amen. And over the cup to say: Make what is in this cup the precious Blood of thy Christ, changing them by thy Holy Spirit.[27]

Here a direct comparison is made between the epiclesis of the Greek liturgy and the *Quam oblationem* of the Latin Canon. (This and other features of the epiclesis will become important when we consider the wording of the 1549 prayers in baptism and the eucharist.) The *Antididagma* also attacks the lack of a consecration of the baptismal water in Hermann's *Consultation*, quoting as authorities for such a usage Pseudo-Dionysius and Basil.[28]

Bucer's reply to the accusation about eucharistic consecration was to attack the Chapter for denying that the words of Christ consecrate the sacraments, preferring the human construction of the Canon. For his part he denied that the recitation of the words of institution in the *Consultation* was used merely as historical description; evidence for this was provided by the Amen said by the congregation after the words were recited, and by the Lord's Prayer which followed, in which the people prayed that the Lord would provide for them his body and blood for food and drink. His reply, then, is important in going some way at least in agreeing with the Chapter that the words of institution cannot be used merely as Paul used them, as a historical narration, but need to be applied, however simply, to the actual service and eucharistic elements.

With regard to the consecration of the water, Bucer is less guarded, indeed to an astonishing degree:

> The seventh accusation is about the consecration of the water of baptism and about the candle, both of ancient usage. However there is nothing handed down about either in the holy scriptures other than what St Paul teaches in 1 Tim. 4 about the sanctification of all things by the word and prayer. And indeed our opponents administer the consecration in a foreign language, contrary to

---

27 *Antididagma*, fol. 113 (author's trans.).
28 *Antididagma*, fol. 58v; quoted by Anonymous (but attributed to F.E. Brightman), 'Capitulum Coloniense: An Episode in the Reformation', *CQR*, 31 (January 1891), pp. 419–37 (429).

ancient custom. From this has arisen a common superstition, as if some particular power can be attributed to the water, and that baptism administered according to the word of the Lord in plain water is not as good or as efficacious as that which is given with consecrated water. That is a grave abuse and a terrible offence against faith in Christ. But if the Church of Christ could truly be built up by this consecration, there might be agreement on some prayer which was in keeping with scripture and in which the Lord was invoked that he might grant that the water would be of service to us for salvation in holy baptism, according to his word, provided that nothing there went beyond what Saint Paul teaches when he says that everything that God made for our use was to be sanctified by the word and prayer, and that there is no trace of superstition.[29]

Bucer here not only concedes that a consecration might be permissible if it were to avoid superstition by being carefully composed (and in the vernacular), but sets out the conditions which would determine such a consecration. First and foremost is the scripture verse 1 Tim. 4.5, that consecration is by the word and prayer. Secondly, the thing is consecrated to a use and nothing else. No magical qualities are instilled. Thirdly, the Lord is invoked that he might grant this. Fourthly, we might add that the consecration of something is in the context of its creation by God for that use. (We shall see all these features included in the Prayer Book of 1549, and also perhaps in the baptism service a hint of Bucer's phrase 'the sanctification of all things'.)

In 1543 Osiander, who in 1533 had forbidden a blessing of the font, subscribed to and indeed is largely held to have been responsible for a eucharistic rite for Pfalz-Neuberg which contained a prayer for consecration.[30] J. Dowden quoted Brightman's views of 1901 in seeing the Pfalz-Neuberger *Kirchenordnung* as a possible model for the 1549 eucharistic prayer, but he believed it served less as a pattern than pointed Cranmer to Eastern parallels. Speculation on the prayer of consecration since then has been sparse. Cuming was evidently entranced by the Pfalz-Neuberg prayer, and included Dowden's translation of it in the texts of his *History*.[31] But whatever he may have speculated, he evidently kept his thoughts to himself.

---

29   *Defensio*, p.184 (author's trans.).
30   'A Striking Departure from the Prevailing Form of the Reformed Churches of Germany', J. Dowden, *Further Studies in the Prayer Book* (London: Methuen, 1908), p. 69.
31   *History of Anglican Liturgy*, p. 285.

iv. The debate in England

The debate about consecration and the role of the words of institution was going on in England as well. It is to be found in a questionnaire, now preserved in the Bodleian library, which seems to have been addressed to conservatives,[32] and which may well be supplementary to or connected with the questionnaires on the Mass sent out over the winter of 1547–48.[33] This document is fascinating for its liturgical agenda; unfortunately the authors of both the questions and the answers are unnamed. The copy is now bound with other traditionalist material, the Bodleian draft of the Vernacular Real Presence Tract (discussed below), and the traditionalist version of Martyr's Oxford Disputation. Some of the questions seem to pre-empt the 1549 or even the 1552 Prayer Book. For instance:

Octava questio

Whether the communion, the supper of our Lorde, the sacrament of the boddie and bludd of Christ And the masse be one in Scripture or no.

Nona questio

Whether the wordes of the institucion of the supper of the Lorde spoken to the appostles are to be understonde at [*sic*] spoken to Laye persons as to preistes or preistes only.[34]

But for our purposes the fifth and tenth items are of most interest:

---

32 *Questiones de missa cum responcionibus eisdem*, Bodleian Library, MS Add. C.197, fols 65–7ᵛ.

33 For the Questions and Answers on some Abuses of the Mass and supplementary questions to the bishops of Worcester, Chichester and Hereford, see Cranmer, PS, II, pp. 150–3. Among the latter set is the following pertinent exchange (p. 152):

The Question

Is there any rite or prayer not expressed in the scripture which Christ used, or commanded at the first institution of the mass, which we be now bound to use; and what the same be?

The Answer

That Christ used rites and prayers at the institution and distribution of the sacrament, the scripture declareth: but what rites and prayers they were, we know not; but I think that we ought to use such rites and prayers as the catholic church hath, and doth uniformly observe.

34 *Questiones de Missa*, fols 66–66ᵛ. Cf. the title of the eucharist in the 1549 Prayer Book and the words of administration in the 1552 eucharist.

Quinta questio

By what Scripture can it be proved that this Sainge, hoc est corpus meum, Shall bring Christes humayne bodie to be contayned in the Sacrament. And that flesshe and bludd and bones as it was borne of the virgyn mary.

Questio decima

Whether the comunion or the supper of the Lorde sholde not be rightlie ministred by Scripture, if there were no mo wordes spoken nor anny other thing don at the admynistracion of the same then that Seint paule reherseth? 1 Corr. 11

Responcio

To Recite a thing don under the waye of narraccion makithe not the Sute for there it shulde folowe that when we reade the last Chapiter of Mathewe and marke 14 and so forthe we do consecratte and make the comunyon, St paules intent is not to make the communyon or the Lordes supper but onlie to teache Corynth how he was taught what the Lorde did and under what manner St paule did consecratte and geve the Lordes Supper by Scripture we cannot tell but this we be sure that many thinges he had in writing he never expressed 1 Corr. 11 *Cetera cum venere disponam*, wherfor seing that in rehersal of St pawles wordes onlie is neither invocacion nor benediccion there canne be no consecracion and consequentlie no communion or Lordes supper. St Aug. *ex exposicione simboli sermone crucis ibi hoc signo crucis consecratur corpus dominicum, sanctificetur fons baptismatis, iniciantur etiam presbiteri et ceteri gradus ecclesiastici, et omnia quaecumque sanctificentur hoc signo dominici crucis cum invocacione xpi nominis consecrantur.*[35]

There is a distinct lack of sympathy on the part of the respondent to the ideas suggested in the questions! It would seem that the respondent was afraid of giving permission for a Lutheran style of eucharist, in which the words of institution stand alone. This, he feels, would be simply the historical narration rather than a form of consecration. He wishes to propose instead the retention of some kind of prayer, no doubt preferably the traditional Canon, and even puts in a plea for the customary ritual actions by invoking Augustine for the sign of the cross used in the prayer.

It is curious that we read here a plea for the same thing as that requested in the *Antididagma*, only with different authorities quoted: a prayer for consecration and the inclusion of the sign of the cross. Where

---

35 *Questiones de Missa*, fols 65ᵛ, 66ᵛ–7. Ps. Augustine, *Sermo de symbolo* (Olim de tempore 181), 3 (*PL*, 40, 1192).

the *Antididagma* quotes Eastern theologians and liturgies, the respondent finds a Latin source in Augustine, though now it is specifically for the sign of the cross which in the Cologne work was mentioned only incidentally. (Do we have here evidence of political reasons for the 'little black crosses' of the 1549 Prayer Book, that they were a sop to the traditionalists? It is hard to imagine that Cranmer would have attached much significance to them. Gabriel Biel in his *Canonis Missae Expositio* maintained that the words of the Canon effected the consecration, but that the sign of the cross represented the passion to the participants in the eucharist.[36] Whatever Cranmer thought about the words, he would surely have agreed about the sign of the cross. It is more difficult to know what these traditionalists wanted to make of it, unless they simply wished to maintain as much of the time-honoured liturgy as possible.)

But it seems very likely from these documents that the debate in England was becoming a second round of that in Cologne.

d. The Order of the Communion

The Order of the Communion was published in March 1548 for use from the Easter of that year.[37] The Order was to be used within the traditional Latin Mass and provides for the communion of the laity along with devotions: an exhortation for the previous Sunday; an exhortation to the communicants, a general confession with introduction and absolution, the Comfortable Words, Prayer of Humble Access, communion with words of administration and blessing. The material was incorporated into the 1549 eucharist with very little change. However, the final rubrics in the 1548 publication reveal a different position from the book of the following year:

> Note, that the Bread that shall be consecrated shall be such as heretofore hath been accustomed. And every of the said consecrated Breads shall be broken in two pieces, at the least, or more by the discretion of the Minister, and so distributed. And men must not think less to be received in part, than in the whole, but in each of them the whole body of our Saviour Jesu Christ.
>
> Note, that if it doth so chance, that the wine hallowed and consecrate doth not suffice or be enough for them that do take the Communion, the Priest, after the first Cup or Chalice be emptied,

---

36 G. Biel, *Canonis Missae Expositio*, Lectio 21, K, ed. H.A. Oberman and W.J. Courtenay, 4 vols (Wiesbaden: Franz Steiner, 1963), Vol. 1, p. 193; Lectio 33 O, p. 362.
37 For the publication and circularization of this Order, see MacCulloch, *Cranmer*, pp. 384–6.

may go again to the altar, and reverently, and devoutly prepare and consecrate another, and so the third, or more, likewise beginning at these words, *Simili modo postquam coenatum est,* and ending at these words, *qui pro vobis et pro multis effundetur in remissionem peccatorum*, and without any levation or lifting up.[38]

The provision for additional consecration, using the words of institution, is based on a provision in the Sarum *Missal* for occasions when the priest discovers at the time of communion that there was no wine in the chalice at the time of consecration. However, it is a novelty that Cranmer should forbid any elevation of the sacrament. MacCulloch points out the fully fledged language of a spiritual feeding in the Order: in the exhortation before the Confession we are told that 'the benefit is great, if with a true penitent heart, and lively faith we receive this holy Sacrament (for then we spiritually eat the flesh of Christ, and drink his blood)'. And, with the proscription of the elevation, he concludes that 'the clear purpose of the Order of the Communion in text and rubric was to attack the notion of Real Presence'.[39] However, it is by no means so clear that we have here Cranmer's mature doctrine. Rather there may be evidence of a rather different theology.

First, the provision for additional consecration is not repeated in either the 1549 or the 1552 Prayer Books. (No doubt it continued in many parishes.)[40] Given the care expended on this rubric in the 1548 Order, it is hard to imagine that the omission was accidental. The words of institution are used as a means of consecration without any other prayer or formula.[41]

Secondly, the language of the rubrics is of interest in that the bread and wine are spoken of as consecrated. (There is no question of support for transubstantiation here.) However, I cannot find the language of consecration in either 1549 or 1552 (except the consecration of bishops).[42] The rubric about the preparation of the bread for the eucharist in 1549 describes it not as 'consecrated bread' but as 'the

---

38   PS, *Liturgies of Edward VI*, p. 8.

39   MacCulloch, *Cranmer*, p. 386.

40   Peter Martyr refers to its continuation when he is discussing the 1549 Prayer Book. See letter to Bucer, 12 January 1551, in G.C. Gorham (ed.), *Gleanings of a few Scattered Ears, during the Period of the Reformation* (London: Bell & Daldy, 1857), p. 228.

41   The use of the words of institution standing alone as words of consecration seems to be implied by Wriothesley in his description of the Mass on 12 May 1548 (cited above). Was this something attempted as an alternative to an English version of the Canon?

42   Cranmer had a low view of bishops (theologically speaking) and believed them to be priests set apart for a particular function. See P.F. Bradshaw, *The Anglican Ordinal* (London: SPCK, 1971), p. 31.

bread prepared for the communion'. In the eucharistic prayer the bread is blessed and sanctified. The water of the font is sanctified, but in neither case is the prayer called a prayer of consecration. The removal of the term from the rubric, its avoidance in the later publications, and the minimalist interpretation given to consecration by Cranmer in his polemical works, all fit together. But what is the earlier sense and use of consecration that has been rejected? It can hardly be the later minimalist form: otherwise why should it be removed from the rubrics?

Thirdly, the Order speaks of the communicants receiving the body and blood of Christ 'in' the sacrament. The exhortation before the communion says that Christ 'hath left in these holy mysteries, as a pledge of his love, and a continual remembrance of the same, his own blessed body and precious blood for us spiritually to feed upon, to our endless comfort and consolation'. The Prayer of Humble Access speaks of eating the flesh and drinking the blood 'in these holy Mysteries'. And the final rubric speaks of the individual pieces of bread (which are directed to be broken at least into two pieces) that 'men must not think less to be received in part, than in the whole, but in each of them the whole body of our Saviour Jesu Christ'. The rubric is not found in the Prayer Book. The use of 'in' survives in the exhortation and the Prayer of Humble Access in the 1549 Prayer Book, but Gardiner's use of it to defend the Real Presence caused Cranmer to excise it carefully by the time of 1552.

Fourthly, the Proclamation which prefaces the Order speaks of the danger facing every communicant:

> lest they by unworthy receiving of so high mysteries become guilty of the Body and Blood of the Lord, and so eat and drink their own damnation: but rather diligently trying themselves, that they may so come to this holy Table of Christ, and so be partakers of this holy communion, that they may dwell in Christ, and have Christ dwelling in them.

This sentiment is even more explicit in the eucharistic prayer of 1549 in which it is prayed that 'whosoever shalbee partakers of thys holy Communion, maye worthely receive the most precious body and bloude of thy sonne Jesus Christe: and bee fulfilled with thy grace and heavenly benediccion, and made one bodye with thy sonne Jesu Christe, that he maye dwell in them, and they in hym'. Here the contrast is with the mature doctrine, that only the worthy communicant may receive the body of Christ at all, the unworthy recipient taking nothing more than the sacramental sign. (Thus the 1552 eucharist prays that the communicants 'maye be partakers of his most blessed body and bloud'.) To 'worthily receive' the body and blood of Christ is, in Cranmer's mature thought, tautological. In 1548 and 1549 the mutual indwelling of the believer and Christ is the result of worthy communion; in the mature Cranmer's thought (though the liturgy of 1552 remains ambiguous) it is the necessary prerequisite.

A final example should be included here which occurs in the 1549 Prayer Book, but again not consonant with Cranmer's mature theology, that the bread and wine of the eucharist and the water of the font can be blessed in one company and then used for communion and baptism in another. The Communion of the Sick in its opening rubrics allows for the priest to reserve 'so much of the sacrament of the body and bloud, as shall serve the sicke person, and so many as shall communicate with hym (if there be any). And so soone as he convenientely may, after the open communion ended in the church, shall goe and minister the same . . .'[43] The water of the font is directed to be changed at least monthly, and the water blessed before any child is baptized in it. This seems to have been a continuation of medieval custom. The blessing of the water is found at the end of the service of private baptism in the Prayer Book, and there is no rubric for its inclusion in the order of public baptism; quite possibly it was performed before the service, and in any large parish with several baptisms a month only a minority of services would have provided even an opportunity for the congregation to hear the form of blessing.

In summary, we have here a liturgy in which the bread and wine of the eucharist and the water of baptism are seen as being at least instruments of the grace signified. By the words of Christ the bread and wine of the eucharist are consecrated as his body and blood in such a way that the recipient receives the signified with the sign. The issue confronting the communicant is not whether they receive the reality signified, but whether that reception is worthy and productive of grace, or whether it brings condemnation. Furthermore there is an objective element to the notion of consecration. Whereas (as we shall see below) for the mature Cranmer 'consecration' as a sign makes no difference at all to the bread, wine or water which may be treated subsequently as ordinary domestic objects, even the limited reservation of the bread and wine and water in the 1549 book implies some special status to those objects, as does the use of the words of institution for supplementary consecration of the wine in 1548.

---

43 This is different from the perpetual reservation of the sacrament in church, which was never officially proscribed but was suppressed during the visitations of 1548: D. MacCulloch, *Tudor Church Militant: Edward VI and the Protestant Reformation* (London: Allen Lane, 1999), pp. 82, 86; Duffy, *Stripping of the Altars*, pp. 462–3. The 1549 Devon rebellion included a demand that 'We will have the sacrament hang over the high altar, and there to be worshipped, as it was wont to be', thereby signifying its former role and importance (Cranmer, PS, II, p.172).

All these features were suppressed by 1552 at the latest and were inconsistent with the general tenor of the 1549 Prayer Book. At the very least Cranmer imposed a strict consistency as he proceeded to the later publications. However, we must ask ourselves what led to these inconsistencies in the first place. When we look at Cranmer's private and public writing throughout this period we will see evidence of a movement from the theological position represented in the 1548 Order to that of the 1552 Prayer Book.

e. Consecration upheld: Questions put concerning some Abuses of the Mass

At the end of 1547, in his answers to 'Questions put concerning some Abuses of the Mass', Cranmer was still holding that it was 'convenient to use the vulgar tongue in the mass, except in certain secret mysteries, whereof I doubt'.[44] It is hard to imagine what may qualify as certain secret mysteries, if not the words of consecration. And that they could be said in Latin would strongly imply that the edification of the people was not the prime purpose in Cranmer's mind; rather some kind of objective consecration of the bread and wine. (Ridley had a similar answer to this question, affirming the general principle that the people should understand the service; 'nevertheless as concerneth that part which pertaineth to the consecration, Dyonise and Basil move me to think it no inconvenience that [that] part should be spoken in silence'.)[45]

f. The Real Presence qualified: Cranmer's Catechism

i. Cranmer and the *Catechism*

The *Nuremberg Catechism Sermons* of 1533, written by Osiander, were translated by Justus Jonas into Latin in 1539 with an eye to a wider readership. Osiander's sermons were based on Luther's *Small Catechism* of 1529. Cranmer's *Catechism* was based on Justus Jonas's translation of the sermons. Cranmer himself is said to have 'overseen and corrected' the *Catechism* according to the Preface. His actual role is uncertain, but it would seem that the above ascription is broadly correct, namely that Cranmer did not translate the work himself but took a role in revising the draft translation. In his own writings he acknowledges the work

---

44 PS, II, p. 151. Selwyn, 'Thomas Cranmer's Writings', p. 292, dates this document to 1547/8. MacCulloch, *Cranmer*, p. 379, n. 103, relates some draft questions to legislation of November–December 1547.

45 Ridley, *Works*, PS, p. 318.

as his own, as well as affirming the same at his examination by Dr Martin.[46]

The *Catechism* was written with children in mind. Selwyn says that 'with its affectionate tone and woodcut illustrations [it] was evidently intended for the younger age group and pitched at a level between the elementary ABC (a special edition of which had been printed for the Prince in 1543) and the school-room catechism such as that compiled by Ponet in 1552 . . .'. But its life was short, as it was overtaken by developments in the sacramental theology of the Reformers, and the theological position shown by the Forty-Two Articles and Ponet's *Catechism* is different at least in eucharistic doctrine.[47]

The theological stance of the *Catechism* is not to be taken as totally square with Cranmer's thought. As a translation which was then revised, it would not contain ideas totally contrary to his beliefs, but in small matters its thoughts, presentation and emphasis might not be corrected by the reviser. MacCulloch points out that Osiander's theology of justification, very different from Cranmer's, is preserved in the translation.[48] Selwyn cites the Lutheran numbering of the Ten Commandments, which was contrary to that in the Henrician formularies, but also says that 'many of the numerous changes and additions to the Latin reflect Cranmer's known interests and doctrinal tendencies at the time'.[49]

ii. The *Catechism* and baptism

The exposition of baptism begins with the theme of the second birth and entry into the kingdom of God (Jn 3.5). The institution of the sacrament is narrated (Mt. 28), and it is said that baptism is one of 'three sacraments or holy seals' instituted by Christ:

> The first of these sacramentes is baptisme, by the whiche we be borne again to a new and heavenly lyfe, and be receaved into Gods churche and congregation, whiche is the foundation and pyller of the trueth. The seconde is absolution or the authoritie of the kayes, whereby we be absolved from suche synnes, as we be fallen into after our baptisme. The thirde sacrament is the communion or

---

46 MacCulloch, *Cranmer*, pp. 387–91; *Cranmer's Catechism*, ed. D.G. Selwyn, Courtenay Library of Reformation Classics 6 (Appleford: Sutton Courtenay Press, 1978), Introduction, pp. 56–61.
47 Selwyn, *Catechism*, Introduction, pp. 17–19.
48 MacCulloch, *Cranmer*, pp. 388–90.
49 Selwyn, *Catechism*, Introduction, p. 60.

the Lordes Supper, by the whiche we be fedde and nourished, and
fortified in the faith of the ghospell and knowlege of Christ, that by
this fode we maye growe more and more in newnes of lyfe, so that
we maye be no longer children, but maye waxe perfecte men, and
ful growen in Christ.[50]

The description of penance as a sacrament equal to baptism and
eucharist is one which has not been found in Cranmer's writings since
the 1530s. Also the permanent efficacy of baptism has been glossed
over.[51] However, it is hard to see how any particular difference of
theology is being implied here, and it may well be simply a matter of
simplification.

Baptism is said to serve as an assurance that one is a Christian and
has put on Christ. It is also for the forgiveness of sins, to which all have
been subject since the time of Adam. The person being baptized asks
for forgiveness and promises to fight against sin. The speaker exhorts
his hearers 'seyng all you that be here are alredy baptysed', to continue
to be sorry and to pray to God for healing and deliverance, and to
beware of falling into sin. 'And yf you do thus, then your baptisme shal
be availeable unto you, and God shall worke in you by his holy Spirit,
and shall fynyshe in you all those thinges which by baptisme he hath
begon.' The hearers are told that baptism is not water alone, but the
work of God. 'For when we be baptized in the name of God, that is as
muche to saye, as God him selfe shoulde baptize us.'[52] Four benefits
are listed: the forgiveness of sins; the gift of the Holy Spirit; the gift of
the whole righteousness of Christ; and sharing in Christ's death. (But
the resurrection is not mentioned here.) In order to help the hearers
understand regeneration and how they are born again, the speaker
recounts their state before they were baptized. Their subjection to sin
is recounted, and it is affirmed that the children of Jews and Turks are
in the unhappy state of lacking the Holy Spirit and knowledge of God.
Furthermore the unbaptized sinner lacks the righteousness of Christ
which is strength in the fight against sin. 'And when they that beleve,
and be baptysed, do continewe in this their faith to the ende of their
lyves, then God shall rayse them up from death to lyfe, that they maye
be immortal and live everlastingly with Christ.'[53] How can water do

---

50 Selwyn, *Catechism*, p. 183.
51 For the English, 'The seconde [sacrament] is absolution or the authoritie of the kayes
wherby we be absolved from suche synnes, as we be fallen into after our baptisme', the
Latin original reads: 'Secundum est potestas clavium, per quam a peccatis, in quae prolapsi
sumus (durante semper efficatia baptismi) absolvimur' (*Catechism*, pp. 183, 248).
52 *Catechism*, pp. 185–6.
53 *Catechism*, p. 189.

this? Answer: it is not the water but the almighty word of God, and faith which receives God's word and promise. 'For with out the worde of God, water is water and not baptisme. But when the worde of the living God is added and joyned to the water, then it is the bath of regeneration, and baptisme water, and the lyvely springe of eternall saluation, and a bathe that wassheth our soules by the Holy Ghoste.'[54] Furthermore, baptism is a token that the old Adam ought to be drowned and killed by daily repentance, and that by the renewal of the Holy Spirit we ought to rise with Christ from the death of sin and walk in new life.

And so in this brief summary we see that the sacrament is concerned not only with initiation but also the whole of the Christian's life. Baptism in the *Catechism* is made to equal justification. Selwyn in his Introduction suggests that in fact, while baptism and justification are so closely related as to be practically interchangeable terms, there is no suggestion that baptism itself justifies. Faith is the necessary condition, it is the word of God which effects the grace, and baptism is a confirmatory sign. The word 'betokens' occurs a number of times in the sermon, and Selwyn suggests that when it does not occur the passages are 'instances of theological "shorthand" and are intended to be understood in the light of this "faith" precondition'.[55] Therefore baptism must always be understood as representing justification rather than as its equivalent.

Do any changes in the translation of the section on baptism show Cranmer's theology or interest? Selwyn gives a list of places in which the translators have departed from the original,[56] and many of the instances seem to be unexceptional. Passages of the Latin are omitted and sentences in English are added, largely to help the reader follow the argument. On pp. 188–9 the instrumentality of baptism is emphasized in the translation by several additions. These are qualified theologically by the faithful translation of the original text, 'Al these thinges doth baptisme worke in us, when we beleve in Christ.'[57] So no theological difference can be suggested. And in other places there is an emphasis on the role of the Holy Spirit. On pp. 183–4 the text is translated, 'A Christen man hathe the certen worde of God, where upon he maye grounde hys conscience, that he is made a Christen man, and is one

---

54   *Catechism*, p. 190.
55   *Catechism*, Introduction, pp. 48–50. The Homily of Salvation also speaks of our 'baptism or justification', Cranmer, PS, II, p. 133, and no doubt is also to be understood in the same way as in the *Catechism*. Null, *Repentance*, p. 228, follows Bromiley (*Cranmer, Theologian*, p. 65) in doubting whether Cranmer had thought out the connection between baptism and justification, but we shall see that it is reasonably clear how he would have envisaged the relationship between them.
56   Selwyn, *Catechism*, pp. 248–51.
57   *Catechism*, p. 189.

which he is of Christes members assured of by baptisme.' And soon
afterwards, the translator adds to the text, 'Wherefore the Holy Gost in
my baptisme assureth me, that I am a Christen man.' This addition hints
at a different sacramental theology, whereby one puts one's trust not
so much in the sacrament and word as in the hidden work of the Holy
Spirit.[58] The other interesting feature of the translator's work is that he
adds several references to our promise or God's promise. This is a theme
which is already prominent in the text, and the additions seem to be little
more than summaries of what has been said or is about to be said; but it
is notable that the translator regards the notion of the promises as a key
to the understanding of baptism and emphasizes them so.[59]

iii. The *Catechism* and the eucharist

Whereas Luther's theology of the eucharist emphasizes the forgiveness
of sins, the *Catechism* starts with the theme of the unity of the believer
with Christ and the eucharist as providing growth in that relationship.
By baptism we are grafted into Christ the true vine and source of life
and salvation. The sacrament of penance allows for restoration of those
alienated from the Christ and the Church through sin. 'But yf we wil
be iustified and saued, it is not ynoughe to be planted in Christ, but
we must also abide and continue in hym . . . Wherefore good children,
forasmuche as ye be alredye planted in Christ by baptisme, learne also
I praye you, howe ye maye contynually abyde and growe in Christ the
whiche thing is taught you, in the vse of the Lordes supper.'[60] The supper
narrative is recited and expounded in four themes: the desirability of
frequent communion; the reality of the presence of the body and blood of
Christ (we shall examine this in more detail below); the body given and
blood shed pointing to Christ's sacrifice – 'For althoughe we are bounde
to do these good workes, yet they be not a sufficient price, raunsome
or satisfaction for oure synnes, but onely the death and bloude of our
Savyoure Christ, was a sufficient and worthy sacrifice, to take away our
synnes, and to obteyne for us forgyvenes of oure offenses'; and finally
faithful obedience to Christ's command to 'do this' is enjoined, and
doubters and quibblers should be ignored.[61] Then the importance of self-
examination is affirmed (following 1 Cor. 11) so that the communicant

---

58   References to spiritual rebirth and to the work of the Holy Spirit are also added on
pp. 182 and 189.
59   Our promises to God in baptism, added on pp. 185, 186; God's promise to us in
baptism, added on p. 190.
60   *Catechism*, pp. 205–6.
61   *Catechism*, pp. 207–10.

may not be condemned but grow in Christ. The sermon finishes with the assertion of the priority of faith: the word of God is added to the outward signs and belief in God's word achieves forgiveness of sins. Indeed, while fasting and religious practice is beneficial, belief and unbelief are what determine worthy or unworthy reception of communion.[62]

iv. The *Catechism* and the presence of the body and blood of Christ

There are a number of statements throughout this section on the presence of Christ in the eucharist, and it is best to examine these together. Our understanding of the precise nuances of meaning can be helped not only by comparison with the Latin version of the *Catechism* but also from changes made in the various English editions, and it is these two sets of comparisons that we must now examine in detail. David Selwyn sets out the most outstanding features of the translation of Jonas's *Catechism* and the subsequent editions of the translation. First there is the famous change made in the translation given below:[63]

LATIN VERSION	ENGLISH VERSION
Deinde de pane dicit, Hoc est corpus meum, et de calice, Hic est sanguis meus. Ideo credere debemus, quod *vere corpus et sanguis eius sit*; nam Deus est omnipotens, ut in symbolo audistis; idea omnia potest facere, quae vult; et vocat ea quae non sunt, tamquam sint, sicut Paulus dicit; *hoc est, quando ipse aliquam rem vocat et nominat, quae ante non erat, tunc mox fit hoc ipsum, sicut Deus nominat.* Ergo quando accipit panem, et dicit, hoc est corpus meum, *tum mox ibi est corpus Domini*; et	Secondarily, Christ saieth of the breade, This is my bodye, and of the cuppe he sayeth, This is my bloud. Wherefore we ought to beleve, that *in the sacrament we receyve trewly the bodye and bloud of Christ.* For God is almyghtye (as ye hearde in the Crede). He is able therefore, to do all thynges what he wil. And as saint Paul writeth *he calleth those thinges whiche be not, as yf they were.* Wherefore when Christe taketh breade, and saieth, Take, eate, this is my body *we ought not to*

---

62 *Catechism*, p. 214.
63 *Catechism*, pp. 207–8. Selwyn, 'A Neglected Edition of Cranmer's Catechism', *JTS*, n.s. 15 (1964), pp. 76–90 (78). Selwyn (p. 91), dates the three editions to the summer and autumn of 1548.

quando calicem accipit, et dicit, hic est sanguis meus, *tunc mox adest sanguis eius.*	*doute, but we eat his veray bodye.* And when he taketh the cuppe, and sayeth, Take, drynke, this is my blod, *we ought to thynke assuredly, that we drynke his veray blode.*

So the *Catechism*'s theology of the eucharistic presence is at one with the liturgy of the Order of the Communion and the 1549 Prayer Book. We see here not only the avoidance of a direct identification of the body with the bread or the blood with the wine, but also the adoption of 'in' to express some connection between the sacrament and the signified. The invocation of the creative power of God's word shown in Genesis 1 is softened in the English. (It is interesting to note that the word *fit* – become – which will be avoided in the 1549 Prayer Book, is omitted here, though too much will happen between the two publications to presume a strong link.) Other translated passages introduce a certain ambiguity about the mode of the eucharistic presence: '*tunc certum est, quod adhuc Christus facit, ut sit ibi corpus et sanguis eius sic ut tunc in coena prima*' is translated as 'it is euident herby, that Christ causeth, even at thys tyme, his bodye and bloude to be in the sacrament, after that maner and fashion, as it was at that tyme, when he made his maundye with his disciples'. At another point the translator inserts a phrase not in the original Latin sentence: 'beleve the wordes of our Lord Jesus, that you eate and drynke his veray body and blode although mans reason can not comprehend' (then the English version adds) 'how and after what maner the same is ther present'.[64] This ambiguity is not far removed from the reverent fence-sitting ascribed to Elizabeth I:

'Twas God the word that spake it,
He took the Bread and brake it;
And what the word did make it;
That I believe and take it.

So in this translation of the *Catechism* we may be justified in seeing a different emphasis from that of the original: whereas the Latin affirms that the bread and wine are indeed the body and blood of Christ, the English version introduces a certain ambiguity about that identification while still wishing to see the sacraments as vehicles making Christ present to the communicant.

---

64 *Catechism*, pp. 208, 209.

However, as Selwyn demonstrates, in the third edition of the translation, published later in 1548, further changes are made in order to remove certain phrases which have now been deemed unacceptable.[65] One particular instance was commented on by Cranmer's opponents:

ALL THREE EDITIONS

For when ye do thus [i.e. worthily prepare yourselves], then ye worthely receave the body and bloud of Christ. And he that so receaveth it, receaveth everlastyng lyfe.

1ST AND 2ND EDITIONS	3RD EDITION
For he doth not *only* with his bodyly mouthe receave the bodye and bloude of Christ, but he doth *also* beleve	For he dothe not with hys bodyle mouthe receave the bodye and bloude of Christ, but he dothe beleve

ALL THREE EDITIONS

the wordes of Christ, wherby he is assured, that Christes bodye was gyven to death for us, and that his bloude was shed for us. And he that this beleveth, eateth and drynketh the bodye and bloude of Christ spiritually.

This instance is most probably the reason why Cranmer was accused of affirming the Real Presence of Christ in his first edition and then inserting a negative in the subsequent edition.[66] Of other examples, an English phrase we have met earlier inserted into the text, that 'mans reason can not comprehend "how and after what maner the same is ther present"', has the word 'ther' omitted in the third edition. 'Ther is the bodye and bloud of our Lorde, which we receaue in the Lordes supper', is changed to 'but in the Lordes supper we receyve the bodye and bloude of Christe'.[67]

Another instance raises a slightly different liturgical issue:

ALL THREE EDITIONS

And let not the foulyshe talke of unbelevers move you, who are wont to aske this question. Howe can the pryest or minister make the bodie and bloude of Christ? To the whiche I answer,

---

65 Selwyn, 'Neglected Edition', pp. 82–3.
66 'Neglected Edition', p. 77.
67 *Catechism*, pp. 208, 209.

1ST AND 2ND EDITIONS	3RD EDITION
that the minister doth not do this *of himself.*	that the minister doth not do this.

ALL THREE EDITIONS
But Christ himselfe doth gyve unto us his fleshe and blode, as his wordes dothe evydently declare.[68]

As Selwyn comments, the effect of this change is to direct attention away from the act of the priest to Christ. But there is probably more to be said here. The comparison between the priest and Christ was a commonplace in Lutheran liturgical commentaries, depending at least partly on patristic precedent, for example in John Chrysostom. The strength of this theme is in the identification of the two actions, one with the other. The action of the minister is that of Christ himself, and so with the eyes of faith we perceive the efficacious working of the grace of the sacrament even in the action of the sacrament itself. But in the wording of the third edition, it is as though the editor has applied the logic of the mature Cranmer, that the sign must not be identified with the signified, whether the sign be the objects of bread and wine or the minister or the action of the sacrament. Do we have here the logic for the removal from Cranmer's baptism service of the Lutheran use of the gospel of Jesus blessing the children (see below, Ch. 6)?

If these documents published in 1548 suggest an 'intermediate' theology, how might we understand it? Cranmer clearly denied transubstantiation. (The word had long disappeared from English formularies, but now the concept, still expressed in the King's Book, that the bread and wine are no longer present in the consecrated sacrament has vanished as well.) The mention of the spiritual feeding on the body and blood of Christ, to which MacCulloch points, suggests that we are not dealing with a Lutheran Real Presence theology either. However, the use of 'in', the description in the earlier editions of the *Catechism* of receiving Christ with the mouth as well as with faith, and the idea of consecration (to be performed in Latin rather than in English if we are to believe the Cranmer of late 1547) which later has to be discontinued, all suggest an intimate relation of the sacramental signs with the grace of the sacrament. The notion of the Real Presence has been qualified, but Cranmer is at this stage loath to abandon it altogether. (Only with the third edition of the *Catechism* and then the House of Lords' Debate do we see the cutting of the Gordian knot and the Archbishop's move to a denial of the Real Presence.)

---

68 *Catechism*, p. 210; Selwyn, 'Neglected Edition', p. 84.

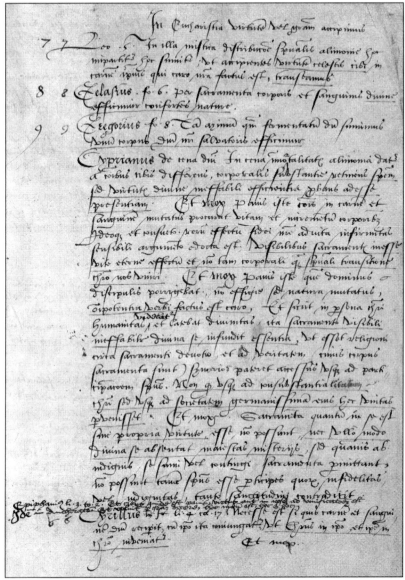

Page 187 from *De re sacramentaria* (CCCC MS 102, reproduced by kind permission of the Master and Fellows of Corpus Christi College, Cambridge). The first three entries refer to folio numbers in an earlier collection of commonplaces. Towards the bottom of the page a passage has been inserted in Cranmer's own hand. The left hand margin carries numbers to put the passages in order: elsewhere the ordering in the ms is the same as in Cranmer's published *Defence*, but this set of passages is not found there. However for the possible influence of these passages on the 1549 eucharistic prayer see pp. 129–30.

g. The presence denied: De re sacramentaria

Why this difficult progress in thought? And need we take the most cynical view of the fact that Cranmer moved to the denial of the Real Presence only when it was politically safe to do so? It is possible that Cranmer found himself driven to his mature position only when he set out his teaching in detail and discovered that the only tenable position was at the extreme wing of the Reformed camp. Might we imagine that Cranmer had hoped to hold to an understanding of the Real Presence, and/or that he had theological sympathy with Bucer, but as his studies continued he could find no moderate position between Rome and Basle? If such a hypothesis is likely, then we might expect to find evidence of it in *De re sacramentaria.*

De re sacramentaria (hereafter *DRS*) is a collection of patristic common-places on the presence of the body and blood of Christ in the eucharist which was used as the basis of Cranmer's appeal to the Fathers in the *Defence.* A full discussion is beyond the bounds of this present work, but it can be briefly described. *DRS* is known to us in two copies, both in Corpus Christi College, Cambridge (MSS 102, pp. 151–93 and 113, pp. 345–91. The latter is a fair copy with some additional passages; the former has a very large number of passages added or noted in Cranmer's own hand and is the version normally referred to. It has often been supposed that the many annotations suggest that he collected them over a period of years from his extensive reading and used them to develop his mature thought. However, K.J. Walsh, who has made the most recent detailed study of the collection, has concluded that in all likelihood the collection was edited in a comparatively brief time with an eye to writing the *Defence,* and that many of the passages were taken not from direct reading of the Fathers but from earlier commonplace collections.[69]

---

69   K.J. Walsh, 'Cranmer and the Fathers', pp. 239–41. A number of passages, at the beginning of several sections (pp. 153, 171, 187, 191) are not written out in full but refer to another commonplace collection by folio number: Walsh says that he was unable to identify it. However, from these references we can construct an order in the earlier collection (popes, councils, other writers; all in date order), and it can be compared with another set of commonplaces in the same library, indeed now bound together with *DRS,* the *Sententiae de Eucharistia* (CCCC, MS 102, pp. 213–45). Examination of the collection *Sententiae de Eucharistia* reveals a great number of parallels not only with *DRS* but also with Cranmer's earlier commonplace collections on the eucharist in the Royal MS 7 B XI. The 'fit' is not exact. Probably the MS 102 version of the *Sententiae de Eucharistia* is not the one used as the basis of *DRS* but there were several different copies just as we now have two different copies of *DRS.* Extra passages were added (and omitted) at each stage, but one interesting example is the quotation from the Council of Nicaea. It was noted by Cranmer in his copy of Oecolampadius's *Dialogus* still extant in the Cambridge University Library. But the reference to it in *DRS* is to a folio number in the prior commonplace collection, and it is to be found in *Sententiae de Eucharistia.*

The selection and arrangement of the patristic quotations in *DRS* are not of themselves strong evidence for a particular theological position, but taken together with the witness of Cranmer's *Catechism* and other documents they do give an incomplete but coherent picture of an 'intermediate' theology of the presence of Christ in the eucharist. Before we consider the quotations themselves, two series of comments at the end in the Archbishop's own hand are of interest. Each set occupies the top of an otherwise blank page. They face each other as though they belong as a pair, but in their theology they are rather different.

Those on the right hand page, 193, express the views that we naturally associate with the writer of the *Defence*.

The foremost points in which we differ from the papists
They declare that Christ is in the bread; we that he is in the person who eats the bread
They that Christ is in the mouth of the one who eats; we that he is in the whole person
They say that the body of Christ flies away when the bread is eaten or consumed; we say that he remains in the person for as long as they are a member of Christ.
They declare that it remains in the bread for a whole year or longer if the bread lasts; we declare that it inhabits the person for as long as they are a member of Christ.
According to their opinion, as far as the real presence is concerned, a human being eats no more than a beast, nor is it any more advantage to a human than to any living being.[70]

Here we have very clearly the Cranmerian line that the wondrous working of God is not in the bread or wine but in the believer. It is no surprise to find this list, enlarged but not changed in its theological bent, repeated in the beginning of the chapter on the Presence of Christ in the *Defence*.[71] The left-hand page of *De re sacramentaria*, (192), is directed against transubstantiation, but from a different perspective:

---

70   Praecipua capita in quibus a papisticis dissentimus.
      Christum papistae statuunt in pane, nos in homine comedente.
      Illi in comedentis ore, nos in toto homine.
      Illi corpus Christi aiunt evolare, masticato vel consumpto pane; nos manere in homine dicimus, quamdiu membrum est Christi.
      Illi in pane statuunt per annum integrum, et diutius, si duret panis; nos in homine statuimus inhabitare, quamdiu templum Dei fuerit.
      Illorum sententia, quod ad realem praesentiam attinet, non amplius edit homo quam bellua, neque magis ei prodest, quam cuivis animanti.

71   *Defence*, 3.2; PS, I, pp. 52–89.

The stupid papists, or Capernaites, affirm many things which
neither Scripture nor any of the Fathers ever said, viz.

That the accidents remain without the substance.

That the accidents of bread and wine, and not the bread and wine,
are the sacraments.

That the sign is not the bread but the accidents of the bread.

That Christ did not call the bread his body.

That when Christ said, 'This is my body', the demonstrative 'This'
refers not to the bread but to the body of Christ.

That we receive as many bodies of Christ, or the body of Christ as
many times, as we receive the bread or as the number of pieces in
which we break it with our teeth.[72]

The last proposition seems to be connected with the rubric we have
seen in the 1548 *Order of the Communion*, that when the consecrated
bread is broken, 'men must not think less to be received in part than
in the whole, but in each of them the whole body of our Saviour Jesu
Christ'.[73] So to some extent popular views are being pilloried, but
other items attacked in the list represent the landmarks of the doctrine
of transubstantiation, as proposed and defended by sophisticated
theologians. This list, then, sets out to attack transubstantiation as being
contrary to Scripture and the Fathers.

How does this list relate to that on p. 193? There again the papists
are the opponents, and their views are contrasted with Cranmer's own.
But there the Real Presence is the issue. What is curious is not only the
difference of subject, but also the fact that the papists are said to affirm

---

72   Multa affirmunt crassi papistae, seu Capernaitae, quae neque Scriptura neque ullus
veterum unquam dixerat.
Viz.
Quod accidentia maneant sine subjecto.
Quod accidentia panis et vini sunt sacramenta, non panis et vinum.
Quod panis non est figura, sed accidentia panis.
Quod Christus non appellavit panem corpus suum
Quod cum Christus dixit, 'Hoc est corpus meum,' pronomen 'Hoc' non refertur ad
panem, sed ad corpus Christi.
Quod tot corpora Christi accipimus, aut toties corpus eius accipimus, quoties, aut in
quot partes, dentibus secamus panem.

73   Gardiner makes a similar attack on popular views of the presence:

The breakynge of the most blessed sacrament by the ministre in the masse doth
no violacion to Christes most precious body there present, ne breaketh the most
precyouse body, whiche is impassible, but only the fourme of bread, under whiche
it is conteyned, and that the same most precyouse bodye is afte hooly in eche of the
partes of the host broken, without any encrease in number: as though there were then
many Christes present, but alwayes one Christ, and the same Christ. (*A detection of
the devil's sophistrie* [London: John Herforde, 1546], fols 17–17ᵛ).

that Christ is present 'in the bread', which strictly speaking (as observed on the previous page) is not so; only the accidents remain without the substance.[74] Now is this careless summarizing by Cranmer, or are we to suppose that the two lists were in fact drawn up at different times, and represent two stages in Cranmer's thought: p. 192 when he wished only to attack transubstantiation and was happy to affirm some kind of Real Presence, somehow spiritualized, and p. 193 when he found himself rejecting the idea of the Real Presence altogether? It is to be noted that Cranmer did not import the list on p. 192 wholesale into his *Defence*, nor could he, without considerable redrafting.[75] And so it may be the case that Cranmer's work in writing the *Defence* proved more difficult than he had supposed, and led him to further changes in his theology.

The headings under which Cranmer arranged his quotations cannot be taken as all supporting his own beliefs: for example, there are quotations which both support and oppose the doctrine of transubstantiation. We cannot take for granted that Cranmer agreed or disagreed with the thesis that 'The body of Christ is taken in the mouth.' By the time that he wrote the *Defence* we know that he disagreed with this notion. But what did he think at the time of compiling *DRS*?

It has been known for many years that some selections of the Fathers in *DRS* are to be found in the *Defence* as though they were copied straight out of the commonplace. Some passages are even numbered with this copying in mind.[76] This is particularly the case in the sections headed:

Christ gave bread to his disciples
The bread is called the body of Christ, and the wine his blood
'This (i.e. the bread) is my body', and 'the cup is my blood' are
    figurative sayings
What this figure signifies, to eat the flesh and drink the blood of
    Christ

---

74   This point is acknowledged in the Latin translation of the *Defence* which adds to the comparison: 'Illi enim docent, Christum in pane et vino (id est, sub speciebus panis et vini)', PS, I, Appendix, p. 45.

75   K.J. Walsh, 'Cranmer and the Fathers', p. 240, seems to have identified this problem, and comes to his own conclusion, when he says of the two lists,

It ought to be noted that neither of the summaries bears directly on the 'new found doctrine' of the sacrament which the collection is supposed to have tested. The crasser views outlined in these summaries would have been rejected by Cranmer well before 1548. They are, however, points which Cranmer pressed hard in the *Defence*, and it is reasonable to think they were drafted by the archbishop with the treatise in mind.

76   See Walsh, 'Cranmer and the Fathers', pp. 239–40; Brooks, *Cranmer's Doctrine of the Eucharist*, pp. 41–2; D. Selwyn, *The Library of Thomas Cranmer* (Oxford: Oxford Bibliographical Society, 1996), p. 198.

The wicked do not eat the flesh and drink the blood of Christ
Christ according to human nature is in heaven
Against transubstantiation
For transubstantiation[77]

Among these sections three in particular seem to gain importance in the editorial process as passages are transferred to them either by annotations to the manuscript or in their equivalent sections in the published *Defence*: '"This (i.e. the bread) is my body", and "the cup is my blood" are figurative sayings' takes a few passages from 'Christ gave bread to his disciples' and 'The bread is called the body of Christ, and the wine his blood' (disrupting the numbering system in those sections) and also many of the passages from 'The bread and the wine manifest the body and blood of Christ' and 'In the eucharist we receive virtue or grace.' The sections 'The wicked do not eat the flesh and drink the blood of Christ' and 'Against transubstantiation' also collect a number of additional passages from other sections. Evidently Cranmer was selecting these three themes as a kind of hermeneutical key to the vast collection of passages.

However, other sections of *DRS* are not represented in the *Defence* in this way. 'The fathers of the Old Testament ate and drank Christ in the same way as we do' has only a few passages which are incorporated in the published work. Other sections simply do not appear:

Just as Christ is present in the eucharist so he is present in baptism
The bread and the wine manifest the body and blood of Christ
In the eucharist we receive virtue or grace
The body of Christ is taken in the mouth[78]

---

77 Panem dedit Christus discipulis
   Panis vocatur corpus Christi, et vinum sanguis
   Hoc scilicet panis est corpus meum, et calix est sanguis meus, figurative sunt locutiones
   Quod significat haec figura, edere carnem et bibere sanguinem Christi
   Mali non edunt nec bibunt corpus et sanguinem domini
   Christus secundum humanam naturam in coelo est
   Contra transubstantiationem
   Pro transubstantiatione

78 Patres veteris testamenti edebant et bibebant Christum sicut et nos
   Sicut in Eucharistia presens est Christus ita et in baptismo est presens
   Panis representat corpus Christi et vinum sanguinem
   In Eucharistia virtutem vel gratiam accipimus
   Corpus Christi ore sumitur

I have translated 'representat' as 'manifests' rather than 'represents' because it must be different from the 'figurative sayings' of the other section. The word covers this range of meaning.

The quotations in these sections are either omitted altogether or they have been transferred to some other section of the commonplace, where they may or may not have been used in the published work. Thus, for example, all the passages under 'The bread and the wine manifest the body and blood of Christ' (p. 185) have been transferred (using cross-references) to the section: '"This (i.e. the bread) is my body", and "the cup is my blood" are figurative sayings' (pp. 157–9). Many of them are then found together in 3.11 of the *Defence*. On the other hand the greater part of the passages in the section 'Just as Christ is present in the eucharist so he is present in baptism', seem to have been omitted. It is hardly coincidental that these sections contain the most positive assertions about the eucharistic presence of Christ. Eventually they will be sifted through the filter of Cranmer's mature theology, but here they are still prominent in the collection.

The mere fact that passages have been moved from one section to another might of itself simply reveal a multi-stage editorial process rather than a radical change of direction. However, there is some evidence that in the process of ordering these passages Cranmer did change his mind.

First there is internal evidence that he had advanced one position considerably before abandoning it. In a number of sections the passages are ordered, by number or letter, as if for copying out. To some extent the order of passages in 2.8 of the *Defence* follows this order in *DRS* pp. 153–6 (though as mentioned above a few passages have been transferred elsewhere, and also some of the numbered passages are omitted from the *Defence*). We find this kind of ordering not only in this section which found its way into the *Defence*, but also in a section which was passed over, namely 'In the eucharist we receive virtue or grace.'

Besides this internal evidence, if we were to take seriously some of these sections as revealing Cranmer's thought when he was composing material in the 1549 Prayer Book, we find some interesting connections.

'Just as Christ is present in the eucharist so he is present in baptism' is a parallel used by the Cranmer of the *Defence* negatively: again and again he stresses the commonality of the sacraments and affirms that there is no reason to imply Christ's presence in the eucharist any more than traditionally has been claimed for baptism. But as we have seen, the 1549 Prayer Book carries an implication of a more positive reading of this parallel: unusually for an evangelical reformer Cranmer includes a blessing of the font, to be carried out at least once a month and the water kept in the font for subsequent baptisms, the language of which is parallel to that used for the bread and wine in the eucharistic prayer.

The section 'In the eucharist we receive virtue or grace' is comparatively lengthy (pp. 187–9) and covers a large number of passages about the spiritual fruit of communion, the receiving of grace and the unity of the communicant with Christ. The theme of the mutual indwelling of the believer and Christ again pervades the thought of the mature Cranmer in his *Defence*: there it is a prerequisite to spiritual communion, and without it sacramental communion, the reception of the bread and wine, is useless or worse. But in *DRS* the passages imply that the indwelling is the fruit of communion. And this is what we see in parts of the eucharistic prayer of the 1549 Prayer Book which are excised in 1552.

De Re Sacramentaria In eucharistia virtutem vel gratiam accipimus	*1549*	*1552*
	And here wee offre and present unto thee (O Lorde) oure selfe, oure soules, and bodies, to be a reasonable, holy, and lively sacrifice unto thee: humbly besechyng thee, that whosoever shalbee partakers of thys holy Communion,	And here we offre and presente unto thee, O lord, our selfes, our soules, and bodies, to be a reasonable holy, and lively Sacrifice unto thee: humbly beseching thee that al we which be partakers of this holy Communion, maye
Gregorius fo. 8. Tam azimum quam fermentatum dum sumimus **unum corpus domini nostri salvatoris efficimur**	**maye worthely receive the most precious body and bloude of thy sonne Jesus Christe: and**	
Cyrillus in Jo. li. 4 ca.17. Necesse est **si quis carnem et sanguinem domini recipit,** cum ipso ita coniungatur, **ut Christus in ipso, et ipse in christo inveniatur** Et mox Sicut parum fermenti totam massam fermentat; sic parvula benedictio totum hominem in seipsum attrahit, et **sua gratia, replet, et hoc modo Christus in nobis manet et nos in Christo**	bee fulfilled with thy grace and heavenly benediccion, and made one bodye with thy sonne Jesu Christe, that he maye dwell in them, and they in hym.	bee fulfylled with thy grace and heavenly benediccion.
	And although we be unworthy (through our manyfolde synnes) to offre unto thee any Sacryfice: . . .	And although we bee unworthy throughe oure manifolde sinnes to offre unto thee any Sacrifice: . . .

We can conclude that the manuscript would strongly suggest a shift in Cranmer's thought. When he compiled the quotations of the Fathers under these different headings he had firmly rejected transubstantiation and sought to affirm that the substances of bread and wine were present in the sacrament. However, he was open to the idea that the sacrament makes present in some way the body and blood of Christ to the communicant. He was sufficiently content with this view to have numbered up some of the sections for use in a published treatise on the eucharist, and also to have carried the themes into his drafts of the eucharistic prayer. However, he then changed his mind. For some reason or other the draft eucharistic prayer was not changed at this point, but the passages from the Fathers were rearranged to support the new theological position.

h. A radical liturgy? A letter from Martin Bucer to Richard Bonner

The main evidence for the shift in Cranmer's thought has been largely outlined above in the history of the various documents. The timing is tied up with them as well. Cranmer espoused a theology different from his mature view in his answer to the 'Questions put concerning some Abuses of the Mass' at the end of 1547, and this view is also seen in *The Order of the Communion* published in March 1548, and again in the first and second editions of the *Catechism* published in the summer of that year.

The successive editions of the *Catechism* suggest theological movement over the summer of 1548. On 4 September Bucer wrote a letter to Richard Bonner in reply to a question about the use of the words of institution in the eucharist.[79] As we have seen, the identity of Bonner is something of a mystery, but his publication of *A Treatyse of the ryght honourynge and wourshyppyng of our Saviour Jesus Christe in the sacrament* in November 1547, using the same printer as that for Cranmer's *Catechism*, and drawing freely on Bucer's *Constans Defensio*, shows that we have here, in modern parlance, a 'source close to Lambeth Palace'.[80] We do not have the original letter from Bonner to which Bucer is replying, but we can reconstruct the gist of it from the way in which it is discussed. On p. 316 Bucer appeals to the precedent, universal in history, of using the words of institution in the eucharist, even though there is no dominically determined form, either of a recitation of these words or of an explanation. The popish practice of addressing the words of institution to the bread and wine rather than to the people is an abuse which can be removed by addressing the people aloud in the vernacular (p. 317). Bucer refers to Bonner having raised the possibility of an explanation or exposition of the words (p. 318), but even this is

---

79 CCCC, MS 113, pp. 315–24. No complete transcript of this letter has yet been made. I am grateful to Professor Diarmaid MacCulloch for sharing with me a rough transcript he made, and hope to publish a more complete version soon.

80 MacCulloch, *Cranmer*, pp. 399–403.

liable to misinterpretation, and abuse should not deprive the faithful of hearing the words, even for a short time (p. 319). After a long discussion of the eucharist, he concludes that the recitation of the Lord's words is altogether necessary (p. 321). We have no justification for change: the revocation of sabbath observance despite the fourth commandment is justified by our Lord's statements about the sabbath (p. 322). And the claims of the 'sophists of Cologne' that the sacrament is consecrated not by the Lord's words but by the canon, a human invention, must be resisted (p. 323).

The whole letter lives up to Bucer's reputation for verbosity, and suggests very strongly that Bonner is proposing an exposition or explanation rather than a recitation of the dominical words. The reason for this unprecedented suggestion is that it is felt the words have been abused by the papists; Bucer repeatedly asserts that abuse does not disqualify right use. Bonner's proposal is certainly radical. Could it be that Cranmer has now abandoned his earlier theological position in which he tried to hold together different theologies of the presence of Christ, and is prepared to sweep away all mediating positions, even to the point of omitting the words of institution from the eucharist? If so, it would be no wonder if these ideas were being sounded out through the disownable person of Richard Bonner. Bucer, however, affirms that the words are appropriate when addressed to the people, clearly and in the vernacular (how different from the Cranmer of 1547 and his mysteries!). 'Consecration' is not a term he seems to use, except in the context of the *novum dogma* of the sophists of Cologne.

Bucer's letter to Bonner marks, in the most dramatic way, the end of a search for some middle way or new language of the sacraments. The words of institution are now directed towards the people, not to the bread and wine. The idea of consecration as seen earlier has been abandoned. The exact dates of the third edition of the *Catechism* and of Bonner's letter to Bucer are unfortunately unknown to us, but these two pieces of evidence coincide in pointing to a decisive shift in Cranmer's thought during the summer of 1548.

i. The Chertsey conference

The authorization of the 1549 Book of Common Prayer was accompanied by a debate in the House of Lords on 15–18 December 1548 on eucharistic theology. Prior to this there had been a conference at Chertsey Abbey in September. Cranmer himself describes the Chertsey (or Windsor, as he calls it) conference in a letter to Queen Mary in September 1555 attacking papal authority and the use of Latin in the liturgy. He says that the conference was unanimously agreed in adopting the vernacular.[81] The House of Lords' debate refers to other points which the Bishop of Chichester had not agreed to: the omission of oil from confirmation, and the wording of the Canon; and these may well have formed part of a document which was referred to as 'the boke of theyre agreements'.[82] Also with regard to eucharistic theology the bishops involved in the conference came to the House of Lords' debate with no unanimity.

The debate referred also to a 'book of doctrine', the identity of which has been much debated. David Selwyn has identified it not with the new Prayer Book under debate but with a vernacular tract on the Real Presence of Christ in the eucharist (the issue specifically being debated in the House of Lords), two different versions of which survive.[83] There are many differences between the two copies, most prominent of which is that the Corpus Christi manuscript does not include the final paragraphs of the Bodley manuscript which discuss, among other things, the adoration of Christ in the sacrament and the eucharistic oblation. It has therefore been suggested by Selwyn that this may be the 'book of doctrine' referred to in the House of Lords' debate of December 1548, given that there were complaints about the omission of the adoration and that, 'there was in the book: Oblation, whiche is left oute nowe'.[84] Selwyn identifies the tract as belonging more to the period 1547/8 when there was still hope of consensus around some statement about the Real Presence of the body and blood of Christ in the sacrament (and as such it will be discussed further below). He suggests that it was used in the House of Lords' debate, but to no avail, because everyone's goalposts had moved: Cranmer and his close associates had moved to a rejection of the Real Presence and the *manducatio impiorum*, and the conservative bishops had fallen back on the traditional theology of transubstantiation.[85]

However, I think it unlikely that either of the surviving versions of the Vernacular Real Presence Tract are the 'book of doctrine' referred to in the debate. Both, whatever their differences, affirm the presence

---

81   PS, II, p. 450.
82   MS Royal 17B XXXIX, fols 2ᵛ–3ᵛ; C.O. Buchanan (ed.), *Background Documents to Liturgical Revision 1547–1549*, Grove Liturgical Study 35 (Bramcote: Grove Books, 1983), p. 18.
83   'The Book of Doctrine, the Lords' debate and the first Prayer Book of Edward VI: An abortive attempt at doctrinal consensus?', *JTS*, n.s. 40 (1989), pp. 446–80.
84   Buchanan, *Background Documents*, pp. 15, 18.
85   Selwyn, 'The Book of Doctrine'. Redworth, *In Defence of the Church Catholic*, pp. 265–7 and n. 58, outlines the effort taken by Gardiner to find conciliatory ways of speaking about the presence of Christ in the eucharist, and concludes that his 'genuine hopes of building upon a eucharistic consensus were outflanked not by his traditionalism but by the subsequent radicalisation of Cranmer's own eucharistic thought'.

of the body and blood of Christ 'in the sacrament'. What is excluded is the standpoint adopted by Cranmer in December 1548, that the body of Christ is not to be found in the sacrament but is eaten spiritually only by the faithful recipient:

> Wher fore noe faithfull Christian man maye thincke that there is in this sacrament none other thing then the onlie presence and substaunce of the outward signes or tokens of breade and wine and wherbie Christ is to us figured or represented or that there is nothing ells besydes and said outward signes but onlie a spiritual virtue, operation, effect or grace. Whereof onlye the wourthie receavers be partakers But men must constantlie beleve that also there is the trew presence of Christes bodie and bludd in verytie of substance.[86]

If this tract had come before the House of Lords as an agreed document in the form of the Corpus Christi manuscript, the traditionalist bishops may well have complained about sections on adoration and oblation being removed, but would surely have used the tract to condemn Cranmer's eucharistic theology as deviant from the consensus that Protector Somerset had requested.[87]

---

86   CCCC, MS 102, Brooks (ed.), *Cranmer's Doctrine of the Eucharist*, pp. 166–7. The Bodley parallel differs in wording but not in substance.

87   Reading again the text of the House of Lords' debate, I am inclined to believe that the 'book of doctrine' is the same as, or at least part of, the book of the bishops' agreements, i.e. a summary of the conclusions from the Chertsey conference covering doctrinal and liturgical principles. Through the relevant section of the debate the emphasis is consistently on 'agreement' of 'doctrine': Thirlby protested: 'the boke whiche was redde touching the doctrine of the Supper was not agreed on among the Busshoppes'. After an adjournment 'the boke of theyre agreements was redde' and the Bishop of Chichester's objections noted. Thirlby gave a justification of his subscription to the book, citing his reservations over the questions of the elevation and the adoration, and then complaining that 'there was in the book: Oblation, whiche is left oute nowe. Things in disputacion are not agreid upon tyll we allowe that whiche is spoken of.' To this Secretary Smith replied, saying, 'Towching this booke of the doctrine all they are agreed so farr as is of me red.' I infer from this that Smith did exactly what he said: he read out those items which were agreed on by the whole or at least the great majority – but he omitted those which had caused greatest division, and these would have included the eucharistic oblation. (It is unclear whether they were omitted from the document itself or just from the reading.) Whether or not a doctrinal section on the adoration was omitted from the reading, Tunstall's attack on the omission of the adoration at the beginning of the debate is different: 'the adoracion is left out of the booke bycause ther is nothing in the sacrament but breade and wyne'. This is a comment on the Prayer Book's theology, not on an omission from the reading of the 'book of doctrine'. Buchanan, *Background Documents*, pp. 17–18, 15. Tomlinson, *Parliamentary Debate*, p. 5, notes a previous occasion on which Cranmer himself had collected bishops' agreements and disagreements under the heading of a 'book of doctrine'.

j. The House of Lords' debate

On 28 September 1548 Bartholemew Traheron, a man with strong links with Zurich and previously a critic of the Archbishop, informed Bullinger that 'Latimer has come over to our opinion respecting the true doctrine of the eucharist, together with the Archbishop of Canterbury and the other bishops, who heretofore seemed to be Lutherans.'[88] McCulloch supposes this to have been a response to the revised edition of the *Catechism*; Tomlinson thinks that news of the Chertsey conference had leaked out.[89] Whatever the source of Traheron's glee, it was becoming clear that Cranmer's views had shifted and consensus had failed. The denouement was staged in the most public arena of the House of Lords.

Cranmer's first major speech as recorded in the notes of the debate effectively summarizes his new theology:

> By scripture our Saviour Christ is our hed, and we his bodie. The worde is in oure hearing, in our eyes the sacrament. '*Qui manducat carnem meam etc.*'
>
> They be twoo things to eate the sacrament and to eate the bodie of Christ.
>
> The eating of the bodye is to dwell in Christe, and this may be thoo a man never tast the Sacrament.
>
> All men eate not the body in the sacrament. '*Hoc est corpus meum*': he that maketh a will beaquiethes certayne Legacies, and this is our Legacy. Remission of synnes, which those onelie receave that ar membres of his body.
>
> And the sacrament is the remembraunce of this deathe which made the wyll good.
>
> '*Indigni judicium sibi manducant.*'
>
> They eate not the bodye of Christe but eate theyr condempnacion for he hath nothing to do with theym that ar not parcells of his bodye.
>
> They ar not fedd of him bicause they dwell not in him . . .
>
> Our faithe is not to beleave him to be in Bread and wyne, but that he is in heaven. This is proved by scripture and Doctors, tyll the Bushshoppes of Romes powre came in. Than no man drinketh Christe or eateth hym, except he dwell in Christe and Christe in him.[90]

This position makes a clear break with Cranmer's previous thought, and will be discussed in greater length below.

---

88 *Original Letters*, PS, p. 322.
89 MacCulloch, *Cranmer*, p. 392; Tomlinson, *Great Parliamentary Debate*, p. 9.
90 Buchanan, *Background Documents*, pp. 16–17.

Chapter 4

CRANMER'S MATURE THEOLOGY
OF THE SACRAMENTS

1 THE 42 ARTICLES AND THE *REFORMATIO LEGUM*

We must now turn to Cranmer's mature theology of the sacraments. For the most part we are gleaning information from his *Defence* and *Answer*, controversial works taken up with the theology of the eucharist. But among the wearisome bulk of polemic, there is sufficient material for us to build up a reasonably coherent picture of Cranmer's theology and even to guess at the advantages he may have seen in his own thought where it differs from contemporary reformers. At some points comparisons will be made with contemporary theologians in order to bring out the distinctiveness of Cranmer's thought.[1]

In brief, it will be seen that Cranmer had his own distinctive theology of the sacraments, based on scripture and his reading of Saint Augustine, and one which evolved out of the disputes of the 1540s over justification outlined above. His basic understanding was of the sacrament as a sign (rather than a seal). Sacraments are differentiated from other signs by God's promise of grace and his command to celebrate the sacraments. Cranmer wished to believe in the instrumentality of the sacraments, but his model was a weak one in which the link between the sacrament and the grace it signifies is effected by faith and prayer, appropriating God's promise. Baptism speaks of the work of redemption throughout the candidate's life, not simply at the moment of administration of the sacrament. Therefore it is legitimate to speak (figuratively) of God's work of redemption and the individual's response of faith without entangling himself in the problems, for example, of the relation of the sacraments to election or to the personal faith of infants.

In concentrating on Cranmer's own writings, we have to step back from other documents in which Cranmer had a share, but not sole

---

1   Lack of space prevents me attempting a fuller comparison between Cranmer and his contemporaries. For more details, see my doctoral thesis 'Signs of God's Promise: Thomas Cranmer's Sacramental Theology and Baptismal Liturgy', University of Wales, Lampeter, 1998, pp. 136–93.

authorship. In particular the 42 Articles and the draft forms of the proposed canon law reform, the *Reformatio Legum*, contain sections on the sacraments which are difficult to assess historically and theologically. MacCulloch very ably exposes the many hands at work in them,[2] and we would do well in all these cases to trust the writings of individuals rather than these composite documents. But before we proceed to examine Cranmer's own works, a very brief survey of the official documents would be pertinent.

Article 26 of the 42 Articles discusses the sacraments, limiting them naturally to baptism and the Lord's Supper. 'Right use' of them is commended; *ex opere operato* efficacy is denied, and it is stated that unworthy reception communicates damnation. It is further stated that sacraments are not just badges or tokens, but rather 'sure witnesses and effectual signs of grace, and God's good will toward us, by the which he doth work invisibly in us; and doth not only quicken, but also strengthen, and confirm our faith in him'. Article 28 discusses baptism, and says that is is 'a sign and seal of our new birth, whereby, as by an instrument, they that receive baptism rightly are grafted into the church: the promises of forgiveness of sin, and our adoption to be the sons of God, are visibly signed and sealed'. In Article 29 the Lord's Supper is described in more guarded language as not only a sign of love but a 'sacrament of our redemption'. Those who receive the sacrament by faith share in the communion of the body and blood of Christ. Transubstantiation is condemned, and also the idea of the 'real and bodily presence . . . of Christ's flesh and blood in the sacrament', since the body of Christ is in heaven.[3] So the three articles each have their own language about the sacraments: in the eucharist it is most guarded and badly defined (as one might expect of the more controversial element); with regard to the sacraments in general, we are told that they are effectual signs by which God works his grace in us, and in the case of baptism the sacrament is a sign and seal of grace. We must examine shortly which of these is Cranmer's own preferred language.

In the *Reformatio Legum* the sacraments are discussed twice. First they are mentioned in a series of condemnations of heretical opinion. There it is denied that the sacraments are bare signs, and affirmed that faith is strengthened and the promise of God is 'symbolized . . . as though by a certain seal' (*quasi sigillo quodam consignatur*). 'As though by a certain seal' is an addition in the manuscript by Cranmer, but it seems difficult to discern what he was seeking to express by it (presuming it was his own opinion anyway rather than a committee decision which

---

2   MacCulloch, *Cranmer*, pp. 500–4.
3   42 Articles, PS, *Liturgies of King Edward VI*, pp. 532–4.

he was inserting). Also inserted in his hand is a statement that 'the Holy Spirit and grace is more abundantly instilled in the minds of the faithful' (*Spiritus sanctus et gratia in mentibus fidelium uberius instillatur*). The covenant between God and humanity is also mentioned. Also in the section against heresies is a chapter on baptism, in which are denied the twin evils of the Anabaptists and Papists: the first believing that baptism is unnecessary or wrong (covenant theology is invoked against them); and the second said to believe that the grace of the Holy Spirit is linked to the water and that baptism is absolutely necessary for salvation. As for the eucharist, transubstantiation and the Lutheran doctrine of the Real Presence are condemned, and it is affirmed that the sacraments do not contain in themselves what they signify.[4] Later in the draft canon law comes a positive discussion of the sacraments. A sacrament is a visible sign instituted by God, and by it the grace of Christ and forgiveness of sins are offered to us. The external signs recall for us the working of salvation by Christ, stir up faith in us and instil in us mutual love and the fear of God. Circumcision in the old covenant is superseded by baptism and the eucharist. A chapter on 'what is to be sought in a sacrament' lists three requirements: a clear sign, the promise of God which is represented and confirmed by the sign, and the command of God to perform the sacrament and to make the remembrance. Next baptism is described: regeneration is sealed by the external washing, forgiveness granted and the power of the Holy Spirit is poured on us. The dipping is described as representing the death and resurrection of Christ, and the cleansing of the soul from sin. Then the eucharist (in a passage in which it is said that people sit at the table of the Lord, despite Cranmer's known views set out in the black rubric of the 1552 Prayer Book) is described as a sacrament in which the grace of the Holy Spirit and the pardon of sins is sealed in those who receive the bread and wine, understanding it in faith to be the body and blood of Christ. The mutual indwelling of Christ and the believer is described, and transubstantiation and the Real Presence are again denied.[5]

There is much here that will be familiar to a reader of Cranmer. However given, for example, his opposition to seated communion, it would be hazardous to take this document as evidence for his own belief. Therefore, while noting the contents of the *Reformatio Legum* and the 42 Articles, we must leave them and concentrate on Cranmer's own writings.

---

4   *Reformatio Legum*, De Haeresibus, cap. 17–19, ed. G. Bray, *Tudor Church Reform: The Henrician Canons of 1535 and the Reformatio Legum Ecclesiasticarum*, Church of England Record Society, 8 (Woodbridge: Boydell Press, 2000), pp. 200–7.

5   *Reformatio Legum*, De sacramentis, cap. 1–4, Bray (ed.), *Tudor Church Reform*, pp. 226–9.

2. CRANMER: WHAT IS A SACRAMENT?

a. Sacrament as sign

Cranmer begins his *Answer* with a definition of his use of the word 'sacrament'. He says that he uses it in two ways: first, 'for the sacramental bread, water, or wine; as when they say, that *sacramentum est sacrae rei signum*, "a sacrament is the sign of an holy thing"', and second, for the 'whole ministration and receiving of the sacraments'. Linked with each use, Cranmer distinguishes his understanding of the presence of Christ. In the former, he speaks 'not of Christ's carnal presence in the outward sacrament, but sometimes of his sacramental presence'. In the latter, 'in the due ministration of the sacraments according to Christ's ordinance and institution, Christ and his holy Spirit be truly and indeed present by their mighty and sanctifying power, virtue, and grace, in all them that worthily receive the same'.[6]

The Archbishop builds on this definition. The sacramental element cannot of itself be holy, for it is a lifeless stuff. But it can be called holy because it is the sign of holiness and it has a holy use.[7] We are often reminded that, to follow Augustine, sacraments 'for their similitude and likeness, commonly . . . have the name of the things, whereof they be sacraments. Therefore, as after a certain manner of speech the sacrament of Christ's body is Christ's body, the sacrament of Christ's blood is Christ's blood; so likewise [in a passage we shall return to later] the sacrament of faith is faith'.[8] This principle is one which Cranmer evokes often in defence of his position whenever any ancient writer speaks too explicitly of the bread and wine as the body and blood of Christ.[9] Indeed, he is able on this basis to speak of the eucharist even as a sacrifice.[10]

Related to this idea is the use of the words 'figure' and 'signify'. 'Signify' is a commonly used term which determines the relationship

---

6   *Answer*, Preface: PS, I, p. 3. In the Latin translation of the *Defence*, 2.11, Cranmer adds the quotation of Augustine (*In Joan Tract.* 80) in which the sacrament is described as 'Accedit verbum ad elementum, et fit sacramentum'. But he quotes it in order to distinguish between the word and the element, not to combine them (PS, I, Appendix, p. 38).

7   *Answer*, 3: PS, I, p. 11.

8   *Defence*, 3.11: PS, I, p. 124, quoting Augustine, *Ep. 23 ad Bonifacium de baptismate parvulorum* (*Ep.* 98).

9   E.g. his treatment of Chrysostom in *Defence*, 4.8: PS, I, p. 226.

10   'Questions and Answers concerning some Abuses of the Mass', PS, II, p. 150: 'The oblation and sacrifice of Christ in the mass is not so called, because Christ indeed is there offered and sacrificed by the priest and the people (for that was done but once by himself upon the cross); but it is so called, because it is a memory and representation of that very true sacrifice and immolation which before was made upon the cross.' Cf. *Defence*, 5.13: PS, I, pp. 351–2.

of the elements to the divine action, both establishing the relationship in itself and respecting the distinct nature of both the earthly and the spiritual. The nature of the sacrament as signifying the working of God requires, for Cranmer, that the original elements remain (in opposition to the theology of transubstantiation). Otherwise how can they signify anything? If the element is taken away, so is the sacrament.[11] However, we would be wrong to apply the same logic to the signified and say that it must be present. For, he says, 'figures be in vain and serve to no purpose, when the things by them signified be present'. So this doctrine of the sacraments depends on the corporal absence of the body of Christ in the eucharist, just as it is denied that 'every man be corporally buried in deed when he is baptized, which is a figure of our burial'.[12]

b. Corporal/ sacramental/ spiritual

Often Cranmer distinguishes between three modes of Christ's presence: the corporal, the sacramental and the spiritual.

> And although Christ in his human nature, substantially, really, corporally, naturally and sensibly, be present with his Father in heaven, yet sacramentally and spiritually he is here present. For in water, bread and wine, he is present, as in signs and sacraments; but he is indeed spiritually in those faithful, christian people, which according to Christ's ordinance be baptized, or receive the holy communion, or unfeignedly believe in him.'[13]

These three notions of presence are clearly stated here. Elsewhere they are not given such clarity but the distinctions are still observed. The spiritual presence of Christ is in the believer, not in the element of the sacrament, and he is corporally only in heaven.[14] And just as there are two modes of presence on earth today, so there are two modes of feeding on Christ: spiritual and sacramental.[15] And we shall see later that there are three forms of the giving of the flesh of Christ: corporally on the cross, spiritually and sacramentally.

---

11   *Answer*, 1: PS, I, p. 37.
12   *Answer*, 2: PS, I, p. 288. Ridley has a similar comment in his Disputation at Oxford (PS, p. 199).
13   *Defence*, 1.17: PS, I, p. 47.
14   Cf. the very clear statement of his theology in the Preface to the *Answer*: PS, I, p. 3.
15   *Answer*, 4: PS, I, p. 205.

Baptism is discussed by Cranmer as a sign in this way: the spiritual reality is of baptism by fire and the Holy Spirit, spiritual regeneration, putting on Christ, dying with Christ. But these cannot be perceived by us, since we are physical beings and fallen ones at that, and so they are shown to us by signs and figures of material washing.[16]

The true nature of the sacrament is recognized by the spiritual person, the true believer. The 'ethnick and carnal', the 'Capernaite', are offended at the language of eating the body and drinking the blood of Christ; they see 'no figure or mystery'. The words are figurative, not to the unfaithful, but the faithful.[17] Cranmer uses 'figure' in the same way as he does 'sacrament'. A figure, like a sacrament or rather being a sacrament, bears the name of the thing of which it is the figure.[18]

c. The dominical sacraments

So far, it cannot be said that Cranmer draws a strict boundary between figures in general and the dominical sacraments. His initial definition, that a sacrament is the sign of a holy thing, can be applied to any number of things, and indeed it was in earlier years by Cranmer himself.[19] But he identifies those two sacraments ordained by Christ as means by which, being physical beings and constrained to the things of this world, we may perceive him as fully as possible and gain strength and faith from the signification of the physical washing, eating and drinking. And, most important, the sacraments are instituted by God and carry his promise of

---

16 *Defence*, 3.12: PS, I, p. 135:

> [After quoting a series of scriptural passages on the theme of baptism and the water of life:] This baptism and washing by the fire and the Holy Ghost, this new birth, this water that springeth in a man and floweth into everlasting life, and this clothing and burial, cannot be understand of any material baptism, material washing, material birth, clothing and burial; but by translation of things visible into things invisible, they must be understand spiritually and figuratively.

Defence, 3.15: PS, I, pp. 197–8:

> And because this Adam is spiritual, therefore our generation by him must be spiritual, and our feeding must be likewise spiritual. And our spiritual generation by him is plainly set forth in baptism; and our spiritual meat and food is set forth in the holy communion and supper of the Lord. And because our sights be so feeble that we cannot see the spiritual water wherewith we be washed in baptism, nor the spiritual meat wherewith we be fed at the Lord's table, therefore to help our infirmities, and to make us the better to see the same with a pure faith, our Saviour Christ hath set forth the same, as it were before our eyes, by sensible signs and tokens, which we be daily used and accustomed to.

17 *Defence*, 3: PS, I, pp. 117–18.
18 *Answer*, 3.15: PS, I, p. 172.
19 Questions and Answers concerning the Sacraments, 1540: PS, II, p. 115.

grace.[20] As well as the sacraments of the New Testament, there are also those of the Old Testament: the eating of manna in particular is equated with the eucharist. Gardiner at one time asks, but Cranmer does not answer, what the difference is between the eucharistic bread and manna, if the former 'be but a figure of Christ's body'.[21] But the answer, of course, is that there is no difference.[22]

Cranmer is insistent that the sacrament is no empty token, 'like a painted fire'. Rather, Christ is present in his sacraments (we have already seen in what sense that must be understood) just as he is present in his word, which works grace in the hearers. In neither case can one talk of a corporal presence, in the bread and wine any more than in the voice, 'but this speech meaneth that he worketh with his word, using the voice of the speaker, as his instrument to work by; as he useth also his sacraments, whereby he worketh, and therefore is said to be present in them'.[23] The notion of the sacrament as an instrument will be discussed further later. Here we shall note particular ways in which Cranmer discusses the sacramental action and which help us to build up a picture both of the language he uses and the theology it reflects and embodies.

Of the action of God, Cranmer says that he 'worketh inwardly in our hearts by his holy Spirit, and confirmeth the same outwardly to our ears by hearing of his word, and to our other senses by eating and drinking of the sacramental bread and wine in his holy supper'.[24] This is the same as what we have just seen, namely the parallel with the preached word. And the sacrament is there to confirm our faith, as assurance.[25] It shows Christ and 'puts him into our eyes, mouths, hands and all our senses'.[26] But we are now told here how the action on our senses relates to the way in which God 'worketh inwardly in our hearts'.

---

20 *Answer*, 3: PS, I, p. 148. 'Although the sacramental tokens be only significations and figures, yet doth Almighty God effectually work in them that duly receive his sacraments those divine and celestial operations which he hath promised, and by the sacraments be signified.'

21 *Explication and Assertion of the True Catholique Fayth, touchyng the moost blessed sacrament of the aultar* (Rouen: Robert Caly, 1551), 4, included in Cranmer's *Answer*: PS, I, p. 219.

22 *Answer*, 3: PS, I, p. 75.

23 *Answer*, 1: PS, I, p. 11.

24 *Defence*, 1.16: PS, I, p. 43.

25 *Defence*, 1.16: PS, I, p. 44.

26 *Defence*, 1.12: PS, I, p. 41.

d. Bucer: the intimate relation of sign and grace

Martin Bucer's long career as a leading reformer saw a development in his sacramental theology, such that it is important to distinguish between different periods.[27] At first he observed a clear distinction between the sign and the signified, but from the 1530s he spoke of a closer link between them, and by the end of his career he communicated a strong sense of the instrumental role of the sacrament. Thus, for example, in *Grund und Ursach*, published in December 1524 as a rationale of contemporary liturgical reforms in Strasbourg, he appeals to the Augustinian distinction between the sacramental sign and the grace signified. The important part of baptism is the inner, spiritual baptism by Christ with the Holy Spirit, which is distinct from the water baptism. When Bucer discusses Ananias's instruction to Paul, 'Rise and be baptized, and wash away your sins, calling on his name', the last phrase is meant to point away from the ritual act and towards the spiritual washing that Christ performs.[28] It is those who believe in Christ, or the elect (there is no difference between the two), who receive the spiritual grace.[29] However, by 1550 he discusses the same biblical passage in a totally different way: 'And in Acts 22, where the Apostle Paul recites the words of Ananias who invited him to receive baptism, reports these words of Ananias, "And now, why do you delay? Arise, be baptized, and wash away your sins, calling on the name of the Lord." And by these words the effect, that is, the forgiveness or washing away of sins, is attributed to baptism.'[30] No longer do we have the distinction between the washing with water and the calling upon the name of the Lord. The two are indeed one, and the divine grace is attributed to the sacramental action, not magically, but by God's promise to his elect.

e. Bucer and 'exhibition'

A cornerstone of Bucer's mature sacramental theology is the term 'exhibition'. René Bornert outlines the importance of this term as, from

---

27   With little German, I rely here on the description of the work in Old, *Reformed Baptismal Rite*, and W. P. Stephens, *The Holy Spirit in the Theology of Martin Bucer* (Cambridge: Cambridge University Press, 1970).

28   Old, *Reformed Baptismal Rite*, p. 55; M. Bucer, *Deutsche Schriften*, ed. R. Stupperich, Martini Buceri Opera series 1 (Paris: Gütersloh, 1960–), Vol. 1, p. 255.

29   Stephens, *Holy Spirit in Bucer*, p. 223.

30   *De vi et usu sacri ministerii explicatio Martini Buceri*, in M. Bucer, *Martini Buceri Scripta anglicana fere omnia iis etiam, quae hactenus vel nondum, vel sparsim, vel peregrino idiomate edita fuere a Conrado Huberto . . . collecta* (Basel: ex P. Pernae officina, 1577), pp. 553–610 (p. 596) (author's trans.).

about 1530 onwards, Bucer sought to reintegrate the external and internal aspects of the sacrament.[31] By 'exhibition' he sought to establish a real and objective relation between the element and the grace while respecting their distinctiveness.[32] Grace is linked to the sign without being limited or conditioned by it. And God works with his Spirit in those who receive the sacrament in order that it be effective in them.[33]

David Wright summarizes the use of the term with regard to baptism, showing how strong the sense of the term is in Bucer's 1536 *Commentary on Romans*, where *exhibition* can only mean 'to impart': 'To infants God only imparted [his blessing through the sacrament], to parents and the church he both signified and imparted them'.[34] He goes on to point out how far a shift this represents in Bucer's thought: 'The wheel has come full circle. Whereas originally Bucer allowed to baptism little more than a purely significative function . . . and was adamant that it actually imparted nothing, now he affirms that for infants the "only" thing it does is actually impart God's blessings, even when its significative force is futile.'[35]

Basil Hall describes how Bucer by no means abandoned the word when he came to England, but canvassed it as of utmost importance in his discussions with fellow reformers.[36] With regard to the eucharist, he maintains that the bread and wine are 'exhibitive signs'. Such he had called them in 1545,[37] and such he maintained when commenting on Martyr's propositions for debate in Oxford, so the proposition 'The Body and Blood of Christ are Sacramentally conjoined to the Bread and the Wine' is amplified by 'so that, to them that believe, Christ is here truly exhibited; to be seen, however, received, enjoyed, by faith, not by any sense or manner of this world'.[38]

---

31   R. Bornert, *La Réforme protestante du culte à Strasbourg au XVIe siècle* (Leiden: Brill, 1981), pp. 317–22.

32   Bornert, *Réforme protestante*, p. 319.

33   Bornert, *Réforme protestante*, p. 320.

34   'Infantibus exhibuit tantum, parentibus et Ecclesiae iuxta et significavit et exhibuit.' In *Metaphrasis et enarratio in epistolam D. Pauli ad Romanos* (Basel: apud Petrum Pernam, 1562), p. 160, quoted by D.F. Wright, 'Infant Baptism and the Christian community', in D.F. Wright (ed.), *Martin Bucer: Reforming Church and Community* (Cambridge: Cambridge University Press, 1994), pp. 95–106 (p. 99).

35   Wright, 'Infant Baptism and the Christian Community', p. 100. Wright also discusses the exact translation of this passage in more detail, but the issues do not affect the basic principle outlined here.

36   Hall, 'Cranmer, the Eucharist and the Foreign Divines', pp. 226, 228, 232.

37   J.V. Pollet, *Martin Bucer: Etudes sur la correspondance*, 2 vols (Paris: Presses universitaires, 1958–62), Vol. 1, pp. 281ff.; Hall, 'Cranmer, the Eucharist and the Foreign Divines', p. 226.

38   Gorham, *Gleanings*, pp. 84–5; Hall, 'Cranmer, the Eucharist and the Foreign Divines', p. 228.

I cannot find any instance of Bucer using the term in his *Censura*.[39] There need not be any significance in this omission: perhaps he simply felt that personal theological terms were out of place in this document, and he was certainly trying to make his comments within the context of the Prayer Book. But in his personal correspondence he says, 'In the Public Prayers [the 1549 Prayer Book], however, at the Lord's Supper, a true exhibition of the Body and Blood of Christ is expressed in words exceeding clear and weighty'.[40]

Bucer's response to the theology of the 1549 Prayer Book was to support vigorously the Prayer of Humble Access and the phrase, 'in these holy mysteries'. He is perfectly happy with the word *in*, himself speaking of 'the reception of Christ the Saviour in the mysteries of the holy supper', and saying that the traditionalists are wrong to maintain that 'we receive [Christ] in these mysteries not only by faith but actually through the medium of the senses'.[41] However, the phrase in question did not survive into the 1552 Prayer Book.

The notion of exhibition is such an important one in Bucer's thought that we must look closely at it in Cranmer's writings to see if he uses it in a similar manner. Cranmer uses the word only very rarely, and then very carefully. In one instance he picks up Bucer's phraseology but qualifies it, saying:

> But in this place he easeth you nothing at all; for he saith no more but that the body and blood of Christ be exhibited unto the worthy receivers of the sacrament, which is true, but yet spiritually, not corporally. And I never said that Christ is utterly absent, but I ever affirmed that he is truly and spiritually present, and truly and spiritually exhibited unto the godly receivers: but corporally is he neither in the receivers, nor in or under the forms of bread and

---

39 For example, we might have expected him to use his favourite word when he says,

   The bread and wine remain in their own nature and in all the properties of their nature. In these mysteries they are nothing other than signs of the body and blood of the Lord, but not of things altogether absent. They are signs of a kind by which in association with his words the Lord offers himself to us again and again, communicates and unites himself to us. (*Censura*, ed. E.C. Whitaker, *Martin Bucer and the Book of Common Prayer*, Alcuin Club Collection, 55 [Great Wakering: Mayhew–McCrimmon, 1974], p. 76).

40 Letter to Theobald Niger, 15 April 1550, *Scripta Anglicana*, p. 862; Gorham, *Gleanings*, p. 143. Gorham in a note links Bucer's favourable opinion with the prayer for consecration, 'With thy Holy Spirit and word', etc., which is hardly correct.

41 *Censura*, in Whitaker (ed.), *Bucer*, pp. 64–81; 'Christi servatoris in sacris Coenae mysteriis Receptio' (pp. 66/7); 'nos eum non fide tantum in his recipere mysteriis, verum etiam sensibus' (pp. 74/5).

wine, as you do teach clearly without the consent of master Bucer, who writeth no such thing.[42]

On another occasion he speaks without reference to Bucer:

But St Augustine saith not, that the thing signified is in the bread and wine, to whom it is not exhibited, nor is not in it, but as in a figure; but that it is there in the true ministration of the sacrament, present to the spirit and faith of the true believing man, and exhibited truly and in deed, and yet spiritually, not corporally.[43]

'To whom it is not exhibited' would seem here to refer to the bread and wine rather than to the recipient, the point being that the divine action of exhibition is directed entirely towards the recipient, as is the divine action of spiritual feeding, and we see this in a further instance where he picks up the word 'exhibit' from Gardiner:

And yet in the Lord's Supper, rightly used, is Christ's body exhibited indeed spiritually, and so really, if you take really to signify only a spiritual and not a corporal and carnal exhibition. But this real and spiritual exhibition is to the receivers of the sacrament, and not to the bread and wine.[44]

In *Defence* 3.15 Cranmer, when dealing with Origen, speaks of Christ being 'exhibited unto us, as it were face to face and sensibly, in his word, in the sacrament of regeneration, and the sacraments of bread and wine', but that the reality of all this is not corporal but spiritual. Gardiner picked him up on 'exhibited sensibly', and Cranmer retorted sharply, attacking his opponent for leaving out the words 'as it were', which effectively (says Cranmer) deny that Christ is exhibited sensibly: it is spiritual.[45]

In a further instance the word is similarly restricted to the spiritual aspect of the sacrament:

And in token hereof he hath prepared bread to be eaten and wine to be drunken of us in his holy supper, to put us in remembrance of his said death, and of the celestial feeding, nourishing, increasing, and of all the benefits which we have thereby; which benefits

---

42 *Answer*, 3: PS, I, pp. 126–7.
43 *Answer*, 2: PS, I, p. 281.
44 *Answer*, 3: PS, I, p. 123.
45 Cranmer, *Defence* 3.15; Gardiner, *Explication*; Cranmer, *Answer*: PS, I, pp. 154–6.

through faith and the Holy Ghost are exhibited and given unto all that worthily receive the said holy supper.[46]

In all these instances 'exhibition' is applied only to the spiritual feeding as distinct from the sacramental action. Cranmer makes no attempt to integrate the external and internal actions, even when the context might have allowed some such approach. The only possible conclusion is that Cranmer uses the same word 'exhibition' in a very different sense from that employed by Bucer.

The *Reformatio Legum*, being a document with many authors, does not provide sure evidence of Cranmer's personal theology, but we must consider a sentence on the nature of the sacraments that was emended in Cranmer's own hand: 'For when they are distributed among us, faith is confirmed by the power of the Holy Spirit, the conscience is awakened, and the promise of forgiveness of sins through Christ is exhibited as made internally, while externally it is sealed by those sacraments as if by some seal.'[47] Again we see that the word 'exhibit' is used in such a way as to respect the distinction between the grace and its sign. We also see here the use of the analogy of the seal for the sacrament. This is very unusual for Cranmer; while he uses 'exhibition' purely for the inward spiritual grace, the seal is for the sign that merely signifies that grace. This is different from the way in which it is used by other reformers.

f. Bullinger and Laski: sacrament as seal

For many reformers the language of the sacraments as signs was complemented by describing them as a seal. In the sixteenth century the seal was a part of everyday life, giving authority to all kinds of legal transactions; for theologians, it had the advantage that it graced something already determined and written and brought it into effect, and so could be used to express some kind of relation between the sacrament and the grace and to accord efficacy to the sacrament while allowing the primacy to grace. Thus Bullinger distinguished between the sign and its reality: sacraments cannot confer grace because they do not possess grace in themselves.[48] The elect people of God do not receive the reality

---

46 *Answer*, 2: PS, I, p. 328.

47 'Quae cum inter nos dispertiuntur, vi divini Spiritus fides confirmatur, erigitur conscientia, promissio etiam veniae peccatorum per Christum facta intrinsecus exhibetur, extrinsecus vero quasi signillo quodam consignatur' (*Reformatio Legum*, 2 De Haeresibus, 17 De sacramentorum natura, Bray (ed.), *Tudor Church Reform*, p. 202). Bray dates the manuscript (BL, MS Harleian 426) to mid October 1552. I have based my translation on Bray.

48 Decade 5.7: *Decades*, ed. T. Harding, PS, 4 vols (Cambridge: Cambridge University Press, 1849–52), pp. 302, 305.

only with the sign, 'for they enjoy the things before they be partakers of the signs'. Abraham was justified before he was circumcised. Likewise the eunuch's pre-baptismal belief points to his justification at that time, and the case of Cornelius is cited.[49] And on the basis of these precedents, Bullinger asks:

> For why, I pray you, do we baptize our infants? Is it because they believe with their heart and confess with their mouth? I think not. Do we not therefore baptize them, because God hath commanded them to be brought unto him? because he hath promised, that he will be our God, and the God of our seed after us? to be short, because we believe that God, of his mere grace and mercy, in the blood of Jesus Christ, hath cleansed and adopted them, and appointed them to be heirs of eternal life? We therefore, baptising infants for these causes, do abundantly testify, that there is not first given unto them in baptism, but that there is sealed and confirmed which they had before.[50]

Despite their lack of individual faith, infants are baptized in obedience to Christ's command to bring them to him, and they already enjoy his grace through the promise of God to those who believe and their offspring. What is conferred or signified in baptism is not redemption itself, since that has occurred already, but its seal and confirmation. Reception into the visible Church signifies regeneration among the elect people of God.

Similarly in Laski's thought the dominant theme for understanding the sacraments is as a seal. 'This is the prime aim of all the Sacraments, of both the old and new Church, that they are seals of the divine mercy towards us, and are affixed to certain promises as if to legal documents made out to us.'[51] In this respect the sacraments are, as it were, at one stage remove from the divine action.

> Scripture has the custom of calling circumcision a covenant, and baptism the washing of regeneration, and the Supper the communion of the body and blood of Christ, but it does so in the same sense as when the Gospel is called the power for salvation for everyone who believes. For we are not saved by the preaching of

---

49　Decade 5.7: PS, pp. 311–12.

50　Decade 5.7: PS, pp. 312–13.

51　*Epitome* §13, in *Joannis a Lasco Opera tam edita quam inedita*, ed. A. Kuyper, 2 vols (Amsterdam: Muller, 1886), Vol. 1, p. 513 (author's trans.). Cf. *Tractatio*, fol. 59 (Kuyper, *Opera*, Vol. 1, p. 164), where the divine action is compared to the custom of kings: 'Apud quos primum fit donatio ipsa, deinde in diplomate ad id scripto declaratur. Postremo per additum diplomati sigillum regium communitur et obsignatur.'

the Gospel, but the Gospel testifies to us the mercy of God through which we are saved.[52]

There is a similar logic applied in a critique of the Zwinglian understanding of the sacraments as analogous to the military oath: Laski holds that the analogy is wrong because the oath is an act which binds the soldier who was not previously bound to the commander, whereas the sacrament firstly is about what God has done, not what we do, and also because we already belong to Christ and the sacrament is a subsequent action.[53] So too the baptism of Cornelius comes as a seal after his having received the Holy Spirit and God's approval of his good works.[54]

g. Martyr: the sacrament as 'relationship'

Peter Martyr Vermigli had another way of speaking of the close relation of the sacraments to the grace they signify. As with all these Reformers, we must remember that they do always emphasize the distinction between the sacrament and the reality. Thus, for example, in his *Treatise* on the Lord's Supper of 1550, Martyr says:

> In a sacrament we put a difference between the outward signs and the things that are signified by them.[55]
>
> When we receive the sacrament we should not stop or tarry in the outward signs with our worshipping but . . . we should in spirit and in truth worship Christ that sitteth in heaven on the right hand of the Father.[56]
>
> We affirm and advouch the proper natures of bread and wine to be kept still and the changing to be only sacramental through grace.[57]

Martyr developed a distinctive theology of the sacraments. This has been examined in detail by Salvatore Corda. For the most part Corda

---

52   *Epitome*, §13; Kuyper, *Opera*, Vol. 1, pp. 512–13 (author's trans.).
53   *Tractatio*, fols 9–9ᵛ (Kuyper, *Opera*, Vol. 1, p. 122). 'Ideo sacramentis utimur, quia ad Christum iam olim pertinemus.'
54   *Tractatio*, fols 87ᵛ–8 (Kuyper, *Opera*, Vol. 1, p. 188).
55   *A Discourse or Treatise of Peter Martyr . . . concerning the Lord's Supper* (London: 'R. Stoughton' [Whitchurch], 1550), fol. 69ᵛ. This work is a translation of his *Tractatio de Sacramento Eucharistiae habita in celeberrima Universitate Oxoniensi* (London, 1549).
56   *Treatise*, fol. 70ᵛ.
57   *Treatise*, fol. 90.

uses Martyr's mature theological works, for example his *Defensio Doctrinae Veteris et Apostolicae de Sacrosancto Eucharistiae Sacramento* published in 1559. Before we turn to earlier works emanating from his time in England, we shall briefly survey some of the points raised by Corda.

For Martyr, the identity of the bread and wine with the body and blood of Christ is affirmed at the sacramental level 'by signification', but denied at the ontological level.[58] He distinguishes between the outward and inward eating of the sacrament,[59] and can speak of the impious eating only the sacrament and not eating the body.[60] The essential factor here is faith, God's own gift, which must precede the sacrament for it to be spiritually received.[61] However, while acknowledging the distinction between sacrament and reality, Martyr also thinks in terms of the sacrament as a *relationship* between the earthly and divine realities. Without any change in themselves the elements are brought into a status in which they are the instruments of the Holy Spirit on the recipient. The Reformer uses the analogy of the stone column whose nature is not changed when it is placed in a building but it becomes a support. It has changed not in its nature but in its relationship.[62] Martyr maintains that a sacrament is more than just a figure and belongs more to grace than to nature.[63] The examples he chooses to explain the sacramental relationship bear this out: the relation of father and son imply one the moment the other is spoken of; the relationship is found between 'word' and 'meaning' which are inseparable but (in those sunny premodern days!) distinct.[64] This close relationship sometimes leads him to speak in a different way where the impious recipient does not share in the *res* but only in the symbol: the suggestion, indeed the logical corollary, is that the impious recipient does not even share in the sacrament.[65]

---

58 *Defensio Doctrinae Veteris et Apostolicae de Sacrosancto Eucharistiae Sacramento* (Zurich, 1559), p. 82; S. Corda, *Veritas Sacramenti: A Study in Vermigli's Doctrine of the Lord's Supper*, Zürcher Beiträge zur Reformationsgeschichte, 6 (Zurich: Theologischer Verlag, 1975), p. 121.

59 *Defensio*, p. 563; Corda, *Veritas Sacramenti*, pp. 138–9.

60 *Defensio*, p. 540; Corda, *Veritas Sacramenti*, p. 158.

61 *Defensio*, p. 311; Corda, *Veritas Sacramenti*, pp. 142–4.

62 *Defensio*, p. 612; Corda, *Veritas Sacramenti*, p. 118.

63 *Defensio*, p. 641; Corda, *Veritas Sacramenti*, p. 117.

64 *Defensio*, pp. 627, 387; Corda, *Veritas Sacramenti*, pp. 102–3.

65 'In Sacramento, ut illius recte, et cum fructu usurpetur, duplicem esse manducationem: alteram carnalem, alteram spiritualem: alteram signorum, alteram veritatis' (*Defensio*, p. 563; Corda, *Veritas Sacramenti*, pp. 138–9. Cf. Corda's comments, *Veritas Sacramenti*, p. 132: 'A true sacramental eating cannot be severed from its beneficial effect upon the partaker. In other words, a sacrament can really occur only when one properly participates in it.'

We find similar ideas in Martyr's earlier works from his time in England. In his *Treatise* he writes: 'The wicked do not receive the Lord's body even like as unskillful or ignorant persons when they hear talk in Greek or Latin do not perceive the sense and meaning thereof.'[66] The failure to understand the words reduces them to gibberish in the hearer's mind. Likewise a sacrament will convey nothing at all to one who does not have faith. In his *Sacrament of Thanksgiving* he puts forward the same argument about recognizing the role and meaning of a seal.[67] We do not have in these works of the Edwardian Reformation the fully worked out theology or examples which we see in Martyr's later *Defensio*, but the same assumptions and principles are present and coherent.

The negative argument is always the most difficult. It can only be said that I have found nothing in Cranmer which is equivalent to Martyr's distinctive treatment of the relationship between the sacrament and the reality. When trying to imagine what in Cranmer might be closest to Martyr's discussion of a sacrament being like the relation of a word to its meaning, what comes to mind is the Archbishop's statement about the true meaning of the sacrament:

> And the authors term it here a figure, not thereby to 'cover the mystery', but to open the mystery, which was indeed in Christ's words by figurative speeches understand. And with the figurative speech were the ethnick and carnal ears offended, not with the mystery, which they understood not. And not to the ethnick and carnal, but to the faithful and spiritual ears, the words of Christ be figurative, and to them the truth of the figures be plainly opened and declared by the fathers: wherein the fathers be worthy much commendation, because they travailed to open plainly unto us the obscure and figurative speeches of Christ. And yet in their said declarations they taught us, that these words of Christ, concerning the eating of his flesh and drinking of his blood, are not to be understanded plainly, as the words properly signify, but by a figurative speech.[68]

Do we have the same model of understanding as Martyr gives? In one sense yes, because the wrong sense is nonsense. But there seems to be a major difference in that Martyr seems to be speaking about the

---

66 *Treatise*, fols 90^V-1.
67 *Of the sacrament of Thankesgeving: a short Treaties of Peter Martir's making*, BL, MS Royal 17 CV, fols 53–4.
68 *Answer*, 3: PS, I, p. 117.

sacrament as a whole being like a word with its literal meaning, whereas that is what Cranmer would have us reject in this case. In other words, while for Martyr the model of a word and its meaning is essentially one of a close relationship, for Cranmer this discussion is about a qualified relationship, a distinction as much as a relationship.

h. The dominical sacraments: are they distinct?

The identity of the two dominical sacraments is a theme to which Cranmer returns almost *ad nauseam* in his *Defence* and *Answer*. Often it is negative in the sense that it is used as an argument against a theology of the Real Presence of Christ in the eucharistic bread and wine: if the water is not understood as conveying the presence of God locally, then nor should this be suggested of the bread and wine.[69] Cranmer can even be led (by a quotation of Ps. Cyprian's *De Coena Domini*) to assert that as the nature of bread is changed, so also is that of water. But he goes on to explain 'nature' in terms of the role or use of water.[70] And, as in the eucharist, the sacrament mirrors the continual presence of Christ and the Holy Spirit in us.[71] The sacrament defines neither who receives the grace nor when; that is determined by God's own election and grace. Others who are baptized receive only the outward sign but not the grace.[72] This

---

69 E.g. *Defence*, 2: PS, I, p. 305: 'But forasmuch as [Christ] is joined to the bread but sacramentally, there followeth no impanation thereof, no more than the Holy Ghost is inaquate, that is to say, made water, being sacramentally joined to the water in baptism.'

70 *Defence*, 2.11: PS, I, p. 308: 'And likewise is the nature of the water changed in baptism, forasmuch as beside his common nature, which is to wash and make clean the body, it declareth unto us that our souls be also washed and made clean by the Holy Ghost.'

71 *Answer*, 3: PS, I, p. 71:

And as the Holy Ghost doth not only come to us in baptism, and Christ doth there clothe us, but they do the same to us continually so long as we dwell in Christ; so likewise doth Christ feed us so long as we dwell in him and he in us, and not only when we receive the sacrament. So that as touching Christ himself, the presence is all one, the clothing all one, and the feeding all one, although the one for the more comfort and consolation have the sacrament added to it, and the other be without the sacrament.

Answer: PS, I, p. 140: I grant that Christ is really, not only in them that duly receive the sacrament of the Lord's supper, but also in them that duly receive the sacrament of baptism, and in all other true Christian people at other times when they receive no sacrament.

72 *Defence*, 4.7: PS, I, p. 221: 'Therefore, as in baptism those that come feignedly, and those that come unfeignedly, both be washed with the sacramental water, but both be not washed with the Holy Ghost and clothed with Christ; so in the Lord's supper both eat and drink the sacramental bread and wine, but both eat not Christ himself, and be fed with his flesh and blood, but those only which worthily receive the sacrament.'

identity of the two sacraments can lead to Cranmer speaking almost of a complete lack of distinction between them: Christ is present in baptism as in the eucharist; we are regenerated in baptism as in the eucharist, and united to Christ's divinity by his manhood.[73] Some comments might seem extreme: 'Infants, when they are baptized, do eat the flesh of Christ.'[74]

But there is a positive side to this approach, in that Cranmer claims that he is defending the proper role and dignity of baptism, and that his opponents are demoting it by claiming that in baptism we do not receive the whole Christ but his spirit only. And he claims that the difference between the sacraments lies not in how intimate our relation with Christ is (we receive him 'whole body and soul, manhood and Godhead, unto everlasting life'), but in the grace received: 'in baptism it is done in respect of regeneration, and in the holy communion in respect of nourishment and augmentation'.[75] (How we reconcile this comment with the one noted above in which we are regenerated in the eucharist is a difficult issue.) And baptism should be received by adults with fear and trembling – just as they do the eucharist.[76]

We shall see Cranmer express this in a parallel structure for the baptism and communion service. A similar structure is found in Laski's Stranger Church in London at the time of Cranmer's Prayer Books, but it is by no means certain which liturgy influenced which.[77]

i. Christ and the Holy Spirit

The two dominical sacraments, because they bring us to the one Christ, function virtually as one sacrament in two forms. Cranmer does distinguish between the grace given: in baptism we receive Christ with respect to regeneration, and in the eucharist with respect to nourishment

---

73 *Answer*, 3: PS, I, p. 176.

74 *Disputation at Oxford*, PS, I, p. 412. Besides the theological principle, this may refer to an entry in *De re sacramentaria*, p. 171, under the heading 'Sicut in eucharistia praesens est Christus, ita et in baptismo est praesens': HIERONIMUS Ad Hebediam quaest.2 Quotquot in Christo baptizamur, Christum induimus et panem comedimus angelorum. (= *Ep.* 120.2; *PL*, 22: 986).

75 *Answer*, 1: PS, I, p. 25. Cf. *Answer*, p. 45.

76 *Answer*, 3: PS, I, p. 146.

77 *Forma ac Ratio tota ministerii in peregrinorum . . . Ecclesia instituta Londini . . . anno post Christum natum 1550*, reproduced in A. Kuyper (ed.), *Opera*, Vol. 2. The precise details of its relation to the practice of the Stranger Church over the years of its existence and to the 1552 book are not beyond doubt. The development is discussed by B.D. Spinks, *From the Lord and 'The Best Reformed Churches': A Study of the Eucharistic Liturgy in the English Puritan and Separatist Traditions, 1550–1633*, Bibliotheca 'Ephemerides Liturgicae', Subsidia, 33 (Rome: CLV, 1984), pp. 100–13.

and growth.[78] This is part of the spiritual process of redemption, not just its sacramental signification: 'And whensoever two or three be gathered together in his name, [Christ] is there in the midst among them, by whose supernal grace all godly men be first by him spiritually regenerated, and after increase and grow to their spiritual perfection in God, spiritually by faith eating his flesh and drinking his blood.'[79]

In the above quotation there is no reference to the sacraments at all, nor are they necessary. What is described would have applied to the righteous of the Old Testament, who shared in the spiritual reality of Christ without enjoying the New Testament sacraments. With or without the sacraments, regeneration and growth are the path of life in Christ. In one description of baptismal grace Cranmer follows scriptural analogies. After quoting a series of scriptural passages on the theme of baptism and the water of life he writes:

> This baptism and washing by the fire and the Holy Ghost, this new birth, this water that springeth in a man and floweth into everlasting life, and this clothing and burial, cannot be understand of any material baptism, material washing, material birth, clothing and burial; but by translation of things visible into things invisible, they must be understand spiritually and figuratively.[80]

Elsewhere his description is based closely on the liturgical symbols:

> And for this cause Christ ordained baptism in water, that as surely as we see, feel and touch water with our bodies, and be washed with water, so assuredly ought we to believe, when we be baptized, that Christ is verily present with us, and that by him we be newly born again spiritually, and washed from our sins, and grafted in the stock of Christ's own body, and be apparelled, clothed and harnessed with him, in such wise, that as the devil hath no power against Christ, so hath he none against us, so long as we remain grafted in that stock, and be clothed with that apparel, and harnessed with that armour. So that the washing in water of baptism is, as it were, shewing of Christ before our eyes, and a sensible touching, feeling, and groping of him, to the confirmation of the inward faith which we have in him.[81]

---

78 *Answer*, 1: PS, I, p. 25.
79 *Defence*, 3.2: PS, I, p. 89.
80 *Defence*, 3.12: PS, I, p. 135.
81 *Defence*, 1.12: PS, I, p. 41.

We have here references not only to the baptismal immersion, but also to the clothing in the chrism cloth, the exorcism of the devil, the sign of the cross with the imagery of Christ's soldier. What is curious about this second passage is that there is no mention of the Holy Spirit: it is entirely Christocentric. It is not always so: in the previous quotation Cranmer picks up the scriptural allusion to fire and the Holy Spirit; elsewhere he speaks of receiving the Holy Spirit and putting Christ upon us in baptism,[82] of being washed with the Holy Spirit and putting on Christ.[83] Chapter 2 of the *Defence* offers imagery concentrated more on the Holy Spirit.

> For as baptism is no perfect sacrament of spiritual regeneration, without there be as well the element of water, as the Holy Ghost spiritually regenerating the person that is baptized, which is signified by the said water; even so the supper of the Lord . . .[84]
>
> Forasmuch as [Christ] is joined to the bread but sacramentally, there followeth no impanation thereof, no more than the Holy Ghost is inaquate, that is to say, made water, being sacramentally joined to the water in baptism.[85]

But elsewhere the most common theme is of the presence of Christ that is enabled by the Holy Spirit. Following a quotation of Hilary, Cranmer speaks of a spiritual union with Christ in baptism of the same kind as in the eucharist.[86] In the eucharist Christ is present, not corporally but spiritually, or, as Cranmer says, by his Spirit. 'It is the Spirit that gives life; the flesh availeth nothing.'[87] In this model of the sacraments the Holy Spirit is expressed most commonly as the agent by which union with Christ is achieved, but there is little attention to receiving the Spirit or living the life of the Spirit. The independent identity of the Spirit at times seems to be lost. The *Defence* 4.5 speaks of the recipients of communion having Christ's Spirit in them, without which they cannot receive Christ's body. Thus the Holy Spirit is seen as an aspect of the incarnate Christ analogous to the model of humans as body and spirit.

The Holy Spirit is the one who enables the individual to appropriate salvation (spiritual reception as opposed to sacramental reception) and therefore is the hidden vehicle of grace. We have seen above in Cranmer's *Catechism* the addition of a mention of the Holy Spirit who assures the individual in baptism of their Christian identity, and also in his

---

82 *Answer*, 3: PS, I, p. 64.
83 *Defence*, 4.7: PS, I, p. 221. *Answer*, 5: PS, I, p. 366.
84 *Defence*, 2.8: PS, I, p. 304.
85 *Defence*, 2.9: PS, I, p. 305.
86 *Defence*, 3.15: PS, I, p. 161.
87 *Defence*, 4.6: PS, I, p. 219. *Defence*, 2.12: PS, I, p. 315.

theology of consecration similar passages in which the Holy Spirit has this role of bringing the individual to Christ. It is a strong and positive theme in Cranmer. It is a pity that the Spirit is so totally subsumed to his Christocentric emphasis.

3 THE EUCHARISTIC PRESENCE OF CHRIST

a. 'The Spirit giveth life, the flesh availeth nothing'

Cranmer denies transubstantiation and the Lutheran doctrine of the Real Presence of Christ in the eucharistic bread and wine. Of that everyone is agreed. It is his relation to the reformers Zwingli, Calvin, Bucer, Martyr and Laski that is hotly debated, often with the assumption spoken or unspoken that Cranmer was 'influenced' by one or more of these and had no mind of his own. But he cannot be claimed for any camp. Cranmer was a Cranmerian. In this respect the work of Richardson, seeking to establish distinctions as well as similarities, presents one of the most careful and accurate studies of Cranmer's work.

Richardson makes particularly strong points when he shows how Cranmer and Zwingli agree together, against Calvin and Bucer, that the communicant does not share, even spiritually, in the body and blood of Christ, but in his divinity. In his second article he pointed out Cranmer's qualifications on the role of the body of Christ; that he believed Christ to be present by his divinity alone. 'The whole Christ is indeed received in spiritual feeding on the Passion, but what is *present* is not the *body* of Christ, but the *grace* of Christ who is there by his divinity.'[88] And, as Cranmer himself said in the Preface to his *Answer*,

> Lest any man should mistake my words, and think that I mean, that although Christ be not corporally in the outward visible signs, yet he is corporally in the persons that duly receive them, this is to advertise the reader, that I mean no such thing; but my meaning is, that the force, the grace, the virtue and benefit of Christ's body that was crucified for us, and of his blood that was shed for us, be really and effectually present with all them that duly receive the sacraments: but all this I understand of his spiritual presence, of the which he saith, 'I will be with you until the world's end'; and, 'wheresoever two or three be gathered together in my name, there am I in the midst of them'; and, 'he that eateth my flesh and drinketh my blood dwelleth in me, and I in him'.[89]

---

88 Richardson, 'Cranmer and the Analysis of Eucharistic Doctrine', p. 427.
89 PS, I, p. 3.

Cranmer, in his *Defence*, is prepared to use the analogy of Christology in order to attack transubstantiation. One has to respect the two distinct natures of Christ, and likewise in the sacrament one must respect the natures of bread and wine and the body and blood:

> As the person of Christ consisteth of two natures, that is to say, of his manhood and of his Godhead, and therefore both those natures remain in Christ; even so, saith St Augustine, the sacrament consisteth of two natures, of the elements of bread and wine, and of the body and blood of Christ, and therefore both these natures must needs remain in the sacrament.[90]

It is at this point that Gardiner suggests that Cranmer's sacrament is 'like a body lying in a trance, whose soul for the while were in heaven'. He suggests that this passage was originally written to support a view of the Real Presence after the Lutheran mode of understanding rather than Cranmer's current theology.[91] But Cranmer seeks to explain Augustine further.

> And very true it is, as St Augustine saith, that 'the sacrifice of the church consisteth of two things, of the sacrament, and of the thing thereby signified, which is Christ's body, as the person of Christ consisteth of God and man'. But yet this resemblance is not altogether like, as you say truly for so much; for the person of Christ consisteth so of his Godhead and manhood, that they be both in him in real presence and unity of person. But in the sacrifice it is otherwise, where neither is any such union between the sacrament and the truth of the sacrament, nor any such presence of the body of Christ . . .
>
> But if Christ's similitudes should be so narrowly pressed, as you press here the similitude of the two natures of Christ in the sacrament, collecting that because the body and blood of Christ be truly present in the due administration of the sacrament, therefore they must be there naturally present, as the two natures of the humanity and divinity be in Christ; many wicked errors should be established by them . . .
>
> And it is not necessary for our eternal salvation, nor yet profitable for our comfort in this life, to believe that the natural body and blood of Christ is really, substantially, and naturally present in the sacrament. For if it were necessary or comfortable

---

90 *Defence*, 2.5: PS, I, p. 277.
91 *Explication* 2: PS, I, p. 281.

for us, it is without doubt, that our Saviour Christ, his apostles and evangelists, would not have omitted to teach this doctrine distinctly and plainly. Yea, our Saviour would not have said, *Spiritus est qui vivificat, caro non prodest quicquam*; 'The Spirit giveth life, the flesh availeth nothing.'[92]

This lengthy quotation summarizes how Cranmer approaches the question. At the end of a long process of exegesis of the Fathers, he comes back to John 6 as a proof text, a key to determining the meaning of scripture and the sacraments.

b. The analogy of the sun and its rays

As a marker, as it were, for the different theologies, Richardson cites the analogy of the sun and its rays. The scientific question of the precise relation between the rays and their heavenly source were answered by different theologians according to their views on the nature of the glorified Christ. For Cranmer (as for Zwingli), the rays do not participate in the sun's substance. By them its power pervades everything, but its substance does not:

They say, that Christ is corporally in many places at one time, affirming that his body is corporally and really present in as many places as there be hosts consecrated. We say, that as the sun corporally is ever in heaven, and no where else, and yet by his operation and virtue the sun is here in earth, by whose influence and virtue all things in the world be corporally regenerated, increased, and grow to their perfect state; so likewise our Saviour Christ bodily and corporally is in heaven, sitting at the right hand of his Father, although spiritually he hath promised to be present with us upon earth unto the world's end. And whensoever two or three be gathered together in his name, he is there in the midst among them, by whose supernal grace all godly men be first by him spiritually regenerated, and after increase and grow to their spiritual perfection in God, spiritually by faith eating his flesh and drinking his blood, although the same corporally be in heaven, far distant from our sight.[93]

In order to affirm that, while Christ's body is locally in heaven, believers may still participate in its substance by the Holy Spirit, Bucer

---

92 *Answer*, 2: PS, I, pp. 282–3.
93 *Defence*, 3.1: PS, I, p. 89.

(like Calvin) held that the rays of the sun were of the same substance as that of the sun itself:

> As the sun is truly placed determinately in one place of the visible heaven, and yet is truly and substantially present by means of his beams elsewhere in the world abroad, so our Lord, although he be comprehended in one place of the secret and divine heaven, that is to say, the glory of his Father, yet nevertheless by his word and holy tokens he is exhibit present truly whole God and man, and therefore in substance in his holy supper.[94]

And so, for Bucer, the bodily presence of Christ in heaven is no bar to his presence in respect of his body and blood on earth in the eucharist. When Gardiner took up the issue and cited this passage, Cranmer maintained his ground:

> If the substance of the sun be here corporally present with us upon earth, then I grant that Christ's body is so likewise: so that he of us two that erreth in the one, let him be taken for a vain man, and to err also in the other . . . and yet if you both said that the beams of the sun be of the same substance with the sun, who would believe either of you both? Is the light of the candle the substance of the candle? or the light of the fire the substance of the fire? Or is the beams of the sun any thing but the clear light of the sun?[95]

We have here a clear instance of a difference between Cranmer and Bucer. For Richardson this passage points both to a clear idea of Cranmer's eucharistic theology and to the nominalist philosophy underlying it: things are discrete objects confined in space. Their substance cannot go beyond this physical confine.[96] Bullinger does not seem to discuss the analogy of the sun, but from his writing one can be confident that he would have sided with Cranmer and Zwingli. It must also be said that Cranmer is somewhat sharper in his distinction between the sun and its rays than are Ridley and Martyr; even though they both maintain that the two are distinct, Martyr emphasizes that they are joined together, by 'conjunction': 'The body or ball of the sun that shineth in the sky, and

---

94 Commentary in Mt. 26, trans. Gardiner; *Explication* 3: Cranmer, PS, II, p. 90.

95 *Answer*, 2: PS, p. 91.

96 Brooks, *Cranmer's Doctrine of the Eucharist*, p. 105, n. 2 notes Richardson's use of this analogy but does not discuss it, even though he acknowledges that it is the cornerstone for the thesis that Cranmer is close to Zwingli. Nor can I find any comment by Hall on the passage, even though he maintains energetically that Cranmer is influenced strongly by Bucer and not by the Zwinglian party.

the light of the said sun have between themselves a natural and most high conjunction; and yet the same body of the sun doth not really and verily reach to all places that the light doth extend itself unto.'[97] We have here a finely nuanced version of this analogy of the sun. Its rays are not identical with it, but nor are they totally separate or different.

Ridley affirms a wider presence, though he does not state the actual mode of this presence:

> Briefly [those who deny transubstantiation] deny the presence of Christ's body in the natural substance of his human and assumed nature, and grant the presence of the same by grace: that is, they affirm and say, that the substance of the natural body and blood of Christ is only remaining in heaven, and so shall be unto the latter day . . . And the same natural substance of the very body and blood of Christ, because it is united in the divine nature in Christ, the second Person of the Trinity, therefore it hath not only life in itself, but is also able to give, and doth give life unto so many as be, or shall be partakers thereof: That is, that to all that do believe on his name . . . though the selfsame substance abide still in heaven, and they, for the time of their pilgrimage, dwell here upon earth; by grace (I say) . . . the same body of Christ is here present with us. Even as, for example, we say the same sun, which, in substance, never removeth his place out of the heavens, is yet present here by his beams, light, and natural influence, where it shineth upon the earth.[98]

The sun is spoken of as remaining in heaven, as regards its substance, yet still present here 'by his beams'. While there may be a difference of nature between the sun and its rays, there is still an identity between them which enables the sun to be present on earth. The humanity also is naturally confined to heaven, and yet is present on earth by virtue of its unity with the omnipresent divinity of Christ. And the presence on earth of Christ's body and blood is not the full story: by virtue of the divinity, the body and blood are not merely present but are life-giving.

c. The sacraments and the incarnation

The distinction between the sign and the signified is taken to the length that even the institution of the eucharist in the Last Supper is said to

---

97   *Treatise*, fol. 95.
98   *A Brief Declaration of the Lord's Supper*, PS, p. 13.

be separate from Christ's self-offering on the cross. There is only one propitiatory sacrifice, on the cross. In the Last Supper Christ made no such offering, but merely instituted the Supper as the means of remembrance and thanksgiving.[99] The sacraments are external to the divine action of atonement on the cross. They speak of Christ giving himself for us and to us, and of our dying with Christ, but they are distinct from these mysteries. To try to identify the work of divine grace in the sacraments or in their institution – even the Last Supper – is as Capernaical as to look for the flesh and blood of a man in bread and wine.

This distinction may underlie the curious feature noted by Richardson, that Cranmer applies to the incarnation realistic language used by the Fathers about the bodily presence of Christ in the eucharist. As Richardson says,

> The Holy Communion teaches [our union with Christ], to be sure, and gives us an occasion to exercise faith so that we may become recipients of the gift, acquire that virtue, force, and grace by which we are united to Christ and made flesh of his flesh. But it is not the *action* of the eucharist which *effects* all this and *imparts* these gifts; rather is this brought about by the incarnation and atonement and by conscious faith in them.[100]

However, while Richardson is right to identify the oddity of applying the realistic language of the eucharist to the incarnation, I am not convinced that Cranmer's approach to the incarnation is different from his understanding of the sacraments. When discussing Cyril and Hilary's statements about Christ dwelling corporally or naturally in us, Cranmer uses the analogy of the incarnation:

> And as St Paul, when he said that in Christ dwelleth the full divinity 'corporally', by this word 'corporally' he meant not that the divinity is a body, and so by that body dwelleth bodily in Christ. But by this word 'corporally' he meant, that the divinity is not in Christ accidentally, lightly, and slenderly, but substantially and perfectly, with all his might and power . . . So St Cyril, when he said that Christ is in us 'corporally', he meant that we have him in us, not lightly and to small effect and purpose, but that we have him in us substantially, pithily and effectually, in such wise that we have by him redemption and everlasting life.[101]

---

99 *Answer*, 1, 3: PS, I, pp. 35–6, 86.
100 Richardson, 'Cranmer and the Analysis of Eucharistic Doctrine', p. 432.
101 *Defence*, 3.15: PS, I, p. 166.

'Corporal' is simply not an appropriate term for describing the activity or presence of the divinity either in the incarnation or in the sacraments; and neither the divinity nor the humanity of Christ are changed in nature by the incarnation or the resurrection. The human body of Christ is in heaven, and his divinity is present to the faithful spiritually but not corporally.

d. Sacrament and anthropology

Richardson identifies one feature of Cranmer's distinction between the sacramental and the spiritual in that it mirrors the body/soul split: spiritual feeding is the property of faith.[102] Physical objects cannot be holy or convey holiness, and the body belongs to the physical world rather than to the spiritual. The body of Christ itself is irrelevant to the spiritual feeding, for it is in heaven, and 'unto the faithful, Christ is at his own holy table present with his mighty Spirit and grace, and is of them more fruitfully received, than if corporally they should receive him bodily present'.[103] 'In them that rightly receive the bread and wine, he is in a much more perfection than corporally, which should avail them nothing.'[104] Richardson criticizes Darwell Stone for his definition of 'virtualism', in which the recipient receives 'those effects of Christ's life and death which would be conveyed if there were a beneficial reception of his actual body and blood'. Richardson answers that 'the virtue of the sacrament is not a substitute for the presence of the actual body. Rather is it the grace and benefit that derive from the Passion; and these are of infinitely more value than the presence of the actual body ever could be.'[105] And we see this most trenchantly maintained by Cranmer himself when he says, expounding Chrysostom, 'we should not fix our thoughts and minds upon the bread, wine, priest, nor Christ's body; but to lift up our hearts higher unto his Spirit and divinity, without the which his body availeth nothing, as he saith himself: "It is the Spirit that giveth life, the flesh availeth nothing."'[106] We have already seen that the action of the recipient in feeding on Christ is a spiritual rather than a physical one; so also the body of Christ is secondary to the Spirit and without it, it is profitless.

Ridley, whose theology otherwise was effectively the same as that of Cranmer, offered a positive account of the presence of the body of Christ in the eucharist in the House of Lords' debate of December 1548:

---

102 Richardson, 'Cranmer and the Analysis of Eucharistic Doctrine', p. 427.
103 *Defence*, 4.6: PS, I, p. 219.
104 *Defence*, 3.15: PS, I, p. 183.
105 *Cranmer Dixit et Contradixit*, pp. 32–3.
106 *Defence*, 2.12: PS, I, p. 315.

The carnall Substaunce sitteth on the right hande of the father after this understanding of the presence, he is not in the sacrament. He is absent for he saythe he will leave the worlde. And in an other sense (he saith) he wilbe with us untill thend of the worlde . . . The manhood is ever in heaven his divinitie is every where present. When he was here he was *circumscriptive* in one place as touching his naturall body. *Secundum ineffabilem graciam*. I wilbe with youe till the consummacion. Christ sittes in heaven. And is present in the Sacrament by his worcking.[107]

Howe the body is present, and in whate manner. *Quia divinitas infundit se elemento*. Therefore the humane nature being in heaven may be sayde to be heare. *Non in unitate naturae sed in unitate personae*. Where the one nature is the other may be sayde to be.[108]

So Ridley proposes an alternative form of the presence of the humanity of Christ. On earth, in the incarnation, his presence was limited – *circumscriptive*. That locally limited nature of existence is not the end of the matter now that Christ's body is in heaven. By virtue of the union of the divine and the human in the one person of Christ, the humanity is said to be wherever the divine presence is, not *circumscriptive* but (rather vaguely) by ineffable grace.[109] Ridley's logic is driven by his christological motif: the divine Christ is present therefore the human Christ must be also.

4 THE SACRAMENTS AS INSTRUMENTS OF GRACE

a. Symbolic memorialism, parallelism, instrumentalism

When discussing the question of the way in which sacraments may be understood as representing or effecting the grace they signify, a useful structure has been provided by Brian Gerrish.

> We need to distinguish within the Reformed camp three conceptions of sacramental signs: symbolic memorialism, symbolic parallelism,

---

107 House of Lords' debate, C. Buchanan (ed.), *Background Documents*, p. 23.

108 House of Lords' debate, p. 29.

109 We may contrast this discussion with Richardson's comments on Cranmer. He maintains the strictly local presence of the humanity in heaven: if he had grasped the real meaning of the Fathers about the presence of Christ, 'he would have had to develop categories, as the Scholastics and Luther developed them (e.g. the *esse definitive* and *repletive*, over against the *esse circumscriptive*), for speaking of diverse modes of the presence of the body of Christ. But this he resolutely refuses to do. The body of Christ is an object only in heaven, and that is that.' 'Cranmer and the Analysis of Eucharistic Doctrine', p. 427. Here we see Ridley fumbling after a new category.

and symbolic instrumentalism. In all three the shared component
is the notion that a sign or symbol 'points to' something else. They
differ in that the reality pointed to is variously thought of as a
happening in the past, a happening that occurs simultaneously in
the present, or a present happening that is actually brought about
through the signs.[110]

Gerrish labels Zwingli as a symbolic memorialist, and attributes symbolic
parallelism to Bullinger and symbolic instrumentalism to Calvin. As we
proceed through this discussion I shall suggest that Cranmer thought of
himself as espousing an instrumentalist approach but that his theology is
really closer to symbolic parallelism.[111]

For Zwingli, the sacraments could not be vehicles of grace. However,
Cranmer insisted that they are not mere tokens: 'They be no vain or
bare tokens, as you would persuade (for a bare token is that which
betokeneth only and giveth nothing, as a painted fire, which giveth
neither light nor heat); but in the due ministration of the sacraments
God is present, working with his word and sacraments.'[112] Hall quotes
a number of passages to suggest that Cranmer believed that 'sacraments
confer grace'.[113] The particular instances are discussed in this chapter
where relevant, and it is apparent that Cranmer does not himself use
that precise term. The Archbishop prefers to speak of God, not the
sacraments, working, and it is more typical for him to say that God
works *by* his sacraments *in* those who rightly receive them. To explore
this issue further we must investigate Cranmer's use of sacramental
language and his understanding of the precise relationship between the
sacramental elements and action on the one hand, and the sacramental
grace on the other.

There is a splendidly graphic passage in which Cranmer affirms and
describes his concept of sacramental efficacy with regard to both baptism
and the eucharist.

> But in your [viz. Gardiner's] handling here of St Ambrose [re. the
> sacramental change in bread and wine], you seem to be utterly
> ignorant, and not to know difference between sacramental signs,
> in the use whereof Almighty God inwardly worketh, and other
> vain signs which be nothing else but outward shews to the eye.

---

110 B. Gerrish, *Grace and Gratitude: The Eucharistic Theology of John Calvin* (Edinburgh:
T&T Clark, 1993), p. 167.
111 MacCulloch identifies Cranmer's theology as the second of the categories. *Cranmer*,
pp. 614–15.
112 *Defence*, 1: PS, I, p. 11.
113 Hall, 'Cranmer, the Eucharist and the Foreign Divines', pp. 239–40.

For if you understand the matter, would you resemble a knave playing in a prince's coat, in whom nothing is inwardly wrought or altered, unto a man being baptized in water, who hath put upon him outwardly water, but inwardly is apparelled with Christ, and is by the omnipotent working of God spiritually regenerated and changed into a new man? Or would you compare him that banqueteth at a feast to represent an anniversary, or triumph, unto that man that in remembrance of Christ's death eateth and drinketh at his holy supper, giving thanks for his redemption, and comforting himself with the benefit thereof? . . . The marvellous alteration to an higher estate, nature, and condition, is chiefly and principally in the persons, and in the sacramental signs it is none otherwise but sacramentally and in signification.[114]

Here Cranmer specifies more closely what he means by God's working by the sacraments. The Zwinglian position is rejected: in the case of baptism it would be 'a knave playing in a prince's coat'; the eucharist cannot be compared with 'a feast to represent an anniversary, or triumph'. But the real working of God is in the person, not in the sacramental signs. This still leaves the relation between the sign and grace unclear: in Gerrish's terms, memorialism has been discounted but parallelism and instrumentalism are both possible. How are we to give substance to Cranmer's claim that the signs are themselves efficacious?

b. Promise, faith, prayer

For Cranmer, the essential element was faith. It is faith that enables the recipient of the sacrament to perceive its sacramental relationship to the grace signified. The unspiritual person is captivated by the elements themselves and does not perceive the spiritual reality to which they point. 'They be figurative rather to the faithful than to the unfaithful. For the unfaithful take them for no figure or mystery at all, but rather carnally, as the Capernaites did.'[115] Faith lifts the recipient to perceive the reality and to share in it.

The eating of Christ's flesh and drinking of his blood is not to be understand simply and plainly (as the words do properly signify), that we do eat and drink him with our mouths: but it is a figurative speech spiritually to be understand, that we must deeply print and

---

114 *Answer*, 2: PS, I, pp. 322–3.
115 *Answer*, 3: PS, I, p. 118.

fruitfully believe in our hearts, that his flesh was crucified and his blood shed for our redemption. And this our belief in him is to eat his flesh and drink his blood.[116]

To believe is to eat and drink. *Crede et manducasti*: believe and thou hast eaten – Cranmer could quote Augustine with great effect.[117] The role of the sacramental sign then is to teach and confirm what God is doing spiritually:

> The true eating and drinking of the said body and blood of Christ is, with a constant and lively faith to believe, that Christ gave his body, and shed his blood upon the cross for us . . . And this faith God worketh inwardly in our hearts by his holy Spirit, and confirmeth the same outwardly to our ears by hearing of his word, and to our other senses by eating and drinking of the sacramental bread and wine in his holy supper.[118]

This is much closer to symbolic parallelism than to instrumentalism.

It is easy to present Cranmer's theology of the sacraments in a 'nothing but' mode: to say that they are nothing more than prayer or faith. Thus Richardson says that 'sacraments *teach*, while incarnation and redemption (with the corresponding faith in them) are what *effects*'.[119] However, like other aspects of his theology which appear to be negative because they are expressed in a polemical context, it is perhaps better to see this as a positive relation, as faith effecting a real relationship between the sacrament and the grace. Faith, as Timms emphasized, is not a mere mental activity, but is a whole-hearted commitment of the self to God.[120] It includes praise, thanksgiving, and prayer. It is the faith of the recipient which makes the sacrament to be an efficacious sign. That is clear in the case of the eucharist. In the instance of adult baptism it cannot go unqualified since, as in the instance of Cornelius, to request baptism in faith, one must be already the recipient of justifying grace and therefore already be spiritually regenerate. Nevertheless, baptism would still represent and celebrate the individual's spiritual rebirth and faith. And in the case of infants, the recipient has not yet come to faith, and we are not told whether an individual candidate has experienced the hidden working of the Holy Spirit. But Cranmer refuses to skirt round

---

116 *Defence*, 3.10: PS, I, pp. 115–16.
117 *Answer*, 3: PS, I, p. 118.
118 *Defence*, 1.16: PS, I, p. 43.
119 Richardson, 'Cranmer and the Analysis of Eucharistic Doctrine', p. 431.
120 'Dixit Cranmer', part 1, pp. 223, 227.

the issue. Here we can turn to his discussion of sacraments being called by the name of what they signify. Cranmer quotes Augustine himself:

> For their similitude and likeness, commonly they have the name of the things, whereof they be sacraments. Therefore, as after a certain manner of speech the sacrament of Christ's body is Christ's body, the sacrament of Christ's blood is Christ's blood; so likewise the sacrament of faith is faith. And to believe is nothing else but to have faith; and therefore when we answer for young children in their baptism, that they believe, which have not yet the mind to believe, we answer that they have faith, because they have the sacrament of faith. And we say also that they turn unto God, because of the sacrament of conversion unto God; for that answer pertaineth to the celebration of the sacrament. And likewise speaketh the apostle of baptism, saying, that 'by baptism we be buried with him into death'; he saith not that we signify burial, but he saith plainly, that we be buried. So that the sacrament of so great a thing is not called but by the name of the thing itself.[121]

And in answer Cranmer explains: to the question of how one can answer for a baby in baptism that he believes and turns to God,

> the answer of St Augustine is this: that forasmuch as baptism is the sacrament of the profession of our faith, and of our conversion unto God, it becometh us so to answer for young children coming thereunto, as to the sacrament appertaineth, although the children in deed have no knowledge of such things.[122]

Therefore it is entirely appropriate in Cranmer's baptismal liturgy to include a sacramental expression of the candidate's profession of faith, spoken by the godparents, even though the infant is unconscious of what is happening.

In *Answer*, 3, Cranmer outlines the distinctiveness of the promise of God which differentiates the sacrament from other signs:

> Although the sacramental tokens be only significations and figures, yet doth Almighty God effectually work in them that duly receive his sacraments, those divine and celestial operations which he hath promised, and by the sacraments be signified. For else they

---

121 *Defence*, 3.11, quoting Augustine, *Epistula 23 ad Bonifacium de Baptismo parvulorum* (*Ep.* 98): PS, I, p. 124.
122 *Defence*, 3.11: PS, I, pp. 124–5.

were vain and unfruitful sacraments, as well to the godly as to the ungodly.[123]

The theme of the promise of God is more prominent in the baptism service, and so too is that of prayer in response to God's promise and command. Hence the faith and prayer of the congregation is an important element in the dynamic of the baptismal rite. Indeed, it is this element above all which affirms the sacramental efficacy of baptism, that Cranmer's sacraments are no 'mere tokens'. And if the baptism service spoke only sacramentally of the candidate's profession of faith, and admitted the infant's actual ignorance and lack of faith, then the sacrament could only signify the general message of salvation directed towards the child but in no way appropriated by it. The faith of the congregation expressed in prayer for the child enables, as it were, the grace of the sacrament to be effective, for it is the only real engagement with the promise of God offered in word and sacrament. This faith is not vicarious in the sense that it supplies the assent of the candidate in the affirmations; rather, as the exhortations make clear, it is our own faith and trust in God which leads us to pray for grace for the child.

This role of the faith of the congregation is similar to Bucer's stress on the faith of the Church in *Quid de baptismate . . . est sentiendum*. For Bucer the response of the Church to baptize infants is one of faith in God's promise and a commitment that the children themselves will belong to the same faith.[124] It is this faith of the community that is more evident than any notion of the individual faith of the child. Later, quoting Bede with evident agreement about the case of infants who 'have no knowledge in themselves and cannot do anything good or evil', he places the onus of belief on the parents or the Church.

When parents have faith in this promise [that God will be the God of his people to a thousand generations] God causes them to believe even as he has promised. Thus the children receive salvation, but only by the gift of God and by the merit and work of Christ alone, but all of this is given to the faith of the parents. And if the parents should believe nothing and be hypocrites, the Church believes, and the children more properly belong to her than to the parents.[125]

---

123 *Answer*, 3: PS, I, p. 148.
124 'Ecclesia ista promissione confisa, non minus testari debet se ei habere fidem et offerentium Domino liberos pronunciare in fide Dei fore et benedictionis Christi esse participes.' *Quid de baptismate infantium . . . est sentiendum* (Strasbourg: ex aedibus M. Apiarii, 1533), sig. B1ᵛ.
125 *Quid de baptismate*, sig. E7 (author's trans.).

Wright maintains that this appeal from the faith of the parents to that of the Church is not a common one in Bucer.[126] But however infrequent it may be, it is an important one in this particular work, for in the earlier passage we hear of the faith of the Church in the covenant promises of God.

The faith of the congregation was also a major theme in the Strasbourg baptismal rites. That of 1525–30 has an introductory exhortation which stresses that Christ answers prayer, and so the congregation is bidden to pray that the child being baptized may be given faith 'which is a gift of grace', and that God will baptize the child with water and the Holy Spirit. After the Lord's Prayer and the Creed, a prayer asks that the child may be given faith and sealed and confirmed with the Holy Spirit 'so that thy inward renewal and the regeneration of the Spirit may truly be signified by this our baptism'. Then after the gospel of Jesus and the children, the minister exhorts the congregation, 'Believe these words and pray that this infant also shall be one of these and that the kingdom of heaven shall be his, and that he may truly have from God the gift of faith, through which he may be a child of God and a fellow heir of Christ.' Then the baptism follows as 'the sign of faith'.[127] The Strasbourg Order after 1537 does not ask for the gift of faith for the child, it merely invokes the Holy Spirit for the effectual ministration of the sacrament. At the same time it puts special stress on the congregation's faith. A prayer invoking the God of Abraham, the God of the covenant, says:

> Grant, O heavenly Father, that we may truly and with our whole heart desire to lay hold on this thy grace and the redemption of thy Son for this child with true faith, and may not doubt that, as we baptize him in thy name, as we now by thy grace purpose to do, thou wilt entirely forgive him his inborn sin through our Lord Jesus . . . In this faith, O heavenly Father, grant that we may baptize this infant . . .[128]

The faith in which the child is baptized is not its own, but that of the parents and godparents, and indeed the congregation. And again the reading of Jesus and the children is included in the rite 'in order that our

---

126 Wright, 'Infant Baptism and the Christian Community', p. 103.

127 Fisher, *Christian Initiation*, p. 36. F. Hubert, *Die Strassburger Liturgischen Ordnungen in Zeitalter der Reformation* (Göttingen: Vandenhoek & Ruprecht, 1900), p. 42. Hubert also notes an edition of the service in which 'gift of faith' is emended to 'gift of the Holy Spirit'.

128 Fisher, *Christian Initiation*, p. 40; Hubert, *Die Strassburger Liturgischen Ordnungen*, p. 48.

faith may with greater consolation see, recognize and perceive the work of the Lord in this holy sacrament'.[129]

It may well be the case that Bucer's writings and the Strasbourg liturgies were influential on Cranmer for the role of the congregation's faith in the performance of baptism and the understanding of it as an efficacious sign. But that must not disguise the difference between the two reformers over the matter of the candidate's profession of faith. In the *Censura*, Bucer has no sympathy whatsoever with the godparents' statements, likening them to the practice reported of the Marcionites, who were meant to have baptized their dead, with the ritual answers being supplied by someone hidden under the bed. Bucer wishes the question to the godparents to be about an undertaking that the child will learn the faith and proclaim it in due course.[130] This is an instance where Cranmer ignored the advice, and with good reason. His theology of baptism is different in this respect, and to have omitted the profession of faith would have torn an essential element out of the heart of the rite.

In later literature much has been made of the question of the faith of the godparents and, in the twentieth century, of the parents also, since they too stand as sponsors. It is beyond the scope of this book to consider the later arguments, but it is pertinent to ask whether the notion of the importance of the personal faith of the godparents would be a correct reading of Cranmer's liturgy. If this study is correct, the profession made by the godparents signifies that of the candidate, and in that respect it could properly be said to be a vicarious act. It might also be said, in the words of Robert Wilberforce, that 'that which a proxy can effect for an infant is not the prognostication of his uncertain will, but the confession of his unquestionable duty'.[131] However Cranmer's presentation of baptism as being 'the sacrament of the profession of our faith' suggests very strongly that the godparents' role is purely significatory. In the commentary on the baptism service in Chapter 6 below, it will be seen that the part which is presented as efficacious – the trust in Christ's promises and the prayer for the child that it will receive God's grace – is the role of the entire congregation. The godparents stand as sureties for the infants and are their guides for the future, but for the grace of the sacrament it is no evasion to appeal from the faithlessness of parents or godparents to the faith of the Church. In Cranmer's baptism service itself the only distinctive role of the godparents is to perform a

---

129 Fisher, *Christian Initiation*, p. 40; Hubert, *Die Strassburger Liturgischen Ordnungen*, p. 49.
130 *Censura*, in Whitaker (ed.), *Bucer*, pp. 94–7.
131 R.I. Wilberforce, *The Doctrine of Holy Baptism* (London: John Murray, 1849), p. 105.

sign, which must not be confused with the reality, and it is the prayer of the congregation that invokes the reality of grace to which the sign points.

c. The dispute with Martyr

We must now move to a discussion about infant baptism in which there was an actual clash between Martyr and the English bishops. Martyr's own position is made clear in his letter to Bullinger:

> But in respect of children, while they are baptized, since on account of their age they cannot have that assent to the divine promises which is faith, in them the sacrament effects this, that pardon of original sin, reconciliation with God, and the grace of the Holy Spirit, bestowed on them through Christ, is sealed in them, and that those belonging already to the church are also visibly ingrafted in it. Although even to those that are baptized, whether little children or adults, it is not to be denied that much advantage and profit come to them from the invocation of the Father, the Son, and the Holy Spirit, which takes place over them: for God never fails to hear the faithful prayers of his church.
>
> We should have wished that these things had been determined and decreed concerning the sacraments, in order that their pure and simple use might at length be restored. But it was exclaimed against: and many will have it, and those otherwise not unlearned nor evil, that grace is conferred, as they say, by the sacraments. Nor are they willing to grant that little children are justified or regenerated before baptism . . . No little displeasure is stirred up against us on this account, that we altogether dissent from Augustine.[132]

Martyr goes on to accuse the bishops of clinging to works-based righteousness, but we may discount that here as mere polemic. What we must consider is the substance of the theological argument between fellow-Reformers. Martyr would wish to have it that children when baptized have grace sealed in them and, being already members of the Church, they are visibly grafted into it. We have here evidence of Martyr's emphasis on the priority of faith (as a gift endowed by God)

---

132 Martyr to Bullinger, 14 June 1552, in A. Townsend (ed.), *Writings of Bradford*, PS, 2 vols (Cambridge: Cambridge University Press, 1848 and 1853), Vol. 2, pp. 404–5; also in Gorham, *Gleanings*, p. 282; Hall, 'Cranmer, the Eucharist and the Foreign Divines', p. 244 quotes this letter but not in full.

and the theology of election, which leaves no room for any work by the sacraments save that of 'sealing'. The advantage of the invocation of the Trinity over the baptismal candidates seems to have no more specific content than generally praying for them.

McLelland quotes and discusses this same passage in *The Visible Works of God*, and offers a fuller account of the Reformer's position: Martyr appeals to the example of Abraham, who was justified by faith before circumcision, which functioned as a seal of what is already received. Baptism fulfils exactly the same function: it is the seal of the faith already placed in our hearts by God.[133] Martyr includes a future reference in that baptism is bound up with growth into the likeness of Christ and 'into a future regeneration'. But McLelland warns us to keep the past reference of the prior justification.[134]

As we turn to consider his opponents, we must exercise some care in ascertaining precisely what the issues were.[135] First, who are Martyr's opponents here? He accepts that they include men who were otherwise not unlearned or evil, so it is not a matter of another battle with the traditionalists; rather, he has fallen out with those he expected to be his allies. Also, the decision against him was to be framed in the theology of the baptism service in the revised Prayer Book that he is criticizing in the letter. So on both counts it is quite possible, and even likely, that Cranmer is among those being attacked by Martyr.[136]

Martyr's first charge against his opponents, that they believe that grace is conferred by the sacraments, tells us little or nothing. This could refer to the traditionalist position (but this is hardly likely in 1552); more probably, it is a biased account of the notion that God uses his sacraments as 'instruments' of grace. However it is not at all clear that Cranmer would have disagreed with the first of Martyr's arguments against the idea that sacraments 'confer' grace, namely,

---

133 J.C. McLelland, *The Visible Words of God: An Exposition of the Sacramental Theology of Peter Martyr Vermigli* (Edinburgh: Oliver & Boyd, 1957), p. 148.
134 *Visible Words of God*, pp. 157–8.
135 Hall, 'Cranmer, the Eucharist and the Foreign Divines', p. 231, raises another case, in the Preface of the *Tractatio de Sacramento Eucharistiae* (1549), in which he says that Martyr attacks Cranmer. He quotes the passage in question: 'Now let me say a little (for your satisfaction) about Christ's body since you so greatly dislike my denial of its Presence . . . why do you deny that we are truly joined to him without any real or corporeal Presence? And if you do not deny it, why do you insist on urging this Presence?' However, it is evident from consulting the Latin original (p. 8 of the Preface) that at this point Martyr is not speaking to the Archbishop (whom he elsewhere addresses as *tu*), but to his Oxford opponents, the *martyromastiges*, whom he addresses here as *vos*. Therefore this passage tells us nothing of Cranmer's theology.
136 MacCulloch, *Cranmer*, p. 520 disagrees, seeing Martyr's opponents as possibly Goodrich and Ridley.

that it is appropriated by faith. The second criticism, that he connects their beliefs with Augustine and with a refusal to allow that children are justified or regenerated before baptism, gives us something slightly more substantial. Martyr was holding out for what he believed to be the logical position against sacraments conferring grace (both the role of faith in receiving the sacrament and its temporal priority to it), and anyone who disagreed with either proposition is accused of agreeing with the contrary position. Anything that smacked of fence-sitting was disallowed. However, Cranmer and his allies were not to be browbeaten in this manner. They had their own position, based on Augustine, which they believed enabled them to talk about regeneration and justification being linked with the administration of baptism. For corroboration we can search the writings of Martyr and Cranmer for their attitudes to Augustine's views on the baptism of infants, and it will be seen that they hold opposing points of view similar enough to the positions that Martyr describes in his account of the dispute.

In Martyr's treatment of Augustine we see two different issues arising. The first can be seen in a letter to Bucer dated 31 August 1550, where Martyr complains that 'Augustine tied the grace of God more than is right to the external Sacrament, which, howsoever it may please him, does not satisfy me. Sometimes, indeed, he acknowledges the baptism of martyrdom; if, by reason of the shortness of time, water cannot be procured; and he seems to make no other exception.'[137] We find another complaint to the same effect, against Augustine's doctrine of the absolute necessity of baptism for salvation, in Martyr's *Commonplaces*. The Reformer maintains that we are under a general obligation to baptize, but failure to do so becomes damnable only when the unbaptized infant grows up and maintains the contempt for God's sacraments. We cannot be condemned for our parents' neglect.[138]

While such a complaint could have been made against the 1549 Prayer Book, that it taught the absolute necessity of baptism, it is hard to maintain the same accusation against the 1552 Book when the earlier rubric that in case of necessity childen ought to be baptized is softened to 'may at all times be baptized'. Strictly speaking, Martyr has no cause for complaint, though he would have looked askance at the provision of even optional emergency baptism. And so we turn to the second of Martyr's complaints against the teaching of Augustine in his later *Commonplaces*, that children are saved by another person's faith. For

---

137 Gorham, *Gleanings*, p. 172.
138 P. Martyr, *The Commonplaces of the most famous and renowned divine doctor Peter Martyr*, trans. A. Marten (London: Henry Denham, 1583), 4.8.18, p. 121.

the Reformer, it is essential that we are saved by our own faith, and in the case of infants by the Holy Spirit who is the root of faith.

> But the cause why our adversaries are so loath to allow of this opinion, is for that they attribute unto the sacraments more than they ought to do. For they think that by the power and efficacy of the work of baptism, sin is forgiven. Neither do they acknowledge that by the sacraments forgiveness is rather sealed, which they of perfect age obtain by believing, and the young children of the faithful, which belong unto election, have it already by the Holy Ghost and by grace. When thou shalt demand of them, wherefore they baptize infants, knowing that they perceive not those things which are spoken, nor yet do consent unto the covenant which is pronounced to them in baptism, perhaps they will answer according to the opinion of Augustine, that they be saved by other men's faith, that is, by the faith of their parents. But the prophet saith [Hab. 2.4] that everyone is saved by his own faith and not by another man's. Wherefore we may more fitly make answer that as touching them which be of ripe age we require a faith expressed and in act, but in the young children of Christians which are offered to be baptized, we say, that the same is begun. I mean in their beginning and root, because they have the Holy Ghost, from whence as well faith as all other virtues do flow.[139]

This point underlies the position Martyr was seeking to argue with the Prayer Book revisers as reported in his letter to Bullinger. If the children already have faith or the Holy Spirit as its equivalent (which they require for the sacrament to be efficacious), then they are already regenerate.

And here we return to the passage of Cranmer quoted above about sacraments being called by the name of what they signify. After quoting Augustine to the effect that 'the sacrament of faith is faith', Cranmer adds, 'forasmuch as baptism is the sacrament of the profession of our faith, and of our conversion unto God, it becometh us so to answer for young children coming thereunto, as to the sacrament appertaineth, although the children in deed have no knowledge of such things'.[140] Cranmer uses the quotation to explain the principle of sacramental figurative language. His own paraphrase of Augustine after a lengthy quotation suggests most strongly that he wholeheartedly agrees with him both on the general principle and on the specific instance of the ascription of faith to infants. But he has included also the instance of baptism being

---

139 *Commonplaces of Peter Martyr*, 4.8.15, p. 120.
140 *Defence*, 3.11: PS, pp. 124–5.

the sacrament of conversion, and we could fairly include Augustine's third example, that of burial with Christ in his death; indeed, on this principle, it is hard to see what grace of regeneration or justification could be excluded from the sacramental signification of baptism. And so the Archbishop's views were of this kind: that sacramental baptism is the sign of spiritual regeneration, baptism by the Holy Spirit, and must not be equated with it. Spiritual regeneration is effected by God's election, and therefore faith as a mental act is not required as a prerequisite. Spiritual regeneration and the work of the Holy Spirit may occur with, before, or after sacramental baptism. Martyr, with his emphasis on the prior need for faith or some equivalent work of the Holy Spirit, and therefore supposing that children must already be regenerate before baptism, portrays the bishops as linking regeneration too closely to baptism. He therefore accuses them (fairly) of following Augustine and (not fairly) of holding that sacraments confer grace.[141]

It must be admitted that there is an element of speculation here, for we are putting together arguments from different contexts and have not the slightest evidence that Cranmer quoted this passage to Martyr. Indeed, we can only presume that Cranmer is included in the latter's attack on the bishops (though as it is by no means unreasonable). But a consistent picture emerges from Cranmer's *Defence* and *Answer*, along with Martyr's acid comments on the revision of the Prayer Book (to say nothing of the liturgy itself).

e. Cranmer and speech acts

Just as the model of the sun and its rays was invoked by some theologians as an analogy for models of the eucharistic presence of Christ, so Peter Martyr used the analogy of speech acts as a model to explain sacramental efficacy:

> Amonge all earthely things I finde no better likenesses then those which I rehersed before. The scepter of the kinge that is crowned

---

141 Another piece of evidence raised by Hall ('Cranmer, the Eucharist and the Foreign Divines', p. 238) is Hooper's dispute with the Council over the Articles he was required to sign when he was appointed Bishop of Gloucester. Most attention is focused on the vestment controversy, but Micronius also reports that he took exception to the statement in the Articles that the sacraments confer grace. Hooper wished to say that they 'seal or testify to' grace instead (PS, *Original Letters*, II, p. 563). This objection, in May 1550, is somewhat surprising since Hooper himself had expressed great satisfaction with the Articles that Cranmer had drawn up at the end of 1549 (PS, *Original Letters*, pp. 71–2, 76). We do not possess any copy of these Articles, which makes any detailed comment extremely difficult.

doth betoken his kingdom and when it is geven him accordingly
into his handes ther is certeynly a kingdom delyverde him. By the
keyes also and the ringe and givinge of handes ther is not only the
possession of the house, true maryage, faith and truth betokened
as evident tokens, but also they be geven in deade and are not to
be thought emptie and voyde signes. And it may be proved that
this coplinge ought to be called sacramentall or holy tokende that
the Lorde when he ordeyned his soper did ordeyne as every man
generally calleth it the sacrament or holy token.[142]

But this does not necessarily imply an automatic conferral of the grace
by the instrumentality of the sacrament. The disposition of the recipient,
as we have already seen, is all important. In the light of what he says
about the need of the recipient of the sacrament to understand the
meaning of a language or a seal, we could apply to this instance Austin's
discussion of speech acts, in which a speech act can only operate within
certain agreed conventions.[143] The unfaithful recipient would receive
only the tokens and remain unaware of their significance, and the result
would be fruitless.

While Martyr (among others) was fond of invoking coronations,
Cranmer, who had the advantage of actually having performed the rite
on Henry's second wife and his son, had a minimalist understanding of
its function. In his speech at the coronation of King Edward VI he says:

The bishops of Canterbury for the most part have crowned your
predecessors, and anointed them kings of this land: yet it was not
in their power to receive or reject them, neither did it give them
authority to prescribe them conditions to take or to leave their
crowns . . .

The solemn rites of coronation have their ends and utility, yet
neither direct force or necessity: they be good admonitions to put
kings in mind of their duty to God, but no increasement of their
dignity. For they be God's anointed, not in respect of the oil which
the bishop useth, but in consideration of their power which is
ordained, of the sword which is authorised, of their persons which
are elected by God, and endued with the gifts of his Spirit for the
better ruling and guiding of his people.[144]

---

142 *Sacrament of Thankesgeving*, fols 33–33ᵛ.
143 J.L. Austin, *How to do Things with Words*, 2nd edn (Oxford: Oxford University Press, 1980), p. 14.
144 Speech at the Coronation of Edward VI, PS, II, p. 126.

Two issues are being argued here. The first is that the ceremony has no efficacy in itself: the election of the king has already been performed by God himself. The second, though logically necessary from the first, is also spelt out in great detail, that the Church and especially the papacy have no right or ability to refuse or set conditions on the coronation. The same principles are set out by Cranmer some seven years earlier, in the Questions and Answers concerning the Sacraments, 1540. Having stated in his answer to Question 9, that clergy are normally appointed by the monarch in the same way as civil ministers, he says:

> In the admission of many of these officers be divers comely ceremonies and solemnities used, which be not of necessity, but only for a good order and seemly fashion: for if such offices and ministrations were committed without such solemnity, they were nevertheless truly committed. And there is no more promise of God, that grace is given in the committing of the ecclesiastical office, than it is in the committing of the civil office.
> *Question 12.* Whether in the New Testament be required any consecration of a bishop and priest, or only appointing to the office be sufficient?
> *Answer*: In the New Testament, he that is appointed to be a bishop or a priest, needeth no consecration by the scripture; for election or appointing thereto is sufficient.[145]

Speech acts, then, seem to be the wrong way of understanding the sacraments as far as Cranmer was concerned. They link the grace too closely with the action and with the minister. That link can only be made in the private world of the individual's relationship with God.

f. Covenant theology: the 'Croydon Commentary'

Until recently the only suggestion that Cranmer had any interest at all in covenant theology has been in the *Confutation of Unwritten Verities*, an anonymous work probably based on his commonplaces but not a reliable authority for his views. The baptismal liturgy in both Prayer Books is silent on the covenant, even when sources use the theme, and it could be safely concluded that Cranmer avoided covenant theology in his liturgical writing just as he was silent on it in his theological works. However, we face a challenge to this picture in the so-called Croydon

---

145 Questions and Answers concerning the Sacraments and the Appointment and Power of Bishops and Priest, PS, II, pp. 116–17.

Commentary on Matthew, to be found in Corpus Christi Library, Cambridge (MS 104). A title in Cranmer's hand attributes it to Bucer, but the editor, Herbert Vogt, uses the evidence of the various hands and in particular corrections in Cranmer's own hand to suggest that the Archbishop was responsible for writing the commentary on Chapters 1–3.[146] In addition to Vogt's work, Ashley Null directs our attention to further pp. 211–14 in the manuscript which, he believes, belong to the Commentary. They contain a discussion of 'The baptism of John and Christ', certainly discussing Matthew Ch. 3, and would fit well under the heading *Loci communes huius capitis tertii*, which at present introduces only a single *locus*, that of 'The Kingdom of Heaven'.[147] The second *locus* discusses the relation of John's baptism to that of Christ and the role of infant baptism.

Ascription of authorship is not an easy matter. The corrections in Cranmer's own hand are important evidence for his close collaboration in the project, but it cannot be ignored that one of Cranmer's own annotations ascribes the work to Bucer. Perhaps the commentary, even that on Chapters 1–3, should be regarded as one in which Cranmer had a share rather than sole authorship. But if we were to follow Vogt and Null in ascribing these various pages wholly to Cranmer, do they affect our earlier impression of his use of covenant theology?

At first sight the Croydon Commentary (using this term with particular reference to the passages ascribed to Cranmer) might suggest that the author was an exponent of covenant theology and should be included with Reformers such as Bucer, Calvin, Martyr, Laski, Bullinger and Zwingli.[148] However, a closer reading of the commentary leads us to ask what sort of covenant theology is being espoused.

Covenant theology exists under myriad forms, and not all of the versions apply to our consideration of baptism now. But with regard to the use of covenant theology as a justification of the baptism of infants, the forms could be briefly distinguished as follows:

---

146 H. Vogt (ed.), *Martin Bucer und Thomas Cranmer: Annotationes in Octo Priora Capita Evangelii secundum Matthaeum, Croydon 1549* (Frankfurt: Athenäum, 1972).

147 CCCC, MS 104, p. 32; Vogt (ed.), *Annotationes*, p. 45; Null, *Repentance*, p. 277.

148 For covenant theology and baptism, see J.G. Møller, 'The Beginnings of Puritan Covenant Theology', *JEH* 14 (1963), pp. 46–67; R.L. Greaves, 'John Knox and the Covenant Tradition', *JEH* 24 (1973), pp. 23–32; J.B. Torrance, 'Covenant or Contract?', *SJT*, 23 (1970), pp. 51–76; B.D. Spinks, 'Calvin's Baptismal Theology and the Making of the Strasbourg and Genevan Baptismal Liturgies 1540 and 1542', *SJT* 48 (1995), pp. 55–78; B.D. Spinks, 'Luther's Timely Theology of Unilateral Baptism', *Lutheran Quarterly*, 9 (1995), pp. 23–45; D.A. Weir, *The Origins of Federal Theology in Sixteenth-Century Reformation Thought* (Oxford: Clarendon Press, 1990).

1. The argument by deduction from the circumcision of infants in the Old Testament applied simply one step further, to God's promise to Abraham that he is the God of his children, and a presumption that baptism accords with circumcision, with the qualification of children being extended to the Gentiles. As will be seen below, Luther includes covenant theology in his justification of infant baptism, and it would best fit with this description.

2. The theology of the covenant implying an agreement between the parties, with God making an undertaking which sets certain obligations on his people. This may become the guiding principle of a systematic theology of God's grace in the Old and New Testaments such as we see in Calvin, Bullinger and others. There is a further issue here as to unilateral and bilateral covenants according to the emphases of the particular theologian.

The first instance above is likely to have little or no influence on the baptismal liturgy. The use of one more defence (among many others) of infant baptism against a minority Anabaptist attack is not going to require its insertion into the national liturgy. On the other hand, the use of the theology of covenant as a principle of the theological understanding of scripture and the Church is likely to become likewise the hermeneutic principle of the baptismal liturgy. The understanding of a unilateral or bilateral covenant will also have its influence on the liturgy, in particular on the role of the baptismal affirmations.

Furthermore, a distinction can be made about the role of baptism under the covenant:

a. The child may by birth within the community simply be an appropriate candidate for baptism which, according to the particular sacramental theology, communicates the grace of God.

Luther and Calvin in their different ways apply sacramental efficacy to baptism. Calvin's language varies in his baptismal rite but we hear that 'All these graces are conferred on us, when it pleases [God] to incorporate us in his church by baptism.'[149]

b. Grace may be granted by virtue of the child's birth within the community of grace and simply sealed or attested by baptism.

---

149 *Form of Prayers*, Fisher, *Christian Initiation*, p. 114.

We see this in Bullinger.[150] Laski also justifies the baptism of infants by
an appeal to covenant theology,[151] and affirms that we are reconciled to
God before baptism, and baptism bears witness to this reconciliation.
This is made clear in his discussion of Jesus and the children:

> The Lord Christ said about unbaptized children that the kingdom
> of heaven belongs to such as these, and when he took them in his
> arms (without any mention of baptism in the meantime) he blessed
> them, so that we may understand that we are not offered to Christ
> in baptism, but rather that it is declared that we all belong to him
> after our weakness has been transferred to him, if we do not disdain
> his generosity. Thus baptism corresponds to its aim for which it was
> instituted, namely that it should be the seal of the divine goodwill
> towards us.[152]

This approach is seen clearly in John Knox's *Order of Baptism*
where the minister says: 'Our infants appertain to [God] by covenant
and therefore ought not to be defrauded of those holy signs and badges
whereby his children are known from infidels and pagans.'[153] But the
clearest example is perhaps in the later *Westminster Directory* when
the minister instructs the congregation to the effect that 'the seed and
posterity of the faithful, born within the Church, have, by their birth,
interest in the Covenant, and right to the seal of it', and that 'they are
Christians, and federally holy before baptism, and therefore are they
baptized'.[154]

Such, very simply, are the versions of covenant theology which must
be considered. It will be suggested that, if he is indeed the author,
Cranmer's use of the idea is essentially similar to that of Luther, namely
that he uses it as a defence of infant baptism but takes it no further in his
theology. Children within the Christian community are by God's promise
suitable candidates for baptism.

Luther's use of covenant theology has been outlined by Bryan Spinks
and Jonathan Trigg. The latter draws our attention to the *Lectures on
Genesis* where the reformer sets out the basic analogy of circumcision to
baptism:

---

150 Decade, 5.7: PS, pp. 312–13, 343–5.
151 *Epitome*, §16; Kuyper, *Opera*, Vol. 1, pp. 520–30.
152 *Epitome*, §15; Kuyper, *Opera*, Vol. 1, p. 519 (author's trans.).
153 Fisher, *Christian Initiation*, p. 120.
154 I. Breward, ed., *Westminster Directory*, Grove Liturgical Studies, 21 (Bramcote: Grove
Books, 1980), pp. 19–20.

If [inclusion in the kingdom, justification] was brought about with the Jews in the Old Testament through the medium of circumcision, why would God not do the same thing with the Gentiles through the medium of the new covenant (*novo pacto*) of baptism? The command pertains to all (*praeceptum universale est*): 'Go therefore and make disciples of all nations, baptizing them . . .' Hence whereas circumcision was commanded only to the descendants of Abraham, baptism is commanded to all the nations, with the promise of salvation if they believe.[155]

Trigg points out that the argument from circumcision is joined with that of the faith of the infants and of *fides aliena*, both hallmarks of Luther's defence of infant baptism, but it is still distinct from them. It is God's command to baptize that is now universal, whereas the command to circumcise had been limited to the children of the Jews.[156] Spinks is concerned to make a clear distinction between Luther and any sense of a bilateral covenant, and he shows how *testament* for Luther was to be understood as God's work entirely: in the early commentary on Galatians, *pactum, testamentum*, and *promissiones* all have the same meaning, and in the *Treatise on New Testament* the word *testament* is defined as God's gift to us. He concludes: 'Thus covenant is explained as God's promise to be present in the sacraments which are signs of justification. The human response is to trust that the covenant is indeed unilateral.'[157]

The relevance of Luther's approach is clear when we notice that in chapters 1 to 3 the Croydon Commentary nowhere speaks of covenant (*foedus, pactum*) but only of God's promise. So although it refers to the standard phrases of God being the God of the patriarchs and of their children, and of the unity of baptism and circumcision, these are in the context of promise, rather than of covenant. It is hard to see how this distinction can have been anything but deliberate, especially when the beginning of the commentary (written, says Vogt, by Bucer) discusses *testamentum* as covenant (*foedus*).

The two *loci* in the Commentary make much of the theme of promise: as well as the one we have seen, that God will be the God of the patriarchs and their children, the first *locus* also discusses a divine promise concerning the kingdom of heaven.

---

155 *WA*, 42, 622, 19–25 = *LW*, 3, p. 104; quoted by J. Trigg, *Baptism in the Theology of Martin Luther* (Leiden: E.J. Brill, 1994), p. 105. The same argument can be found, e.g., in *Concerning Rebaptism*, *LW*, 40, pp. 244–5.
156 Trigg, *Baptism in the Theology of Martin Luther*, p. 105.
157 Spinks, 'Luther's Timely Theology', p. 32.

This kingdom was given to the ancient people, and it flourished among all those who received this promise of God with true faith: 'And you will be to me a royal priesthood and a holy nation.' Indeed it existed and flourished before Christ was glorified, however among the nation of Israel alone, and without the extent of its revelation and power; and after his glorification it held sway among the nations throughout the world, and it was taken away from the ancient people, the children of the kingdom, because of their obstinate rejection of this kingdom.[158]

The treatment of the promise of the kingdom of heaven is similar to that of the promise which was sealed by circumcision or baptism: after the glorification of Christ, it was 'more richly poured out on the whole human race'. Indeed, even the baptism of John in this text undergoes a similar process.

In the baptismal liturgy Cranmer makes nothing of the Old Testament promises. There are a number of references to the kingdom of heaven, largely focused on the gospel reading, and in this respect not going beyond Cranmer's sources (except in the 1552 version of the Flood prayer, which now ends 'that finally they maye come to the lande of everlasting lyfe, there to reygne with thee, worlde without ende'.) The final thanksgiving prayer ends by praying that the child 'may be an inheritor of thine everlasting kingdom'. But the theme of the promise is centred exclusively on Christ, where again Cranmer does not go beyond his sources but rather focuses on what they say with greater clarity: 'Ye have heard also that our Lorde Jesus Christe hath promysed in his gospel, to graunte all these thynges that ye have prayed for: whiche promyse he for his parte, will moste suerly kepe and perfourme. Wherfore, after this promyse made by Christe, these infantes muste also faythfully for theyr parte promise by you, that be theyr sureties . . .' This paragraph is the closest Cranmer will move to covenant theology. There is no agreement with God. His promises are faithful and evoke a response.

We might also note a passage earlier in the Commentary, where the author might seem to part company with at least some followers of covenant theology: 'At this point, turn your mind, you whoever wish to

---

158 Hoc regnum datum fuit veteri populo, viguitque in omnibus iis, quicumque hanc dei promissionem vera fide, receperunt, *Et vos eritis mihi regium sacerdotium, et gens sancta.* Verum extitit et viguit ante Christum glorificatum, tantum in sola gente Israelis, neque tam revelate et potenter, atque post eius glorificationem obtinuit per universum orbem in gentibus, et est a veteri populo, filiis regni propter obstinatam regni huius reiectionem ablatum. (CCCC, MS 104, p. 34; Vogt, *Annotationes*, p. 46)

seek God and learn what amount or of [what] capacity there be in us: I will not speak of a preparation to faith in Christ in our nature; whoever is from Adam, we are born with as much as there is in stones, that they may be sons of Abraham and, consequently, sons of God.'[159]

This is a comment on Mt. 3.9. But the form of the comment could offer a connection with Cranmer and possibly shed light on his rejection of covenant theology. The rejection of any preparation to faith is shown by Null to be an important feature of the development of Cranmer's thought on justification, where he argues against the understanding propounded by John Fisher and others and enshrined in the King's Book. It is against this view of grace that the Article 'Of Works before Justification' is directed. The Archbishop had struggled hard to maintain the understanding of salvation as by God's grace alone, and we may see in the Croydon Commentary evidence that he was still aware of the danger of 'a preparation to faith' against which he maintained firmly that 'we are born with as much as there is in stones, so that they may be sons of Abraham and, consequently, sons of God'. As a result Cranmer may well have been resistant to any idea of a relationship of a child to God by virtue of its birth to believing parents.

Whatever the nature of Cranmer's part in the writing of the Croydon Commentary, it does not affect our picture of his rejection of covenant theology as used by some other Reformers in their baptismal theology and liturgy.

f. Sacramental signification and instrumentality

Why is it that Cranmer seems to emphasize the distinction between the sacrament and the reality when many of his fellow Reformers, like Bucer and Martyr, are so concerned to establish the relationship? In part at least the answer must be that for Cranmer the distinction was one which needed to be taught to a Church still wedded to the traditional sacramental theology. Almost any reformer's book in this period seems to give a disproportionate amount to polemic. Perhaps also the distinction is a notion Cranmer is still coming to grips with. But it needs to be asked, what are the losses and gains of his approach? He rejects the vocabulary of exhibition, he thinks of the sacraments as signs rather than seals of God's grace, he chooses the language of the three modes

---

159 'Hic adverte mentem quisquis quaeris deum, et disce quantum sit in nobis vel capacitatis, taceo preparationis ad fidem Christi in nostra natura: quicumque ex Adam tantum geniti sumus, quantum scilicet est in lapidibus, ad id ut sint filii Abrahae ac proinde filii dei.' (CCCC, MS 104, p. 32; Vogt, *Annotationes*, p. 44, following Null's translation, *Repentance*, p. 232).

of the corporal, spiritual and sacramental presence of Christ. Rightly or wrongly, he must have seen certain advantages in his own approach. We must take this seriously and try to follow him in this path.

The negative side of Cranmer's theology is all too obvious. Richardson is merciless in exposing the confusion of his attempts to squeeze quotations from the Fathers about the presence of Christ into the Procrustean bed of his own eucharistic theology. And the dictum that the sign can only be operative when the thing signified is absent gets him into real trouble when he attempts to use other analogies of the sacramental relationship. When he addresses the issue of transubstantiation, Cranmer in his *Defence* uses the old illustration of the incarnation as a model for understanding the presence of Christ in the eucharistic bread and wine. Gardiner acutely notices the problem here: if Christ is absent from the sacrament, 'then were the sacrament like a body lying in a trance, whose soul for the while were in heaven'. Gardiner goes on to accuse Cranmer of writing this section in order to maintain the Lutheran view of the Real Presence against that of transubstantiation: whether true or no, it suited Winchester's purpose to present Canterbury as inconsistent.[160] And he certainly has a point. Cranmer is forced to retract, or at least to qualify his statements in a less than satisfactory manner, and is left with very little ammunition at this stage for alternative models of understanding the sacrament. And just as the presence of Christ proves a difficult concept in Cranmer's model, so too does sacramental efficacy. The elements and the action of the sacrament are left somewhat exterior and incidental to the private engagement of faith between God and the recipient.

There are, however, advantages, the first of which is that Cranmer has more freedom in expressing what the sacrament signifies since it is less tightly linked to the actual engagement between the believer and God. Biblical and patristic language can be appropriated and used without apology. Thus he is able to speak positively even about the eucharist as a sacrifice because, to quote Augustine, it is a sign or representation of the true sacrifice.[161] Secondly, Cranmer can use 'sacramental' language to describe positively and confidently the liturgical action, both in his theological and liturgical writings. The caveat that the grace is effected only in the elect is spoken of as rarely as the doctrine of election itself. The rhetorical confidence of the rite stands on a very narrow theological

---

160 *Explication*, 2, Cranmer, PS, I, p. 281.
161 *Defence*, 5.13: PS, I, p. 351. Of course, Cranmer still opposes what he sees as traditional misunderstandings or abuses in the notion of sacrifice, but that he can relate the eucharist to the sacrifice of Christ in this way is quite remarkable.
162 Gerrish, *Grace and Gratitude* (p. 172) is right in saying (of Calvin's theology) that election limits rather than negates an understanding of sacramental efficacy.

foundation.[162] Thirdly, this approach enables Cranmer to sit loose when necessary to the relation between the sacrament and the grace signified. In particular, it is the mechanism by which he is able to circumvent the problems raised by Redman and the traditionalists about justifying grace in the 1540s. If Cornelius is saved before baptism, which signifies his justification rather than causes it, then Cranmer can avoid the trap of dealing with the idea of prior faith or works leading to justification.

Cranmer opposed Peter Martyr, I believe, because he wanted to protect a positive facet of his own theology which he found in the pages of Augustine. An important element of this, I have already suggested, could have been the elimination of any place for grace before justification. But there is an additional advantage in the Cranmerian approach of signification, namely that it avoids the trap into which Martyr and Laski fall in their baptismal theology when they distance the sacrament from the divine work of regeneration. In order to maintain one model of sacramental instrumentality, they have to posit prior faith (or in the case of infants, the prior grace of the Holy Spirit) in the recipient. Logically the recipient is therefore already regenerate, and baptism, while witnessing to the original regeneration, communicates grace, which is said explicitly to be subsequent to the initial act of justification. There is, then, a dislocation between the signification and the grace. Cranmer avoids this problem by sticking resolutely to the sacrament as signification; it is called by the name of what it signifies. The distinction between the sacramental action and the spiritual grace frees us from the entanglements of saying that God must justify the recipient and at this moment in time, but also the relationship of signification leaves it open that God might indeed do that very thing and now. Cornelius, the just thief or the unelect infant might be rare exceptions to a rule in which God in his freedom works salvation in his children in the very moment of baptism. By and large, however, Cranmer does not press the point, preferring instead to present a picture of the sacrament as pointing to the work of God as a continuous action in the elect:

> As [Christ] is spiritually present, so is he spiritually eaten of all faithful christian men, not only when they receive the sacrament, but continually so long as they be members spiritual of Christ's mystical body . . . And as the Holy Ghost doth not only come to us in baptism, and Christ doth there clothe us, but they do the same to us continually so long as we dwell in Christ; so likewise doth Christ feed us so long as we dwell in him and he in us, and not only when we receive the sacrament.[163]

---

163 *Answer* 3: PS, I, p. 71.

The sacraments help us to experience spiritually the immediate presence of Christ. There is an element of the 'continuous present' both in the individual's faith and in the presence of Christ in the Old and New Testaments. One might almost talk of the sacraments as the tip of the iceberg, except that Cranmer's sacraments are distinct from, not part of, the hidden presence of Christ. Working from the standpoint of the eucharist, Cranmer does not explore the relationship in baptism between sacrament and grace in any detail. But there is nothing exceptional in the way in which in the 1540s he posited the possibility of even a temporal delay before the communication of the grace of baptism. This view was entertained at times by both Luther and Bucer.[164] Bullinger disliked the notion of simultaneity which was part of Calvin's sacramental theology. For Calvin, the idea of sacraments as instruments of grace required that the grace should be conferred through the actual administration of the sacrament.[165] Bullinger disagreed, and in the *Consensus Tigurinus* a compromise was sought which affirmed that the action of grace in baptism, and also in the eucharist, is not restricted to the administration of the sacrament but is operative throughout the recipient's life.[166]

These are the advantages of using the language of signification. The idea of sacramental efficacy is weakened as a result. Yet Cranmer assiduously affirms that the sacraments are not mere tokens, that baptism is not a knave playing in a prince's coat. He seems genuinely to believe that he has preserved a sound notion of sacramental instrumentality. However, as we look more closely at his theology, symbolic parallelism rings more true.

---

164 P. Althaus, *The Theology of Martin Luther*, trans. R.C. Schultz (Philadelphia, PA: Fortress Press, 1966), p. 39; Wright, 'Infant Baptism and the Christian Community', p. 97.
165 Calvin to Bullinger, 25 February 1547, in J. Calvin, *Ioannis Calvini opera quae supersunt omnia*, ed. W. Baum, E. Cunitz and E. Reuss, CR, Vols 29–87 (Berlin: Brungswig, 1863–1900), Vol. 40, p. 482: 'Dominus quod signo repraesentat simul efficit'. Gerrish, *Grace and Gratitude*, p. 166 and n. 29.
166 *Consensus Tigurinus*, 20, in B.J. Kidd (ed.), *Documents Illustrative of the Continental Reformation* (Oxford: Oxford University Press, 1911), p. 655.

Utilitas porro quam ex sacramentis percipimus, ad tempus quo ea nobis administrantur, minime restringi debet: perinde ac si visibile signum, dum in medium profertur, eodem secum momento Dei gratiam adveheret. Nam qui in prima infantia baptizati sunt, eos in pueritia vel ineunte adolescentia, interdum etiam in senectute regenerat Deus. Ita Baptismi utilitas ad totum vitae decursum patet, quia perpetuo viget quae illic continetur promissio. Cf art. 19 [re adult baptism and communion:] Sic Baptismo abluta sunt Pauli peccata, quae iam prius abluta erant. Sic idem Baptismus Cornelio fuit lavacrum regenerationis, qui tamen iam Spiritu sancto donatus erat. Sic in Coena se nobis communicat Christus, qui tamen et prius se nobis impertierat et perpetuo manet in nobis.

Chapter 5

THE PRAYER BOOKS OF 1549 AND 1552

1 THE 1549 BOOK OF COMMON PRAYER

a. The new Prayer Book

The new Prayer Book was passed by parliament on 21 January, and was required to be in use on Whit Sunday, 9 June, 1549. It was entitled *The Booke of the Common Prayer and Administracion of the Sacramentes, and other Rites and Ceremonies of the Church after the Use of the Churche of England.* In effect there are three categories of service: 'Common Prayer', referred to Morning and Evening Prayer, with a calendar and lectionary for the year (and the book's Preface refers only to this section); next the introit psalms, collects, epistles and gospel readings for the communion service and then the service itself (with the Litany added afterwards); and thirdly services effectively covering the life cycle of baptism, confirmation, matrimony, the visitation and communion of the sick and the burial service. The purification of women (in 1552 more accurately entitled the Thanksgiving of Women after Childbirth) and the Ash Wednesday devotions complete the list. In one book the Church of England was given the equivalent of the medieval Breviary, the Missal and the Manual.

b. The shape of the baptism service

A detailed examination of the text of the baptism service will be undertaken in the final chapter of this book. Here I wish simply to outline its structure and contents and, pre-empting to some extent the final chapter, note the probable textual sources used by the Archbishop.

The baptismal rite of 1549[1]

(Service begins at the church door)
Introduction
Flood prayer
Signing
Seeking prayer
Exorcism
Gospel
First exhortation
Lord's Prayer
Creed
Hermann's prayer
Approach to font
(Blessing of font)
Second exhortation

Renunciations	*When more than one child is*
Interrogatory Creed	*baptized, this section is to be used*
Queries	*individually with each child.*
Immersion	
White garment	
Anointing	

Final exhortation to godparents

i. The end of the Sarum rite

It will be seen below that the 1549 baptism service was probably modelled on a Lutheran rite. But those on whom it was imposed would have compared it with the Sarum rite, and so we shall do likewise here. If we follow the descriptions of the *Declaracion of the Seremonies a nexid to the Sacrament of Baptyme* and the *Rationale of Ceremonial*, most elements highlighted by them are to be found preserved in the new rite. First, the various distinctions between parts of the service are omitted, so there is no separate Order for making a catechumen. The blessing of the water is a separate item, but it is placed, as it were, as an appendix

---

1   The titles of the various elements of the service as given here will be those I will use. The service may be found in the PS edn of *Liturgies of Edward VI*, pp. 106–19, and also in the Everyman edition of the *First and Second Prayer Books of King Edward VI* (London and Toronto: J.M. Dent, 1910), pp. 236–46. A tabulated version may be found in Brightman's *English Rite*, Vol. 2, pp. 724–61. References to the baptism and communion services and to other parts of the Edwardine Prayer Books will not normally be paginated.

after the service of private baptism, and there is no instruction in the text where it was meant to be used in the rite of public baptism. As for the elements of the service, the service begins, as formerly, at the church door, but the Introduction and the Flood prayer give a totally new feel to the rite. The initial signing on the forehead and breast which once had opened the service then follows, and then the Seeking prayer, which is based mainly on a prayer from the Sarum *Manual*. The giving of salt with its attendant exorcism and prayer is also omitted, though both commentaries had made much of it, and the eight exorcistic formulas (most of them different for a boy or a girl) are reduced to one. The Sarum reading of Jesus blessing the children in Matthew is replaced by the Marcan version, and followed by an exhortation to the congregation, holding the gospel narrative as a justification of infant baptism and encouraging the people to have faith in Christ. This then proceeds to the Lord's Prayer and Creed (in Sarum there had been the *effeta* rite, followed by the Lord's Prayer, Hail Mary and Creed) and to Hermann's prayer (I have labelled it thus because it is taken wholesale from the *Deliberatio*), giving thanks for the faith of the congregation and praying for the Holy Spirit to be given to those being baptized. Then (omitting a signing of the hand, described in the *Rationale* but passed over by the *Declaracion*, and a blessing) the priest, as formerly, takes the child to the font. In the Sarum rite an exhortation to the godparents instructs them to teach the child the three formulas just recited and to ensure that the child is confirmed in due course. Also instructions are given about the return of the chrisom cloth, and they are told to wash their hands to remove the baptismal oils before they leave church. Cranmer replaces all this with an exhortation telling the godparents that, as Christ has promised to receive the child being baptized, so the child through them must promise to forsake the devil and follow Christ. Here the Sarum *Manual* has the blessing of the font and, if it was performed in the course of the ceremony, no doubt it would have happened in 1549 at around this point. But now that the exhortation looks forward to the renunciation and affirmation of faith, a blessing here would have disrupted the flow of the service.

The 1549 blessing of the font is printed separately, after the provision for private baptism. The rubric states simply that the water in the font is to be changed at least every month, and the prayers are to be said before any child is baptized in the new water. The provision is much simpler than that in the *Manual*. The litany of the saints is omitted altogether, and after a prayer of blessing there follow the Grant prayers (the form of which may have been reminiscent of the staccato nature of a litany) and a prayer for the candidates of baptism. (This final prayer will become the Invocation prayer in the 1552 baptism service.) Ceremonial actions – once so rich in the Sarum blessing with making the sign of the cross in the water by hand, by breathing on it, with wax from a candle and with the candle itself, then adding oil and chrism – are now replaced by only a single signing of the water, noted by a sign of the cross in the text of the prayer of blessing.

The central section of the baptism rite, the renunciation and profession of faith, the immersion, clothing and anointing, are directed to be administered individually to each child being baptized. This would have provided a solemn emphasis on the individual child, and perhaps been pastorally sensitive for people used to private baptisms. I have made no attempt to calculate how often there would have been several candidates on a given Sunday, but the service as a whole is worded with plural candidates. No doubt the repetition of the large section would have been wearisome, and it is no surprise that this directive was omitted in 1552.

The formula of renunciation in 1549 is fuller than in the *Manual*; and likewise the affirmation of faith is now the interrogatory form of the Apostles' Creed in full. (An anointing in Sarum is omitted in 1549.) Then after questions in which the child, through the godparents, requests baptism, it is immersed three times. The 1549 rite retains the older practice of dipping first one side, then the other, then finally the child is dipped face down. A rubric allows here the pouring of water on a sick child. A similar rubric is found at the end of the Sarum rite in the case of emergency baptism.[2] Tyndale's mocking of the baptism rite (see Chapter 1, pp. 13–14), seems to suggest that the alternative was used in church as well as in emergencies, otherwise we would not have the disapproval of the onlookers.

The 1549 rite says the godparents 'shall take and lay their hands upon the child'. This is reminiscent of the *Declaracion* in which they 'lay hand on the child's head for they be witnesses of his baptism and receive the charge to teach it and the truth of his belief'.

Of the final post-baptismal symbols in the *Manual*, only the candle is omitted. The chrismation and vesting of the child are preserved, though their order is inverted, as happens in Ryce's rite; as noted above, this may reflect actual practice. The Sarum final readings of Mk 9.16–28 (effective against epilepsy) and of Jn 1.1–14 are not found in 1549.

ii. The shape of the 1549 baptism service compared with Lutheran rites

The shape of Cranmer's 1549 rite can be shown to be very close to that of the German Lutheran rites. It is necessary to provide a full comparison only with the 1540 rite of Albertine Saxony.[3] This rite follows Luther's

---

2   *Manual*, p. 38.
3   E. Sehling (ed.), *Die evangelischen Kirchenordnungen des xvi. Jahrhunderts* (Leipzig: 1902–), Vol. 1, pp. 266–7.

second *Taufbüchlein* of 1526 very closely,[4] but is notable for the addition of the exhortations after the gospel and at the Approach to the font.[5] In this it is distinctive; along with some other rites, it is preceded by material for a homily, and it replaces the shorter formula of adhesion with an interrogatory Apostles' Creed. For these reasons, as much as the question of detailed content which will be considered below, the Albertine Saxony rite must be considered to be an important source for Cranmer's service. However, if we look back before 1540 we may be entitled to look to Luther himself or, for example, to the Brandenburg–Nuremberg rite of 1533.

A comparison of the baptism service of 1549 with that of the Albertine Saxony *Kirchenordnung* of 1540

1549	*Albertine Saxony, 1540*
Introduction	Preliminary material (not in Luther)
Flood prayer	
	'Come out, thou unclean spirit . . .'
Signing	Signing
Seeking prayer	Seeking prayer
	Flood prayer
Exorcism	Exorcism
Gospel	Gospel
Exhortation	Exhortation (not in Luther)
	Rubric – priest lays hand on child
Lord's Prayer	Lord's Prayer
Creed	
Hermann's prayer	
Approach to font	Approach to font
(Blessing of font)	
Exhortation	Exhortation (not in Luther)
Renunciations	Renunciations
Interrogatory Creed	Interrogatory Creed
Queries	Queries
Immersion	Immersion
Vesture	(Vesture with words of Anointing)
Anointing	
Final exhortation	
	'Peace be with you'

---

4   Sehling (ed.), *Die evangelischen Kirchenordnungen*, Vol. 1, pp. 17–23, trans. in Fisher, *Christian Initiation*, pp. 23–5.
5   Brightman became aware of the importance of the Albertine Saxony material late in the preparation of his *English Rite* and included some of the parallels only as *corrigenda* in the

Apart from the exhortations that depend on the Albertine Saxony material, the features in the structure of 1549 which most closely evoke that of the Lutheran rites, as opposed to the Sarum *Manual*, are perhaps the prominent position of the Seeking prayer, the single exorcism and the choice of Mark's gospel for the account of Jesus and the children. In having a final exhortation about the duties of the godparents, a parallel can be found in Brandenburg–Nuremberg, but also, and perhaps more appropriately, in the Sarum rite. However, even in Sarum the godparents' duties were also specified in the middle of the service, at the approach to the font. Cranmer moves it all to the end and the future upbringing of the child is not made a precursor to baptism.

The synopsis also makes clear what distinguishes Cranmer from the Lutheran rites. Joining the Flood prayer to the Introduction is an elegant alteration, and one made necessary by certain changes, as we shall see below in the commentary on the text (Chapter 6). The fact that the Lord's Prayer, Creed and Hermann's prayer are all together is likely to reflect plans for 1552: in the later rite a simpler version closer to the Lutheran rites (only with Hermann's prayer rather than the Lord's Prayer concluding the exhortation) suggests that 1549 might here be seen as a 'half-way house' from the position of the Sarum *Manual* to the 1552 rite. The omission of the rubric found in the Lutheran rites, that the priest lay his hand on the child's head while the Lord's Prayer is said, is theologically very important and will also be considered in the commentary. The blessing of the font is said monthly at most, and so could be said to have little structural importance. However, its theological importance is immense and will need to be examined in detail when we consider Cranmer's principles of consecration.

iii. Lutheran and Reform sources

As well as the structure following Lutheran precedent, some of the content also came directly from such a source (see commentary in Chapter 6 below). The gospel reading of Mark (rather than Matthew

---

Preface. It is a pity that he did not make this more clear, since these later discoveries have for the most part gone unnoticed, with the result that scholars have gone on attributing to Hermann material which Brightman himself in 1915 showed was more closely linked with the Albertine Saxony *Kirchenordnung* of 1540. Geoffrey Cuming, who in his *Godly Order*, pp. 84–5, missed most of the Albertine Saxony parallels, in his *History of Anglican Liturgy*, p. 84, correctly identifies them. However Cuming earlier on the same page keeps alive the possibility of the determining influence of Hermann at a particular stage in the evolution of the rite: 'If all traces of Hermann be removed from the 1549 Baptism, the remainder is very similar to Luther's form.'

as in Sarum) is a translation from the Latin, which is different to any published translation, suggesting that it might have been executed before the authorization of the English Bible in the 1537 ('Matthew's Bible') and the 1539 ('Great Bible').[6] The Flood prayer is based either on Luther's own rite or some other dependent on it, rather than on Hermann's *Consultation*, and it is taken as evidence by Cuming for liturgical drafting by Cranmer before he had access to Hermann, whose rite, says Cuming, he used so freely.[7]

However, Hermann's rite contributes very little if we follow the synopsis provided in Brightman's *English Rite*: the short introduction to the service; the formula for the signing; two sections of the exhortation after the gospel and the whole of the prayer following it; and the final exhortation concluding the service.[8] In fact, as will be seen below, the texts of the signing and the final exhortation have closer parallels in other works than Hermann, and the introduction is taken from Coverdale's translation of a Danish Lutheran rite. Of the remainder, which is clearly taken from the *Deliberatio*, Hermann's prayer takes the place of the Lord's Prayer and Creed, which are moved to more central positions in 1552. The sections of the exhortation that depend on Hermann could be removed and the passage could still make good sense, which tempts one to guess that they were simply inserted into an earlier draft. Certainly they are very much of a kind, emphasizing the love of God towards infants and forbidding doubt.

This leads me to believe that Hermann's material was introduced at a late stage into a rite that was for the most part already composed. It may well have come at a time when Cranmer was already thinking towards the 1552 shape of the service, and was looking for material to fit in with it. We may suppose that earlier drafts of the service had been in line with the 1549 edition, but, lacking Hermann's prayer, would have retained the Lord's Prayer after the gospel exposition. The Creed may well have been there also, and not merely as an interim measure, if it was not already inserted as the formula for the affirmation of faith. But Cranmer without Hermann was not Luther's *Taufbüchlein*, but rather Justus Jonas's Albertine Saxony *Kirchenordnung*. The question that perforce remains open is whether there was another Lutheran stage before Albertine Saxony.

---

6   Cuming, *History of Anglican Liturgy*, p. 31.

7   Cuming, *History of Anglican Liturgy*, p. 60.

8   C. Hope (Hopf), 'Lutheran Influences on the Baptismal Services of the Anglican Prayer Book of 1549', in F. Hildebrand (ed.), *'And Other Pastors of thy Flock': A German Tribute to the Bishop of Chichester* (Cambridge: privately printed, 1942), pp. 61–100 argues for a considerable dependence on Hermann.

iv. Sarum

When the text of the service is examined in detail, it will appear that while the structure of the 1549 service owes much to Lutheran sources, the content of the prayers looks to the Sarum *Manual* almost whenever possible. Thus, the first part of the signing formula and the opening of the Seeking prayer, addressing it to the Father, follow Luther, and then the main text reverts to a translation of Sarum (though we shall see another important change in the Seeking prayer). The opening part of the exorcism could have been based on Luther (there is no difference to enable us to distinguish it), but the remainder of the material is most probably based on Sarum. It is as though Cranmer possessed, either on paper or in his mind, the Lutheran rite as a series of brief formulas and headings, but relied on the text of the Sarum *Manual*. The longest passage taken from the German rites in preference to an existing Sarum formula is the first half of the signing.

Unlike Luther and the other rites described (but like, e.g., Electoral Brandenburg of 1540), the vesture and unction are retained from the Sarum rite, albeit in an inverted order.

v. The Mozarabic rite

The Grant prayers in the baptismal liturgy, in the 1549 rite found in the material for the blessing of the font, seem to be derived from a Mozarabic or possibly Gallican source. This will be discussed below. Apart from the advantages of being non-Roman, such a source would demonstrate above all Cranmer's wide scholarship and (non-Roman) catholic tastes.

vi. English formularies: the King's Book and *Rationale of Ceremonial*

It will be seen that significant passages bear resemblance to material in the King's Book and the *Rationale of Ceremonial*. The importance of these documents has already been described. In part they no doubt provided theological material congenial to Cranmer, but they also supplied him with politically convenient resources, in that by following them he might seek to satisfy the demands of other schools of thought.

c. Private baptism

The 1549 Prayer Book included provision for private baptism, which, it was emphasized in the opening rubrics, could be administered only in emergency. Much of the form of service for the reception in Church is based on the provision of the 1540 Albertine Saxony *Kirchenordnung*, with an interrogation of those who had baptized the child. There then follow elements taken from the public baptism service, which are amended where necessary: the gospel reading and exhortation, Lord's Prayer, Creed, renunciation and affirmation of faith, vesting, Hermann's prayer and final exhortation.[9] The service is more brief than the provision in the Sarum *Manual*, where the entire service is used except for the immersion itself and the candidate's request for baptism immediately preceding it.[10] The emphasis of the service is, naturally, shifted slightly from the baptism itself to the Christian life. Thus, the vesting appropriately speaks of the innocency of the Christian life lived faithfully to the end, and Hermann's prayer is amended in a similar direction.

d. The communion service

At first sight the eucharist, like the baptism service, was extremely conventional by Reformation standards. The whole service was now in the vernacular rather than mainly in Latin, but vestments and, for the time being, the medieval altars and furnishings were retained. The service was entitled 'The Supper of the Lord and the Holy Communion, commonly called the Mass': this serves as a clue that Reformation theology is to be found disguised, as it were, in medieval dress. The structure of the service as a whole is very close to the Sarum Mass.[11] The Collect for Purity and the Lord's Prayer continue (but out loud) the priest's private prayers of preparation. The Introit Psalm, Kyrie and Gloria are followed by the Collect (with an additional collect for the king), then the Epistle and Gospel (but without the intervening Gradual, Alleluia and Sequence). The Creed follows, and then the sermon, which in the Sarum rite had come later. An exhortation to faithful communion is delivered. At the Offertory, members of the congregation place their gifts in the poor men's box, which had been set up by the altar; those who are to receive communion remain in the chancel and the remainder leave altogether. The Offertory is accompanied by sentences exhorting the people to generosity towards the poor, but there are no traditional Offertory prayers commending the

---

9   The service is to be found following the service of Public Baptism in the editions of the Prayer Book already cited. Brightman's *English Rite* (Vol. 2, pp. 748–61) sets out the probable sources. I have not attempted a detailed discussion of this service.
10   *Manual*, p. 39.
11   The text of the Sarum Mass can be conveniently followed in Cuming, *History of Anglican Liturgy*, pp. 233–51.

oblation of bread and wine to God. The service of 1549 also omits the vernacular Bidding of the Bedes: the later intercessions effectively replace this item. The Sursum corda, Preface and Sanctus are preserved as usual (there are rather fewer Proper Prefaces than previously), as is the Canon itself, which will be discussed in more detail below. The priest's private prayers are omitted, but the public Communion devotions are rather fuller than in the Sarum rite, comprising the Lord's Prayer and Peace, as before, and then the Confession and Absolution, Comfortable Words and Prayer of Humble Access from *The Order of the Communion*. The Agnus Dei is sung during the communion, then afterwards there are sentences on the theme of service, love and trust in God. A postcommunion Prayer of Thanksgiving concludes with the blessing, but the Sarum dismissal and reading of the last gospel are omitted.

While modern readers might feel there is little active participation for the congregation, contemporary worshippers – and especially clergy – might have been struck more by the absence of the many private prayers said by the celebrant. Now every word was spoken out loud and could be understood by the congregation. Participation was also required by emphasis on more frequent communion: the rubrics at the end of the service require there to be someone to receive communion with the priest, otherwise the service ends with the Offertory.

The eucharistic prayer in 1549 is totally unlike any provision in the Lutheran or Reformed churches. It bears a very close similarity to its medieval predecessor. It begins with the Sursum corda, Preface, Sanctus and Benedictus. The remainder of the prayer is referred to in the Prayer Book as the Canon, again like its predecessor, and would have been seen as separate from what came before. It begins with a lengthy intercession – the old Canon had included several elements of intercession and it might have seemed like simple common sense to put them altogether.

The prayer continues with a remembrance of Christ's one 'full, perfect, and sufficient sacrifyce, oblacion, and satysfaccion, for the sinnes of the whole worlde', which we are commended to commemorate, and the prayer that God will 'with thy holy spirite and word, vouchsafe to bl✠esse and sanc✠tifie these thy gyftes, and creatures of bread and wyne, that they may be unto us the bodye and bloude' of Christ. 'May be unto us' was correctly criticized at the time as ambiguous: did this mean that they become the body and blood of Christ, or only represent them? The unambiguous answer is to be found after the words of institution, when, most significantly, there is to be no elevation of the bread. This had been the high-point of the medieval Mass, when the consecrated bread, now the body of Christ, was worshipped by the congregation, and the omission of this ritual action speaks more clearly of the character of the revised service than the ambiguous wording: it is not to be worshipped because it is not

Christ. As Tunstall had correctly observed in the House of Lords' debate, 'The adoracion is left out of the booke bycause ther is nothing in the sacrament but bread and wyne'.[12] However, the priest is directed to take the bread and cup in his hands while pronouncing the words of institution: there is still some emphasis on the sanctification of the bread and wine.

The remainder of the Canon carries a close verbal similarity to the medieval rite, but in a very different sense. Gone is any offering of the consecrated bread and wine to God: now the congregation simply 'make the memorial' of Christ's death and resurrection, and the only offering is of praise and thanksgiving and the self-offering of the worshippers. Cranmer's use of Sarum as a source by no means demonstrates his allegiance to its theology!

The communion devotions from the *Order of the Communion* follow with minimal change. In the light of Cranmer's mature theology we must pause to consider how he would have understood the words of administration of the sacrament: 'The body of our Lorde Jesus Christe whiche was geven for thee, / the bloud of our Lorde Jesus Christe which was shed for thee / preserve thy bodye and soule unto everlastyng lyfe'. These words could be taken to imply that the sacrament of the body and blood (which is how the rubrics describe the bread and wine, with no mention of their being still bread and wine!) indeed convey to the communicant the body and blood of Christ. However, we know that Cranmer believed otherwise, and the words must be understood as a prayer for spiritual communion, asking that the communicant receiving the sacrament may also receive by faith the body and blood of Christ.

The service concluded with a prayer of thanksgiving (which will be examined in more detail when we look at the 1552 Prayer Book) and a blessing.

2 CRANMER'S MATURE UNDERSTANDING OF CONSECRATION

a. Cranmer's theology of consecration

One of the most remarkable features of Cranmer's liturgy, which we must examine in some detail, is the different ways in which he applies his theology of consecration to the liturgies of 1549 and 1552. First we remember the later Cranmer's own doctrine about the consecration of physical objects. On this he is quite explicit.

> Consecration is the separation of any thing from a profane and worldly use unto a spiritual and godly use. And therefore when usual

---

12　Buchanan, *Background Documents*, p. 15.

and common water is taken from other uses, and put to the use of baptism in the name of the Father, and of the Son, and of the holy Ghost, then it may rightly be called consecrated water, that is to say, water put to an holy use. Even so, when common bread and wine be taken and severed from other bread and wine to the use of the holy communion, that portion of bread and wine, although it be of the same substance that the other is from the which it is severed, yet it is now called consecrated, or holy bread and holy wine. Not that the bread and wine have or can have any holiness in them, but that they be used to an holy work, and represent holy and godly things.[13]

The marvellous working of God . . . is in the spiritual receivers, not in the bread, wine and water, nor in the carnal and ungodly receivers.[14]

Against his opponents, Cranmer sought to score a particular point in comparing consecration in the eucharist with that in baptism, and in claiming that the two are effectively the same. Therefore, nothing more should be attributed to consecration in one than in the other. The parallel structure of the services of baptism and eucharist has a polemical point, but that point is made too often for us to imagine that he was being solely or cynically polemical. It was Cranmer's sincere belief that the two sacraments should be understood together and celebrated in like manner. But his reservations about consecration go further than this. It is his basic precept that physical objects cannot contain or communicate holiness. Only people can be holy, and only people can be the recipients of spiritual grace. The physical objects and actions of the sacraments remain outside this engagement with the divine. Thus consecration marks nothing more than a change of use of the objects.

Cranmer has an ambivalent attitude to the question whether consecration be effected by the words of institution or associated with them. At times he seems to accept the idea; at other times he derides it. In both cases it can be seen that he takes the line that suits his polemical purpose. In so far as he has a genuine opinion, it is linked with his notion of consecration as a setting apart for a holy work, and is connected with his use of sacramental or figurative language:

Not that the bread and wine have or can have any holiness in them, but that they be used to an holy work, and represent holy and godly things. And therefore St Dionyse called the bread holy bread,

---

13 *Defence*, 3.15: PS, I, p. 177.
14 *Answer*, 2: PS, I, p. 341.

and the cup an holy cup, as soon as they be set upon the altar to the use of the holy communion. But specially they may be called holy and consecrated, when they be separated to that holy use by Christ's own words, when he spake for that purpose, saying of the bread, 'This is my body', and of the wine, 'This is my blood'.[15]

We may note Cranmer's concessive use of language: 'they may be called holy and consecrated'. That suggests very strongly Cranmer's personal unhappiness with the notion of consecration. He wants to avoid any idea of consecration making any change in the elements themselves. When discussing Ambrose's description of the bread which is called Christ's body after the consecration, Cranmer takes a figurative interpretation of Ambrose's words, relying on his quotation of the contemporary Milanese liturgy that it is a figure of the body and blood, and goes on to say that the bread 'is neither Christ's mystical body (for that is the congregation of the faithful dispersed abroad in the world) nor his natural body (for that is in heaven), but it is the sacrament both of his true natural body, and also of his mystical body, and for that consideration hath the name of his body'.[16]

It is very convenient for Cranmer at times to identify the words of institution with the consecration, because some liturgies would speak of there being still bread and wine after that point. Indeed, he misinterprets John Damascene on this very issue. When Damascene says that the liturgy of Basil called the bread and wine the figures of the body and blood of Christ only before they were consecrated (ἀντίτυπα τοῦ σώματος καὶ αἵματος . . . οὐ μετὰ τὸ ἁγιασθῆναι . . . ἀλλὰ πρὶν ἁγιασθῆναι) Cranmer understands ἁγιασθῆναι as 'the consecration', and by identifying that with the words of institution misrepresents Damascene (who is clearly referring to the words of the epiclesis: εὐλογῆσαι καὶ ἁγιάσαι καὶ ἀναδεῖξαι . . .) and thus invokes Basil as evidence that after consecration the bread and wine are still present as ἀντίτυπα.[17] So basic is this misreading of Damascene that it is hard to

---

15 *Defence*, 3.15: PS, I, p. 177.

16 *Answer*, 3: PS, I, p. 180. Cf. Ambrose, *De sacramentis* 4.21, ed. B. Botte, *Des Sacrements, Des Mystères, Explication du symbole*, 2nd edn (Paris: Cerf, 1980).

17 *Defence*, 3.15: PS, I, p. 196: the relevant text of Damascene, *De fide orthodoxa* 4.14, is quoted on p. 197; cf. the Liturgy of St Basil, ed. F.E. Brightman, *Liturgies Eastern and Western*, Vol. 1 (Oxford: Clarendon Press, 1896), pp. 405–6. A Latin translation of Damascene is used by Cranmer in his commonplaces, MS 7B XII, fols 100–1ᵛ; trans. J. LeFèvre, *De fide orthodoxa* (Paris: Henry Stephanus, 1507). The relevant passage is there rendered as 'Et si quidam examplaria corporis et sanguinis domini panem et vinum vocaverunt, ut deifer vocavit Basilius, non tamen post sanctificationem dixit, sed priusquam sanctificaretur ipsa oblatio, ita vocabant' (fol. 101ᵛ). So even in translation the reference to the liturgical text has been preserved.

avoid the conclusion that, willingly or unwillingly, Cranmer allowed himself to be swept away by polemical interest.[18]

At other times Cranmer takes a contrary view; in his *Answer* he mocks the notion of a point of consecration:

> But all truths agree to the truth, and falsehood agreeth not with itself: so it is a plain declaration of untruth, that the papists vary so among themselves. For some say that Christ consecrated by his own secret power without sign or words: some say that his benediction was his consecration: some say that he did consecrate with these words, *Hoc est corpus meum* . . .[19]

And Gardiner ascribes to Cranmer an even wider set of alternatives, including a passage after the words of institution, from the *Supplices te rogamus* of the Canon:

> The Papists do not know what words serve for the consecration. For Scotus and Innocent III say that the consecration is in the word, 'he blessed'. Others say it is in the words, 'command these things to be brought [. . . to your altar on high'; others, in 'This is my body'. This diversity reveals the ignorance.[20]

In no case does Cranmer wholeheartedly adopt the language of consecration. His manipulation of the idea of a moment of consecration suggests that his concern here is polemical and negative, and that by the time he was writing the *Defence* he had no positive theology of consecration. The liturgy of both Prayer Books accords with Cranmer's mature theology. In both eucharist and baptism, the elements are sanctified 'unto a spiritual and godly use': in 1549 the bread and wine are blessed only 'that they may be unto us the body and blood' of Christ, and the water 'that all those that shall be baptized therein may be spiritually regenerated'. In 1552, we shall see that there is no language of blessing of the objects

---

18 But see B.D. Spinks, *The Western Use and Abuse of Eastern Liturgical Traditions* (Rome and Bangalore: Centre for Indian and Inter-Religious Studies and Dahram Publications, 1992), p. 56 for a different reading of Cranmer at this point.

19 *Answer*, 2: PS, I, p. 249.

20 'Papistae nesciunt quibus verbis consecratio fiat. Nam Scotus et Innocentius Tertius dicunt consecrationem esse in verbo, *Benedicit*. Alii dicunt in iis verbis, *Iube haec perferri*, alii in iis, *Hoc est Corpus meum*. Haec varietas arguit ignorantiam' (*Confutatio Cavillationum quibus sacrosanctum Eucharistiae Sacramentum, ab impiis Capernaitis, impeti solet, Authore Marco Antonio Constantio, Theologo Lovanensi*. [*sic*: i.e. Stephen Gardiner] [Paris: Jean de Roigny, 1552], Ob. 84). Quoted by H.G.C. Moule in *A Brief Declaration of the Lord's Supper written by Nicholas Ridley*, ed. H.C.G. Moule (London/ New York: Seeley/Thomas Whittaker, 1895), pp. 177–8.

whatsoever. They are simply taken and used. They are referred to, but there is not even any reference to a change of status. The water of the font is no longer retained after a baptism, even for a month. The bread and wine that remain unconsumed may be taken home by the priest for his own use.

b. The 1549 prayers of 'sanctification'

Although the 1549 equivalents of the 1552 Invocation prayers might be called 'prayers of consecration', Cranmer deliberately avoided the term and so I shall call them 'prayers of sanctification', picking up his own language and acknowledging the role of the elements and actions that are more integral to the prayer than in the case of the invocations, which look wholly to the recipients.

The prayers are part of much larger structures: in the eucharist we are looking simply at one paragraph within the eucharistic prayer of 1549, still occasionally called the Canon. The baptismal prayer is part of the lengthy set of prayers used when the water of the font is changed (there is no title or heading, which is very convenient when Cranmer does not want to say what the prayers actually do). The prayer of sanctification is followed by the 'Grant' prayers and the prayer of Invocation for those to be baptized, which is slightly different from its 1552 form but ready for use in its more central position.

The 1549 eucharistic petition for sanctification begins with an address to the Father and a recital of the Son's self-sacrifice on Calvary in the same way as its 1552 counterpart, with only stylistic differences. The eucharist is instituted, however, so that we may celebrate a perpetual memory of it rather than continue it; the 1549 version is more ambiguous than that in 1552. The second part of the prayer is wholly different, in 1549 looking very similar to the *Quem oblationem* of the Canon and asking God that he may bless and sanctify the bread and wine with his Holy Spirit and word so that they may be to the communicants the body and blood of Christ. Cranmer's own meaning of the words is spelt out explicitly elsewhere: there is no objective change of the elements and the words 'unto us' are an essential qualification; figurative language is implied.[21] And we may be assured that Cranmer is allowing for the caveat that only the elect will actually receive the grace of the sacrament. But besides these qualifications, it is notable that the prayer includes the elements in the action, as it were.

---

21 *Answer*, 3: PS, I, p. 79. 'And therefore, in the book of the holy communion, we do not pray absolutely that the bread and wine may be made the body and blood of Christ, but that unto us in that same mystery they may be so; that is to say, that we may so worthily receive the same, that we may be partakers of Christ's body and blood.' Essentially Cranmer (in 1551!) interprets 1549 by 'quotation' of the 1552 Prayer Book.

While the 1552 Invocation keeps its attention solely on the recipient, the 1549 petition for sanctification, having moved from Calvary to the eucharist, proceeds to focus its attention first on the bread and wine and then, through them, on the recipient.

It is the same with the 1549 prayer of sanctification of the baptismal water. Here we have a totally different prayer from the 1552 counterpart (if only to avoid repetition since they are published almost side by side), beginning with an address to Christ who, it is said, instituted the sacrament in his own baptism in the River Jordan.[22] He is asked to send the Holy Spirit on those who invoke his name, and by the power of his word to sanctify the fountain of baptism so that those baptized in it may be spiritually regenerate. Once again we have the same movement of the prayer through the institution of the sacrament and the sanctified elements to the grace communicated to the recipient. The 1552 distinction between the sacramental elements and actions on the one hand, and the grace on the other, are disguised in the 1549 prayers, and this needs to be read into them rather than being naturally read out of them.

c. Liturgical principles

We have already seen Cranmer's theology of consecration. What liturgical principles does he apply when composing a prayer of consecration/ sanctification? We can see in the prayers of 1549 the same principles as those outlined by Bucer in his defence against the *Antididagma*.[23] First,

---

22 Alone of the four prayers under consideration, the 1549 blessing of the font is addressed to Christ rather than to the Father. So also are the following Grant prayers, as is evident from the fourth petition: 'Whosoever shal confesse the, o lorde: recognise him also in thy kingdome.' The address to Christ follows the Mozarabic precedent, but also that of Osiander. It is hard to see what the attraction would have been for either reformer to have composed such a prayer (I find the idea of the Mozarabic precedent a weak one for determining the question of the addressee of the entire section). In the thanksgiving prayer of the eucharist, Cranmer nodded and asked the Father that 'we may be very members incorporate in thy mystical body': this error left congregations wincing until 1662. Dowden devotes some pages of his *Further Studies* to this subject (see pp. 286–95).

23 'Capitulum Coloniense' speculates on Cranmer's debt to the debates in Cologne and in particular to the *Antididagma* to which he refers several times in his commonplace books. The author curiously believes that Cranmer owed no debt to Bucer, but rather that he was rescued by the *Antididagma* from the 'well-intentioned but mischievous work of Herman and Bucer' (p. 436). Among the items of controversy in the *Antididagma* highlighted by the article are the consecration of the font and the invocation of the Holy Spirit and word in the communion service. (The article does not claim, however, that Cranmer notes these particular points.) The writer notes how unusual it was to have a consecration in a Reformed liturgy (p. 427). The article proceeds to suggest that the position of the blessing of the font in the 1549 book is 'as if it were brought in by an afterthought'.

Likewise, commenting on the *Antididagma*'s criticism of the lack of a eucharistic prayer, the article proceeds to ask: 'Have we here an explanation of the insertion of the words of

consecration is by the word and prayer: and we have prayers which include reference to the scriptural warrant. Secondly, the things are consecrated to a use: eating, drinking, immersion; there is no suggestion that the things in themselves are changed in any way. Thirdly, there is always the explicit invocation of God that he might grant the grace. Fourthly, looking back to 1 Tim. 4.3, it is emphasized that the things consecrated have been created by God for our use: 'thy gyftes, and creatures of bread and wyne'; 'ordeyned the element of water for the regeneracion of thy faythful people . . . Sanctifie ✠ this fountaine of baptisme, thou that art the sanctifier of al thynges.' 'Sanctifier of all things' contrasts markedly with Brightman's suggested source for this prayer from the Mozarabic rite: 'Sanctify this fountain, thou sanctifier of the human race.'[24] Whether or not the source is correct, the contrast is pertinent. For Cranmer, there is no simple connection between the sanctification of the thing and the sanctification of any person. God has created and sanctified all things – for the uses for which they are ordained, and nothing more. There are also differences between the 1549 prayers and Bucer: in particular, the use of the sign of the cross and the similarity to *Quem oblationem* in 'may be unto us' suggest attention to traditionalist concerns. In the 1552 versions these have disappeared altogether, and also the very theme of consecration. There is nothing in them that equates to Bucer's suggestion that the Lord be invoked and that the elements might be of service to us for salvation.

i. The use of the sactification prayer once a month

The water of the font was meant to be changed, and the new water blessed, at least once a month. Therefore, for at least a large number of children baptized the water would already have been blessed on a previous occasion. How did Cranmer theologically justify this? Bucer in his *Censura* entirely disliked the idea of a consecration and bid for its removal altogether. He does not discuss the problem here of blessing the object in the absence of the recipient of the sacrament, and so is of no help for our purposes. However, he refers to his discussion of the consecration of bread and wine, and we too may follow him in drawing the analogy with the eucharist and the Communion of the Sick, where in 1549 the sacrament may be taken from church to a sick person's house, though that is meant to happen as soon as practically possible after the eucharist that day, and reservation for longer is forbidden. Just as a eucharist without communicants is forbidden,

---

invocation, and of their apparently unusual position in this Prayer?' (p. 434). But Cranmer's liturgy of consecration is more in accord with Bucer than with the *Antididagma*.

24   'Sancti✠fica fontem hunc sancti✠ficator generis humani.' Brightman, *English Rite*, Vol. 2, p. 738.

so the font is blessed only when there is a child to be baptized and not on other occasions, such as had formerly been the case.

> For every Easter and Whitsun-even, until this time, the fonts were hallowed in every church, and many collects and other prayers were read for them that were baptized. But alas! in vain, and as it were a mocking with God: for at those times, except it were by chance, none were baptized, but all were baptized before.[25]

We must suppose, then, that however he may have justified the practice in detail, the blessing of the water and its retention was by analogy with the eucharist and reservation of the sanctified bread and wine. Cranmer was allowing the retention of an ancient custom in his first prayer book; the monthly renewal of the water was also required by the Marian bishops, who appealed to the traditional rules in this respect.[26] However, there is one thing we must bear in mind: for Cranmer, consecration effects no change in the elements. It sets something apart for a holy use, but since God created it with that use in mind already, consecration makes no essential difference.

Thus Cranmer might have justified the 1549 blessing of the font from the standpoint of his mature theology.

ii. The sanctification prayers of 1549: structure

It is useful to note how closely the two baptism prayers reflect each other, and also the form of the petition for sanctification in the eucharist. (We shall see later that the Invocation prayer of the 1552 communion service also follows the same shape.) In all these cases there is an equivalent structure:

- Address to God (1549 baptism: to the Son)
- Recitation of a salvific event (1549 baptism: baptism in Jordan, in the others the death of Christ)
- Institution of the sacrament (1549 baptism: ordains water for regeneration; 1552 baptism: words of institution from Matt. 28)
- Invocation of God (1549: blessing of the elements of water or bread and wine)
- Grace imparted to the recipients (Eucharist: words of institution)

---

25 Cranmer, Answer to the Fifteen Articles of the Rebels, Devon, Anno 1549, 6th Article: PS, II, p. 175.

26 Bonner's Articles for London Diocese 1554, Article 58, 'Whether the water consecrated, being in the font, be once a month, at the least, duly changed and renewed, according to the old custom of the Church?'; Frere (ed.), *Visitation Articles*, Vol. 2, p. 346. (A note observes that in 1236 Abp Edmund ordered it to be renewed weekly.)

The structure of the sanctification prayers

1549 eucharist	*1549 baptism*	*1552 baptism invocation prayer*
O God heavenly father, which of thy tender mercie diddest geve thine only sonne Jesu Christ to suffre death upon the crosse for our redempcion, who made there (by his one oblacion once offered) a full, perfect, and sufficient sacrifyce, oblacion, and satysfaccyon, for the sinnes of the whole worlde, and did institute,	O MOSTE mercifull god our savioure Jesu Christ, who hast ordeyned the element of water for the regeneracion of thy faythful people, upon whom, beyng baptized in the river of Jordane, the holye ghoste came down in the likenesse of a doove:	ALMIGHTYE everliving God, whose moste derely beloved sonne Jesus Christe, for the forgevenesse of our sinnes did shead out of his moste precious side bothe water and bloude,
and in his holy Gospell commaund us, to celebrate a perpetuall memory of that his precious death, untyll his comming again:		and gave commaundemente to his disciples that they shoulde goe teache all nacions, and baptize them in the name of the father, the sonne, and the holye ghoste:
Heare us (O merciful father) we besech thee;	Sende down we beseche thee the same thy holye spirite to assiste us, and to bee present at this our invocacion of thy holy name:	Regarde, we beseche thee, the supplicacions of thy congregacion, and
and with thy holy spirite and worde, vouchsafe to bl✠esse and sanc✠tifie these thy gyftes, and creatures of bread and wyne,	Sanctifie ✠this fountaine of baptisme, thou that art the sanctifier of al thynges, that by the power of thy worde,	
that they maie be unto us the bodye and bloude of thy moste derely beloved sonne Jesus Christe. Who . . .	all those that shall be baptized therein, maye be spirituallye regenerated, and made the children of everlasting adopcion. Amen.	graunte that all thy servauntes which shall bee baptized in this water prepared for the mynystracion of thy holy sacrament, maye receive the fulnesse of thy grace, and ever remaine in the noumbre of thy faithful, and elect children, through Jesus Christ our Lord.

iii. The relation of the 1549 and 1552 prayers to one another: evidence
of Cranmer's settled position

The 1552 baptism prayer of invocation began its public life in the 1549
set of prayers for the new water in the font as the final prayer in the
section, being a prayer for the recipients. Considering how it is parallel
in content and form to the Invocation prayer in the eucharist of 1552,
with the quotation of the scriptural words of institution of the sacrament
and the prayer for grace for the recipients, one may naturally suppose
that the two were linked in Cranmer's mind when he composed them
(together or at different times). Furthermore, given the close relationship
in structure and content between the 1549 prayers of sanctification
and the 1552 prayers of invocation, they are evidently composed as
alternative approaches to the same problem, namely, how liturgically one
may express the way in which the grace of the sacrament is applied to
the recipient. Clearly, the 1549 book presents us with the two alternative
forms sitting side by side in the blessing of the font. By the time of the
publication of the 1549 book, Cranmer must have worked out the
option of the baptismal invocation prayer that he adopted in 1552, and
it is quite likely that he had also in mind the equivalent for the eucharist.
The two sacraments were linked far too closely in his theology for them
to be much out of step liturgically.

This leads on logically to the question of how far Cranmer's revision
of the sacramental rites in 1552 was caused or affected by Gardiner or
Bucer, or the other critics of 1549, or to what extent he had already
sketched out the options in his own mind. Given that theologically he
seems to have reached his mature position on the sacraments by the
end of 1548, it is likely that he was one step ahead of his critics and,
for example, already had alternatives to the eucharistic petition for
sanctification which Bucer was to criticize in his *Censura*. It is by no
means impossible that in 1549 he had in his mind the 1552 structure of
the services, just as he already had composed a form of invocation.

d. The sanctification prayer in 1549: Holy Spirit and word

As well as the presence of prayers of 'sanctification', the mention
of the Holy Spirit and 'word' in the 1549 prayers, and the theology
suggested by it, have been much discussed. It would be useful to review
the discussion in order to understand the place of the formula within
the context of the 1549 Prayer Book, and to identify Cranmer's own
intentions and theological understanding.

In the 1549 eucharistic prayer, the prayer for the blessing of the bread
and wine runs as follows: 'Heare us (O merciful father) we besech thee;

and with thy holy spirite and worde, vouchsafe to bl✠esse and sanc✠tifie these thy gyftes, and creatures of bread and wyne . . .' We find the parallel version in the first prayer of the 1549 blessing of the font: 'Sende down we besethe thee the same thy holye spirite to assiste us, and to bee present at this our invocacion of thy holy name: Sanctifie ✠this fountaine of baptisme, thou that art the sanctifier of al thynges, that by the power of thy worde . . .' The overall structure of both prayers is the same: God is invoked so that the elements may be sanctified for the recipients of the sacrament to receive the relevant grace. In both prayers there is mention of the Holy Spirit and the 'word', closely related in the eucharist but rather different in the case of baptism.

The passage in the 1549 eucharistic prayer has been much discussed over the years, mainly with regard to its possible sources rather than its meaning, and without reference to its parallel in the baptism service. The Holy Spirit is clear enough in identity (though the Spirit's role must be discussed). The 'word' is generally and correctly taken to refer to the word of institution rather than to the Word or Logos. (The Scottish-American Anglican tradition picked up this prayer, and in the American prayer book of 1793 'Word' was capitalized and thus taken to refer to the Logos.)[27]

Cranmer's own mature theological understanding of the notion of 'Holy Spirit and word' is nowhere exactly described, but we may easily discern what he would have meant. In one example in which he speaks of the two together, we read:

> This spiritual meat . . . is received with a pure heart and a sincere faith . . . And this faith God worketh inwardly in our hearts by his holy Spirit, and confirmeth the same outwardly to our ears by hearing of his word, and to our other senses by eating and drinking of the sacramental bread and wine in his holy supper.[28]

The primary cause of grace is the Holy Spirit, who works in the heart of the receiver. The word is that of scripture, heard with comfort, and accompanying the sacramental sign. The recipient of the sacrament, granted faith by the Holy Spirit, is open to the true meaning of the word and the true nature of the sacrament as pointing to the reality of spiritual grace.

---

27 R.C.D. Jasper and G.J. Cuming (eds), *Prayers of the Eucharist, Early and Reformed,* (New York: Pueblo, 1987; 3rd edn), p. 312.
28 *Defence*, 1.16: PS, I, p. 43.

i. The King's Book: the basis?

Such was the importance of the King's Book as the benchmark of orthodoxy in Henry's last years that we must consider a quotation from the article on baptism which affirms that all the sacraments 'have all their virtue, efficacy, and strength by the word of God, which by his holy Spirit worketh all the graces and virtues which be given by the sacraments to all those that worthily receive the same'. However, while the reference is similar, the theology is very different. That of 1543 discusses the worthiness of the minister, and thus it is still in the traditionalist understanding whereby the sacrament is the primary cause of grace,[29] whereas in the Reformed doctrine of the Prayer Book (as interpreted by Cranmer himself) the prime cause of grace is the right relationship of the recipient with God, in which the sacrament has (at most) an instrumental role.

ii. 'Spirit and word' as a basis of consensus

We have already met the Vernacular Real Presence Tract in its two surviving versions published by Peter Brooks[30] and by David Selwyn.[31] I have stated above that I do not think the versions we possess can be the 'book of doctrine' produced by the Chertsey conference and discussed in the House of Lords' debate of December 1548. However, they are still interesting as discussion documents of the period. And they agree in affirming

> that Christe the sonne of god, as he is the author of his Sacrament, so by his mightie worde he is the contynuall wourker and doer in the ministracion of the same. And therfore when soever thes wourdes of Christ, This is my bodye, and this is my bludd, bee duelye pronounced in the ministracion of this sacrament, thei ought to be taken not for the wourdes of any other but of our Saviour

---

29   That this is a convention of traditional theology can be seen, e.g., by a passage of Rabanus Maurus, *De Institutione Clericorum*, 1.24:

> Quae [sacramenta] ideo fructuose penes Ecclesiam fiunt, quia sanctus in ea manens Spiritus, eumdem sacramentorum latenter operatur effectum. Unde seu per bonos seu per malos ministros intra Ecclesiam Dei dispensentur, nec bonorum meritis dispensatorum amplificantur haec dona, nec malorum attenuantur, quia neque qui plantat est aliquid, neque qui rigat, sed qui incrementum dat, Deus. (*PL*, 107, col. 309, [quoted in MS Royal 7 B XI, fol. 59]).

30   CCCC, MS 101, pp. 195–204, Appendix, *Cranmer's Doctrine of the Eucharist*, pp. 163–71.

31   Bodleian Library, MS Add. C. 197, fols 61–4, Selwyn, 'Vernacular Tract', pp. 217–29.

Christ himsef whoe wourketh the same thyng that he did at his laste Supper being with his apostles.[32]

Thus far we see phraseology that would suggest a liturgy based solely and entirely on the words of institution as words of consecration. However, again in both versions, the document goes on to attack the 'Capernaite' wrong emphasis on the fleshly understanding of the eucharist:

Christe therefore in this matter putting awaie and dissolving all the vain phantazes, ymaginacions, and questions moved by carnall reason, saith that yt is the spirit that gyveth lief, the flessh propheteth nothing meaning thereby that all carnall ymaginacions of man wherwith the Caphernaites wer trobeled is to be excluded, for as for the flesshe of Christ, it is alwaies ioyned unto the spirit and so the eternall wourde of god, and therby it must neded [*sic* Bodleian MS: needs] profitt yf thei be not altogither in flesshe and not in spirit the which receave it; for then if thei receave it unwourthelie thei eate and drinck ther owne dampnacion because thei have noe considercion of the bodye of our lord.[33]

To compare the King's Book and the Vernacular Real Presence Tract, there would seem to be a certain continuity of theology running through these two documents: the 'virtue, efficacy, and strength' of the sacrament is effected by the word of God (to quote the King's Book), and this theme remains in the Vernacular Tract. However, there is a change of emphasis in the role of the Holy Spirit: in the earlier book it makes irrelevant the unworthiness of the minister and thereby renders the sacrament a trustworthy means of grace. In the later tract the Holy Spirit is active in the case of those who worthily receive the sacrament. This is linked in turn to the spiritual perception of the sacrament and the words 'It is the spirit that giveth life, the flesh profiteth nothing.' In whatever way that verse was used in the discussions that led to these drafts, we see its radical import when Cranmer produces it at the Lords' debate and emblazons it on the title page of his *Defence*. So in the Tract we have moved a long way from the King's Book and towards Cranmer's own mature theology. But whatever the theological allegiance of Cranmer of whatever period, and whatever the status of the Vernacular Tract,

32 CCCC, MS, Brooks, *Cranmer's Doctrine of the Eucharist*, p. 165; cf. Bodleian Library, MS, Selwyn, 'Vernacular Tract', pp. 222–3.
33 CCCC, MS, Brooks, *Cranmer's Doctrine of the Eucharist*, p. 170; cf. Bodleian Library, MS, Selwyn, 'Vernacular Tract', p. 226.

it would seem that anyone whose views were reflected in it could read the petition for sanctification in the 1549 eucharist as affirming these views. Therefore a formula such as that in the 1549 eucharist, 'with thy Holy Spirit and word', might imply to many both the traditional theology of the efficacy of the sacraments (including the Real Presence of Christ in the eucharist) and the need, stressed by traditionalists and reformers alike, for careful preparation on the part of the recipients of the sacrament if they are to receive the sacramental grace.

iii. Eastern liturgies: the epiclesis

Brightman, as we have seen, originally believed that the source for the mention of the Holy Spirit, and the idea of the prayer altogether, lay in the Eastern liturgies. Cranmer had probably studied the liturgies of Basil, certainly John Chrysostom and possibly James.[34] The epiclesis in the Eastern rites came after the words of institution (Cranmer did not know the Egyptian tradition of the epiclesis coming earlier, or the epiclesis of the Word in Sarapion) but the position in 1549 is suggested more by the *Quam oblationem* of the Roman Canon. Such was Brightman's position when he produced *The English Rite*. However, he later abandoned the idea of an Eastern source, in 1927 when he was intent on criticizing, perhaps one should say anathematizing, the proposed new Prayer Book. Now only Western sources were proposed, and an appeal to Eastern precedents for the 1927 revision was attacked.[35] The search for Western rather than Eastern, and medieval as well as Patristic, parallels was now undertaken with gusto. Frere and Ratcliff added their evidence and as a result, says Spinks, the wealth of Western sources 'makes it almost impossible to make any convincing appeal to the Eastern anaphoras'.[36] Indeed, Spinks himself, as we shall see below, has carried on the process of excluding possible Eastern sources by seeking Western ones.

However, if 'Holy Spirit and word' can be seen as functioning as a formula of religious consensus, it is perfectly reasonable to see some influence from the Eastern liturgies. It is not necessary to show that Cranmer was influenced theologically by them. Rather, we need to ask whether they were seen as authorities for doctrine and worship at the time, and whether contemporaries might have seen the connection between the phrasing of 1549 and the Eastern liturgy. In fact, both links in the chain are easily made, and it is reasonable to propose the Eastern

---

34 Summarized by Spinks, 'And with thy Holy Spirite and Worde', in M. Johnson (ed.), *Thomas Cranmer*, pp. 94–102 (p. 95).

35 'The New Prayer Book Examined', *CQR*, 104 (1927), pp. 219–52.

36 Spinks, 'And with thy Holy Spirite and Worde', p. 96.

epiclesis as a convenient source for consensus liturgy, if this is what Cranmer was attempting to produce.

Explicit borrowings from the liturgies were few, as Spinks shows, but discussion was wider. During the debates on the Bishops' Book, we find the conservative Bishop Tunstall carrying 'an old Greek book', and likewise Bishop Stokesley; and using their arsenal of liturgies and canons they cornered the faint-hearted Bishop Sampson of Chichester in the barge on the Thames and in the gallery at Lambeth and bullied him in support of traditional ceremonies. In particular the custom of praying for souls was justified as not being Popish by appeal to the Greek liturgy.[37] At this time the Greek liturgies were also appealed to by the reforming lobby, as we have seen in the essay *De sacramentis*, where the eucharistic sacrifice is interpreted in the light of them.[38]

We have also seen how in the 1540s the *Antididagma* could appeal to the epiclesis of the Greek liturgies as a parallel to the *Quam oblationem*, without any hint that this was in any way inappropriate. There is much in this passage about the words of Christ, but nothing about the 'word' in the singular; otherwise the role of the Holy Spirit and the sign of the cross make good connections with the 1549 rite. It is likely that this discussion influenced the English debate in the reply to the *Questiones de missa* examined above. The Greek epiclesis was abandoned as evidence in favour of Augustine, but its influence may be detected.

Also, the Greek epiclesis is referred to by Bucer in his *Censura* when he discusses the 'Holy Spirit and word' formula. Indeed, the Greek formula 'Make this bread the precious body of thy Son' is quoted and 'changing them by thy Holy Spirit', second only to scriptural verses for God sanctifying things by his word. Bucer has clearly done his homework. But he does not suggest that there is anything incongruous either in invoking the Greeks or in any change of position of an element of the eucharistic prayer.[39]

In Cranmer's commonplaces there are a number of marginal notes to extracts from Patristic writers of both East and West that draw attention to the role of both the 'word' and the Holy Spirit.[40] One passage in particular deserves comment, because it concerns a theological discussion

---

37   J. Strype, *Ecclesiastical Memorials*, Vol. 1/1 (Oxford: Clarendon Press, 1822), pp. 502–4; Vol. 1/2, pp. 381–2.
38   Jeanes, 'Reformation Treatise', p. 176. And Cranmer's commonplaces quote a section of the Liturgy of St John Chrysostom concerning prayer for the departed (ibid., p. 177).
39   *Martin Bucer*, ed. Whitaker, pp. 54/5.
40   MS Royal, 7B XI, fol. 81 on (Ps.) Cyprian, *De coena domini*; fol. 81ᵛ on Irenaeus, li. 5 *contra Valentinum*; fol. 87ᵛ on Chrysostom, *de proditione Jude hom*. 30; fol. 93 on Ambrosius, *De mysteriis*.

by John Damascene of the role of the Holy Spirit in the eucharist, based on the actual liturgical use of the epiclesis in Basil, and because Cranmer returns to the same passage years later in his *Defence*. It therefore functions as an example of how he could use such theological terminology at different times.

First, in the commonplaces (in a collection of patristic passages supporting the eucharistic Real Presence) Cranmer places beside the following passage the comment, 'In a way which surpasses nature by the operation of the Holy Spirit the body of Christ is made in the sacrament.'

> If, then 'the word of the Lord is living and effectual', and if 'whatsoever the Lord pleased he hath done'; if he said, 'Be light made, and it was made' . . . then can he not make the bread his body and the wine and water his blood? . . . [Drawing on the analogy of rainfall as the instrument by which God's command to the earth to bring forth vegetation continues to this day, Damascene explains the fulfilment of 'This is my body', and 'Do this in remembrance of me'.] And through the invocation the overshadowing power of the Holy Ghost becomes a rainfall for this new cultivation. For, just as all things whatsoever God made he made by the operation of the Holy Ghost, so also it is by the operation of the Spirit that these things are done which surpass nature and cannot be discerned except by faith alone.[41]

Cranmer's underlining and his marginal comment follow the way in which Damascene explains the mystery of Christ's presence as effected by the Holy Spirit in the invocation, fulfilling the creative word of God which says 'This is my body' and the command to do this. The marginal note in particular focuses the issue on the bread and wine as the body and blood of Christ. Such is Cranmer's position in the 1530s. In 1550 the same passage of Damascene is discussed at length by Cranmer in

---

41   MS Royal 7 B XI, fols 100–100ᵛ on John Damascene li. 4 orthodoxe fidei ca. 13.

Si igitur verbum dei vivens est et efficax et omnia quaecumque voluit deus fecit, si dixit, fiat lux, et facta est lux . . . non potest panem suum ipsius corpus facere? et vinum et aquam sanguinem? . . . et fit pluvia novae huic agriculturae per invocationem spiritus sancti obumbrans virtus. Nam quemadmodum omnia quae fecit deus spiritu sancto cooperante fecit, sic et nunc spiritus sancti operatione haec supra naturam operatur quae non potest cognoscere nisi sola fides. [marg: supra naturam per spiritus sancti operationem fit corpus Christi in sacramento.

(The marginal note comes by the beginning of this section, but the fact that it echoes the words at the end shows that it refers to the whole section.) Trans. F.H. Chase, Jr, *St John of Damascus Writings* (New York: Fathers of the Church, c. 1958).

his *Defence*, and it is clear from his paraphrase of this section how far his theology has moved from the time he made the underlinings in the commonplaces.

> And as Almighty God by his most mighty word and his holy Spirit and infinite power brought forth all creatures in the beginning, and ever sithens hath preserved them; even so by the same word and power he worketh in us, from time to time, this marvellous spiritual generation and wonderful spiritual nourishment and feeding, which is wrought only by God, and is comprehended and received of us by faith.[42]

Now the focus is not the bread and wine at all, but the recipients in whom God works. The terminology used by Damascene, the word, Spirit and power, are still cited. But their role is subsumed into Cranmer's new sacramental understanding.

The conclusion must be that, although Spinks is right to look for a Reformed theology in the 'Holy Spirit and word' formula, he is wrong to discount the Eastern epiclesis as a distant source, perhaps even as a 'red herring' to placate the traditionalists.

iv. Theological parallels

Spinks has made an important step forward in looking first and foremost at Cranmer's intentions, which were to have a service 'embodying sound doctrine as judged by reformed standards'.[43] It is in the light of this theological criterion that he renews a search, this time for contemporary sources, and he considers and rejects Luther, Zwingli and Calvin, and prefers as possible sources Bucer and, he believes, the closest parallel and so the most likely source, Peter Martyr. But if the phraseology of 'Holy Spirit and word' might seem to fit with the search for a general consensus, then it is plainly advantageous that the term finds parallels in many theologians whom Cranmer would have held to be important at the time.

Spinks quotes a relevant passage of Luther's Sermon against the Fanatics in which he says: 'For as soon as Christ says, "This is my body", it is his body through the word and power of the Holy Spirit.'[44] As Spinks says, this is not typical of Luther's approach, but it may

---

42 *Defence*, 3.15: PS, I, p. 198.
43 Spinks, 'And with thy Holy Spirite and Worde', p. 97.
44 *WA*, 19: 491, trans. in *LW* 36: 341; Spinks, 'And with thy Holy Spirite and Worde', p. 97.

well have enjoyed some following in England. We must consider some quotations in Cranmer's commonplaces from Calvin's Institutes under the heading *De sacramentis*. They are taken from the 1536 edition and effectively serve as a summary of iv.14 (according to the numbering of later editions). If we were looking for a Reformed rather than Lutheran precedent, there is adequate material here. Spinks mentions the possibility, and doubts the likelihood, of the influence of this very passage. But among the lengthy quotations it is worth considering comments such as: 'The sacraments have the same office as the Word of God: to offer and set forth Christ to us, and in him the treasures of heavenly grace . . . And they are of no further benefit unless the Holy Spirit accompanies them. For he it is who opens our minds and hearts and makes us receptive to this testimony.'[45] So for Calvin, along with a strong sense of the reality of grace administered using the sacraments, there is always the proviso that the Holy Spirit is necessary for the role of faith and the effective working of that grace.

Spinks gives us parallels in Bucer and Martyr. He points out how Bucer dislikes the idea of consecrating the elements in the 1549 Prayer Book, preferring the prayer to be for the recipients, but retains the mention of 'word' and Holy Spirit.[46] His own preference as a source is Peter Martyr, who through 1549 defended an understanding of the sacraments around the working of the Holy Spirit and the 'word' or institution of Christ.

He is able to make common bread and wine a most effectual sacrament . . . such a change in it, in which bread and wine are translated from the natural order, and profane degree in which they were, to a sacramental state and order, both by the work of the Holy Spirit and by the institution of the Lord.[47]

As Spinks says, the theology of consecration here is very similar to that of Cranmer.

---

45   Trans. Battles, *Institutes*, pp. 91–2; *Institutes*, iv.14.17, CR 29, col. 107; MS Royal, 7B XI, fol. 61. 'Quamobrem fixum maneat, non esse alias sacramentorum, quam verbi Dei partes; quae sunt, offerre nobis ac proponere Christum et in eo coelestis gratiae thesauros . . . nec ulterius proficiant, nisi accesserit spiritus sanctus, qui mentes ac corda nostra aperiat, nosque huius testimonii capaces reddat.'
46   *Censura*, in Whitaker (ed.), *Bucer*, pp. 52–4; Spinks, 'And with thy Holy Spirite and Worde', p. 98.
47   Disputation at Oxford: IV.Q2, quoted by Spinks, 'And with thy Holy Spirite and Worde', p. 99. Spinks also quotes similar passages from Martyr's tract 80 and his letter to Bucer, 15 June 1549.

However, lest we should believe that this Holy Spirit and 'word' theology is the preserve of the reform camp, we may look at the Catholic *Encheiridion* of Cologne. We do not possess Cranmer's copy or quotations from it in his note books, but its influence is seen in the liturgy and so the following passage may be included here, if for no other reason than to show the breadth of thought on the theme of Spirit and 'word'.

> The sacrament consists of two things, namely the physical element which is the sign, and the word. The word is the invocation of the Trinity which depends on the word of promise. The element is water, oil and other suchlike things. Just as the word is the instrument by which the will of God is signified and apprehended, and through which the Holy Spirit is efficacious (as Paul says, 'Faith comes by hearing, and hearing by the word of Christ', and again, 'The Gospel is the power of God for salvation to everyone who believes'), so the Holy Spirit works efficaciously salvation and confers grace through the sacraments which are like signs and testimonies of God, by which he declares his goodwill towards us for the sake of Christ his Son. And so in the sacrament we should consider not simply the element or the external appearance but rather the word.[48]

Through this ambiguous phrase 'Holy Spirit and word', we are as close to ecumenical consensus as we could possibly be.

v. Holy Spirit and word: a range of meanings

The evidence as presented now suggests a multiplicity of sources which might have struck Cranmer and been known to his colleagues and opponents in England. In the first instance the immediate source of the expression 'Holy Spirit and word' was quite possibly the King's Book.

---

48 *Canones Concilii Provincialis Coloniensis . . . quibus adiectum est Encheiridion Christianae institutionis* (Cologne, 1537), fol. 77.

> Constat enim sacramentum duobus, nempe elemento sensibili uti signo et verbo. Verbum est invocatio trinitatis verbo promissionis innixa. Elementum est aqua, oleum et caetera eiusmodi. Quemadmodum vero verbum instrumentum est quo dei voluntas significatur et apprehenditur et per quod spiritus sanctus efficax est, sicut Paulus ait: Fides ex auditu, auditus autem per verbum Christi. Et iterum: Evangelium est potentia Dei ad salutem omni credenti. Ita per sacramenta tanquam quaedam indicia seu testimonia dei (quibus testatur se nobis placatum propter Christum filium suum) spiritus sanctus efficaciter operatur salutem et conferit gratiam. In sacramento ergo non tantum elementum seu exteriorem speciem respecimus sed magis verbum.

All that is presumed is that the liturgical use of the phrase was penned at
a time when the Book was still the touchstone of doctrine, which was the
case into the first months of Edward's reign. Even when that Book was a
thing of the past, the language continued in the Vernacular Real Presence
Tract, and so could have been part of the furniture of early Edwardian
consensus. Beyond those discussions, almost any writer imaginable seems
to have used language that could claim an echo in these words. We know
that Cranmer was aware of the notions of eucharistic consecration in
ancient writers. Contemporary writers were known and could have been
noted. The range would have made such a liturgical expression tempting
in any rite which looked for acceptance from a wide spectrum of
theological opinions. Incidentally, there is no quotation of any liturgical
source here (apart from the reference to the *Quam oblationem* of the
Canon and the Eastern epiclesis). Cranmer was influenced by theological
considerations rather than liturgical precedents.

But besides the use of 'Holy Spirit and word', the important question
is the meaning of the term. There are two basic approaches. One has its
focus on the reality and efficacy of the sacrament itself, and the occasion
for this is often doubt raised concerning the worthiness of the minister.
In this category can be included the King's Book and the Cologne
Encheiridion, and also Luther: the word and Spirit are the means by
which this bread and wine are connected with the loaf and cup over
which once Christ himself spoke and effected that which he said. Very
different is the approach of Cranmer himself, Martyr, Calvin and Bucer.
For them, the emphasis is on the work of the Holy Spirit, not on the
sacrament, but on the recipient. The wording of the eucharistic prayer of
1549 could be read according to either understanding. In itself it seems
to have passed muster as a piece of consensus liturgical writing, but the
Prayer Book as a whole had moved beyond acceptable consensus, and so
publicly had its principal author before it was published. The House of
Lords' debate marked the end of consensus.

3 THE OBLATION

There was much to discuss about the eucharistic presence of Christ,
but less about the idea of the eucharist being a propitiatory sacrifice
or oblation to God the Father. From *De sacramentis* in the late 1530s
Cranmer was already opposing the medieval theology, attacking the
concept of priests offering the Mass for a particular purpose. Instead of
this the principle was that the people receive the sacrament with regard
to the remission of their own sins, and that the sacrifice of the Mass is
one of thanksgiving. It is allowed, however, that there are prayers in the
service for the living and the dead, and this is acknowledged using the

Greek liturgical language of the λογικὴ λατρεία or spiritual sacrifice (or 'reasonable' sacrifice as we find it literally translated in the Prayer Book's Prayer of Oblation).[49] By 1547 Cranmer had incorporated his critique of sacrifice into his maturing theology of the sacrament as sign:

> The oblation and sacrifice of Christ in the mass is not so called, because Christ indeed is there offered and sacrificed by the priest and the people (for that was done but once by himself upon the cross;) but it is so called, because it is a memory and representation of that very true sacrifice and immolation which before was made upon the cross.[50]

The scholarly understanding of the traditional doctrine of the eucharistic offering was in fact not so different from the above statement. Gardiner could state, 'The catholic doctrine teacheth not the daily sacrifice of Christ's most precious body and blood to be an iteration of the once perfected sacrifice on the cross, but a sacrifice that representeth that sacrifice, and sheweth it also before the faithful eyes, and refresheth the effectual memory of it.'[51] However, the language of sacrifice depended for its rationale on the identity of the bread and wine with the body and blood of Christ, and the self-giving of Christ at the Last Supper with his self-giving on the cross. 'To call the daily offering a "sacrifice satisfactory" must have an understanding that signifieth not the action of the priest, but the presence of Christ's most precious body and blood, the very sacrifice of the world once perfectly offered being propitiatory and satisfactory for all the world.'[52] So this understanding of the eucharist as a sacrifice depended on a theology of the presence of Christ that Cranmer had rejected.

The fifth book of his *Defence* is devoted to the 'Oblation and Sacrifice'. It is a brief piece, but heartfelt all the same, beginning with the declaration that 'The greatest blasphemy and injury that can be against Christ . . . is this, that the priests make their mass a sacrifice propitiatory, to remit the sins as well of themselves, as of other, both quick and dead, to whom they list to apply the same.'[53] Cranmer distinguished between the propitiatory sacrifice for sin and the sacrifice of praise and thanksgiving. 'The first kind of sacrifice Christ offered to God for us;

---

49   *De Sacramentis*, Jeanes, 'Reformation Treatise', p. 176.
50   Questions and Answers concerning some Abuses of the Mass, Cranmer, *PS*, II, p. 150.
51   Gardiner, *Explication*, Cranmer, PS, I, p. 360.
52   Gardiner, *Explication*, Cranmer, PS, I, p. 361. Fisher took the same approach: Rex, *Fisher*, pp. 132–3.
53   *Defence*, PS, II, p. 345.

the second kind we ourselves offer to God by Christ. And by the first kind of sacrifice Christ offered also us unto his Father, and by the second we offer ourselves and all that we have unto him and his Father.'[54] It is affirmed that the Mass was called a sacrifice because it represented the sacrifice of Christ, but even the Last Supper was no propitiatory sacrifice, only one of praise and thanksgiving.[55] The communion of the people is set in opposition to the priestly sacrifice:

> If we put the oblation of the priest in the stead of the oblation of Christ, refusing to receive the sacrament of his body and blood ourselves, as he ordained, and trusting to have remission of our sins by the sacrifice of the priest in the mass . . . we do not only injury to Christ, but also commit most detestable idolatry . . . The true use of the Lord's Supper is to be restored again; wherein godly people assembled together may receive the sacrament every man for himself, to declare that he remembereth what benefit he hath received by the death of Christ, and to testify that he is a member of Christ's body, fed with his flesh, and drinking his blood spiritually.[56]

There is, for Cranmer, no real difference between the lay person and the priest: the latter are simply the necessary functionaries.

> The priests and ministers prepare the Lord's supper, read the gospel, and rehearse Christ's words, but all the people say thereto, Amen. All remember Christ's death, all give thanks to God, all repent and offer themselves an oblation to Christ, all take him for their Lord and Saviour, and spiritually feed upon him, and in token thereof they eat the bread and drink the wine in his mystical supper.[57]

The 'Prayer of Oblation', as it is often called in its 1552 form, formed the section of the 1549 Canon after the words of institution. The wording is based closely on the medieval Canon, but the theology is very different. We may usefully consider it section by section.

> WHERFORE, O Lorde and heavenly father, accordyng to the Instytucyon of thy derely beloved sonne, our saviour Jesu Christ, we thy humble servauntes do celebrate, and make here before thy

---

54 *Defence*, PS, II, p. 346.
55 *Defence*, PS, II, pp. 351, 359.
56 *Defence*, PS, II, pp. 349–50.
57 *Defence*, PS, II, p. 350.

> divine Majestie, with these thy holy giftes, the memoryall whyche thy sonne hath wylled us to make, havyng in remembraunce his blessed passion, mightie resurreccyon, and gloryous ascencion, renderyng unto thee most hartie thankes, for the innumerable benefites procured unto us by the same, entierely desiryng thy fatherly goodnes, mercifully to accepte this our Sacrifice of praise and thankesgeving: most humbly beseching thee to graunt, that by the merites and death of thy sonne Jesus Christ, and through faith in his bloud, we and al thy whole church, may obteigne remission of our sinnes, and all other benefites of hys passyon.

The anamnesis, picking up Christ's command to do this in remembrance of him, follows the medieval Canon in commemorating not only the death of Christ (as we find in the petition for sanctification which follows 1 Cor. 11.26) but also the resurrection and Ascension. However, while the Canon proceeds immediately to offer the consecrated bread and wine to God, the 1549 prayer contents itself with 'rendering hearty thanks' and offering the sacrifice simply of praise and thanksgiving. That is why the eucharist was instituted by Christ: to remember his death, not to offer it to the Father. This section received considerable criticism at the House of Lords' debate, with Bishop Day of Chichester having proposed words to be added to include an offering in the style of the old Canon.[58] The prayer continues by asking that the congregation, and the whole Church, may receive the benefits of the passion. The emphasis is on faith in Christ's blood – in other words, not trust in the sacramental elements or action. The primacy of Christ's own sacrifice has already been stated in the petition for sanctification: that God gave his Son 'Jesu Christ to suffre death upon the crosse for our redempcion, who made there (by his one oblacion once offered) a full, perfect, and sufficient sacrifyce, oblacion, and satysfaccyon, for the sinnes of the whole worlde.' We merely receive the benefits of the propitiatory sacrifice of Christ, and respond with thanksgiving.

> And here wee offre and present unto thee (O Lorde) oure selfe, oure soules, and bodies, to be a reasonable, holy, and lively sacrifice unto thee: humbly besechyng thee, that whosoever shalbee partakers of thys holy Communion, maye worthely receive the most precious body and bloude of thy sonne Jesus Christe: and bee fulfilled with thy grace and heavenly benediccion, and made one bodye with thy sonne Jesu Christe, that he maye dwell in them, and they in hym.

---

58 Buchanan, *Background Documents*, p. 18.

The worthy reception and mutual indwelling of the faithful with Christ have already been discussed. Here we see the context of fruitful communion being the self-oblation of the worshippers to God, again as the response of those who have accepted the propitiatory sacrifice of Christ.

> And although we be unworthy (through our manyfolde synnes) to offre unto thee any Sacryfice: Yet we beseche thee to accepte thys our bounden duetie and service, and commaunde these our prayers and supplicacions, by the Ministery of thy holy Angels, to be brought up into thy holy Tabernacle before the syght of thy dyvine majestie; not waiyng our merites, but pardonyng our offences, through Christe our Lorde . . .

The final section of the prayer is again reminiscent of the old Canon with the ministry of the angels. But now they bring before God not the offering of the Church but the petitions of the congregation. Also gone is the theme of reciprocity from the original prayer, in which God responds to the people's offering by pouring on them his blessing and grace. Now there is a reminder of our unworthiness and sin which impedes even our response to Christ and our petitions to the Father, but which God in his love overlooks and forgives.

This section may well owe its wording (and even its existence) to a search for consensus, in that it echoes a phrase to be found in the *Questiones de missa* where the etymology of the word 'Mass' is being discussed:

> The Etymologie after the hebriue is this: *communis et voluntaria oblacio que manu offertur* And therfor Deut. 16 where we have *spontaneam oblacionem* the hebriue hath *massha*. Summe deducte it *a mittendo* ffor the prest being a mediator betwene god and the people in this publique accion sendethe up this oblacion the desyres and Requestes of the people.[59]

Here the author is borrowing from John Fisher, and provides a very moderate account of what the oblation consists of.[60] It is as though Cranmer could use these thoughts for his own scheme.

---

59 *Questiones de missa*, fol. 67[v].

60 J. Fisher, *Defensio Regie Assertionis contra Babylonicam captivitatem* (Cologne: Quentel, 1525), fols 84–84[v]:

> Porro, quantum ad Etimologiam spectat, parum refert unde deductam hanc misse vocem putes, an ab emittendo, an ab demittendo, an a promittendo, aut demum ut

4 THE RECEPTION OF THE 1549 PRAYER BOOK

We know from contemporary sources that the reception of the 1549 Prayer Book was mixed. The popular reaction was often unfavourable. The rebels of Devon expressed their disgust in the new service book, describing it as 'but like a Christmas game'. They demanded the restoration of the Latin Mass 'celebrated by the priest, without any man or woman communicating with him', of general communion only at Easter, and of the sacrament being reserved. Also they attacked the practice of administering baptism on a Sunday rather than a weekday. Cranmer could exercise his learning at the expense of the less erudite longing after the familiar, mocking the Cornish preference for Latin over English, and after pointing out that baptism on any day is permitted in case of necessity made an attack on baptism *quam primum* and on the blessing of fonts at Easter and Whitsun when there were none to be baptized.[61]

Articles of Enquiry around this time give other evidence of reactions. Ridley's Articles for London Diocese 1550 include the following queries:

37. Whether the minister receiveth the Sacrament except there be one at the least to communicate with him?

38. Whether the minister useth any elevation or showing the Sacrament before the distribution thereof?

39. Whether the minister or any other doth reserve the Sacrament, and not immediately receive it?

40. Whether any tarrieth in the choir after the Offertory, other than those that do communicate, except clerks and ministers?

45. Whether there be any that privately in their private houses have their Masses contrary to the Form and Order of the book of Communion?

47. Whether baptism be ministered (out of necessity) in any other time than on the Sunday or holy-day, or in any other tongue than English?

48. Whether any speaketh against baptism of infants?

57. Whether any useth to hallow . . . the font on Easter-even . . .

58. Whether the water in the font be changed every month once, and then any other prayers said than is in the Book of Common Prayer appointed?[62]

---

nonnullis placet a transmittendo . . . [fol. 85ᵛ] Aliis visa fuit a transmissione vocari, quod, per sacerdotem qui mediatoris vice fungatur inter deum et homines, preces et vota simul et oblationes deo transmittantur.

61   'Answers to the Fifteen Articles of the Rebels, Devon, Anno 1549', Article 6, PS, II, pp. 169–80.
62   Ridley's Articles for London Diocese, 1550: Frere, *Visitation Articles*, Vol. 2, pp. 237–9.

The Articles about the eucharist show how it was not just the rebels of Devon who disliked the requirement for more frequent communion, and how determined the Reformers had to be to remove those who wished to remain simply to see but not receive the sacrament. Article 48 suggests worries about the influence of Anabaptists. But Articles 47, 57 and 58 are evidently mainly concerned with the possibility of traditional ceremonies being retained. The baptism of infants other than on a Sunday is now to be allowed for emergency only (no doubt raising for many the same concern that the rebels of Devon entertained). The monthly changing of the water is to be accompanied only by the prayers specified in the new Prayer Book, and the banning of the Easter hallowing of the font, effected by the demise of the old rite, is enforced.

There are many instances of popular unhappiness or simply confusion. People's worshipping patterns were not going to change overnight, and it is by no means clear how well prepared congregations, or even the clergy, were for this innovation. Eamon Duffy gives various instances of wills requesting traditional observances within the framework of the new regulations.[63] Martin Bucer mentions, among other examples of conservatism, such unwillingness to receive communion that people were paying poor people to communicate in their place, and a popularity for private Masses which was fully prepared to accept the Antecommunion, referred to as a 'memorial', as at least better than nothing.[64]

Another source of information is the baptism registers extant from the period: it was one thing for central government to demand that healthy babies be baptized on the Sunday or holy day, but was this actually carried out? It was clearly a matter of concern, as has been seen in Ridley's Visitation Articles for London Diocese in 1550. A full survey of the available evidence would go beyond this particular study, but a brief perusal of a number of surviving baptism registers in Somerset would suggest very wide variety of practice. In West Buckland the Sunday rule seems to have been applied rigorously with very few exceptions. In Trull and Milverton, on the other hand, it would appear to have been ignored altogether with no change of practice from beforehand. In the author's home parish of North Curry the response was somewhat fitful, with careful observance in the middle of 1549 soon waning and the old practice re-establishing itself by October. The clergy seem to have tried again, somewhat half-heartedly, in the first half of 1550, and then to have given up until the advent of the 1552 Prayer Book. Nearly all the baptisms in 1553 were on Sundays or holy days, but slipped back into traditional practice as the reign of Edward closed.

---

63 *Stripping of the Altars*, pp. 470–1.
64 *Censura*, in Whitaker (ed.), *Bucer*, pp. 20, 30.

One interesting example of liturgical adjustment of the baptismal service can be found in annotations to a copy of the Prayer Book now in the Bodleian Library in Oxford, where after the blessing of the font are to be found (subsequently crossed out) the words spoken after the blessing in the Sarum *Manual*, when consecrated oil and chrism are added to the water separately and then together:

coniuncio olii uncionis & aqua baptismatis in nomine –
fecundetur et sanctificetur fons iste salutifero crismate in nomine
coniuncio crismatis sanctificationys & olii uncionis
aqua baptismalis in nomine patris – [65]

The insertion of these words is a clear example of the kind of practice we hear about, in which the 1549 rite was administered in as similar a way to the Sarum rite as possible. Less controversially, the annotator also prefixes the signing with the cross at the beginning of the rite with 'wat shal be the name of thes chyld'.

On the side of the Protestant reformers, we hear little comment. Francis Dryander, writing to Bullinger in June 1549, comments favourably on the Prayer Book. He concentrates on the issue of the communion service, but he comments, 'certain ceremonies are retained in that book which may appear useless, and perhaps hurtful, unless a candid interpretation be put upon them'. He goes on to complain about the obscurity of the language, and obviously regards it as not a masterpiece of liturgical prose.[66] Martin Bucer and Paul Fagius wrote to the ministers at Strasbourg, welcoming the new Prayer Book and saying that it is regarded as an interim revision: traditional ceremonies are retained as a concession, but 'they are only to be retained for a time'.[67]

---

65 Bodleian Library press mark S. Seld. d.40. This is a copy of the 1st edn, published by Whitchurch, 7 March 1549. Cf. the Sarum *Manual*, p. 35:

    Post hec mittat sacerdos oleum sanctum cum ipsa billione que est in vase eius in aquam: signum crucis faciens et dicens

    Coniunctio olei unctionis et aque baptismatis. In nomine patris et filii et spiritus sancti. Amen.

    Simili modo mittat chrisma dicens

    Fecundetur et sanctificetur fons iste hoc salutifero chrismate salutis. In nomine patris etc.

    Postea mittat simul oleum cum chrismate modo supra dicto dicens

    Coniunctio chrismatis sanctificationis et olei unctionis et aque baptismatis. In nomine patris etc.

66 Dryander to Bullinger, 5 June 1549, trans. in PS, *Original Letters*, Vol. 1, pp. 350–1.

67 Trans., PS, *Original Letters*, Vol. 2, pp. 535–6.

6 TOWARDS 1552

We know very little about the process of revision that led to the second Prayer Book. The first step was the production in March 1550 of the Ordinal as a separate volume from the Prayer Book (though it was to be revised and bound with subsequent editions later). The official business of producing the Ordinal was swift. An act of parliament on 31 January 1550 set up the committee, whose members were named on 2 February and completed the work on 8 February. Ratcliff sensibly sees their work as being to approve a form set before them, especially when Strype records an ordination on 31 December 1549 which used the 'order that was soon after established'.[68] In the summer of 1550 Cranmer's *Defence of the True and Catholic Doctrine of the Body and Blood of our Saviour Christ* was published, making clear for all the theological understanding which the main author of the 1549 Prayer Book had of his liturgy.[69]

Besides these publications, we hear of steps being taken in matters of ceremonial and practice which were to be enshrined in the 1552 revision. In November 1550, following Ridley's initiative in the Diocese of London, the Council ordered the removal of altars, to be replaced by a table.[70] In the Diocese of Gloucester, Hooper ordered the Ten Commandments to be recited along with the Creed, Lord's Prayer and General Confession by those who were to receive communion.[71] His attempt to eschew vestments was less successful, and had to be abandoned. Reform (but not total abolition) of vestments would come in the new Prayer Book, but only then by due authority, not by the whim even of a bishop.[72] Seated communion was on the agenda of the more extreme reformers. John Laski's Stranger Churches recommended it by example; Hooper asked for it in sermons.[73] They were not to sway the commission which oversaw the revision of the Prayer Book, but the issue did not go away easily. In 1551 appeared Gardiner's reply to Cranmer's *Defence. An Explication and Assertion of the Catholic Faith Touching the most Blessed Sacrament of the Altar* relied, among

---

68   E.C. Ratcliff, *The Book of Common Prayer of the Church of England: Its Making and Revisions 1549–1661* (London: SPCK, 1949), p. 67; J. Strype, *Memorials of Archbishop Cranmer*, 3 vols and Appendix (Oxford: Ecclesiastical History Society, 1848–54), Vol. 2, p. 128.
69   For the date of publication, see MacCulloch, *Cranmer*, p. 462.
70   Cuming, *History*, p. 72.
71   Injunctions, Gloucester Diocese, 1551; PS, *Later Writings of Bishop Hooper*, pp. 132–3.
72   MacCulloch, *Thomas Cranmer*, pp. 479–84.
73   MacCulloch, *Thomas Cranmer*, pp. 479–80; Hooper, Sixth Sermon on Jonas, PS *Early Writings of Bishop Hooper*, p. 536. The sermons were preached before the King and Council in the Lent of 1550.

other more obvious authorities for a defence of Catholic theology, on the eucharist of 1549. Gardiner quotes the petition for sanctification as supporting the consecration of the bread and wine to be the body and blood of Christ, and the words of Christ, 'This is my body', etc., to be 'not only a memory but an effectual memory, with the very presence of Christ's body and blood, our very sacrifice: who doing now, as he did then, offereth himself to his Father as he did then'.[74] Likewise, the words of administration are taken to affirm the presence of Christ in the sacramental bread and wine, and also the note ordering the bread to be broken at communion, stating that 'menne muste not thynke lesse to be receyved in parte then in the whole, but in eache of them the whole body of our saviour Jesu Christ'.[75] The adoration of the sacrament in the elevation had been banned, but Gardiner claimed to find it in the Prayer of Humble Access.[76] This wilful manipulation of Cranmer's consensus approach to liturgical writing (which Gardiner would probably have maintained was deceitful in any case) made the earlier Prayer Book indefensible as a standard of Reformed worship. Certainly the door to that kind of understanding of the liturgy would have to be closed, but disagreements with fellow Reformers during this period suggest that Cranmer may have expended more time and energy defining details of theology within the spectrum represented by his colleagues and allies and determining the pace of change in matters of ceremonial.

In the winter of 1549/50 the Convocation of Canterbury discussed, among other details of the authorized Prayer Book, saints' days and the words of administration at the eucharist.[77] On 12 January 1550 Bucer, in a letter quoted by Beza, said that no foreigners were being consulted about the revision.[78] But a year later, Peter Martyr and Martin Bucer made their submissions on the Prayer Book in January 1551, and it is evident from Martyr's comments in his letter to Bucer of 12 January that

---

74 *Explication*, Cranmer, PS, I, pp. 79, 83.
75 *Explication*, Cranmer, PS, I, pp. 55, 142.
76 *Explication*, Cranmer, PS, I, p.229. These citations by Gardiner and others are noted by Buchanan, *What did Cranmer think he was Doing?*, p. 32.
77 MacCulloch, *Cranmer*, p. 505; P. Heylin, *Ecclesia Restaurata, or the History of the Reformation of the Church of England*, ed. J.C. Robertson, Vol. 1 (Cambridge: Ecclesiastical History Society, 1849), pp. 227–8. MacCulloch understands Heylin's note about conversations concerning 'the different manner of administering the holy Sacrament' to refer to 'nationwide variety', but it could refer to the new prescriptions in the 1549 Prayer Book of administering the chalice to the laity and breaking the consecrated wafer before administration.
78 Quoted by Richard Lawrence, *An Attempt to Illustrate those Articles of the Church of England which the Calvinists improperly consider as Calvinistical*, Bampton Lectures, 1804 (Oxford: W. Baxter, 1838; 3rd edn), p. 246: 'Quod me mones de puritate rituum, scito hic neminem extraneum de his rebus rogari.'

the bishops had already agreed on revision. By February, Martyr could report that they had agreed on a large number of alterations. He himself had seen a copy of the 1549 book with the emendations annotated in it. He could not read English and so could make nothing of them; however, he suspected that the reform would be a half-hearted one, failing to meet his and Bucer's observations. Martyr was concerned that a second interim reform after the pattern of 1549 would bring the process into disrepute: frequent changes help no one. Cranmer, he believed, would have performed the work well if it had been his task alone, but he had to carry with him the other bishops.[79] Martyr presents us with the picture of a task half done. The agenda seems to have been agreed in 1550 and the opinions of people like Bucer and Martyr sought at the end of that year. The main hard work of the revision must therefore have been undertaken in 1551. Martyr speaks as though a large amount was achieved in January and early February, but it is hard to imagine that those months, taken up with Hooper's vestments controversy and the trial of Bishop Gardiner for disobedience, can have been congenial for liturgical composition. There was time enough for Martyr to be further disenchanted with the process. In a letter to Bullinger of 14 June 1552, which we have considered above (Chapter 4, pp. 171–5), he commented on the completed reform of the book, and added a long complaint about the failure of the bishops to achieve unanimity in sacramental theology.

The most important document surviving from this process is Bucer's *Censura*, a discussion and critique of the entire 1549 Prayer Book with recommendations for further reforms. One manuscript version of this document says (in an annotation by another hand) that it is addressed to the Bishop of Ely, Thomas Goodrich, and Charles Whitaker, the editor of the modern edition, believes that the internal evidence of the *Censura* supports this view.[80] Peter Martyr's comments, relying in part on a copy of Bucer's work, have not survived.[81] It is difficult to assess what influence Bucer's *Censura* had on the revision process: the Reformers were all pulling in broadly the same direction, and while it is easy to see where Cranmer was making political concessions to the traditionalists it is more difficult to say where he went out of his way to include Bucer's contributions. Cuming suggests that Martyr's comments may have been of more influence, if only by arriving before Bucer's did, and many changes may have been decided upon already by Cranmer. According to Cuming, of some 60 criticisms made by Bucer, about two dozen were

---

79 Martyr to Bucer, letters of 12 January 1551 and undated (probably February 1551), trans. Gorham, *Gleanings*, pp. 227–33.
80 Whitaker (ed.), *Bucer*, pp. 2–3.
81 Cf. Peter Martyr's letter to Bucer of 10 January 1551, Strype, *Memorials of Cranmer*, Vol. 2, pp. 661–4.

adopted and about the same number ignored. Others were dealt with in various ways. In particular, his concerns about the theology of the eucharist would not be treated positively in the new book.[82]

Bucer's main comments on the eucharist are as follows:[83]

- The initial notes requiring communicants to give their name to the minister beforehand and giving the minister the right to exclude evil-livers is praised.
- The use of traditional vestments is criticized.
- The provision for the Antecommunion is criticized as providing room for superstitious abuse.
- The communion service in private chapels should not be allowed at all.
- The directions for the bread used for the service should allow for the use of leavened bread.
- The note about reception of a piece of the bread should be rephrased to explain the symbolic nature of the breaking of bread, or omitted altogether.
- The minimum requirement of annual communion should be replaced by an expectation of frequent communion.
- The requirement for frequent and attentive attendance in the parish church is supported.
- Receiving the sacrament in the mouth is criticized: it is better to receive it in the hand.
- It is observed that few parishes are practising the offertory collection in the poor man's box: this should be encouraged more.
- The division of communicants into men and women on either side of the chancel is accepted, but the position of the table needs to be reconsidered, and the small number of communicants challenged.
- The rubric limiting the bread and wine to what is needed for communion suggests that it is wrong to use what remains afterwards for ordinary purposes. People should be disabused on this matter.
- In many churches the clerks were singing the Sanctus and Agnus Dei during the priest's prayers, contrary to the rubrics. This should be stopped.
- The prayer for the departed should be removed from the prayer for the Church.

---

82 Cuming, *History*, pp. 73–4. N. Scott Amos, 'Martin Bucer and the Revision of the 1549 Book of Common Prayer', *Reformation and Renaissance Review*, 2 (1999), pp. 107–26, argues for Bucer having greater influence on the 1552 Prayer Book.
83 *Censura*, in Whitaker (ed.), *Bucer*, pp. 16–81.

- The Canon should ask for the people, not the bread and wine, to be blessed and sanctified for communion. The signs of the cross and the directions to the priest to take the bread and wine at the words of institution should also be omitted.
- The reference to the angels bringing the people's prayers to God should be omitted: it is appreciated that the motive was to preserve reminiscences of the traditional rite, but such abuses should be avoided rather than imitated.
- Finally Bucer asks, at great length and with deep passion, that the Prayer of Humble Access should continue to speak of the communicants receiving the body and blood of Christ in the holy mysteries of bread and wine. The bread and wine are indeed signs of the body and blood, but not signs of things absent.

With regard to baptism, Bucer makes the following points:[84]

- The practice of baptizing children in the presence of the congregation is praised.
- Baptisms should therefore be performed not in morning or evening prayer, but after the sermon in the communion service, when the greatest number of people is present.
- Pastors should be given notice of a baptism in advance, in order to enhance respect for the sacrament.
- The whole service should be said in the church, rather than part at the door. The children of the faithful, being already holy, can be brought straight into church.
- The white robe and the chrism should be discontinued.
- The Flood prayer should omit the reference to the sanctification of Jordan and other waters through Christ's baptism.
- The sign of the cross on the forehead and breast may be retained as long as it is properly understood.
- Liturgical statements should not be addressed to the unconscious infant but to God or the congregation.
- 'They, coming to holy baptism', should be amended to 'who are brought to thy holy baptism'.
- The exorcism be no longer a casting of demons out of the child but a prayer for deliverance from the power of the devil.
- Godparents should not speak in the child's name but should themselves promise to bring up the child in the faith.
- Concerning emergency baptism, Bucer is more concerned with Anabaptist attacks on baptism than on any superstitious addiction

---

84 Whitaker (ed.), *Bucer*, pp. 82–101.

to the custom. He affirms that baptism in such cases should not be delayed. What he said about godparents above also applies here.
• The consecration of the baptismal water should be amended (presumably to become a prayer for the recipients of the sacrament).

It will be evident that some of these points made by Bucer were met in 1552 and others were ignored, including some of the most important and distinctive points. In the eucharist, as Cuming observed, the point that Bucer stressed most urgently, that of the theology of the body and blood of Christ being received in the holy mysteries, was rejected. This was not just a defensive ploy against Gardiner's liking for the phrase: Cranmer's theology was different from Bucer's. Of the many points in which the new service was in accord with Bucer's recommendations, one cannot be confident that the Strasbourg Reformer's comments were the cause of change. The 1552 invocation prayer was already foreshadowed by its baptismal parallel in the 1549 book. Hooper was already challenging vestments and Ridley was experimenting with the position of the communion table. In the baptism service, the Flood prayer was in fact revised, but the clause to which Bucer objected remained. The alterations to the affirmations by the godparents do not in any way meet his objections. Those changes which he sought, such as the omission of the exorcism and certain ceremonies, and holding the entire service at the font, might easily have been decided on anyway as part of a simplification of the rite. The 1552 baptism service, with its many prayers, short exhortations and the prominent role of the godparents, still looks closer to Lutheran than to Reformed rites. In short, it is hard to say that Bucer had any significant influence on the revision process.

In addition one might wonder at certain things which Bucer failed to comment on. In the eucharist he had pleaded for the close linking of the sacramental sign and the signified grace. In the preface to the 1549 baptism service, as we shall see, the rite suggests that these two are distinct. Bucer does not comment on this in the *Censura*, but someone did, for the most obvious passages, in the Introduction and the Flood prayer, were amended in 1552. And Bucer failed to commend the exhortations which speak of the congregation praying for the child to be baptized, a feature which he used in his own rites in Strasbourg. It is as though the finer points of theological detail have been omitted from the *Censura*. And here we must remember that it was addressed to Goodrich and would presumably have worked its way through the various revision committees, not all of whose members would have been sympathetic to the venture. Did Bucer write separately to Cranmer, and if so, what would he have said as one liturgist to another? It is hard to imagine that he would have contented himself with the comments in the *Censura*.

The Uniformity bill relating to the revised book was read in the House of Lords on 9 March 1552, and was finally passed on 14 April. The new Prayer Book was to come into use on All Saints Day. According to the Act of Uniformity, the former Prayer Book was a 'very godly order', which had been misunderstood. The revision was therefore 'as well for the more plain and manifest explanation [of divers doubts], as for the more perfection of the said order of common service'.[85] Politically, the emphasis was on the former aspect of making plain what was obscure in the 1549 book. Theologically, it could be said to be true also of Cranmer's own intent. But the 'more perfection' was perhaps an honest appraisal of the revision, in that the changes went far beyond explanation and clarification. The former policy of seeking a consensus across the broad spectrum of religious thought had been abandoned, and the new liturgy enshrined an explicit Reformed theology of the sacraments.

In September and October 1552 an argument broke out over whether congregations should receive communion kneeling or seated. On 27 September the Council ordered Grafton to stop the work of printing the new Prayer Books. Cranmer's letter to the Council of 7 October successfully defended the Prayer Book as authorized by parliament, sealed with the Great Seal and deposited with the clerk of parliament. (It seems from his comments that the Council had tried to change details under the pretext that they were printers' errors.) As for the matter of seated or kneeling communion, he stated that it had been considered by 'a great many bishops and others of the best learned within this realm and appointed for that purpose'.[86] The eventual resolution was that kneeling communion should be maintained and explained by what was to be known as the Black Rubric, appended to the book by order of Council on 22 October.[87]

MacCulloch presents the September discussion over seated communion as a bolt from the blue and an aspect of the rivalry between Cranmer and Northumberland. No doubt the latter was true, but there is some evidence that the former was not. Hooper and Laski had already raised the issue earlier in the process of reform, and as Cranmer says in his letter to the Council, it had been discussed and rejected by the commission. But we need to look more closely at the process of authorization in parliament of the new Prayer Book. The long gap between the Act being passed in April and the enforcement of it in November makes good

---

85   Brightman, *English Rite*, Vol. 1, pp. cxlix–cxlx, 9–23.
86   *Calendar of State Papers Domestic Edward VI*, ed. C.S. Knighton (London: HMSO, 1992; rev. edn), no. 725, p. 264.
87   MacCulloch, *Cranmer*, p. 525.

sense for proper arrangements to be made (though the publication of the books was still not ready and could be halted at the end of September). However, there are hints of rush and dissent at this crucial phase. First, the Bill for Uniformity which was read in the Lords on 9 March absorbed another bill, 'For the appointing an order to come to divine service', enforcing attendance at the 1549 rites. This bill had been read for the third time in the Lords and the first time in the Commons on 26 January, but then its progress had stalled.[88] So in January or February of 1552 there was some change of policy at least in the matter of the timing of legislation. This was awkward from the point of view of the enforcement of worship, in that the necessary legal backing would not grow its teeth until All Saints Day.[89] Perhaps the two bills were joined together for the sake of tidiness, in which case we might suppose that either the draft Prayer Book was ready earlier than expected, or that other parliamentary business forced a change in the timetable. However, dissent might be surmised from comments by Roger Hutchinson, Fellow of Eton, in a sermon preached on the Sunday before Easter, 10 April 1552. In the period that the bill for the Prayer Book was progressing through parliament, Hutchinson criticized the 1549 eucharist for blessing the bread and wine, held out hopes for the administration of the bread into the communicant's hand rather than the mouth, and went on to mention the possibility of seated communion. But however excellent these things, Hutchinson reminded his hearers that they must wait on due authority for any changes.[90] He was obviously well enough connected to know something of the discussions behind the new Prayer Book. Some changes he presented as very likely, that of seated communion less so. This may have simply reflected his hopes, but it raises the possibility that the sudden bringing forward of the authorization of the Prayer Book left the more extreme Reformers disappointed and feeling that they had not been heard. Perhaps the discussions of the commission finished without any satisfactory conclusion on the matter. If so, then for the second time Cranmer went to parliament with a completed Prayer Book but with less than complete consensus. For the time being, the losers would have had to accept the situation, but the leisurely, indeed slack, progress in publication then gave Northumberland his opportunity for raising the matter again at the very last moment, this time using Knox rather than Hooper.

---

88 Brightman, *English Rite*, Vol. 1, p. cl.
89 MacCulloch, *Cranmer*, p. 528, links Ridley's moves against the Stranger churches in November 1552 to Cranmer's victory over Knox and Northumberland in October, but it could also relate to the Act of Uniformity which only now came into force.
90 The First Sermon on the Lord's Supper, R. Hutchinson, *Works*, ed. J. Bruce, PS (Cambridge: Cambridge University Press, 1842), pp. 226, 231–2.

7 THE 1552 PRAYER BOOK

Colin Buchanan describes the 1552 communion service as 'no accident, no afterthought, and no overreaction'.[91] This judgement is entirely correct when comparing that service with its 1549 predecessor. One could not make the same assessment about everything in the second Prayer Book, but certainly it reflects much more clearly Cranmer's mature theology than did the first book. The title is slightly changed: *The Boke of Common Prayer, and administracion of the Sacramentes and other rites and Ceremonies in the Churche of Englande*; and the order of contents similarly shows little difference. The note on ceremonies is now found after the Preface rather than at the end, the Litany has been moved to a more sensible position, and the Ordinal is now bound in the book. However, virtually every service shows a marked step away from conservative sensibilities in the direction of reform.[92] Here we have space to consider only the two sacraments.

a. The core of the two sacraments compared

Before we examine the communion and baptism services of the new Prayer Book it is important to note that there is now a marked similarity in the structure and content of the administration of the sacraments. Their structures are not completely identical but they are so close that this must have been a deliberate and self-conscious feature of the liturgy, reflecting also Cranmer's repeated assertion in his *Defence* and *Answer* that the two sacraments should be understood together.

Structure of the 'core' of the services compared	
Baptism	*Eucharist*
	Sursum corda, Preface, Sanctus
Grant prayers	Prayer of Humble Access
Invocation prayer	Invocation prayer
Administration of baptism	Administration of communion
Reception and signing with cross	
Lord's Prayer	Lord's prayer
Thanksgiving prayer	Thanksgiving prayer or Prayer of Oblation

Within this structure the two Invocation prayers and the two Thanksgiving prayers can be compared. The Invocation prayers follow the same

---

91   Buchanan, *What did Cranmer Think he was Doing?*, p. 21.
92   For an overview of the whole book see Cuming, *History*, pp. 75–86.

structure of (1) remembrance of the saving death of Christ; (2) mention of the institution of the sacrament (with the eucharist Invocation prayer concluding with the words of insititution); (3) petition that God will hear the prayer; (4) asking that those who receive the sacramental washing or food will also receive the grace signified.

The Invocation prayers compared

Baptism	*Eucharist*
ALMIGHTYE everliving God, whose moste derely beloved sonne Jesus Christe, for the forgevenesse of our sinnes did shead out of his moste precious side bothe water and bloude,	ALMIGHTY God oure heavenly father, whiche of thy tender mercye dyddest geve thine onely sonne Jesus Christ, to suffre death upon the crosse for our redempcion, who made there (by hys one oblacion of hymselfe once offered) a full, perfecte and sufficiente sacrifice, oblacion, and satisfaccion, for the synnes of the whole worlde,
and gave commaundemente to his disciples that they shoulde goe teache all nacions, and baptize them in the name of the father, the sonne, and the holye ghoste:	and dyd institute, and in hys holye Gospell commaund us to continue, a perpetuall memorye of that his precious death, untyll hys comynge agayne:
Regarde, we beseche thee, the supplicacions of thy congregacion, and	Heare us O mercyefull father wee beeseche thee; and
graunte that all thy servauntes which shall bee baptized in this water prepared for the mynystracion of thy holy sacrament,	graunt that wee, receyving these thy creatures of bread and wyne, accordinge to thy sonne our Savioure Jesus Christ's holy institucion, in remembraunce of his death and passion,
maye receive the fulnesse of thy grace, and ever remaine in the noumbre of thy faithful, and elect children, through Jesus Christ our Lord.	maye be partakers of his most blessed body and bloud: who, in the same night . . .

The Invocation prayer of the communion service continues the preamble of the 1549 petition for sanctification of the bread and wine, but changes the essence by focusing on the communicants rather than on the elements. Nevertheless, a solemn tone is achieved by the fulsome description of Christ's sacrifice upon the cross and by the full narration of the words of institution, albeit without any taking of the bread and wine on the table.

Both prayers lead directly into the administration of the sacrament without even an Amen interposed. Negatively, this sidesteps the argument (used for example by Bucer in his *Constans Defensio*) that the Amen turns the historical narration of the Last Supper into a prayer for consecration. Positively, the administration becomes the climax of the invocation, and the prayers are focused entirely on the recipients: the bread, wine and water are almost incidental and there is certainly no notion of consecration. (This is underlined not only by the fact that, as for 1549, there is no provision for additional consecration, but also a note at the end of the service states that the priest can take for his own domestic use any remaining bread and wine.)

Thanksgiving Prayers Compared

Baptism	*Eucharist*
WE yelde thee heartie thankes, most merciful father, that it hathe pleased thee to regenerate this infant with thy holy spirite, to receyve him for thy owne chylde by adopcion, and to incorporate him into thy holy congregacion.	ALMIGHTIE and everliving God, we most hartely thank thee, for that thou dooest vouchsafe to fede us, whiche have duely receyved these holye misteries, with the spirituall foode of the most precious body and bloud of thy sonne our saviour Jesus Christ, and doest assure us thereby of thy favoure and goodnes towarde us, and that we bee verye membres incorporate in thy mistical body, which is the blessed companie of all faythfull people, and be also heyrs, through hope, of thy everlasting kingdom, by the merites of the most precious death and Passion of thy deare sonne.
And humbly we beseche thee to graunt that he, being dead	We now most humbly beseche thee, O heavenly father, so to

unto sinne, and lyving unto righteousnes, and beeinge buried with Christ in his death, may crucify the old man, and utterly abolishe the whole body of sine: that as he is made partaker of the death of thy sonne, so he may be partaker of his resurreccion: so that finalli, with the residue of thy holy congregacion, he may be enheritour of thine everlasting kingdom: through Christ our lord. Amen.

assiste us with thy grace, that we may continue in that holy felowship, and do al such good workes, as thou hast prepared for us to walk in:

through Jesus Christ our Lord, to whom, with thee and the holy ghost, be all honour and glorye, world without ende. Amen.

The Thanksgiving prayer returns to the theme of the sacrament and the grace signified. (This prayer is found in the eucharist of 1549 and a parallel prayer for baptism is added in 1552.) In both the communion and the baptism services Cranmer uses the most fulsome and confident language about the grace received by the recipients of the sacrament. He knew that he was exercising the unspoken caveat that this only applies to the elect, but would the clergy and congregations of the Church of England also have known this? Nevertheless, both thanksgiving prayers point to the unseen company of the elect: the residue of the holy congregation and the spiritual body of Christ which is the company of the faithful.

b. The shape of the 1552 baptism service

The shape of the 1552 baptism service, compared with that of 1549, is set out below. Overall, the service is much simpler. In particular there is no move from the church door to the font, but the entire service is held around the font.

The section of the service which is italicized in the box is that which is parallel to the central section of the eucharist in 1552, and it is immediately obvious that, whereas elsewhere in the baptism service there has been little change, essentially contraction and simplification, there has been considerable rearrangement and introduction of material in the centre effectively creating a whole new element, almost as radical as its counterpart in the eucharist. (However, there is no requirement to repeat the section for each individual child, as there was with the immersion and attendant material in 1549.)

There are other clear changes of mind between 1549 and 1552. The Flood prayer in the earlier book, a translation little altered from Luther's original, is rewritten. The signing is moved from the beginning of the service to a position of the greatest importance, directly after the immersion. For the rest, the 1552 service is simplified by the loss of the exorcism and the ceremonial features of the entry into the church and the white garment and the anointing. The occasional blessing of the font is changed and becomes the central prayer of invocation for those baptized.

c. Private baptism

The baptismal rites of 1549 and 1552 compared.[93]

1549	*1552*
Introduction	Introduction
Flood prayer	Flood prayer
Signing	
Seeking prayer	Seeking prayer
Exorcism	
Gospel	Gospel
First exhortation	First exhortation
Lord's Prayer	
Creed	
Hermann's Prayer	Hermann's prayer
Approach to font	
(Blessing of font)	
Second exhortation	Second exhortation
Renunciations	Renunciations
Interrogatory Creed	Interrogatory Creed
Queries	Queries
	Grant prayers
	Invocation
Immersion	*Immersion*
	Reception and signing
White garment	
Anointing	
	Bidding and Lord's Prayer
	Thanksgiving prayer
Final exhortation to godparents	Final exhortation to godparents

---

93   The 1552 service may be found in the PS edn of *Liturgies of Edward VI*, pp. 284–94; and Everyman edn of the *First and Second Prayer Books of King Edward VI*, pp. 394–403. A tabulated version may be found in Brightman's *English Rite*, Vol. 2, pp. 724–61.

Private baptism is retained in the 1552 Prayer Book. It is emphasized in the opening rubric to public baptism that private baptism can only be sought in emergency, and then is optional: 'children may at all times be baptized at home' (1549: 'children ought at all times to be baptized, either at the church or else at home'). Minimal changes are made in the service from 1549: the vesting disappears, the duplication of the Creed removed (though the congregation is still bidden to recite it after the Lord's Prayer – an unusually obvious case of a drafting error in the 1552 Prayer Book), and details of wording of the declarations by the godparents.

d. The 1552 communion service

The eucharist is now entitled: 'The Order for the Administracion of the Lordes Supper, or Holye Communion'. Gone is any mention of the Mass, and as far as possible any memory of it. The traditional vestments are replaced by the surplice. The Introit psalm is omitted (sung material is much reduced) and the Ten Commandments are now recited after the Collect for Purity. After the sermon or homily, offerings for the poor are collected, and the intercession block from the 1549 Canon now follows as a separate prayer for the Church Militant here on earth (the dead are no longer included). This would now be the conclusion of the Antecommunion service on days when there was no one to communicate with the priest. Although it was now required that people make their communion at least three times a year rather than once, as in 1549, in all probability many Sunday services would have concluded at this point.

Those who are to receive communion are now meant to move into the chancel which is no longer a place reserved for the clergy but effectively a room for the communion service. The altar has been replaced by a table standing 'in the body of the Churche, or in the chauncell . . . and the Priest standing at the north syde of the Table'.[94] After the exhortation come the confession, absolution and comfortable words, Sursum corda, Preface, Sanctus and Prayer of Humble Access. Buchanan gives a very useful analysis of this section. The last sentence of the comfortable words, speaking of Jesus as our advocate with the Father, leads naturally into the Sursum corda where the congregation is bidden to lift their

---

94   The priest is thus positioned at the middle of the table lengthwise, but why the north side, as opposed to the south? I suppose this was determined by the daylight, which with medieval stained glass would not have been good. Standing on the north side, the priest would not have the table in his shadow, and evangelicals would have no need, and traditionalists no excuse, for candles on the table.

hearts to heaven. The transition from the Sanctus to the Prayer of Humble Access is explained by Buchanan:

> The Benedictus Qui venit was removed from the end of the Sanctus, and the whole biblical order of Isaiah 6 came to light. If we catch the vision of God and sing the angels' song, then, if Isaiah is to be believed, we immediately express our own unworthiness. What could be more natural than the location of humble access at this point?[95]

This explanation certainly makes good sense of the sequence. However, I am not convinced that the same forethought is evident here that we can see, by contrast, in the core structure of the administration of the sacrament or the prayers of invocation. While each unit follows naturally enough from the one before it, the overall effect is something of a spiritual rollercoaster ride of alternating acceptance and unworthiness; and I find it hard to imagine that that is what Cranmer planned from the outset. If he had, we might have expected the sequence to carry through with the theme of the coal cleansing the prophet's lips (a notion which coincidentally is found in some Eastern liturgies). As it is, the Prayer of Humble Access is but slightly revised, beginning as before with the theme of the unworthiness of eating the crumbs from the table (Mt. 15.27; Lk. 16.21), but removing the reference 'in these holy Misteries' which had given such comfort to Gardiner, and inverting the final clauses so as to finish with the mutual indwelling of Christ and the believer. Therefore I am inclined to think that here Cranmer was trying to find a new and creative use for older material which had been composed earlier. In allowing that not everything was organized equally well we do not need to subscribe to the out-of-date view that he was dismembering ancient structures without any theological rationale.

The Invocation prayer, as described above, is now no more than a prayer for those receiving the sacrament that they may also receive the grace signified. The words of administration follow, or rather, conclude the prayer without even an intervening Amen:

> *And when [the minister] delyvereth the bread, he shall saye.*
>   Take and eate this, in remembraunce that Christ dyed for thee, and feede on him in thy hearte by faythe, with thanksgeving.
>   *And the Minister that delyvereth the cup, shal saye,*
>   Drinke this in remembraunce that Christ's bloude was shed for thee, and be thankefull.

---

95 Buchanan, *What did Cranmer Think he was Doing?*, p. 27.

These words are entirely new drafting. They with the action of communion are the heart and focus of the service when Christ's command is obeyed and the faithful communicant not only receives the bread and wine but also is graced by the spiritual presence of Christ. Buchanan describes these words as 'anamnetic': they fulfil the same function in Cranmer's rite as did the anamnesis in the old, picking up and responding, as it were, to the words of institution. As Buchanan says, the response to Christ's command to eat and drink is to do precisely that, and so the words of institution are followed immediately by the action they prescribe.[96] Strictly speaking that is correct, but there may be more to this form of words. They are so close to the words of institution as to be virtually identical with them. Here we must bear in mind two points.

First, the administration of the sacrament is parallel to that in the baptism service. There the words of administration are taken from the end of Matthew's gospel where Jesus commands his disciples to baptize people in the name of the Father and of the Son and of the Holy Spirit. Our familiarity with the baptismal formula might lead us to forget how it is a verbal adaptation of the traditional institution of the sacrament. Secondly, we may remember that in the summer of 1548 Bucer had written to Richard Bonner to dissuade him from a policy of replacing the words of institution of the eucharist with some paraphrase which would have avoided popish superstition.

In the light of these observations it is possible that we should understand the words of administration in some way as a paraphrase of the institution of the Lord's Supper. In this case 'anamnesis' is not really a strong enough term. The institution narrative, a historical narration, is explained and made present, as it were, with the administration. In 1549, as in the medieval Canon, the narrative had to be complemented with the petition for the bread and wine to represent or be the body and blood of Christ. It was actualized through sanctification. Now the narrative is actualized through the act of communion.

What do the words of administration teach us of Cranmer's understanding of the institution of the sacrament? Not surprisingly, 'This is my body . . . this is my blood' are the words not found. They are replaced by an expansion of 'Do this in remembrance of me' when the communicant is bidden to remember Christ's death to which the sacrament bears witness. The feeding on Christ is of course by faith, and in the administration of both bread and cup we find the theme of thanksgiving, echoing Jesus giving thanks at the Last Supper and responding with the Christian's sacrifice of thanks to God. Curious is

---

96 Buchanan, *What did Cranmer Think he was Doing?*, p. 22.

the term, 'this': 'Take and eate this . . . drinke this.' The demonstrative pronoun is not expanded or explained. In the Mass the same pronoun had been the subject of 'This is my body.' Now it is the object of the command to eat and drink. In medieval speculation on the consecration there had been much discussion of the precise meaning of '*hoc*'. Cranmer does not give us an explicit answer here, though we know it already. 'This' is bread and wine, mere signs, empty in themselves but pointing to a spiritual reality elsewhere. Like the angels at the tomb, they bid us not to stop here but to look elsewhere for the living Christ. The bread is further desacralized by the use of ordinary bread placed in the hand of the communicant rather than in the mouth. But still communion is received kneeling; for Cranmer this signifies the unworthiness of the communicant rather than the significance of the sacramental elements. (After the protest raised by Knox this interpretation was enshrined in the Black Rubric.)

The Lord's Prayer and Prayer of Thanksgiving follow. Cranmer commonly uses the Lord's Prayer to introduce a section of prayers. It is found in 1549 at Matins and Evensong and in the marriage and burial services.[97] But it is hard to avoid the notion that here the congregation is reminded of its most essential Christian identity and oneness with Christ as children of God. The Prayer of Thanksgiving takes up the Cranmerian confidence of sacramental language, speaking as though every communicant has indeed spiritually fed on Christ and is a member of the elect. The Prayer of Oblation which was originally part of the Canon is now an alternative to the Prayer of Thanksgiving. Given the parallel thanksgivings in the two sacraments, it is hard to avoid the conclusion that (as in the case of the Prayer of Humble Access) Cranmer has made the best of material he did not want to lose. Theologically it is in the right place, representing the communicant's response to Christ's grace of which communion is a sign. It is just odd that such an important theme in Cranmer's understanding of the eucharist should be made optional.

The Gloria in Excelsis is the only part of the whole service which is directed to be sung (at least as an option). Buchanan notes a long history of scholars who reckon that this was based on the hymn sung at the end of the Last Supper, and certainly it works as a fitting conclusion to the service. The culmination of praise is no longer the Sanctus at the beginning of the Canon but the Gloria in Excelsis as a response to communion. The service concludes, as before, with the blessing.

---

97 Buchanan, *What did Cranmer Think he was Doing?*, p. 26.

Chapter 6

THE ADMINISTRATION OF BAPTISM:
A COMMENTARY ON THE TEXT OF THE SERVICE

1 THEMES IN THE SERVICE AS A WHOLE

This commentary seeks largely to apply to the service the principles and issues which have already been discussed. Naturally other issues will be raised as well, but they cannot receive equal treatment.

The two versions of the service will be considered together. The various elements will be discussed according to the 1552 order (thus the signing on the forehead in both the earlier and later versions of the liturgy is considered after the immersion), except that items in 1549 omitted in 1552 (the exorcism, white garment and anointing) are included at their original position.

I have made no attempt to imagine a congregation being taken through the service, or to picture how it might react to the sequence of events. The very nature of liturgy is that it is a repeated experience, and so, while some elements have the importance of a particular position in the rite and there is a clear sense of progress through the service, we must also bear in mind that the congregation will hear, for example, the Introduction while already knowing the Thanksgiving prayer from previous occasions. Generally the aim will be to ask what concerns Cranmer brought to the service, and to what degree he was successful.

Before we approach the elements of the service in order, it is useful to summarize some themes which present themselves in it.

a. Sacrament and grace

The problem of the relation of the sacrament to the grace it signifies has been discussed already at great length with regard to the basic principles and also with specific reference to the sanctification and Invocation prayers. There are a number of other cases where the distinction between the outward and inward aspects of the sacrament or, following the Johannine picture, the aspects of water and the Holy Spirit, are stressed.

- The 1549 Introduction exhorts the congregation to pray that the child may be baptized with the Holy Spirit – something which by nature we cannot have. In 1552 the dualism is softened and 'water and' is inserted.
- The same dualism and its remedy is to be found in the Flood prayer of the two Prayer Books.
- While the dualism of these passages is resolved in 1552, the same revised liturgy re-introduces the dichotomy in the Thanksgiving prayer, giving thanks to God 'that it hathe pleased thee to regenerate this infant with thy holy spirite'.

b. The question of faith in the baptismal liturgy

We have already seen how Martyr and Laski were forced by their notion of sacramental efficacy to distance their understanding of baptism one remove from regeneration and faith, since these must already be present in some way in one who receives a sacrament efficaciously; for Cranmer on the other hand, one advantage of holding to sacramental signification is that the sign can still refer immediately to these central issues. Now we need to examine how the baptism services of the Prayer Books, especially that of 1552, dealt with the question of faith.

Cranmer was in no doubt about the lack of a personal faith in infants, as we read in the *Defence*:

> Hitherto I have rehearsed the answer of St Augustine unto Boniface . . . that forasmuch as baptism is the sacrament of the profession of our faith, and of our conversion unto God, it becometh us so to answer for young children coming thereunto, as to the sacrament appertaineth, although the children in deed have no knowledge of such things.[1]

However, it is also clear here that the faith of the baptismal candidate should not be ignored in the rite. If baptism is the sacrament of the profession of our faith, then the profession of faith cannot be omitted from the liturgy. When an infant, lacking faith, cannot make the profession, the godparents are necessary to make it on its behalf. But in addition to the godparents' profession, there is also the theme of the faith of the congregation which is prominent throughout the service. We shall look at all three of these facets – infant lack of faith, the godparents' profession of faith and the faith of the congregation – in turn.

---

1   *Defence*, 3.9; PS, I, pp. 124–5.

In the baptism services, the absence of personal faith on the part of the child is seen in

- changes in the wording of the Flood prayer
- changes in the wording of the Seeking prayer
- the avoidance of the Lutheran motif of Christ instilling faith in the child, expressed in the priest laying his hand on the child's head after the example of Christ

and, in 1552:

- the softening of the language of the renunciation and declaration of faith, so that it is no longer spoken 'by' the child but rather by the godparents in the child's name
- the change of formulas which in the medieval and 1549 rites were addressed to the child and are now, except for the baptismal formula itself, speaking about the child rather than to it.
- the change of position of the signing of the cross which in 1549 told the child that it was 'in token that thou shalt not be ashamed to confesse thy fayth in Christe crucifyed', and which in 1552 became 'in token that hereafter *he* shal not be ashamed'. Whereas the earlier formula had allowed for the possibility of infant faith expressed in baptism (and the formula, originating in the liturgy of adult catechesis and baptism, would have been looking explicitly to the confession of faith at baptism), the later formula implicitly rules out that option, looking to a later event or time in which the child confesses the faith.

The sacramental profession of faith by the godparents on behalf of the child is seen in the renunciation of the world, the flesh and the devil; and in the affirmation of faith.

The faith of the congregation, expressed in intercession for the candidates, has a prominent role in the services:

- The Introduction sets the agenda of intercession from the very beginning of the rite.
- The revised Seeking prayer focuses on the intercessory role of the congregation.
- Hermann's prayer emphasizes the faith of the congregation and intercession for the infant.
- The exhortation to the godparents and congregation, seeking to dispel their doubts and affirm their faith in the Christ who accepts and embraces the child, stresses the role of faith in the one who answers prayer.

- The Grant prayers in 1552, immediately before the baptismal invocation, maintain the emphasis on the role of intercession at the most central part of the service.

c. The emphasis on the individual and the corporate

It is useful briefly to summarize the different emphases on the individual and corporate aspects of baptism.

The individual aspect of baptism is seen above all in the renunciation and the affirmation of faith spoken in the candidate's name. The emphasis is on the individual rather than (as in other liturgies which use covenant theology) the community in which the child is brought up. Also the theme of Christ receiving the child has a strong individualist tone in the service in that it effectively portrays a personal interaction between the two.

The corporate, however, is not forgotten. We have already seen the role of the community in praying for grace to be given to the child. In the 1549 service, the new additions to the exorcism formula portray the candidate's defence against evil to be vested in membership of the body of Christ and his congregation, and being one of his flock. The 1552 formula of signing begins by speaking of reception of the child into the congregation (but see my comments when I discuss the formula below on how central this may have been to the meaning of baptism), and the thanksgiving prayer includes reference to the congregation. However, here a final mention of salvation being extended to the 'residue' of the congregation opens the question of the corporate nature of baptism. The body of Christ, the Church, is real and important for Cranmer, but it cannot be identified with the earthly, sacramental Church or congregation. Any corporate image has to cope with that caveat.

Bridget Nichols describes how, as a theme in the service, the kingdom of heaven effectively represents the goal of the Christian life in opposition to earthly society. From the Introduction, in which entry to the kingdom is impossible for all people except by God's grace, through to the Prayer of Thanksgiving, in which one has to die with Christ in order to appropriate the kingdom, it is held up as the fulfilment of all God's promises. In this respect it presents a strong transcendence to the social order, in which the modern baptismal service of the Church of England Alternative Service Book (and the more recent Common Worship) is weak, concentrating instead on the analogy of the Church as family.[2] Nichols is right in outlining this goal and promise which is held

---

2   *Liturgical Hermeneutics* (Frankfurt am Main: Peter Lang, 1996), pp. 157–66.

before the congregation. However, the weakness of the liturgy, as we discover, is that the promise is available only to the elect, and we are not told how it may be appropriated except through God's own hidden will. The kingdom relativizes the earthly society and also the congregation, and we are not given a way of linking it to either.

d. Christ and the Holy Spirit

It has been described above how in his polemical writings Cranmer portrays the sacraments principally in a Christocentric context. In his liturgical writing also we see the same emphasis on baptism as a meeting with Christ, and the Holy Spirit is portrayed usually as enabling that meeting. The motif of Christ receiving the child is of course the most important aspect here, and will be discussed in detail below. As for the Holy Spirit, we may summarize the various references as follows:

In 1549 Cranmer departs from his Lutheran models in omitting the initial formula, 'Come out, thou unclean spirit, and give place to the Holy Spirit.'[3] This may represent his distaste for the idea of exorcism of the unbaptized (and it was never in the Sarum *Manual*), but the second part of the formula is one of the few places in the rite which speaks of baptism imparting the Holy Spirit.

The Introduction speaks of the child being baptized with the Holy Spirit, in fulfilment of Jn 3.5.

The Flood prayer asks for the children to be sanctified with the Holy Spirit, as an alternative to the Lutheran model in which faith is prayed for for the infants.

Hermann's prayer asks for the Holy Spirit to be given to the infants so that they may be born again.

In the 1549 blessing of the font, the Holy Spirit is invoked on the congregation rather than on the candidates or font, though in the Grant prayers the priest prays that 'all thynges belongyng to the spirite' may grow in the children.

In 1549 the anointing describes the unction of the Holy Spirit. This is replaced in 1552 by the Thanksgiving prayer which mentions regeneration of the infant with the Holy Spirit. And in so far as the signing replaces the anointing, the pneumatological motif is replaced by the Christological one of the soldier of Christ.

In nearly all of these instances, the Holy Spirit could be seen as being the agent of regeneration, sanctification, etc. – in other words the one who communicates to the elect individual the word and grace of Christ

---

3   Luther, Second *Taufbüchlein*, Sehling (ed.), *Kirchenordnungen*, p. 22; Fisher, *Christian Initiation*, p. 23.

– but there is very little interest (in 1552 only the Grant prayer) on the presence and life of the Holy Spirit *per se*.

e. Baptism and the Christian life

The theological understanding of baptism as referring to God's work of justification and sanctification throughout the Christian's life, and the Christian's following the commandments of God, is inevitably to be seen in the liturgy, and something of what this involves is mentioned in the final exhortation to the godparents. If there is any surprise, it is that this theme is so little found in the baptism service; the idea of regeneration is much more to the fore. Most significantly, the introductory rubrics tell us that the baptism is meant to take place in Sunday worship and is to be administered in the vernacular so that 'every manne presente maye be put in remembraunce of his owne profession made to God in his Baptisme'. So the experience of baptism is not so much when I am baptized as an unconscious infant as when I, a conscious person knowing God, am reminded of my baptism by its administration to another person. And the congregation present at the baptism, the community as a whole, is that company of the baptized which welcomes and receives the child into its corporate life.

Significant passages within the service which look to the Christian life are

- the new words of the signing (in both the 1549 and the 1552 positions)
- the bidding and thanksgiving prayer after the immersion
- the final exhortation to the godparents which deals with specific duties.

Also, less prominently, we read at the end of the Introduction the priest directing the people to pray that the baptized may be 'received into Christ's holy Church, and be made lively members of the same'. At the second exhortation he says they are to 'constantly believe God's holy word and obediently keep his commandments'. The Grant prayers and the Invocation prayer return to the same theme.

f. The use of ceremony

Apart from the baptismal immersion itself, all the ceremonial acts in the service can and should be interpreted in the light of the comments in the Appendix to the Prayer Book, 'On Ceremonies', in which

Cranmer explains their purpose: that they 'dooe serve to a decente ordre and godlye discipline, and . . . bee apte to stirre uppe the dulle mynde of manne to the remembraunce of his duetie to God, by some notable and speciall significacion whereby he myght bee edified'. Therefore some ceremonies are suppressed because they 'dyd more confounde and darken, then declare and sette forth Christes benefites unto us'. And other ceremonies are retained which 'be neyther darke nor dumme ceremonies, but are so set forth that every man may understande what they dooe meane, and to what use they do serve'.[4] The presumption underlying these comments is that ceremonies are essentially didactic aids. When the sacrament itself cannot be understood as a performative act, as we have already seen, then there is no room for any such role for the ancillary ceremonies of the rite. They too are figurative. This principle will be seen to hold for the three ceremonial actions in the service: the signing on the forehead, the white garment, and the anointing. All are meant to signify something rather than convey anything.

2 THE SERVICE TO BE USED IN CHURCH, 1549 AND 1552

a. Note on the sources cited for the baptism service of 1549

Every form of synopsis is to some extent hypothetical, and presents the views of the compiler rather than some 'objective' process of the development of the text. The present synopsis is based on that by Brightman in *The English Rite*. Changes represent partly new insights, such as the importance of the Albertine Saxony baptism service, which was recognized, at least in part, by Brightman himself and noted in the Preface to his work. Other supposed sources, in particular the texts from the King's Book and the *Rationale of Ceremonial*, are more circumstantial and are given prominence here through the cumulative effect of a number of possible parallels rather than any single convincing instance such as we see with Albertine Saxony. As such, the presumed importance of the two English documents in the history of the Prayer Book is the result of a particular hypothesis rather than evidence for it. Some prayers from the Strasbourg rite will be included more for comparison than a claim that Cranmer was influenced by them.

---

4   'Of Ceremonies', *First Prayer Book of King Edward VI*, (London: J.M. Dent, Everyman, 1910), pp. 287–8.

Key to sources
AS   Albertine Saxony *Kirchenordnung*, 1540[5]
C   Coverdale[6]
H   Hermann, *Pia Deliberatio*, Latin version of *Einfaltigs Bedencken*, 1545.[7]
KB   The King's Book, 1543[8]
L   Luther, Second *Taufbüchlein*, 1526,[9] or some rite derived from it
M   Mozarabic rite[10]
R   *Rationale of Ceremonial*, c. 1542[11]
S   Sarum *Manual*[12]
ST   Strasbourg *Taufordnung*, 1537[13]

* *Note*: Denotes material not cited in Brightman's text (but including additional material included in his neglected preface).

Passages are normally cited in English translation.

Notes refer to a number of passages which function either as less immediate sources or as parallels which might illuminate our understanding of the Prayer Book phrase.

b. Opening rubrics

1549

ADMINISTRACION OF
PUBLYKE BAPTISME

TO BE USED IN THE
CHURCHE

H Among the ancient fathers baptism was openly ministered only at two times in the year, at Easter and Whitsuntide

It appeareth by auncient wryters, that the Sacramente of Baptisme in the olde tyme was not commonly ministered, but at two

5   Sehling (ed.), *Evangelischen Kirchenordnungen*, Vol. 1, pp. 264–9.
6   M. Coverdale, *The order that the churche and congregacion of Christe in Denmarke and in many places, countreis and cities in Germany doth use, not onelye at the holy supper of the Lorde, but also at the ministration of the blessed Sacrament of Baptisme and holy Wedlocke* (n.p., ?1548).
7   Fisher, *Christian Initiation*, pp. 54–69.
8   *Formularies of Faith*, pp. 253–7.
9   Fisher, *Christian Initiation*, pp. 23–5.
10 *Missale Mixtum secundum regulam Beati Isidori, dictum Mozarabes*, in PL Vol. 85, col. 465–7.
11 *Rationale*, pp. 6–12.
12 Translation in Whitaker, *Documents of the Baptismal Liturgy*, pp. 284–307.
13 Fisher, *Christian Initiation*, pp. 38–42.

which constitution because it would be hard perchance to renew

tymes in the yeare, at Easter and whytsontyde, at whiche tymes it was openly mynistred in the presence of all the congregacion: Whiche custome (now beeyng growen out of use) although it cannot for many consideracions be wel restored again, yet it is thought good to folowe the same as nere as conveniently maybe be: Wherfore the people are to bee admonished, that it is

we will that baptism be ministered only upon the Sundays and holy days when the whole congregation is wont to come together.

moste conveniente that baptisme shoulde not be ministred but upon Sondayes and other holy dayes, when the most numbre of people maye come together. As well for that the congregacion there presente may testifie the receyvyng of them, that be newly baptysed, into the noumbre of Christes Churche, as also because in the Baptisme of Infantes, every manne presente maye be put in remembraunce of his owne profession made to God in his Baptisme. For whiche cause also, it is expediente that Baptisme be ministred in the Englishe tounge. Neverthelesse (yf necessitie so requyre) children ought at all tymes to be baptised, eyther at the churche or els at home.

The basic principle of public baptism is set out in these introductory rubrics. The emphasis is on the presence of the congregation which will both receive the child after baptism and also is put in mind of their baptism. This second element is, as has been noted above, the common experience of baptism, when adults are reminded through a child's baptism of their own baptismal relationship to God. In the rubrics 'commonly' means 'publicly'.

The private administration of baptism is allowed and even encouraged, but it is not obligatory by the rubric of 1549. Despite complaints about this, the 1552 rubric softens the passage even further to make private baptism a concession: 'Neverthelesss (yf necessitie so requyre) chyldren maye at all tymes be baptized at home'.

c. The Introduction

| | 1549 |
| | PUBLIKE BAPTISME |

H the parents of the infants shall signify the matter betimes to the pastors and . . . shall humbly require baptism for their infants

When there are children to be Baptised upon the Sonday, or holy daye: the parentes shall geve knowledge over nyght or in the mornyng, afore the beginning of Mattens, to the curate. And then the Godfathers, Godmothers, and people, with the children muste be ready at the Church dore, either immediatly afore the laste Canticle at Mattens or els immediatly afore the last Canticle at Evensong, as the Curate by his discrecion shall appoynte. And then, standyng

S Let the priest ask of the midwife whether the infant is a male or female. Then if the infant has been baptized at home

there, the prieste shall aske whether the chyldren be baptised or no. If they aunswere No, then shall the priest saye thus.

***C** for asmuche as all men are conceyved and borne in synne, and that seynge it is unpossible for a man to come into the kyngdome of God, excepte he be borne a new and regenerate: they wyll shewe and declare theyr Godly love, and call upon God the father thorow Jesus Christ and in his name, that he wyll mercifullye

DEARE beloved, forasmuche as all men bee conceyved and borne in sinne, and that no manne borne in synne, can entre into the kingdom of God (except he be regenerate, and borne anewe of water, and the holy ghost) I beseche you to

call upon God the father through our Lord Jesus Christ, that of his bounteouse mercy he wil graunt to these children that thing, which by nature they cannot have, that is to saye, they may be baptised with [1552: water and] the holy ghost, and receyved into Christes holy Church,

baptyse that chylde (or those children) wyth the holy goste, and receyve hym (or them) to grace.

KB made again the lively members of Christ's mystical body

and be made lyvely membres of the same.

Coverdale's account of the Danish liturgy first appeared probably between 1543 and 1546. It describes a Lutheran liturgy, with some prayers which are also found in the Strasbourg rite of 1537 and the Cassel *Kirchenordnung* of 1539.[14] This section is the only one used by Cranmer (with the addition of Jn 3.5), and the borrowing is very close. This includes a clear distinction between the sacramental sign and the grace signified: the candidates will receive the washing of baptism, but the congregation prays that they will also be baptized with the Holy Spirit. Cranmer adopts this wording in 1549, though for 1552 he corrected it to unite more closely the physical washing and the spiritual grace.

d. The Flood prayer

	1549
	Then the prieste shall saye.
L Let us pray.	Let us praye.
Almighty and eternal God, who hast through the flood, according to thy righteous judgement, condemned the unfaithful world, and, according to thy great mercy, hast saved faithful Noah, even eight persons, and hast drowned hard-hearted Pharaoh with all his in the Red Sea, and hast led thy people Israel dry through it, thereby prefiguring this bath of thy holy baptism, and through the baptism of thy dear child, our Lord Jesus Christ, hast sanctified, and set apart the Jordan and all water for a saving flood, and an ample washing away of sins: we pray that through thy same infinite mercy thou wilt graciously look upon this N, and bless him with a right faith in the spirit, so that through this saving flood all	ALMYGHTIE and everlastyng God, whiche of thy justice dydest destroy by fluddes of water the whole worlde for synne, excepte viii persones, whome of thy mercy (the same tyme) thou didest save in the Arke: And when thou didest drowne in the read sea wycked kyng Pharao with al his armie, yet (at the same time) thou didest leade thy people the chyldren of Israel safely through the myddes therof: wherby thou didest fygure the washyng of thy holy Baptisme: and by the Baptisme of thy wel beloved sonne Jesus Christe, thou dydest sanctifie the fludde Jordan, and al other waters to this misticall washing away of synne: We beseche thee (for thy infinite mercies) that thou wilt mercifully looke upon these children, and

---

14 The fullest description of Coverdale's work is in R.A. Leaver, *'Goostly psalmes and spirituall songes': English and Dutch Metrical Psalms from Coverdale to Utenhove 1535–1566* (Oxford: Clarendon Press, 1991), pp. 103–7. The earliest surviving copy of the translation dates from 1548.

that was born in him from Adam and all which he himself has added thereto may be drowned and submerged: and that he may be separated from the unfaithful, and preserved in the holy ark of Christendom dry and safe, and ever fervent in spirit and joyful in hope serve thy name, so that he with all the faithful may be worthy to inherit thy promise of eternal life, through Christ our Lord. Amen.

sanctifie them with thy holy gost, that by this holesome laver of regeneracion, whatsoever synne is in them, may be washed cleane away, that they, being delivered from thy wrathe, may be received into tharke of Christes churche, and so saved from peryshyng: and beeyng fervente in spirite, stedfaste in fayth, joyfull through hope, rooted in charitie, maye ever serve thee: And finally attayne to everlastyng lyfe, with all thy holy and chosen people. This graunte us we besche the, for Jesus Christes sake our Lorde. Amen.

The Flood prayer in 1549 is a translation of the Lutheran original. For the most part the translation is a faithful one, with various insignificant changes which one would expect in providing a liturgical text rather than an accurate rendering of an original ('received' is inserted at one point). However, there is a consistent difference between the original and the translation, in that all references to faith in the former have been removed in the latter. The unfaithful world and faithful Noah are replaced by a reference to the sin of the world and eight persons without any epithet (the reference now being to 1 Pet. 3.20, a correct but somewhat literary allusion to a biblical verse for the Flood prefiguring baptism); Pharaoh is wicked rather than hard-hearted. Whereas Luther prays that God may bless the child with a right faith in the spirit, Cranmer asks that he may 'sanctifie them with thy holy gost'. Finally Cranmer asks that the child may attain everlasting life 'with all thy holy and chosen people', omitting any reference to the faithful in the original.

The removal of faith in the case of the child and the emphasis on the work of the Holy Spirit and election is consistent with the rest of the baptism service. But in the 1552 service the prayer undergoes a radical revision, as set out below:

1549

ALMYGHTIE and everlastyng
God, whiche of thy justice dydest
destroy by fluddes of water the
whole worlde for synne, excepte
viii persones, whome of thy mercy
(the same tyme) thou didest save
in the Arke: And when thou didest
drowne in the read sea wycked
kyng Pharao with al his armie,
yet (at the same time) thou didest
leade thy people the chyldren of
Israel safely through the myddes
therof: wherby thou didest fygure
the washyng of thy holy Baptisme:
and by the Baptisme of thy wel
beloved sonne Jesus Christe,
thou dydest sanctifie the fludde
Jordan, and al other waters to this
misticall washing away of synne:
We beseche thee (for thy infinite
mercies) that thou wilt mercifully
looke upon these children, and
sanctifie them with thy holy gost,
that by this holesome laver of
regeneracion, whatsoever synne
is in them, may be washed cleane
away, that they, being delivered
from thy wrathe, may be received
into tharke of Christes churche,
and so saved from peryshyng: and
beeyng fervente in spirite, stedfaste
in fayth, joyfull through hope,
rooted in charitie, maye ever serve
thee:
And finally attayne to
everlastyng lyfe, with all thy holy
and chosen people. This graunte us
we beseche the, for Jesus Christes
sake our Lorde. Amen.

1552

ALMIGHTY and everlasting God,
which of

thy great merce diddest save Noe
and his familie in the Arke from
perishing by water:

and also dyddest safely
leade the chyldren of Israel, thy
people throughe the redde Sea:
figuring thereby thy holy Baptisme
and by the Baptisme of thy
welbeloved sonne Jesus
Christe, dyddest sanctifye the
floud Jordane,
and al other waters, to the
mistical washing away of sinne:
We beseche thee for thy infinite
mercies, that thou wylt mercyfully
loke upon these chyldren, sanctifie
them and washe them with thy
holy ghoste,

that they, beyng delivered from
thy wrath, may be receyved into
the Arke of Christes Church,
and beyng   stedfast in fayth,
joyeful through hope, and rooted
in charitie, may so passe the
waves of this troublesome world,
that finally they maye come to the
lande of everlasting lyfe, there to
reygne wyth thee, worlde without
ende, through Jesus Christ our
Lord. Amen.

The resulting version is generally more brief and polished. The obscure reference to 1 Peter is lost, and Noah reappears. But the emphasis of the prayer is now more firmly on salvation: the destruction of the world in the Flood and of Pharaoh and his army in the Red Sea are forgotten. Cranmer's treatment of the prayer is the same as that of the exhortations in the Albertine Saxony rite (below), in which the themes of damnation and condemnation are omitted in the Prayer Book versions. Cranmer does not deny the doctrine, but nor does he wish to dwell on it. He is concerned with a promise and sacrament of salvation.

The 1552 version of the Flood prayer also seeks to amend a problem raised by an initiative Cranmer took in the first version: 'sanctifie them with thy holy gost' made a good substitute to the Lutheran original's petition for faith to be given to the child, but the resulting text invited the interpretation that the physical washing was altogether separate from the spiritual grace and unimportant. Just as this problem was identified and addressed in the Introduction, so too in the Flood prayer it is corrected by being expanded to, 'sanctifie them and washe them with thy holy ghoste'.

e. The Seeking prayer

	1549
*L Let us pray	Let us praye.
Almighty and eternal God, S. the immortal defence of all that beg, the deliverer of those that beseech, the peace of those that ask, the life of those that believe, the resurrection of the dead, I invoke thee upon this thy servant N. who, seeking the gift of thy baptism, desires to obtain eternal grace by spiritual regeneration. Receive him, Lord: and because thou hast vouchsafed to say, Ask and ye shall receive, seek and ye shall find, knock and it shall be opened unto you, grant a reward to him that asks, and open the door to him that knocks, so that having obtained the eternal blessing of the heavenly washing, he may	ALMIGHTIE and immortall God, the ayde of all that nede, the helper of all that flee to thee for succour, the life of them that beleve, and the resurreccion of the dead: we call upon thee for these infantes, that they cummyng to thy holy Baptisme, may receyve remission of theyr sinnes, by spirituall regeneracion. Receyve them (o Lorde) as thou haste promysed by thy welbeloved sonne, saying: Aske, and you shall have: seke, and you shall fynde: knocke, and it shalbe opened unto you. So geve nowe unto us that aske: Lette us that seke, fynde: open thy gate unto us that knocke: that these infantes maye enjoy the

receive the promised kingdom of thy bounty, who livest and reignest with God the Father in the unity of the Holy Spirit God, throughout all ages. Amen.	everlastyng benediccion of thy heavenly washing, and may come to the eternall kyngdome whiche thou haste promysed, by Christe our Lorde. Amen.

In the medieval rites this prayer is one of the prayers for the catechumen, originally looking towards the adult candidate's progress in faith towards baptism. Luther gave the prayer prominence in his second *Taufbüchlein* as the first prayer in the service, coming immediately after the signing of the cross. In the traditional and Lutheran forms, the prayer is for acceptance of the candidate who asks for entry to the Church, a very fitting opening to the service.

Cranmer would seem to be following the *Taufbüchlein* both in the selection of the prayer from the many in the Sarum *Manual*, and in the opening which addresses the Father rather than the Son. Dowden points out the incongruity of Cranmer's translation in that (unlike Luther) he leaves the description of the addressee as 'the Life of them that believe, and the Resurrection of the dead'.[15] It would seem that in his work of translation Cranmer followed Luther to the extent of the *incipit*, and then turned straight back to the familiar Latin without noticing the incongruity. But there is a more important change, and no doubt a deliberate one, in making the prayer one of asking the Father to accept the candidate in answer to the prayers of the congregation. The Latin (followed by Luther) takes the one who is seeking and knocking to be the candidate referred to in the third person throughout the prayer. Cranmer makes the congregation – 'us that ask' – to be the ones seeking and knocking on behalf of the unconscious infant. The role of the prayer has changed, and it is fitting that in the English Prayer Book it should take second place in the service: the Flood prayer sets the scene, as it were, and concentrates on the history of redemption as applied to the candidates. The Seeking prayer focuses on the role of the congregation as praying for the candidates.

---

15 *Further Studies*, pp. 292–3.

f. The exorcism

S	1549
	Then let the priest lokyng upon the chyildren, saye.
I exorcize thee, unclean spirit, in the name of the Father, and of the Son and of the Holy Spirit, that thou come out and depart from this servant of God . . .[16] our God and Lord Jesus Christ has vouchsafed to call him to himself by the grace of the Holy Spirit to his holy grace and blessing and to the fount of baptism . . . Therefore, accursed devil, hearken to thy sentence . . . that day which is about to come as a fiery furnace, in which eternal death will overtake thee and all thine angels.	I COMMAUNDE thee, uncleane spirite, in the name of the father, of the sonne, and of the holy ghost, that thou come out, and departe from these infantes, whom our Lord Jesus Christe hath vouchsaved, to call to his holy Baptisme, to be made membres of his body, and of his holy congregacion. Therfore thou cursed spirite, remembre thy sentence, remembre thy judgemente, remembre the daye to be at hande, wherin thou shalt burne in fyre everlasting, prepared for thee and thy Angels. And presume not hereafter to exercize any tyrannye towarde these infantes, whom Christe hathe bought with his precious bloud, and by this his holy Baptisme calleth to be of his flocke.

In the 1549 rite Cranmer includes an exorcism, but he omits it in 1552. Bucer had criticized its inclusion in his *Censura*; while it is possible that Cranmer is following the German's advice here, it is hard to see in any case how the exorcism would have been included in a revised version of the service.

The text of the exorcism suggests a somewhat complicated origin and development. The first section mirrors that of Luther's *Taufbüchlein*, and so could be based on it, but it then continues with other material. Most of it is based on other passages from the exorcisms in the Sarum *Manual*, but there are one or two phrases which look like Cranmer's own composition: that the infants are 'to be made membres of his body,

---

16   Luther's exorcism formula in the second *Taufbüchlein* also breaks off at this point in the medieval text. Is Cranmer following the Lutheran rite and then adding more material?

and of his holy congregacion', and the Devil is enjoined, 'And presume not hereafter to exercize any tyrannye towarde these infantes, whom Christe hathe bought with his precious bloud, and by this his holy Baptisme calleth to be of his flocke.' The first addition contains themes found throughout the service, and the second picks up the theme that in baptism the candidate rejects the Devil and walks in the way of God's commandments. Bucer had criticized the exorcism on the basis that it implied that the unbaptized infants were demoniacs. That is certainly the case with the traditional material which Cranmer retains. But what seems to be his own composition is very close to the alternative suggested by Bucer, which asks that God will drive out the deception and violence of Satan from the infant, that the infant may be freed from the power of darkness and brought to the kingdom of Christ, and that no unclean spirit may harm it in body or soul.[17] Both Reformers think in terms of demon oppression rather than demonic possession, and prefer to write prayers which are apotropaic rather than exorcistic. On this understanding of what Cranmer is trying to do, we must suppose that he is seeking to present as conservative a baptismal liturgy as his conscience will allow, and mentally he must have invoked the principle of sacramental language as figurative language in the broadest sense possible: the Christian life includes victory over Satan, which may be traditionally expressed in the language of exorcism.

g. The gospel and exhortations

	1549
S *When these things have been said, let the priest say:*	*Then shall the priest saye:*
The Lord be with you.	The Lorde be with you.
And with thy spirit.	*The people.* And with thy spirite.
*L Let us hear the holy Gospel of St Mark.	*The Minister.* Heare nowe the gospell written by S. Marke.
	Marke x
*Vulgate[18]	At a certayne tyme they brought
[In illo tempore] offerebant	children to Christe that he should
illi parvulos ut tangeret illos.	touche them, and hys disciples
Discipuli autem comminabantur	rebuked those that brought them.
	But when Jesus sawe it, he was

---

17 *Censura*, in Whitaker (ed.), *Bucer*, pp. 92–3.
18 The text, uniquely for Bible readings in the Prayer Book, is not taken from the Great Bible, and may be a separate translation (cf. Brightman, *English Rite*, Vol. 1, p. cxviii). Cuming, *Godly Order*, p. 84, says that it is closer to the Latin than to the German.

offerentibus. Quos cum videret Iesus, indigne tulit, et ait illis: Sinite parvulos venire ad me, et ne prohibueritis eos: talium enim est regnum Dei. Amen dico vobis: Quisquis non receperit regnum Dei velut parvulus, non intrabit in illud. Et complexans eos, et imponens manus super illos, benedicebat eos.

displeased, and sayed unto them: Suffre lytle children to come unto me, and forbyd them not; for to suche belongeth the kingdom of God. Verely I say unto you: whosoever doeth not receyve the kyngdom of God, as a lytle chylde: he shall not entre therin. And when he had taken them up in his armes: he put his handes upon them, and blessed them.

*AS *After the Gospel . . . he shall give this short instruction and exhortation based on the gospel.*[19]

After the gospell is red, the Minister shall make this briefe exhortacion upon the woordes of the gospell.

1549

*AS Dear friends in Christ, we hear in this short gospel . . . that Christ . . . is so ready and willing graciously to help the children who are brought to him and us all who come to him that he is angry that people hinder them and do not bring them trustingly to him.

FRENDES you heare in this gospell the woordes of our Saviour Christe, that he commaunded the children to be brought unto him:[20] howe he blamed those that would have kept them from hym: howe he exhorteth all men to folowe their innocencie.[21] Ye perceyve howe by his outwarde gesture and dede he declared his good wyll towarde them.[22] For he embraced them in his armes, he layed his handes upon them, and blessed them: doubte ye not therfore,

. . . He takes them in his arms and embraces them . . . he lays his . . . hand on them . . . and blesses them.

---

19 Auf das evangelion . . . sol er diese kurze unterricht und vermahnung aus dem evangelio thun.
20 Cf. 'De sacramentis' (Jeanes, 'Reformation Treatise', p. 171): 'Nam Christus iussit adduci parvulos ad se, 1) accipit in ulnas, 2) imponit manus, 3) benedicit.'
21 From the same exhortation in Albertine Saxony: Und drauet uns alten, das wir ja zusehen, das wir auch in einfeltigem glauben bleiben und als die kindlein im himelreich, das ist im reich der gnaden und des lebens für im wandeln und in unschuld und reinigkeit anfahen und fortfaren ewig zu leben.
22 Cf. Melanchthon, *Loci Communes*, CR, col. 468: 'Sacramenta . . . sunt signa . . . principaliter fidei, item voluntatis Dei erga nos.' Calvin, *Institutes*, CR, col. 102: 'Sacramentum est autem signum externum quo bonam suam erga nos voluntatem Dominus nobis repraesentat ac testificatur.'

H Have faith . . . and doubt not but that he will so receive your children also, and embrace them with the arms of his mercy, and give them the blessing of eternal life and the everlasting communion of the kingdom of God.

And be ye most certain hereof, that our Lord Jesus Christ will mercifully regard this work of your charity towards this infant *AS therefore let us now baptize the same in the Lord's name and first in addition to the prayers we speak let us also pray the Our Father.[23]

but earnestly beleve, that he wyll lykewyse favourably receyve these present infantes, that he wyll embrace them with the arms of his mercy, that he wyll geve unto them the blessyng of eternall lyfe: and make them partakers of his everlasting kingdome. Wherfore we beyng thus perswaded of the good wyll of our heavenly father towarde these infantes, declared by his sonne Jesus Christe; and nothyng doubtyng but that he favourably alloweth this charitable worke of ours, in bringing these children to his holy baptisme: let us faythfully and devoutly geve thankes unto him; And say the prayer which the Lorde himselfe taught. And in declaracion of our fayth, let us also recyte the articles conteyned in our Crede.

We have already seen the importance of the story of Jesus and the children in the theological writings of some of Cranmer's contemporaries. Bucer constantly appeals to it in his understanding of infant baptism. Bullinger even uses it as the scriptural warrant for baptism. But Cranmer's own use of the passage owes more to Lutheran sources, and may be one of the older parts of the service. It will be discussed in more detail with the second exhortation at the font below.

---

23 Lieben freunde Christ, wir hören in diesem kurzen evangelio . . . das Christus . . . so ganz bereit und willig ist, den kindern, so im zugetragen werden und uns allen, so zu im kommen, gnediglich zu helfen, also das er auch drüber unwillig wird, das man sie hindert und nicht treulich zu im fodert . . . nimpt sie an arm und herzet sie . . . und leget seine . . . . hand auf sie . . . und segenet sie . . . so wöllen wir nu dasselbige auch ins herrn namen teufen und zuvor uber die gesprochene gebet auch das vater unser beten.

h. Hermann's prayer

	1549
S *Afterwards let the priest say to the godfathers and godmothers together with all that stand about* . . .	Here the minister with the Godfathers, Godmothers, and people presente, shall saye. Our father whiche art in heaven,
Our Father *and* Hail Mary *and* I believe in God	halowed bee thy name, &c. *And then shall saye openly.* I beleve in God the father almightie, &c. *The priest shall adde also this prayer.*
H Almighty and everlasting God, heavenly Father, we give thee eternal thanks that thou hast vouchsafed to call us to this knowledge of thy grace and faith towards thee. Increase and confirm this faith in us evermore. Give thy Holy Spirit to this infant, that he may be born again and be made heir of everlasting salvation, which of thy grace and mercy thou hast promised to thy holy church, to old men and to children, through our Lord Jesus Christ, which liveth and reigneth with thee now and for ever. Amen.	ALMIGHTIE and everlastyng God, heavenly father, we geve the humble thankes, that thou haste vouchesaved to call us to knowledge of thy grace, and fayth in thee: Increase and confyrme this fayth in us evermore: Geve thy holy spirite to these infantes, that they may be borne agayne, and be made heyres of everlasting salvacion, through our Lord Jesus Christ: Who lyveth and reigneth with thee and the holy spirite, nowe and for ever. Amen.
S *Next let him introduce the catechumen by the right hand into the church, having asked his (or her) name, saying:*	*Then let the priest take one of the children by the ryght hande, thother being brought after him. And cumming into the Churche towarde the fonte saye.*
N. enter into the temple of God, that thou mayest have eternal life. Amen.	THE Lorde vouchesafe to receyve you into his holy housholde, and to kepe and governe you alwaye in the same, that you may have everlasting lyfe. Amen.

Hermann's prayer, a close translation of a composition in the *Pia Deliberatio*, is elegantly introduced at the end of the first exhortation. In the Lutheran rites, based on the traditional services, the Lord's Prayer was used here. In 1549 Cranmer retained the Lord's Prayer and Creed of the Sarum *Manual*, omitting only the Hail Mary. However, with the full interrogatory Creed being put to the godparents shortly afterwards, we have a clumsy repetition. In 1552 the Lord's Prayer is moved to just after the immersion and signing, and so it is tempting to wonder whether in 1549 Cranmer was simply allowing an old pattern to remain for the time being, but all along had the new shape in mind and the place of Hermann's prayer in it.

As for the content of the prayer, it fits well within Cranmer's understanding of baptism, in which faith is enjoyed by the adult members of the congregation, and they pray for an increase of faith for themselves, but for the gift of the Holy Spirit to the child being baptized. Whereas in Cranmer's revision of the Flood prayer, the notion of faith is replaced by that of the gift of the Holy Spirit, here the two sit together in one prayer, with reference to the adult intercessors and the infant candidate.

The entry into the church in the 1549 book is accompanied by a new formula, emphasizing the theme of the child being received by God. This is removed in 1552 when the whole service takes place at the font.

i. Exhortation at the font

	1549
	Then standyng at the fonte the priest shall speake to the Godfathers and Godmothers, on this wyse.
*AS Dear friends, you have brought this child to the Lord Christ and asked that he will receive him, lay his hands upon him, bless him and also grant to him the kingdom of heaven and everlasting life.	Wel beloved frendes, ye have brought these children here to bee Baptized, ye have prayed that our Lorde Jesus Christ would vouchsafe to receyve them, to lay his handes upon them, to blesse them, to release them of theyr sinnes, to geve them the kyngdome of heaven, and everlastyng life.[24]
You have also heard that our Lord Christ is so heartily willing to do this, and has promised him all this	Ye have heard also that our Lorde Jesus Christe hath promysed in his gospel, to graunte all these thynges

---

24 'De sacramentis' (Jeanes, 'Reformation Treatise', p. 171): '(1) accipit in ulnas, (2) imposuit manus, (3) benedicit, id est sanctificat, remittendo peccata et imparciendo Spiritum sanctum.'

in the gospel, which for his part he will keep entirely although it has been promised and undertaken by the mouth of men and sponsors. And so in return for such a promise the child also must promise a sure faith in Christ through you his godparents and sponsors who have brought him to him, that he will honour God and believe such a promise which is made to him in the gospel and baptism, and that he will renounce the devil and all his lies, deceits and works, that he will not follow after him and his false lies and shameful works, but will put his faith in God as his dear father, whose heir he wishes to be . . .[25]

that ye have prayed for: whiche promyse he for his parte, will moste suerly kepe and perfourme. Wherfore, after this promyse made by Christe, these infantes muste also faythfully for theyr parte promise by you, that be theyr suerties, that they wyll forsake the devyll and all his workes, and constantly beleve Gods holy woorde, and obediently kepe his commaundementes.

The gospel reading was of Jesus blessing the children, and Cranmer chose the Markan account in preference to the Matthean version which had previously been standard in England. The difference is that Mark, but not Matthew, has Jesus say that 'whosoever doeth not receyve the kyngdom of God, as a lytle chylde: he shall not entre therin', and, while in Matthew he laid his hands on them and departed, in Mark, 'when he had taken them up in his armes: he put his handes upon them, and blessed them'. Cranmer now uses these elements in Mark as a commentary on the baptismal immersion, as Stephen Sykes describes:

The emotionally powerful image of the child being embraced in the arms of Jesus' mercy forms the affective heart of this liturgy. The word 'receive' significantly continues to echo at regular intervals

---

25 Lieben freunde, ir habt dieses kindlein dem herrn Christo zugetragen, gebeten das ers annemen wolt, seine hand auflegen, segnen, und im auch das himelreich und ewiges leben geben. So habt ir auch gehört das unser herr Christus so herzlich willig darzu ist und im solches alles im evangelio zugesagt hat, welches er auf seiner seiten alles also wil halten, ob es wol durch menschen stim und mittel person zugesagt und versprochen worden.
    So sol im das kind auf solche zusage durch euch als seine paten und mittelperson, durch die es zu Christo getragen, auch ein festen glauben zusagen, das es gott die ehre thun und solcher zusagung, die im im evangelio und der taufe geschicht, glauben wolle und dem teufel auch allen seinen lugen, gespenst und werken absagen . . .

throughout the rest of the service . . . When the priest, at the height of the drama, takes the child into his arms he is doing what Christ himself did. The congregation witnesses Christ's own embrace. The sacrament is God's own act.[26]

Contrary to the use by Cranmer of the traditional ceremonies as tokens, his concentration on the notion of receiving is understood by Sykes, surely correctly, as in some way an effective sign. But for us to see how Cranmer arrived at this use of the gospel in reflecting on the immersion, we need to look to the Lutheran origins of the motif, first to Luther's own theology and then to liturgical antecedents.

As a natural course Luther would quote in favour of infant baptism the verses in the gospels about Jesus's dealings with children, and we have discussions of Mt. 19.14, when Jesus both tells the disciples to let the children come to him and declares that the kingdom of heaven belongs to children. Luther defends the literal meaning of the parable against those who would qualify it in some way, and we can see here the germs of the treatment of the story (taken from the version in Mark) that is to be found, much developed in detail, in the Lutheran rites and in Cranmer's service.

But Luther develops more fully another theme which is close to his own theology and also feeds the other picture just described, that of the meeting of Jesus and John the Baptist *in utero* in Luke 1. Luther is discussing the problem: can infants have faith? He cites the example where John leaps in his mother's womb (Lk. 1.41, and cf. 1.15), and takes it as evidence of faith. He continues:

What if all children in baptism not only were able to believe but believed as well as John in his mother's womb? We can hardly deny that the same Christ is present at baptism and in baptism, in fact is himself the baptizer, who in those days came in his mother's womb to John. In baptism he can speak as well through the mouth of the priest, as when he spoke through his mother. Since then he is present, speaks, and baptizes, why should not his Word and baptism call forth both spirit and faith in the child as then it produced faith in John? He is the same one who speaks and acts then and now.[27]

---

26 'Baptisme doth represente unto us oure profession', in Johnson (ed.), *Thomas Cranmer*, pp. 122–43 (130–2).
27 'Concerning Rebaptism', *LW*, Vol. 40, pp. 242–3.

The validity of infant baptism depends, then, not only on the possibility that the infant may possess some kind of faith, but also on the conviction that the true minister of the sacrament is Christ, whose word and work are all-powerful. Luther extends the argument from John the Baptist to the children brought to Jesus: '[A child] comes to Christ in baptism, as John came to him, and as the children were brought to him, that his word and work might be effective in them, move them, and make them holy, because his word and work cannot be without fruit.'[28]

This principle of Jesus as the true minister of the sacrament is not restricted to baptism but underlies much of his thinking. Vilmos Vajta describes the principle:

> As a matter of fact the ministry is Christ's continued activity on earth. In the pulpit he speaks through the mouth of the preacher, at the font he himself is the Baptist, at the altar he imparts the remission of sins through the hands of the minister. There is no delegation of authority here. The minister is simply an instrument of the Holy Spirit, and his office a kind of stewardship.[29]

Sykes is no doubt correct, but only partly so, when he speaks of the image of the child being embraced by Jesus as 'the affective heart of this liturgy', and that 'the justification for baptizing infants lies . . . in the quality of [Christ's] response to little children.'[30] But this is not just sentiment. The Jesus who 'embraces with the arms of his mercy' is also, if we follow Luther, the one whose 'word and work cannot be without fruit'. The gospel passage in the liturgy then serves both to appeal to the hearts of the congregation and to give a theological defence for the practice.

So much for the gospel passage in itself and the theology that derived from the notion of Christ as the minister of the sacrament. Now we may turn to see how this was applied to the composition of the liturgy. The earliest form that we meet could be described as following the principle of interpretation by ceremonial. However, the interpretation is as much in the wording of the rubric as in the ceremonial action itself.

Both Luther's first and second *Taufbüchlein* demonstrated the theme by a subtle adaptation of the traditional rite. The gospel reading finished with the words, 'And he embraced them and laid his hand on them and blessed them.' The following rubric then reads, 'Than shall the priest lay his hand upon the child's head and pray Our Father, together with the

---

28 'Concerning Rebaptism', *LW*, Vol. 40, p. 244.
29 Vilmos Vajta, *Luther on Worship* (Philadelphia, PA: Muhlenberg Press, 1958), p. 112.
30 'Baptisme doth represente', p. 132.

godparents, kneeling.'[31] In other words, the priest's action here directly parallels that of Christ in the gospel story.

Luther's simple juxtaposition of gospel and action were evidently not enough for some, for in 1540 the meaning is spelt out in the revised baptism service of the Albertine Saxony *Kirchenordnung*, where an exhortation links the gospel reading and the rubric. This exhortation is the basis of Cranmer's exposition of the gospel in 1549 and 1552.[32] Where Cranmer differs, however, is that he omits any mention of laying a hand upon the child at this point. Rather the symbolism is attached to and centred exclusively on the act of baptism proper, where the priest then takes the child into his arms for the administration of the sacrament.

This move by Cranmer has a threefold result.

First it resists the accumulation of new ceremonies in a rite that has just been cleared of old ones, and concentrates instead on a theological interpretation of the sacramental act, using scripture and other written texts.

Secondly, the concrete linking action has changed. In the Lutheran rites it was the laying-on of the hand by the priest which echoed and communicated the action of Christ. In Cranmer the link is the action of the priest and congregation receiving the child, and the many verbal references to that effect.

The third effect of the shift from the Lutheran original is that Cranmer has moved one step closer to the theology of the Reformed rites. Gone is the idea of the power of the word of God administered directly through the priest doing what Christ did and effecting what he had effected. Now the reception of the child is primarily a response to the action of Christ: we trust in the promise of God that the child is spiritually regenerate. The sacramental sign of this is that the child is received into the Church. And so, in 1552, the signing of the cross has the words, 'We receyve this child into the congregacion of Christes flocke . . .' Incidentally, this is one place where it is possible that we might perhaps see the influence of Calvin's baptismal liturgy on Cranmer.[33] For while Hermann, for example, has simply the one reference and Albertine Saxony several,

---

31 Sehling (ed.), *Kirchenordnungen*, pp. 19, 22; trans. Fisher, *Christian Initiation*, pp. 14, 24. There was a similar action in the Magdeburg rite on which Luther based his service, but the rubric there reads, 'Then the presbyter holding his hand with his stole upon the head of the infant shall say Our Father and I believe in God.' (Fisher, *Christian Initiation*, p. 14.) The practice of holding the hand on the child's head originated with the priest speaking in the child's name at this point, and had nothing to do with the gospel reading. Luther is the first to make anything of the juxtaposition of the two elements.

32 Sehling (ed.), *Kirchenordnungen*, pp. 266–7; cf. Brightman, *English Rite*, p. cxviii.

33 Pace Fisher, *Christian Initiation*, p. 112.

but all to Christ receiving the child, it is Calvin who builds up a modest literary construction around the word, looking both to reception by Christ and reception by the Church:

> For this reason our Lord Jesus Christ received the children when they were presented to him . . .
>
> Since he declares that the kingdom of heaven belongs to them, and lays his hands on them and commends them to God, his Father, he teaches us sufficiently that we must by no means exclude them from his church. So following this rule, we will receive this infant into his church . . .
>
> Lord God . . . we pray thee . . . that thou wouldest receive him into thy holy protection . . .
>
> Since it is a matter of receiving this infant into the company of the Christian church, do you promise . . .[34]

We must explore this motif in a little bit more detail. The word 'receive', as Sykes points out, is used ten times besides its occurrence in the opening rubric. Naturally it is used in different ways, and a brief examination brings out the essential emphases.

i. God or Christ receiving the child being baptized

In the introduction it is used in the passive sense: the child is received into Christ's Church. We do not have a close source for this passage, so it may be an original composition by Cranmer.

Very similar is the phrase in Cranmer's translation of the Flood prayer (it survives in the 1552 version unchanged from 1549): for Luther's prayer that the children be preserved safe and dry in the Ark, Cranmer asks that they 'be received into the Ark of Christ's Church'.

And in the Seeking prayer, the request that God will receive the children is again a direct translation, this time of the Sarum prayer.

In the exhortations after the gospel and at the font the wish that Christ will 'receive' the infant does find the word in the sources. In the first case this follows Hermann's *suscepturum* and so is a natural translation, but in the second case we find a precedent only in the essay *De sacramentis*, which I claim has Cranmerian authorship and is an important witness for the growth of the motif.

The 1549 formula for the procession to the font seems to be a Cranmerian invention, with 'The Lorde vouchesafe to receyve you

---

34 'Form of Prayers', 1542, Fisher, *Christian Initiation*, pp. 115–16.

into his holy housholde.' (The Lutheran version is very different here.) The use of 'receive' could well be an instance of the removal of active movement by the child in the liturgy which might be implied by the Sarum version, 'Enter into the temple of God.' But Cranmer resisted a similar emendation suggested by Bucer in the Seeking prayer, that 'they coming to thy holy baptism' be changed.

Finally the Thanksgiving prayer includes the mention that God has received the child by adoption. The 1537 Strasbourg rite, with which I have compared this prayer, does not include the phrase.

ii. The child as the one who receives

The most important instance is that in the gospel reading, which presents itself as the key to the service. Here it is not Christ who 'receives' the candidate, but the candidate who 'receives' the kingdom like a child.

In the 1549 service the child receives the sign of the cross on the forehead and breast. But this instance of addressing the child and involving it actively in the liturgical performance is suppressed in 1552.

In the Seeking prayer, paired with the petition that God may receive the infants is the other request that the children may 'receyve remission of theyr sinnes'. 'Receive' here is a translation of *consequi*; this is hardly forced but the repetition of 'receive', translating two different Latin words, suggests that Cranmer is deliberately constructing a relationship between the two petitions. The child's reception of forgiveness of sins is linked intimately and necessarily with God's reception of the child.

The Invocation prayer, including the wish that the candidate 'may receive the fulness of thy grace' seems to be pure Cranmer.

iii. The congregation as those who receive

The opening rubrics speak of the congregation's role in testifying to the receiving of the baptized into Christ's Church. While this has a natural reference to God's work as signified by the sacrament, the congregation's role is self-evidently important.

The sign of the cross after baptism in 1552, 'We receyve this child into the congregacion of Christes flocke', inverts the use of 'receive' in 1549: now it is the child who is received. Who is receiving? It might refer to the priest's act of taking the child into his arms to baptize it, as in the Lutheran rites and Sykes's understanding of Cranmer, but I suspect the term includes the godparents, now representing the congregation, receiving the child, newly baptized, from the font. The act was important in the late medieval rite, as we see in the commentaries on it and in the odd rubric in 1549 (omitted in 1552, effectively absorbed into the formula of the signing?) in which the godparents 'shall take and lay theyr handes upon the childe'. Reception into the congregation is the recurring theme, normally expressed as God's action, and is now signified by the godparents' action.

How are we to understand the relation between the various persons who are the subjects of the word, 'receive'? How is the word used to build connections? The dual use in the Seeking prayer sets up a kind of pairing or reciprocity which we will see in the promise made by Christ, to which the promise of the child, made by the godparents, responds. And the act of reception by the congregation signifies or testifies to the divine act of reception of the child. Thus in their various ways the three acts of reception are bound together and are sacramentally enacted at the same time.

Such is the picture that Cranmer wishes to compose. However, as we look more closely at the composition we see another issue coming to the fore – the justification of infant baptism against the Anabaptists – and also we must raise the question of how the various uses of 'receive' are meant to relate to the gospel reading. The two must be discussed together, taking into account the way in which there is a difference between the text of the gospel ('whosoever doeth not receyve the kyngdom of God, as a lytle chylde') and the exhortations (Christ receives the children) which are meant, in part at least, to expound it. From the point of view of the congregation hearing the text, the gospel use of the word 'receive' is suppressed and twisted round. Stylistically this is extremely awkward. From the point of view of one of Cranmer's theological aims, to justify the baptism of infants against Anabaptist criticisms, this clash of meaning is quite disabling and a major fault in the service. An Anabaptist could quite legitimately ask, 'Yes, I am meant to receive the Kingdom as a child, but how does a newborn baby, unconscious of what is happening, do that, and in what way does this action relate to the use of "receive" elsewhere in the service?' The importance of the gospel narrative is such that, for the purposes of the liturgical context and the exhortations, Cranmer should have translated 'complexans eos' (or ἐναγκαλισάμενος αὐτὰ) as 'received them into his arms' instead of 'taken them up in his arms'. Then the connections between the gospel and the exhortations in particular would have been clear and straightforward.

j. The profession of faith

<table>
<tr><td></td><td>

1549

Then shall the priest demaunde of the childe (which shalbe first Baptized) these questions folowing: first naming the childe, and saying.

</td></tr>
</table>

S N. Dost thou renounce Satan . . . and all his works?

I renounce.

And all his pomps?

H And the world also and all his concupiscences?

S I renounce.

*KB . . . carnal and fleshly lusts and desires . . . And by the same grace also conferred unto us in baptism, we be made more strong and able to resist and withstand the said concupiscence and carnal desires than is another man which never was christened.[35]

S I renounce.

*AS Dost thou believe in God the father almighty, creator of heaven and earth?

S I believe.

*AS Dost thou believe in Jesus Christ his only Son our Lord, born of the virgin Mary, crucified, died and buried, was raised from the dead and sits at the right hand of God, and who is to judge the living and the dead?

N. Doest thou forsake the devill and all his workes?

Aunswere. I forsake them.

Minister. Doest thou forsake the vaine pompe, and glory of the worlde, with all the covetouse desyres of the same?

Aunswere. I forsake them.

Minister. Doest thou forsake the carnall desyres of the flesh, so that thou wilt not folowe, nor be ledde by them?

Aunswere. I forsake them.

Minister. Doest thou beleve in God the father almightie, maker of heaven and earth?

Aunswere. I beleve.

Minister. Doest thou beleve in Jesus Christe his only begotten sonne our Lorde, and that he was conceyved by the holy gost, borne of the virgin Mary, that he suffered under Poncius Pilate, was crucified, dead, and buryed, that he went downe into hell, and also dyd ryse agayne the thyrde daye; that he ascended into heaven, and sitteth on the ryght hande of God the father almighty: And from thence shall come agayne at the ende of

---

35 Lloyd (ed.), *Formularies of Faith*, pp. 254–5; Spinks, 'Treasures Old and New', p. 183.

S I believe.

*AS Dost thou believe in the Holy Spirit, one holy Christian church, the communion of saints, forgiveness of sins, the resurrection of the flesh and everlasting life after death?[36]

S I believe.

What seekest thou?

Baptism.

Dost thou wish to be baptized?

I wish.

the worlde, to judge the quicke and the dead: Doest thou beleve this?

Aunswere. I beleve.

Minister. Doest thou beleve in the holy gost, the holy Catholike Churche, the communion of sainctes, remission of Sinnes, resurreccion of the fleshe, and everlastyng lyfe after death?

Aunswere. I beleve.

Minister. What doest thou desyre?

Aunswere. Baptisme.

Minister. Wilt thou be baptized?

Aunswere. I wyll.

The traditional form of a renunciation of Satan and of belief in God, Father, Son and Holy Spirit, are retained by Cranmer. For him, as we have seen already, baptism is the sacrament of faith and so it is important that this element is retained in the service, even though the infants are not yet capable of faith.

In 1549 the godparents answer as the mouthpiece of the child. In 1552 this is modified slightly, and the rubric states that the priest puts the questions to the godparents, not (as in 1549) to the child. However, the preliminary exhortation saying that the children must promise 'by you that be theyr suerties' remains unchanged, the questions are addressed 'thou', and the question, 'wilt thou be baptized' is retained, indeed expanded slightly. It is wrong, therefore, to suppose that the godparents' faith is that demanded at this point. They clearly make proxy statements on behalf of the child, whose faith (as yet not existing) they sacramentally signify by their answers. The parallel provision for the questions and answers after private baptism have a slightly different form: the priest asks the name of the child (presumably because otherwise it would not be heard in the public liturgy), and then asks the questions, 'Doest thou in the name of this childe forsake? etc.' This form recurs in the beginning of the interrogatory creed, and then at the

---

36 Gleubestu an gott den allmechtigen vater, schöpfer himels und der erden? . . . Gleubestu an Jesum Christ seinen einigen son unsern hern, geborn von Maria der jungfrauen, gekreuziget, gestorben und begraben, auferstanden von den todten, sitzend zur rechten gottes, zukünftig zu richten die lebendigen und die todten? . . . Gleubestu an den heiligen geist, eine heilige christliche kirche, gemeine der heiligen, vergebung der sünde, auferstehung des fleisches und nach dem tode ein ewiges leben?

third section it is included a third time, but slightly differently: 'And doe you in *hys* name beleve in the holy gost, etc.' Perhaps there is some confusion on the part of the busy reviser, but this cannot all be blamed on confusion. The evidence perhaps points to a desire to maintain the profession of faith as a vicarious act, sacramentally signifying the faith of the candidate, but there is uncertainty how this may best be expressed.

The renunciation and profession of faith are somewhat fuller than in the Sarum *Manual*. They are threefold in structure in 1549 and a single formula each in 1552. The Creed is used for the profession of faith instead of the shorter phrases of the Sarum *Manual*. Here Cranmer may well be following the example of Albertine Saxony or some other Lutheran rite. The renunciation of Satan also needs to be expanded, or it would be somewhat thin in contrast to the statement of belief. Hermann may have suggested an expansion of one element, and the King's Book another.

The second exhortation which introduces this element of the service combines within itself several important themes. In the 1549 rite the priest and baptism party have now arrived at the font, and the opening words of the exhortation carry a sense of drama: 'Ye have brought these children here to bee baptized.' The godparents are themselves brought physically to a special point in the service, in which their role is now explicit and, in this space around the font, the child's faith is sacramentally enunciated and the redeeming work of God enacted. In 1552 the service began at the font, so the exhortation, though unchanged, seems to have lost this particular strength. Now it stands simply as a second exhortation after the first, and there is a certain lack of direction in this reiteration.

But still the exhortation is important: the priest recaps the first part of the service. He refers to the gospel narrative of Jesus and the children, and also (with reference to the Seeking prayer) to the promise of Jesus to grant what we pray for. The word 'grant' (which up to now has been used sparingly) will soon gain great prominence in the Grant prayers. So here the exhortation links together several elements. Yet another link is made: the promise of Jesus is paired with that now demanded of the children that they will forsake the devil and believe in and follow God. Sykes rightly speaks of this as the 'covenant' between God and the baptizand.[37]

---

37 'Baptisme doth represente', p. 138. No connection is suggested with 'covenant theology' which is a different thing altogether.

k. The Grant prayers

The water in the fonte shalbe chaunged every moneth once at the lest, and afore any child be Baptized in the water so chaunged, the priest shall say at the font these prayers folowing.

M I exorcise thee, creature of water: through God the Father . . . who ordered us to consecrate thee . . . for the regeneration of the human race: and through Jesus Christ our Lord . . . who . . . revealed himself to be baptized by John in thee for our salvation: and the Holy Spirit who appeared over him in the Jordan in the likeness of a dove.
Be present, we pray, at the invocation of thy name. Amen. Sanct✠fy this font, thou Sancti✠fier of the human race. Amen.

O MOSTE mercifull god our savioure Jesu Christ, who hast ordeyned the element of water for the regeneracion of thy faythful people, upon whom, beyng baptised in the river of Jordane, the holye ghoste came down in the likenesse of a doove: Sende down we benseche thee the same thy holye spirite to assiste us, and to bee present at this our invocacion of thy holy name: Sanctifie ✠this fountaine of baptisme, thou that art the sanctifier of al thynges, that by the power of thy worde, all those that shall be baptized therein, maye be spirituallye regenerated, and made the children of everlasting adopcion. Amen.

Here may the old Adam be buried, and the new rise up. Amen.

O MERCIFULL God, graunte that the olde Adam, in them that shalbe baptized in this fountayne, maye so be buried, that the newe man may be raised up agayne. Amen.

Here may all that is flesh die, and all that is spirit rise up. Amen.

GRAUNT that all carnal affeccions maie die in them; and that all thynges, belongyng to the spirite maye live and growe in them. Amen.

Whoever here renounce the devil, grant that they may triumph over the world. Amen.

GRAUNT to all them which at this fountayne forsake the devill and all his workes: that they maye have power and strength to have victorye and to triumph againste

Whoever shall have confessed thee in this place, acknowledge him in your kingdom. Amen.

May crimes be so extinguished in this font that they rise not again. Amen.

Whoever here begins to be thine, may he never cease to be thine. Amen.

Whoever here denies self for thee, may he win thee. Amen.

That the one consecrated to thee by our ministry, may be consecrated for thee with eternal virtues for eternal rewards. Amen.

hym, the worlde, and the fleshe. Amen.

WHOSOEVER shal confesse the, o lorde: recognise him also in thy kingdome. Amen.

GRAUNT that al sinne and vice here maie bee so extinct: that thei never have power to raigne in thy servauntes. Amen.

GRAUNTE that whosoever here shall begynne to be of thy flocke: maie evermore continue in the same. Amen.

GRAUNT that all they which for thy sake in this life doe denie and forsake themselfes: may winne and purchase thee (o lord) which art everlasting treasure. Amen.

GRAUNT that whosoever is here dedicated to thee by our office and ministerie: maye also bee endewed with heavenly vertues, and everlastinglye rewarded through thy mercie, O Blessed lorde God, who doest live and governe al thinges world without ende. Amen.
The Lorde be with you.
Answere. And with thy spirite.

The Grant prayers form a distinct unit within the service. Their position just before the baptismal Invocation is obviously important. Their style, almost that of a litany with the short, simple phrases, all beginning with 'Grant . . .' and the repeated Amens, is unique in the Prayer Book. Their source, in the Mozarabic liturgy, is also distinctive. In 1549 there was a series of eight petitions in the form of blessing of the font. In 1552 their position before the invocation, now moved into the service, is retained, but their number reduced to four (the first three and the last are retained, with only stylistic changes). But the oddity of their origin and structure must not be allowed to disguise their importance, for here the role of intercession by the congregation for the infants being baptized is focused in the most acute manner. The word 'grant' picks up the use of the word in the second exhortation with its reference to the promise of

Jesus in the gospel, and also in the Introduction to the service, where the congregation is bidden to pray that Christ 'will grant to these children that thing which by nature they cannot have'. At this point immediately before baptism, the faith of the congregation is exercised in praying for the child that it may receive the grace signified by the sacrament. And so the content of the Grant prayers summarizes the grace of baptism: death and burial of the old Adam, raising up of the new; putting to death of the flesh, prospering of the things of the Spirit; triumph over the devil, the world and the flesh; a virtuous life and admission to heaven. The 1549 form also prays for the grace of perseverance, and there is a stronger theme of judgement and the opposition of the world to the things of God: denial of self for Christ's sake being the way of winning Christ, and the petition that 'whosoever shall confess thee, O Lord, recognize him also in thy kingdom'. There is a certain loss of drama in the 1552 simplification. Probably simplicity was the aim of the revision: not only do we have a succinct group of petitions, but the addressee of the prayers, who in 1549 is clearly Christ, now is ambiguous ('merciful God'), which enables the prayers to flow naturally into the Invocation which is clearly addressed to the Father.

The source of the Grant prayers is the Mozarabic blessing of the font, of which the published edition was available in the *Missale Mixtum secundum regulam beati Isidori, dictum Mozarabes*, published in 1500. The Mozarabic form is distinctive for breaking up a series of petitions by the repeated Amen. The petitions are found as a single unit in the Gallican blessing of the font in the *Missale Gallicanum Vetus*, a single manuscript which was first published in 1680, and so would have been unknown to Cranmer. However, some scholars have seen points in which the 1549 Grant prayers follow the text witnessed to by the extant Gallican rather than the Mozarabic prayers. What are we to make of these? Two points of content are trivial in the extreme: the omission of 'here' (*hic*) in the second petition (that all carnal affections may die in them); and the inclusion of 'thee' (*te*) in the fourth petition (whosoever shall confess *thee*). However, the latter is a most obvious insertion in an English translation, and the former omission is paralleled by the omission of 'in this place' (*in hoc loco*) from the fourth petition (found in both the Mozarabic and Gallican forms). I am inclined to reject any idea that these two points can stand as evidence of a different source. A third point is stronger, namely that the position of the sixth petition, that 'whosoever shall begin to be of thy flock, may evermore continue to be in the same', follows the order of the Gallican rather than the Mozarabic petitions. If Cranmer, using only the *Missale Mixtum*, moved it to this place for some obscure reason of his own, then we must hypothesize a coincidence with the Gallican order. But there is no reason why such a coincidence should be less likely than the existence of a hypothetical source. Reliance on imaginary sources for insignificant changes underrates the creative aspect of Cranmer's work. The existence of a different Mozarabic source, a manuscript with the distinctive series of Amens but which followed the Gallican order of petitions, is not impossible, but is neither necessary nor likely. Sources must not be multiplied beyond necessity.[38]

l. The baptismal invocation

	1549
	ALMIGHTYE everliving God,
S I bless thee ✠through Jesus Christ	whose moste derely beloved sonne
his only Son . . .	Jesus Christe, for the forgevenesse
who shed thee together with	of our sinnes did shead out of
blood from his side, and gave	his moste precious side bothe
command to his disciples that	water and bloude, and gave
those who believed should be	commaundemente to his disciples
baptized in thee saying, Go, teach	that they shoulde goe teache all
all nations baptizing them in the	nacions, and baptise them in the
name of the ✠ Father and of the	name of the father, the sonne, and
✠ Son and of the Holy ✠ Ghost.	the holye ghoste: Regarde, we
	beseche thee, the supplicacions
	of thy congregacion, and graunte
M that . . . for these who are	that all thy servauntes which
washed by us in you or from you:	shall bee baptized in this water
and are baptized in the name of	prepared for the mynystracion of
the threefold majesty: may receive	thy holy sacrament, maye receive
divine grace and be counted	the fulnesse of thy grace, and
worthy to be included in the	ever remaine in the noumbre of
number of the faithful.	thy faithful, and elect children,
	through Jesus Christ our Lord.

The role of the 1552 Invocation prayer and of the 1549 Sanctification prayers has been discussed in detail already. Here I wish to make some observations on the content of the prayer in the context of its position immediately before the immersion. We might at this point expect some

---

38 Some of those in favour of the 'two source' hypothesis are Brightman, *English Rite*, Vol. 1, p. cxix; Frere in Procter and Frere, *New History of the BCP*, p. 571, note 1; H. Boone Porter, 'Hispanic Influences on Worship in the English Tongue', in J.N. Alexander (ed.), *Time and Community* (Washington: Pastoral Press, 1990), pp. 171–84, 176. On the other hand J. Dowden rejects the Gallican link: see *The Workmanship of the Prayer Book* (London: Methuen, 1899), p. 54, n.

kind of summary or kernel of the theology of baptism. The first half of the prayer does indeed fulfil this expectation: the concentration on the death of Christ and his shedding water and blood from his side brings us by baptism to the centre (as Cranmer sees it) of the mystery of our faith. The command of the risen Christ to his disciples to baptize includes mention of the resurrection more satisfactorily than does the Invocation prayer in the communion service. But the final section of the prayer is extremely sparse by comparison: God is asked simply that the candidates may 'receive the fulness of thy grace, and ever remain in the number of thy faithful and elect children'. Why not something stronger? Perhaps Cranmer felt constrained to write something bland in order to gain the acceptance of as many people as possible. But elsewhere in the rite he has made the most of the freedom which his sacramental language permits. In particular, the Thanksgiving prayer and its bidding use the strongest language possible. The Grant prayers likewise expatiate on the manifold grace of baptism. Brightman's suggestion that here Cranmer is following the Mozarabic source seems likely to answer the question 'how' but not 'why'. It is as though Cranmer brings us to the very threshold of the sacrament, and himself arrives exhausted. Rhetorically he has shot all his arrows. We are not bidden with the same intensity as in the eucharist to see in the symbols Christ offering himself to us. Nor is any strong connection made with the first half of the prayer. Perhaps he hoped that the immersion should speak for itself, but even that approach leaves the Invocation looking lame. The very intensity of the subject seems to have defeated him. Indeed, the final words raise the spectre of the doctrine of election: the petition that the child remain 'in the number of thy faithful and elect children'.

When examining Cranmer's funeral office, Bridget Nichols speaks of 'an imposed world where the dead are not prayed for, and the non-elect not saved'. And she quotes Eamon Duffy's comments on the same service:

> The burial rite of 1552 spoke only of the elect . . . This was to make the most universal of all popular rituals, burial, into a rite not of inclusion, but of separation, and the logical working out of this drastic redrawing and limiting of the Christian community to the elect was the fenced communion table and, ultimately, separation.[39]

The separation is not so strong in the baptism service, but it is there. The Invocation prayer raises the problem but does not resolve it.

---

39 B. Nichols, *Liturgical Hermeneutics*, p. 204; E. Duffy, 'Cranmer and Popular Religion', in Ayris and Selwyn (eds), *Cranmer, Churchman and Scholar*, pp. 199–216 (215).

m. The immersion

	1549
S *Then let the priest receive the infant sideways in his hands, and having asked his name let him baptize him with a threefold dipping invoking the Holy Trinity once saying thus:*	*Then the prieste shall take the childe in his handes, and aske the name. And naming the childe, shall dyppe it in the water thryse. First dypping the ryght syde: Seconde the left syde: The thryd tyme dippyng the face towards the fonte: So it be diseretly and warely done, saying.*
N. I also baptize thee in the name of the Father (*and let him dip him once with his face turned towards the north and his head towards the east*) and of the Son (*and again let him dip him once with his face turned towards the south*) and of the Holy Ghost. Amen (*and let him dip him the third time with his face towards the water*).	N. I Baptize thee in the name of the father, and of the Sonne, and of the holy gost. Amen.
If necessity arise they may know how to baptize . . . I christen the N, in the name of the fadir and of the sone and of the holy gost. Amen: *or in the Latin tongue* . . . *sprinkling water upon the infant or dipping him in the water three times or at least once.*	*And if the childe be weake, it shall suffice to powre water upon it, saying the foresayed woordes. N. I baptize thee, &c.*

In 1549 the traditional threefold dipping is retained, even to the details of dipping the right side of the child, then the left, then face down. This detail, which most of his fellow Reformers must have regarded as contrary to the spirit of a proper liturgy, is perhaps the most outstanding case of the retention of a traditional ceremony. Even the *Kirchenordnung* of Electoral Brandenburg, which retained very many details rejected elsewhere, gives no directions for a triple immersion, let alone the provision for turning the child this way and that.[40] Only in 1552 is all this material swept away and the child is dipped, we presume once only,

40 Sehling (ed.), *Kirchenordnungen*, Vol. 3, p. 58.

in accordance with the Lutheran emphasis on the baptismal immersion as dying and rising with Christ.[41] Pouring water over the head of the child when it is sick is permitted, as had been the case in the *Manual*, as second-best. Cranmer does not adopt the Reformed preference for baptism by pouring water over the head. This may be his innate conservatism, but more probably he preferred to retain the fullness of the sign as figuring death and resurrection.

n. The signing

The signing is perhaps the most important of all the passages which concern the future Christian life, and certainly it encapsulates the theme most dramatically. The 1549 version and its sources read as follows:

	1549
S *and by what name he is to be called*	*Here shall the priest aske what shall be the name of the childe, and when the Godfathers and Godmothers have tolde the name, then shall he make a crosse upon the childes forehead and breste, saying.*
L Then he shall make a cross on his forehead and breast and shall say:	
Receive the sign of the holy cross both on thy forehead and on thy breast.[42]	N. Receyve the signe of the holy Crosse, both in thy forehead, and in thy breste, in token that thou shalt not be ashamed to confesse thy fayth in Christe crucifyed, and manfully to fyght under his banner against synne, the worlde, and the devill, and to continewe his faythfull soldiour and servaunt unto thy lyfes ende. Amen.
R *entokening that he is coming to be professed and totally to be dedicated to Christ crucified: whom he will never be ashamed openly before men to confess and acknowledge.*	*And this he shalt doe and saye to as many children as bee presented to be Baptised, one after another.*

---

41   Luther, *Holy and Blessed Sacrament of Baptism*, 1: *LW*, Vol. 35, p. 29.
42   King's Book, Article of Justification, Lloyd (ed.), *Formularies of Faith*, p. 366: sworn to be servants of God, and to be soldiers under Christ, to fight against our enemies, the Devil, the world and the flesh.
    D. Erasmus, *Encheiridion militis Christiani*, sig. A3v, in A.M. O'Donnell (ed.) (Oxford: Oxford University Press, 1981), p. 35 marginal note: 'In tyme of Baptysme we professe with protestacion to fyght ever under the standard of christ.'

The first part of the new signing formula is based on Luther's *Taufbüchlein*, and an explanation is added to it. It has to be said that this explanation has its origin in the common consent of sixteenth-century Christendom, so widespread are the parallels to its sentiment. However, I have given prominence to the explanation in the *Rationale*, since it seems to have functioned as an important source of the formulas for the white garment and the post-baptismal anointing. Also there is an important feature of the *Rationale* which 1549 does not reproduce (and the contrast is significant whether or not we see the *Rationale* as a direct source of 1549). The passage quoted above of the *Rationale* is the explanation of the signing on the forehead. But it then proceeds to the second signing:

> Then he maketh another cross upon the breast, from whence cometh the belief, signifying that it is not enough to confess Christ with mouth openly unless he doth steadfastly believe in heart inwardly, and therefore the minister prayeth Almighty God to take away the blindness of his heart and to make him apt to receive the grace given in baptism.[43]

Inward belief is something which Cranmer could not ascribe to the infant. While this section of the *Rationale* was probably written by those who would have been impatient with Luther's notion of infant belief, Cranmer himself had in all probability once subscribed to it (if we accept *De sacramentis* as representing his personal views) and he now had replaced it with his own notion of baptism as sacrament of faith, with no room or reason for the individual faith of the child. Therefore any discussion of the inward faith of the child at the time of the signing of the breast would have been most difficult. Far easier to concentrate on the token which distinguishes a Christian from the pagan world.

The 1552 version of the signing is moved to a position directly after the immersion, and its wording is significantly different:

> We receyve this child into the congregacion of Christes flocke, and doe signe him with the signe of the crosse, in token that hereafter he shal not be ashamed to confesse the fayth of Christ crucified, and manfully to fight under his banner agaynst synne, the world,

---

Luther, *Holy and Blessed Sacrament of Baptism*, 1519; LW, Vol. 35, p. 29: 'Baptism is an eternal sign or token which so separates us from all men not baptized that we are thereby known as a people of Christ, our Leader, under whose banner of the holy cross we continually fight against sin.'

43 *Rationale*, p. 7.

and the devyll, and to continue Christ's faythfull souldiour and
servaunt unto his lyves end. Amen.

The signing is now addressed to the congregation rather than to the
child. 'We receyve this child into the congregacion of Christes flocke'
may be paralleled with the 1549 formula of approach to the font: 'The
Lord vouchsafe to receive you into his holy householde . . .' Both themes,
reception into the Church and bearing the cross of Christ, are now
focused together on this point next to the immersion. They can be seen
as explanatory rites, and are part of the entire unit which is omitted at
emergency baptism.

What is the significance of the formula? Bearing the cross of Christ
was the common understanding of baptism as a mark identifying the
Christian and setting them apart from other people. It is the theology of
baptism identified with Zwinglianism,[44] and other theologians are happy
to include it in their discussion of baptism but hasten to emphasize that it
is insufficient by itself.[45] It is perhaps for this reason that Cranmer joins
with the 1549 formula the theme of reception into the congregation:
baptism is not primarily about what we say or do. For the evangelical
Reformers' attitude to ceremonies was that they detracted from the
centrality and importance of the immersion. Therefore to have a separate
ceremony at this very point in effect says that, what this ceremony
signifies is not central to baptism. All of which begs the question for the
participant of what is central. The answer for Cranmer is the sacramental
signification of regeneration.

Marion Hatchett has suggested that the signing in the 1552 baptism
service owes something to the rite of confirmation. The connections he sees
are: we 'signe him with the signe of the crosse' is borrowed from the 1549
confirmation rite: 'I signe thee with the signe of the crosse'; the signing
is performed on the forehead rather than on the head (again following
1549 confirmation rather than baptism); and that the explanation of
the sign of the cross belongs to medieval discussions of confirmation.[46]
Taken cumulatively, the evidence seems impressive. However, it is hard
to imagine what might have led someone of Cranmer's theology and
outlook to try to patch a piece of the confirmation service into baptism.
We know he had consistently played down the status of confirmation;

---

44 W.P. Stephens, *The Theology of Huldrych Zwingli* (Oxford: Oxford University Press,
1986), pp. 184–5, 194–217.

45 E.g. Calvin, *Institutes* (1536), 4, 'De Baptismo', CR 29, col. 110: trans. Battles,
Institutes, p. 94; Jan Laski, *Brevis et Dilucida de Sacramentis Tractatio*, fols 9–9ᵛ, in
Kuyper (ed.), *Opera*, Vol. 1, p. 122.

46 M.J. Hatchett, 'Prayer Books', in S. Sykes and J. Booty (eds), *The Study of Anglicanism*
(London: SPCK, 1988), pp. 121–33 (128).

why rescue what he had so long ago abandoned? So we must look again at the evidence. First, with regard to explanations of the cross, there is an equally strong tradition discussing the sign of the cross in baptism as well as in confirmation. In particular, as we have seen, the *Ordynary of crysten men* discussed the post-baptismal anointing and signing in this way. Secondly the formula of we 'signe him with the signe of the crosse' is quite possibly borrowed from confirmation, but, given the limited number of ways in which this could be said, it is hard to see how this must have been deliberate or significant. Lastly, the idea that Cranmer was preserving the significance of the medieval tradition of confirming with a sign of the cross on the forehead is to project onto him a notion which is totally foreign to his outlook both on confirmation and on medieval symbolism. It is better by far to invoke a biblical reference, to those who have the sign of God on their foreheads (Rev. 7.2ff., 9.4). In short, there is nothing which need distract us from seeing Cranmer as altering the traditional pre-baptismal signing on the forehead and placing it later in the service in order to convey the importance of the whole Christian life.

The signing looks forward to the baptized fulfilling their baptism through their life. This is explicit in the 1549 version, but even more prominent when the formula is brought to a position after the immersion. And the remainder of the service looks strongly towards the future. The final exhortation to the godparents is almost exclusively concerned with the issue of the Christian's fulfilment of what is promised on their behalf in baptism, even to the extent of saying that 'baptism doth represent unto us our profession'. In the sense that it is the 'sacrament of faith', this is indeed so. It would not have been an adequate definition, but within the context of God's election and grace, the human response of faith is expected and required.

o. The bidding, Lord's Prayer and prayer of thanksgiving

In the 1552 Prayer Book the Lord's Prayer and Prayer of Thanksgiving maintain a structure parallel to that which we see in Cranmer's eucharist. The bidding is an addition to the basic structure. It affirms again the importance of vicarious faith and intercession in the baptism service. But the confidence of its declaration, 'Seeyng nowe, derely beloved brethren, that these chyldren be regenerate and grafted into the bodye of Christes congregacion: lette us geve thankes unto God for these benefites, and with one accorde make our praiers unto almighty god, that they may leade the rest of theyr lyfe according to this beginninge', is the most adventurous use of Cranmer's sacramental language.

The Lord's Prayer's position here and in the eucharist is a curious one, following rather than preceding the administration of the sacrament. A clue to the reason for this might be found in Cranmer's commonplaces, where prayer is discussed. In MS Royal 7B XII, fol. 202 we find the headings, 'We pray that those things may occur which we certainly know from the promises of God will happen', and 'We pray so that glory, praise and dominion be to God for ever and ever.'[47] Then on fol. 202ᵛ comes a series of passages under the heading, 'We must always pray to God that he will forgive the sins even of his own children, whose sins have already all been forgiven.' The passages, from Augustine, all speak of the need even for the saints to pray for the forgiveness of their sins. And in each of the passages, reference to the Lord's Prayer and 'forgive us our sins' is underlined. It might be that here we have the reason for the position of the Lord's Prayer: by baptism we are placed in the position where indeed we can pray for forgiveness of our sins in the confidence that they are indeed forgiven. It is evident from the propositions quoted here that Cranmer saw the assurance of the event happening to be a source of confidence in prayer rather than any notion that prayer be redundant. We respond to God's promise shown in the sacrament by praying confidently for its fulfilment. And in this respect the congregation who witness the child being baptized are reminded of their own baptism and pray for the forgiveness of their own sins as well as for forgiveness for the child. Thus the Lord's Prayer, as well as Hermann's prayer, provides for the participation of the congregation in the service and their appropriation of grace offered in baptism. Otherwise they would be gazers only, and liable to bring judgement on their heads.

The Thanksgiving prayer could be said to compensate for the weakness of the Invocation. Here the meaning and the spiritual grace of baptism are dwelt on in detail. The child is regenerated with the Holy Spirit and received by God (no room for individual faith or initiative) and incorporated into the congregation. And by baptism it has died to sin and is living to righteousness, after the pattern of Christ whose death and resurrection have been described in the Invocation prayer. The child's sacramental death and resurrection must now be enacted throughout its life, and the sharing in the resurrection is held as an eschatological hope at the end. At this very moment there is a glimpse, as in the Invocation, of the doctrine of election: only the residue of the congregation will enjoy the fulfilment of that promise.

The structure and content of the Thanksgiving prayer invite comparison with a prayer in the 1537 rite of baptism from Strasbourg. It was rare to have any sort of prayer or formula after the immersion apart

---

47 'Oramus ut eveniant ea quae ex Dei promissis certe novimus eventura. Precamur ut Deo sit gloria, laus et imperium in saecula sacculorum.'

from a dismissal, and the similarities between these two prayers invite a synopsis, whether or not Cranmer was imitating Bucer's composition.

*ST Almighty God, heavenly Father, we give thee everlasting praise and thanks for that thou hast given this child to thy church, and hast granted him a new birth through thy holy baptism, and hast incorporated him in the body of thy dear Son, our eternal Saviour, and hast now made him thy child and heir. Grant, O loving and faithful Father, that we all may show ourselves thankful all our lives for this thy great mercy, and may faithfully bring up this child who is now thine to please thee in all things, and also that together with this child we may evermore die to ourselves and daily increase in the life of thy Son, our Lord Jesus, so that thou mayest always be praised by us and our neighbour be edified; through our Lord Jesus Christ. Amen.	*1552* WE yelde thee heartie thankes, most merciful father, that it hathe pleased thee to regenerate this infant with thy holy spirite, to receyve him for thy owne chylde by adopcion, and to incorporate him into thy holy congregacion. And humbly we beseche thee to graunt that he, being dead unto sinne, and lyving unto righteousnes, and beeinge buried with Christ in his death, may crucify the old man, and utterly abolishe the whole body of sine: that as he is made partaker of the death of thy sonne, so he may be partaker of his resurreccion: so that finalli, with the residue of thy holy congregacion, he may be enheritour of thine everlasting kingdom: through Christ our lord. Amen.

The first half of each prayer is very similar. The 1552 prayer speaks of regeneration with the Holy Spirit (cf. Tit. 3.5?) instead of the 1537 'new birth through thy holy baptism'. The later version is making a higher claim (justified by sacramental language) but falls into the trap of begging the question what has become of the water baptism. Its second half is theologically much stronger in linking intimately the candidate's life and death with the death and resurrection of Christ. By comparison, Bucer's effort lacks any vision which raises us beyond the confines of a good life and an edified neighbour.

The Invocation prayer and the Thanksgiving prayer are evidently meant to function as a doublet around the sacramental administration and Lord's Prayer, both in baptism and eucharist. The construction of the two prayers here reinforces that overall structure. We have a sequence of

Invocation prayer   Death and resurrection of Christ
                        Grace given to recipient

Thanksgiving prayer   Grace given to recipient
                        Death and resurrection of Christ

The Thanksgiving prayer, however, describes the grace given to the recipient in a manner much more satisfactory than is achieved in the Invocation prayer.

p. The white vesture and anointing

1549

S *Then let the godparents receiving the infant from the hands of the priest raise him from the font.*[48] *Next let the infant be clad in his chrismal robe, the priest asking his name and saying thus:*
N. receive a white robe, holy and unstained . . .
R it signifieth also a Christian purity and innocency which after the washing away of old sin he ought studiously to conserve and keep . . .
S . . . which thou must bring before the tribunal of our Lord Jesus Christ, that thou mayest have eternal life and live for ever and ever. Amen.
S Almighty God, the Father of our Lord Jesus Christ, who hath regenerated thee by water and the Holy Ghost, and who hath given thee remission of all thy sins, (*here let him anoint the infant with the chrism with his thumb on the head in the form of a cross,*

Then the Godfathers and Godmothers shall take and lay theyr handes upon the childe, and the minister shall put upon him his white vesture, commonly called the Crisome; and saye.
TAKE this white vesture for a token of the innocencie, whiche by Gods grace in this holy sacramente of Baptisme, is given unto thee: and for a signe wherby thou art admonished, so long as thou lyvest, to geve thyselfe to innocencie of living, that, after this transitorye lyfe, thou mayest be partaker of the lyfe everlasting. Amen.
Then the prieste shall annoynt the infant upon the head, saying.
ALMIGHTY God the father of our lorde Jesus Christ, who hath regenerate thee by water and the holy gost, and hath geven unto thee remission of al thy sinnes: he vouchsave to annoynte thee with the unccion of his holy spirite, and

---

48 Cf. *Declaracion of Seremonies*, sig. A iv, The priest 'commaundyth the gossipis to ley hond on the chyldes heed for they ben wytnesses of his baptim and receve the charge to teach it and the trewthe of his beleve'.

saying) himself anoints thee with
the chrism of salvation in the same
his Son our Lord Jesus Christ unto
eternal life.
R he is anointed with the spiritual
unction of the Holy Ghost, that
by his assistance and grace he may
attain everlasting life.

bryng thee to the inheritaunce of
everlasting lyfe. Amen.

These two ceremonies are retained from the *Manual*, although that
of handing the child the lighted candle is omitted. It is hard to see the
reasons for Cranmer's choice in the matter. The formula for placing
the white garment on the child has been moved to a position before
the anointing, and this may reflect actual practice in a cold climate.
The reason for the chrisom cloth in the traditional rite was to cover the
chrism oil on the head. That element is omitted from the new service:
now the cloth is the white garment which symbolizes the purity of
the newly baptized. This had been the case in the early Church, being
mentioned by Chromatius of Aquileia around AD 400, complete with its
eschatological dimension.[49] The *Stowe Missal* is the first service book
in which the rubrics direct the clergy to use the robe to cover the brow
of the head.[50] Thus we find the formula used even in the *Manual* was
directed to one end, but it was confused, as it were, with the second
role. Whether or not Cranmer was aware of the historical development
(there is no mention of the issue in his commonplaces), by moving the
formula to the earlier position he freed the original symbolism from this
confusion.

The two formulas accompanying the ritual actions show a link with
the work of the *Rationale of Ceremonial*. The innocence of life in the
formula for the white garment is a more explicit version of what is to
be found in the *Manual*, and is very similar to the description of this
ceremony in the *Rationale*, while the explanation of the anointing as
being the unction of the Holy Spirit is, as far as I have been able to
discover, unique to 1549 and the *Rationale*. This document was never
formally submitted for authorization, unlike the King's Book which was

49 '"Let your garments be white at all times and let your head never be lacking oil": We
never lose our white garments if we keep whole and entire the grace of baptism. We never
lose the oil from our head, if we keep safe the saving chrism we received, and so we shall
not be put to shame on the day of judgement.' (*Chromatius of Aquileia, Sermons*, ed.
J. Lemarié, Sources chrétiennes, 154, 164, 2 vols [Paris: Cerf, 1969–71], Sermon 14.4,
Vol. 1, p. 244.)
50 Whitaker, *Documents of the Baptismal Liturgy*, p. 282.

produced at the same time. Cranmer himself was busy on the latter; he had no formal connection with the work of the *Rationale*, though no doubt he was aware of its contents. Given that the *Rationale* was never authorized in the same way as the King's Book, its use by Cranmer would suggest an attempt to be politically sensitive to the conservative groups in the country. In the light of this, we should also give due weight to the similarity of the formula for the signing in 1549 to the explanation of the ceremony in the *Rationale*.

How did Cranmer want us to understand these ceremonies? In the first, we are told most explicitly, that the ceremony is a token and sign of the innocency of baptism and the Christian life. In other words this is simply a didactic aid. In the second formula one might suppose that we have here a performative speech-act: that the anointing should convey the gift of the Holy Spirit. However, it is best to understand the text within the general logic of Cranmer's theology: that this is 'sacramental' and therefore figurative, and the anointing with the Holy Spirit by God is separate and distinct from the physical anointing, though symbolized by it.

The themes of both these ceremonial actions are not lost in the 1552 Prayer Book but are taken into the Prayer of Thanksgiving, which speaks of regeneration by the Holy Spirit, and the Christian life as dead to sin and living to righteousness. However, it is strange that the picture of putting on Christ, which is not only biblical but often mentioned in the *Defence*, should disappear.

q. The final exhortation

1549

FORASMUCH as these children have promised by you to forsake the devill and al his workes, to beleve in God, and to serve him: you must remember that it is your partes and duetie to see that these infantes be taught, so soone as they shalbe able to learne, what a solemne vowe, promyse, and profession, they have made by you. And that they maye knowe these thynges the better: ye shall call upon them to heare sermons, and chiefly you shal provide

*AS You should instruct him in this or send him to church so that he can be instructed, also look to it that he be taught the ten commandments, the Christian creed, the Our Father and what is necessary to know and believe for salvation.

Also you should admonish and keep him in an honourable Christian life and behaviour. [51]

KB And we again, upon our part, ought . . . to remember and keep the promise that we in baptism have made to Almighty God, that is, to believe only in him, only to serve and obey him, to forsake all sin, and the works of Satan, to mortify our affections of the flesh, and to live after the Spirit in new life. Of which promise and covenant by us made to God, St Paul putteth us in remembrance saying, Know ye not that all we which are baptized in Jesus Christ are baptized to die with him? For we be buried with him by baptism to die, that likewise as Christ was raised up from death by the glory of his Father, even so we should walk in a new life . . . and to walk and proceed in a new life of grace and the Spirit.

that thei may learne the Crede, the Lordes prayer, and the ten commaundementes, in thenglish tounge: and all other thinges which a christian manne ought to knowe and beleve to his soules health. And that these children may be vertuously brought up to leade a godly and christian life; remembring always that Baptisme doeth represent unto us our profession, which is to folow thexample of our Saviour Christe, and to be made lyke unto him, that as he dyed and rose againe for us: so should we (whiche are Baptised) dye from synne, and ryse agayne unto righteousnesse, continually mortifying all our evyll and corrupte affeccions, and dayly procedyng in all vertue and godlynesse of lyvyng.

---

51 Solches wolt es unterrichten oder das es unterricht werde zur kirchen halten, auch dran sein, das es gelert werde, die zehen gebot gottes, den christen glauben, vater unser und was zur seligkeit zu wissen und zu gleuben von nöten. Woltet es auch zu einem erbaren christlichen leben und wandel vermanen und anhalten.

The Sarum *Manual* had included provision for an exhortation at the end of the service in which the godparents are told to teach the child the Lord's Prayer, the Hail Mary and the Creed and to see that it is confirmed when the bishop is in the vicinity. The chrisom cloth must be returned to the church. The instructions are all very practical, and these are continued in a rubric at the end of the 1549 service (simplified in 1552 when the chrisom is no longer relevant). The main difference is that confirmation is to be sought, not when the bishop is in the area, but when the child can say the Creed, the Lord's Prayer and the Ten Commandments and be instructed in the Catechism. Didacticism, but also personal appropriation of the faith, are now to the fore.

In addition to this set of general instructions, Cranmer provides a formal exhortation to the godparents. The formal composition, as opposed to instructions which can be delivered in an informal or extempore fashion, suggests a different status, as does the fact that much of the material is based on the Albertine Saxony exhortation at the font. The promises made on the child's behalf are binding on it, and the godparents are entrusted with the role of ensuring that the child be taught the meaning of their promise and be brought up to live a Christian life. It is by no means a definition of baptism, but it is an important element of it, that 'baptism doth represent unto us our profession, which is to follow the example of our Saviour Christ'. At this point in the service the divine promise is passed over in silence, for the word of promise has already been definitively spoken in the sacrament. Now Cranmer concentrates on the human response to the divine promise. The formal part of the service finishes with the theme that baptism looks forward to a life of rejecting evil and following Christ in the way of righteousness.[52]

---

52 The practical way in which this might have been envisaged is described by B.D. Spinks, 'Cranmer, Baptism and Christian Nurture; or, Toronto Revisited', *Studia Liturgica*, 32 (2002), pp. 98–110.

CONCLUSION

This study of Cranmer began as the first chapter of the history of the Anglican baptismal liturgy up to the present day. But I quickly discovered that there was a rich vein of material to be mined, and that any discussion of Cranmer's sacramental theology would be incomplete without detailed discussion of the eucharist as well. In the event this book covers by no means all that we know of these services in the two Prayer Books (and ends without any discussion of their later history), and opens further questions still to be explored. The old model of Cranmer's theological development, that he moved through a number of discrete positions – traditional, Lutheran, Reformed – can no longer be seen as a helpful picture, but the new portrait as presented here is by no means complete. This work has identified an early interest in sacrament as sign in the late 1530s and moves in his sacramental theology in the mid 1540s which come to fruition in his understanding of the eucharist only on the eve of the first Prayer Book. There is evidence presented here for a distinctive position in around 1547. But all this needs to be explored further to understand Cranmer fully.

But much has been usefully described here. As for the liturgy, its historical development has been laid bare in more than mere extra detail. The identification of the baptism service with the Lutheran rites rather than with a revision of Sarum, and its subsequent reshaping to bolster a Reformed theology, is of major significance in understanding the history of the service and indeed of the whole Prayer Book. The influence of Hermann has been diminished, but that of the whole debate over the Cologne reforms has been magnified and its effects on England, in at least one small way, identified. The debate on consecration had a marked effect on the *Order of the Communion* and on the 1549 Prayer Book, even though Cranmer had abandoned that approach by the autumn of 1548. The liturgy had evolved over a number of years before it was published, and carried with it evidence of the earlier stages and principles. I approached the history of the 1549 Prayer Book intensely sceptical of the idea that it may also have within it an attempt at compromise and consensus. I am now won over to that approach, although I believe that the consensus had already collapsed by the time it was published. Likewise, the 1552 Prayer Book was unable to hold together the various wings of the Reformed party. Just as Bucer was disenchanted over the theology of the eucharistic presence of Christ, so Martyr was offended by the sacramental theology implicit in the baptism service. Cranmer's fellow reformers had to acknowledge his independent mind when they met it.

The theological integrity of the Prayer Book is admirable, and evidence of the close personal attention of the Archbishop himself. Occasionally the great man nodded: in baptism the theme of 'receiving' the child is flawed theologically, and the retention of the double exhortations, the second one based on the move to the font which was excised in 1552, produces a somewhat inconsequential structure. In the eucharist the paired options of the Thanksgiving prayer and the Prayer of Oblation after communion, and the sequence of confession and absolution, Sanctus, Prayer of Humble Access and Invocation prayer suggest that it was not easy to fit in all the material Cranmer had to hand. But the text of the Invocation prayer in the eucharist is perhaps one of the greatest pieces of liturgical prose ever written, magnificently setting out the saving death of Christ of which the bread and wine were a sacramental sign. That text, in various revisions, has remained popular down to our own time.

The popularity of the Prayer Book is broad: the eucharist (though admittedly less the baptism service), morning and evening prayer and the marriage service have all fostered affection and spiritual depth down the centuries with familiar phrases and musical settings which are embedded deep in the Anglican religious psyche. There is always warmth felt for Cranmer himself, the great craftsman of liturgical prose and perhaps the most sensitive personality to emerge from the pages of a turbulent chapter of England's history.

And Cranmer is recognized as a theologian in his own right, not merely imitative of others, but with his own concerns and priorities arising out of the debates and experience of his archiepiscopate. In particular his concentration on the sacrament as sign rather than as seal of grace may seem weak in the context of his time, but it carried certain particular strengths which must not be ignored. People often talk of someone having a 'high' or 'low' sacramental theology, and it seems that those terms are given according to the prominence of the notion of the efficacy or instrumentality of the sacrament in the grace given to the recipient. Cranmer's sacramental theology would be, on that scale, 'low'. But that is not an adequate appreciation of what he has achieved. Rather his theology is coherent, prominent in what in the twentieth century we would call spirituality, and able to speak of the grace of God with a clarity and immediacy lacking in many other theologies of the time. His theology has its weaknesses, but any definition of what a 'high' sacramental theology means has to be able to include Cranmer among its exponents.

BIBLIOGRAPHY

UNPUBLISHED MANUSCRIPTS

Bucer to Bonner, 4 September 1548, Corpus Christi College Cambridge (CCCC), MS 113, pp. 315–24.
Collectanea satis copiosa, British Library (BL), Cotton MS Cleop. E.VI.
Cranmer's 'Great Commonplaces', BL, MSS Royal 7B XI, 7B XII.
'Croydon Commentary', CCCC, MS 104.
De re sacramentaria, CCCC, MS 102, pp. 151–93.
Of the sacrament of Thankesgeving: a short Treaties of Peter Martir's making, BL, MS Royal 17 C V.
Orders and Regulations for an Earl's House, Bodleian Library, MS Eng. Hist. b.208, fols 15–22.
Questiones de missa cum responcionibus eisdem, Bodleian Library, MS Add. C.197, fols 65–7$^\text{v}$.

BOOKS WITH CRANMER'S MARGINALIA

Ambrosius, *Opera omnia*, 3 vols (Basle: A. Petri, 1516), BL, press mark 1355.k. 9.
Augustinus, *Omnium operum primus (-decimus) tomus*, 10 vols (Paris: Chevellonii, 1531–32), BL, press mark C. 79. c.1.

PRIMARY MATERIAL

Aless, A., *Of the auctorite of the word of God agaynst the bisshop of London* (Leipzig?, 1537?).
——, *A treatise concernynge generalle councilles, the bisshopes of Rome and the clergy* (London: Berthelet, 1538).
Ambrose, *De sacramentis*, ed. B. Botte, *Des Sacrements, des mystères, explication du symbole* (Paris: Cerf, 1980; 2nd edn).
'Articles Ordained by King Henry VII for the Regulation of his Household', 1494, in *A Collection of Ordinances and Regulations for the government of the Royal Household, made in Divers Reigns from King Edward III to King William and Queen Mary, also Receipts in Ancient Cookery* (London: Society of Antiquaries, 1790), pp. 103–33.
Bale, J., *A declaration of Edmonde Bonners articles concerning the cleargye of London dyocese* (London: Jhon Tysdall, for Frauncys Coldocke, 1561).
Biel, G., *Canonis Missae Expositio*, ed. H.A. Oberman and W.J. Courtenay, 4 vols (Wiesbaden: Franz Steiner, 1963).
Bonner, R., *A Treatyse of the ryght honourynge and wourshyppyng of our Saviour Jesus Christe in the sacrament of breade and wyne . . .* (London: W. Lynne, 1548).
Bradford, J., *Writings of Bradford*, ed. A Townsend, Parker Society (PS), 2 vols (Cambridge: Cambridge University Press, 1848, 1853).

Bray, G. (ed.), *Tudor Church Reform: The Henrician Canons of 1535 and the Reformatio Legum Ecclesiasticarum*, Church of England Record Society, 8 (Woodbridge: Boydell Press, 2000).

Breward, I. (ed.), *Westminster Directory*, Grove Liturgical Studies, 21 (Bramcote: Grove Books, 1980).

Brewer, J.S. *et al.* (eds), *Letters and Papers, Foreign and Domestic, of the Reign of Henry VIII, 1509–47*, 21 vols and 2 vols Addenda (London: HMSO, 1862–1932).

Brightman, F.E., *Liturgies Eastern and Western*, Vol. 1 only (Oxford: Clarendon Press, 1896).

Bucer, M., *Censura*, in E.C. Whitaker, (ed.), *Martin Bucer and the Book of Common Prayer*, Alcuin Club Collection, 55 (Great Wakering: Mayhew–McCrimmon, 1974).

——, *Constans Defensio ex sacra Scriptura . . . Deliberationis de Christiana Reformatione, quam Reverend. Hermannus Archiep. Colon. iam ante publicavit* (Geneva: P. & I. Chouët, 1613).

——, *Deutsche Schriften*, ed. R. Stupperich, *Martini Buceri Opera*, ser. 1 (Paris: Güttersloh, 1960–).

——, *Martini Buceri Scripta anglicana fere omnia iis etiam, quae hactenus vel nondum, vel sparsim, vel peregrino idiomate edita fuere a Conrado Huberto . . . collecta* (Basel: ex P. Pernae officina, 1577).

——, *Metaphrasis et enarratio in epistolam D. Pauli ad Romanos* (Basel: apud Petrum Pernam, 1562)

——, *Quid de baptismate infantium . . . est sentiendum* (Strasbourg: ex aedibus M. Apiarii, 1533).

Buchanan, C.O. (ed.), *Background Documents to Liturgical Revision 1547–1549*, Grove Liturgical Study, 35 (Bramcote: Grove Books, 1983).

Bullinger, H., *Decades*, ed. T. Harding, PS, 4 vols (Cambridge: Cambridge University Press, 1849–52).

Calendar of State Papers Domestic Edward VI, ed. C.S. Knighton (London: HMSO, 1992; rev. edn).

Calfhill, J., *Answer to John Martiall's Treatise of the Cross*, ed. R. Gibbings, PS (Cambridge: Cambridge University Press, 1846).

Calvin J., *Ioannis Calvini opera quae supersunt omnia*, eds W. Baum, E. Cunitz, E. Reuss, Corpus Reformatorum, Vols 29–87 (Berlin/Brunswick, 1863–1900).

——, *Institutes of the Christian Religion, 1536 edition*, trans. F.L. Battles (Grand Rapids, MI: Eerdmans, 1975).

Canones Concilii Provincialis Coloniensis . . . quibus adiectum est Encheiridion Christianae institutionis (Cologne, 1537).

Cardwell, E., *History of Conferences* (Oxford: Oxford University Press, 1849; 3rd edn).

Chromatius of Aquileia, *Sermons*, ed. J. Lemarié, Sources chrétiennes, 154, 164, 2 vols (Paris: Cerf, 1969–71).

Cologne Cathedral Chapter, *Antididagma, seu Christianae et Catholicae religionis per reverendos Canonicos metropolitanae Ecclesiae Coloniensis Propugnatio* (Louvain: S. Zassenus, 1544).

Coverdale, M., *The order that the churche and congregacion of Christe in Denmarke and in many places, countreis and cities in Germany doth use, not onelye at the holy supper of the Lorde, but also at the ministration of the blessed Sacrament of Baptisme and holy Wedlocke* (n.p., 1548?).

Cranmer, T., *Works*, ed. J.E. Cox, PS, 2 vols (Cambridge: Cambridge University Press, 1844, 1846).

——, *Cranmer's Liturgical Projects*, ed. J. Wickham Legg, Henry Bradshaw Society (HBS), 50 (London: Harrison & Sons, 1915).

——, *Cranmer's Catechism*, ed. D.G. Selwyn, Courtenay Library of Reformation Classics, 6 (Appleford: Sutton Courtenay Press, 1978).

Cranmer, T. and Bucer, M., *Martin Bucer und Thomas Cranmer: Annotationes in Octo*

Priora Capita Evangelii secundum Matthaeum, Croydon 1549, ed. H. Vogt (Frankfurt: Athenäum, 1972).

De sacramentis, ed. G.P. Jeanes, 'A Reformation Treatise on the Sacraments', *JTS*, n.s. 46 (1995), pp. 149–90.

Epistolae Tigurinae, ed. H. Robinson, PS (Cambridge: Cambridge University Press, 1847).

Erasmus, D., *Encheiridion militis Christiani*, ed. A.M. O'Donnell (Oxford: Oxford University Press, 1981).

First and Second Prayer Books of King Edward VI (London: J.M. Dent/Everyman, 1910).

Fisher, J., *Assertionis Lutherane Confutatio* (Antwerp: Hillenius, 1523).

——, *Defensio Regie Assertionis contra Babylonicam captivitatem* (Cologne: Quentel, 1525).

Fisher, J.D.C., *Christian Initiation, the Reformation Period*, Alcuin Club collection, 51 (London: SPCK, 1970).

Foxe, J., *Acts and Monuments*, ed. J. Pratt and J. Stoughton, 8 vols (London: Religious Tract Society, n.d.; 4th edn).

Frere, W.H. (ed.), *Visitation Articles and Injunctions of the Period of the Reformation*, Alcuin Club Collections, 14, 3 vols (London, New York: Longmans, Green, 1910).

Gararde, Fr (Gherit van der Goude), *The interpretacyon and sygnyfycacyon of the Masse . . . composed and ordeyned by frere Gararde frere mynoure of the ordre of the Observauntes* (London: Ro. Wyer, 1532).

Gardiner, S., *A detection of the devil's sophistrie* (London: John Herforde, 1546).

——, *Explication and Assertion of the True Catholique Fayth, touchyng the moost blessed sacrament of the aultar* (Rouen: Robert Caly, 1551), included in Cranmer's *Answer*. PS, I.

——, *Confutatio Cavillationum quibus sacrosanctum Eucharistiae Sacramentum, ab impiis Capernaitis, impeti solet, Authore Marco Antonio Constantio, Theologo Lovanensi.* (sic) (Paris: Jean de Roigny, 1552).

Gibson, T., *Declaracion of the Seremonies a nexid to the Sacrament of Baptyme, what they Sygnyffie and how we owght to understande them* (London?: James Nicholson?, 1537).

Gorham, G.C. (ed.), *Gleanings of a few Scattered Ears, during the Period of the Reformation* (London: Bell & Daldy, 1857).

Henry VIII, *Assertio septem sacramentorum* (London: in aedibus Pynsonianis, 1521).

Hermann V (von Wied), *Nostra Hermanni, Archiepiscopi Colon. et Principis Electoris, etc., Simplex ac Pia Deliberatio, qua ratione Christiana et in verbo Dei fundata Reformatio . . . instituenda sit* (Bonn: L. Mylius, 1545).

Hubert, F., *Die Strassburger Liturgischen Ordnungen in Zeitalter der Reformation* (Göttingen: Vandenhoek & Ruprecht, 1900).

Hutchinson, R., *Works*, ed. J. Bruce, PS (Cambridge: Cambridge University Press, 1842).

Jasper, R.C.D. and G.J. Cuming (eds), *Prayers of the Eucharist, Early and Reformed* (New York: Pueblo, 1987; 3rd edn).

John of Damascus, *De fide orthodoxa*, trans. J. LeFèvre (Paris: Henry Stephanus, 1507).

——, *Writings*, trans. F.H. Chase (New York: Fathers of the Church, c. 1958).

Jungmann, J.A., *The Mass of the Roman Rite*, trans. F.A. Brunner, 2 vols (New York: Benzinger Bros, 1951).

Kidd, B.J. (ed.), *Documents Illustrative of the Continental Reformation* (Oxford: Oxford University Press, 1911).

Langforde, B., 'Meditations in the Time of the Mass', in J. Wickham Legg, *Tracts on the Mass*, Henry Bradshaw Society, 27 (London: Harrison & Sons, 1904), pp. 17–29.

Laski, J., *Joannis a Lasco Opera tam edita quam inedita*, ed. A. Kuyper, 2 vols (Amsterdam: Muller, 1886).

Latimer, H., *Sermons*, ed. G.E. Corrie, PS (Cambridge: Cambridge University Press, 1844).

Liturgies: *The Two Liturgies AD 1549 and AD 1552 with other Documents set forth by Authority in the Reign of King Edward VI*, ed. J. Ketley, PS (Cambridge: Cambridge University Press, 1844).

Lloyd, C. (ed.), *Formularies of Faith put forth by Authority during the Reign of Henry VIII* (Oxford: Clarendon Press, 1825).

Luther, M., *D. Martin Luthers Werke: Kritische Gesamtausgabe*, ed. J.F.K. Knaake *et al.* (Weimar, 1833–).

——, *Luther's Works*, ed. J. Pelikan and Helmut Lehmann, 55 vols (Philadelphia, PA: Muhlenberg Press, 1955–)

Manuale ad Usum Percelebris Ecclesiae Sarisburiensis, ed. A.J. Collins, Henry Bradshaw Society, 91 (Chichester: Moore & Tillyer, 1958).

Martyr, P., *A Discourse or Treatise of Peter Martyr . . . concerning the Lord's Supper* (London: 'R. Stoughton' [Whitchurch], 1550).

——, *Disputatio de Eucharistiae Sacramento habita in celeberrima Universitate Oxoniensi* (Zurich: apud And. Gesnerum, 1552).

——, *Defensio Doctrinae Veteris et Apostolicae de Sacrosancto Eucharistiae Sacramento* (Zurich, 1559).

——, *The Commonplaces of the most famous and renowned divine doctor Peter Martyr*, trans. A. Marten (London: Henry Denham, 1583).

——, *Tractatio de Sacramento Eucharistiae habita in celeberrima Universitate Oxoniensi* (London, 1549).

Maskell, W., *Monumenta Ritualia Ecclesiae Anglicanae*, 3 vols (London: William Pickering, 1846–47).

Melanchthon, P., *Opera quae supersunt omnia*, eds C.G Bretschneider and H.E. Bindseil, Corpus Reformatorum, Vols. 1–28 (Berlin, Brunswick, 1834–).

Mirk, J., *Instructions for Parish Priests*, ed. G. Kristensson, Lund Studies in English, 49 (Lund: Gleerup, 1974).

Ordinaire des chrétiens (Paris: Iehan Petit, 1502).

Thordynary of crysten men (London: Wynken de Worde, 1506).

Original Letters Relative to the English Reformation, ed. H. Robinson, 2 vols, PS (Cambridge: Cambridge University Press, 1846–47).

Pilkington, J., *Works*, ed. J. Scholefield, PS (Cambridge: Cambridge University Press, 1842).

Rationale of Ceremonial, ed. C.S. Cobb, Alcuin Club collections, 18 (London: Longmans, Green, 1910).

Ridley, N., *Works*, ed. H. Christmas, PS (Cambridge: Cambridge University Press, 1841).

——, *A Brief Declaration of the Lord's Supper written by Nicholas Ridley*, ed. H.C.G. Moule (London: Seeley; New York: Thomas Whittaker, 1895).

Ryce, R. *The Right Institucion of baptisme sett forth by the Revd Father in Christ Herman Archbishop of Coleyne, translated by the unproffytable Servant of Christ Richard Ryce* (Ipswich: A. Scoloker, 1548).

Sehling, E. (ed.), *Die evangelischen Kirchenordnungen des xvi. Jahrhunderts* (Leipzig: 1902–).

Selwyn, D.G., 'A New Version of a Mid-sixteenth-century Vernacular Tract on the Eucharist: A Document of the Early Edwardian Reformation?' *JEH*, 39 (1988), pp. 217–29.

Smith, R., *A Confutation of a certain Book, called a Defence of the True and Catholic Doctrine of the Sacrament etc, set forth of late in the name of Thomas Archbishop of Canterbury* (Paris: Chaudière, 1550).

State Papers, Henry VIII: Letters and Papers Foreign and Domestic of the Reign of King Henry VIII, 21 vols (London: HMSO, 1920–).

Strype, J., *Ecclesiastical Memorials*, 3 vols in 6 (Oxford: Clarendon Press, 1822).

——, *Memorials of Archbishop Cranmer*, 3 vols and Appendix (Oxford: Ecclesiastical History Society, 1848–54).

Tyndale, W., *Works*, ed. H. Walter, PS, 3 vols (Cambridge: Cambridge University Press, 1848–50).

Whitaker, E.C., *Documents of the Baptismal Liturgy*, ed. M.E. Johnson (London: SPCK, 2003, 3rd edn).

Wriothesley, C., *A Chronicle of England during the reign of the Tudors from AD 1485–1559 by Charles Wriothesley, Windsor Herald*, ed. W.D. Hamilton, 2 vols (London: Camden Society, 1875, 1877).

Zurich Letters, ed. And trans. H. Robinson, PS, 3 vols (Cambridge: Cambridge University Press, 1842,47).

SECONDARY MATERIAL

Alexander, J.N. (ed.), *Time and Community* (Washington, DC: Pastoral Press, 1990).

Althaus, P., *The Theology of Martin Luther*, trans. R.C. Schultz (Philadelphia, PA: Fortress Press, 1966).

Amos, N. Scott, 'Martin Bucer and the Revision of the 1549 Book of Common Prayer', *Reformation and Renaissance Review*, 2 (1999), pp. 107–26.

Anderson, M., 'Rhetoric and Reality: Peter Martyr and the English Reformation', *Sixteenth Century Journal*, 19 (1988), pp. 451–69.

Anon., 'Capitulum Coloniense: An Episode in the Reformation', *CQR*, 31 (January 1891), pp. 419–37.

Aston, M., *Faith and Fire* (London and Rio Grande: Hambledon Press, 1993).

Austin, J.L., *How to Do Things with Words* (Oxford: Oxford University Press, 1980; 2nd edn).

Ayris, P. and Selwyn, D. (eds), *Thomas Cranmer: Churchman and Scholar* (Woodbridge: Boydell Press, 1993).

Beesley, A., 'An Unpublished Source of the Book of Common Prayer: Peter Martyr Vermigli's *Adhortatio ad Coenam Domini Mysticam*', *JEH*, 19 (1968), pp. 83–8.

Bernard, G.W., 'The Making of Religious Policy, 1533–1546: Henry VIII and the Search for the Middle Way', *Historical Journal*, 41.2 (June 1998), pp. 321–49.

——, *The King's Reformation: Henry VII and the Remaking of the English Church* (New Haven, CT, and London: Yale University Press, 2005).

Black, P.M., 'Matthew Parker's Search for Cranmer's "Great Notable Written Books"', *The Library*, 5th ser. 29 (1974), pp. 312–22.

Boone Porter, H., 'Hispanic Influences on Worship in the English Tongue', in J.N. Alexander (ed.), *Time and Community* (Washington: Pastoral Press, 1990), pp. 171–84.

Bornert, R., *La Réforme protestante du culte à Strasbourg au XVIe siècle* (Leiden: Brill, 1981).

Bowers, R., 'The Vernacular Litany of 1544 during the Reign of Henry VIII', in G.W. Bernard and S.J. Gunn (eds), *Authority and Consent in Tudor England* (Aldershot: Ashgate, 2002), pp. 151–78.

Bradshaw, P.F., *The Anglican Ordinal* (London: SPCK, 1971).

Brigden, S., *London and the Reformation* (Oxford and New York: Clarendon Press, 1989).

Brightman, F.E., *The English Rite*, 2 vols (London: Rivington, 1915).

——, 'The New Prayer Book Examined', *CQR*, 104 (1927), pp. 219–52.

Bromiley, G.W., *Baptism and the Anglican Reformers* (London: Lutterworth Press, 1953).

——, *Thomas Cranmer, Theologian* (London: Lutterworth Press, 1956).

Brooks, P.N., *Thomas Cranmer's Doctrine of the Eucharist* (Basingstoke: Macmillan, 1992; 2nd edn).

Buchanan, C.O., *What did Cranmer Think he was Doing?*, Grove Liturgical Study, 7 (Bramcote: Grove Books, 1982; 2nd edn).

——, *Anglican Confirmation*, Grove Liturgical Study, 48 (Bramcote: Grove Books, 1986).

Buxton, R.F., *Eucharist and Institution Narrative*, Alcuin Club Collection, 58 (Great Wakering: Mayhew–McCrimmon, 1976).

Collinson, P., 'Thomas Cranmer', in G. Rowell (ed.), *The English Religious Tradition and the Genius of Anglicanism* (Wantage: Ikon Productions, 1992), pp. 79–104.

Corda, S., *Veritas Sacramenti: A Study in Vermigli's Doctrine of the Lord's Supper*, Zürcher Beiträge zur Reformationsgeschichte, 6 (Zurich: Theologischer Verlag, 1975).

Courtenay W.J., 'Cranmer as a Nominalist, *Sed contra*', *Harvard Theological Review*, 57 (1964), pp. 367–80.

Cressy, D., *Birth, Marriage and Death: Ritual, Religion and the Life-Cycle in Tudor and Stuart England* (Oxford: Oxford University Press, 1997).

Cuming, G., *A History of Anglican Liturgy* (London: Macmillan, 1982; 2nd edn).

——, *The Godly Order*, Alcuin Club collection, 65 (London: SPCK, 1983).

Dickens, A.G., *The English Reformation* (London: Batsford, 1989; 2nd edn).

Dix, G., *The Shape of the Liturgy* (Westminster: Dacre, 1945).

——, *Dixit Cranmer et non Timuit: A Supplement to Mr Timms* (Westminster: Dacre, 1948) (*CQR*, 145 [1948], pp. 145ff.; 146 [1948], pp. 44ff.).

Dowden, J., *The Workmanship of the Prayer Book* (London: Methuen, 1899).

——, *Further Studies in the Prayer Book* (London: Methuen, 1908).

Duff, E.G., *A Century of the English Book Trade* (London: The Bibliographical Society, 1948).

Duffy, E., *The Stripping of the Altars: Traditional Religion in England 1400–1580* (New Haven, CT, and London: Yale University Press, 1992).

——, 'Cranmer and Popular Religion', in Ayris and Selwyn (ed.), *Cranmer: Churchman and Scholar*, pp. 199–216.

——, *The Voices of Morebath: Reformation and Rebellion in an English Village* (New Haven, CT, and London: Yale University Press, 2001).

Dugmore, C.W., *The Mass and the English Reformers* (London: Macmillan, 1958).

Gasquet, F.A. and Bishop, E., *Edward VI and the Book of Common Prayer* (London: John Hodges, 1891; 2nd edn).

Gerrish, B.A., *Grace and Gratitude: The Eucharistic Theology of John Calvin* (Minneapolis, MN: Fortress Press and Edinburgh: T&T Clark, 1993).

Greaves, R.L., 'John Knox and the Covenant Tradition', *JEH*, 24 (1973), pp. 23–32.

Haigh, C., *English Reformations: Religion, Politics and Society under the Tudors* (Oxford: Clarendon Press, 1993).

Hall, B., *John à Lasco 1499–1560: A Pole in Reformation England* (London: Dr Williams Trust, 1971).

——, 'Cranmer, the Eucharist and the Foreign Divines', in Ayris and Selwyn, *Cranmer, Churchman and Scholar*, pp. 217–58.

Hatchett, M.J., 'Prayer Books', in S. Sykes and J. Booty (eds), *The Study of Anglicanism* (London: SPCK, 1988), pp. 121–33.

Heal, F., 'The English Reformation Revisited', *Ecclesiastical Law Journal*, 4 (1996), pp. 446–53.

——, *Reformation in Britain and Ireland* (Oxford: Oxford University Press, 2003).

Heylin, P., *Ecclesia Restaurata, or, the History of the Reformation of the Church of England*, ed. J.C. Robertson, 2 vols (Cambridge, Ecclesiastical History Society, 1849).

Hope (Hopf), C., 'Lutheran Influences on the Baptismal Services of the Anglican Prayer Book of 1549', in F. Hildebrand (ed.), '*And Other Pastors of thy Flock': A German Tribute to the Bishop of Chichester* (Cambridge: privately printed, 1942), pp. 61–100.

——, *Martin Bucer and the English Reformation* (Oxford: Basil Blackwell, 1946).

——, 'An English Version of Parts of Bucer's Reply to the Cologne *Antididagma* of 1544', *JTS*, n.s. 11 (1960), pp. 94–110.

Johnson, M. (ed.), *Thomas Cranmer: Essays in Commemoration of the 500th Anniversary of his Birth* (Durham: Turnstone, 1990).

Kreider, A., *English Chantries: The Road to Dissolution* (Cambridge, MA: Harvard University Press, 1979).

Lawrence, R., *An Attempt to Illustrate those Articles of the Church of England which the Calvinists improperly consider as Calvinistical, in eight Sermons*, Bampton Lectures, 1804 (Oxford: W. Baxter, 1838; 3rd edn).

Leaver, R.A., '*Goostly psalmes and spirituall songes': English and Dutch Metrical Psalms from Coverdale to Utenhove 1535–1566* (Oxford: Clarendon Press, 1991).

Lehmberg, S.E., *The Later Parliaments of Henry VIII, 1536–1547* (Cambridge: Cambridge University Press, 1977).

Leuenberger S., *Archbishop Cranmer's Immortal Bequest* (Grand Rapids, MI: Eerdmans, 1990).

Litten, J., *The English Way of Death: The Common Funeral since 1450* (London: Robert Hale, 1991).

MacCulloch, D., *Thomas Cranmer: A Life* (New Haven, CT, and London: Yale University Press, 1996).

——, *Tudor Church Militant: Edward VI and the Protestant Reformation* (London: Allen Lane, 1999).

Mason, A.J., *Thomas Cranmer* (London: Methuen, 1898).

McConica, J., *English Humanists and Reformation Politics under Henry VIII and Edward VI* (Oxford: Clarendon Press, 1968).

McGee, E.K., 'Cranmer and Nominalism', *Harvard Theological Review*, 57 (1964), pp. 189–216.

——, 'Cranmer's Nominalism Reaffirmed', *Harvard Theological Review*, 59 (1966), pp. 192–6.

McGrath, A., *Iustitia Dei*, 2 vols (Cambridge: Cambridge University Press, 1986).

McLelland, J.C., *The Visible Words of God: An Exposition of the Sacramental Theology of Peter Martyr Vermigli* (Edinburgh: Oliver & Boyd, 1957).

McLelland, J.C. and G.E. Duffield (eds), *The Life, Early Letters and Eucharistic Writings of Peter Martyr*, Courtenay Library of Reformation Classics, 5 (Abingdon: Sutton Courtenay Press, 1989).

McNair, P.M.J., 'Peter Martyr in England', in J.C. McLelland (ed.), *Peter Martyr Vermigli and Italian Reform* (Waterloo, Ontario: Wilfred Laurier University Press, 1980), pp. 85–105.

Møller, J.G., 'The Beginnings of Puritan Covenant Theology', *JEH*, 14 (1963), pp. 46–67.

Nichols, B., *Liturgical Hermeneutics* (Frankfurt am Main: Peter Lang, 1996).

Nijenhuis, W., 'Traces of a Lutheran eucharistic doctrine in Thomas Cranmer', in *Ecclesia Reformata: Studies on the Reformation* (Leiden: Brill, 1972), pp. 1–22.

Null, A., *Thomas Cranmer's Doctrine of Repentance* (Oxford: Oxford University Press, 2000).

Old, H.O., *The Shaping of the Reformed Baptismal Rite in the Sixteenth Century* (Grand Rapids, MI: Eerdmans, 1992).

Parker, T.M., review of Dugmore, *The Mass and the English Reformers*, *JTS*, n.s. 19 (1961), pp. 132–46.

Pollet, J.V., *Martin Bucer: Etudes sur la correspondance*, 2 vols (Paris: Presses Universitaires, 1958–62).

Porter, J.R., review of Richardson, *Cranmer Dixit et Contradixit*, *JTS*, n.s. 4 (1953), pp. 62–3.

Proctor, F. and Frere, W.H., *New History of the Book of Common Prayer* (London: Macmillan, 1905; 2nd edn, 3rd cor. Imp.).

Pruett, G.E., 'Thomas Cranmer's Progress in the Doctrine of the Eucharist, 1535–1548', *Historical Magazine of the Protestant Episcopal Church*, 45 (1976), pp. 439–58.

Raitt, J., 'Three Interrelated Principles in Calvin's Unique Doctrine of Infant Baptism', *Sixteenth Century Journal*, 11 (1980), pp. 51–61.

Ratcliff, E.C., *The Book of Common Prayer of the Church of England: its Making and Revisions 1549–1661* (London: SPCK, 1949).

——, 'The English Use of Eucharistic Consecration, 1548–1662' in A.H. Couratin and D.H. Tripp (eds), *Liturgical Studies* (London: SPCK, 1976), pp. 184–202.

Redworth, G., *In Defence of the Church Catholic: The Life of Stephen Gardiner* (Oxford: Basil Blackwell, 1990).

Rex, R., *The Theology of John Fisher* (Cambridge: Cambridge University Press, 1991).

——, *Henry VIII and the English Reformation* (Basingstoke: Macmillan, 1993).

Richardson, C., *Zwingli and Cranmer on the Eucharist: Cranmer Dixit et Contradixit* (Evanston, IL: Seabury-Weston Theological Seminary, 1949).

——, 'Cranmer and the Analysis of Eucharistic Doctrine', *JTS*, n.s. 16 (1965), pp. 421–37.

Ridley, J., *Thomas Cranmer* (Oxford: Clarendon Press, 1962).

Rorem, P., *The Medieval Development of Liturgical Symbolism*, Grove Liturgical Study, 47 (Bramcote: Grove Books, 1986).

Sawada, P.A., 'Two Anonymous Tudor Treatises on the General Council', *JEH*, 12 (1961), pp. 197–214.

Scarisbrick, J.J., *The Reformation and the English People* (Oxford: Basil Blackwell, 1984).

Selwyn, D.G., 'A Neglected Edition of Cranmer's Catechism', *JTS*, n.s. 15 (1964), pp. 76–90.

——, 'The Book of Doctrine, the Lords' debate and the first Prayer Book of Edward VI: An Abortive Attempt at Doctrinal Consensus?', *JTS*, n.s. 40 (1989), pp. 446–80.

——, 'Cranmer's Writings: A Bibliographical Survey', in Ayris and Selwyn, *Cranmer: Churchman and Scholar*, pp. 281–302.

——, *The Library of Thomas Cranmer* (Oxford: Oxford Bibliographical Society, 1996).

Spinks, B.D., 'Luther's *Taufbüchlein*', *Liturgical Review* (part 1) 5 (1975), pp. 17–20; (part 2) 6 (1976), pp. 13–21.

——, *From the Lord and 'The Best Reformed Churches': A Study of the Eucharistic Liturgy in the English Puritan and Separatist Traditions, 1550–1633* (Bibliotheca 'Ephemerides Liturgicae', Subsidia, 33; Rome: CLV, 1984).

——, 'And With thy Holy Spirite and Worde', in M. Johnson (ed.), *Thomas Cranmer*, pp. 94–102.

——, *The Western Use and Abuse of Eastern Liturgical Traditions* (Rome: Centre for Indian and Inter-Religious Studies, and Bangalore: Dahram Publications, 1992).

——, 'Treasures Old and New: A Look at Some of Thomas Cranmer's Methods of Liturgical Compilation' in Ayris and Selwyn (eds), *Cranmer: Churchman and Scholar*, pp. 175–88.

——, 'Luther's Timely Theology of Unilateral Baptism', *Lutheran Quarterly*, 9 (1995), pp. 23–45.

——, 'Calvin's Baptismal Theology and the Making of the Strasbourg and Genevan Baptismal Liturgies 1540 and 1542,' *SJT*, 48 (1995), pp. 55–78.

——, 'Cranmer, Baptism and Christian Nurture; or, Toronto Revisited', *Studia Liturgica*, 32 (2002), pp. 98–110.

——, *Reformation and Modern Rituals and Theologies of Baptism: From Luther to Contemporary Practices* (Aldershot: Ashgate, 2006).

Stephens, W.P., *The Holy Spirit in the Theology of Martin Bucer* (Cambridge: Cambridge University Press, 1970).

——, *The Theology of Huldrych Zwingli* (Oxford: Oxford University Press, 1986).

Strudwick, V., 'English Fears of Social Disintegration and Modes of Control, 1533–1611', in R. Griffiths (ed.), *The Bible in the Renaissance* (Aldershot: Ashgate, 2001), pp. 133–49.

Sykes, S., 'Baptisme doth represente unto us oure profession', in M. Johnson (ed.), *Thomas Cranmer*, pp. 122–43.

Targoff, R., *Common Prayer: The Language of Public Devotion in Early Modern England* (Chicago, IL and London: University of Chicago Press, 2001).

Timms, G., 'Dixit Cranmer', Part 1, *CQR*, Vol. 143 (January–March 1947), pp. 217–34, and Part 2, Vol. 144 (April–June 1947), pp. 33–51; (also published separately; London: A.R. Mowbray, 1947).

Tjernagel, N.S., *Henry VIII and the Lutherans: A Study in Anglo-Lutheran Relations from 1521 to 1547* (St Louis, MO: Concordia, 1965).

Tomlinson, J.T., *The Great Parliamentary Debate in 1548 on the Lord's Supper* (London: J.F. Shaw, n.d.; 2nd edn)

——, *The Prayer Book Articles and Homilies* (London: Church Association, 1897).

Torrance, J.B., 'Covenant or Contract?' *SJT*, 23 (1970), pp. 51–76.

Trigg, J., *Baptism in the Theology of Martin Luther* (Leiden: E.J. Brill, 1994).

Vajta, V., *Luther on Worship* (Philadelphia, PA: Muhlenberg Press, 1958).

Walsh, K.J., 'Cranmer and the Fathers, especially in the *Defence*', *Journal of Religious History*, 11 (1980), pp. 227–47.

Warner G.F. and J.P. Gilson, *Catalogue of the Western Manuscripts in the Old Royal and King's Collections in the British Museum*, 4 vols (Oxford: Oxford University Press, 1921).

Weir, D.A., *The Origins of the Federal Theology in Sixteenth-Century Reformation Thought* (Oxford: Clarendon Press, 1990).

Whitaker, E.C., *The Baptismal Liturgy* (London: Faith Press, 1965; 1st edn; SPCK, 1981; 2nd edn).

Wilberforce, R.I., *The Doctrine of Holy Baptism* (London: John Murray, 1849).

Wilson-Kastner, P., 'Andreas Osiander's Probable Influence on Thomas Cranmer's Eucharistic Theology', *Sixteenth Century Journal*, 14 (1983), pp. 411–25.

Wright, D.F., 'Infant Baptism and the Christian Community' in D.F. Wright (ed.), *Martin Bucer: Reforming Church and Community* (Cambridge: Cambridge University Press, 1994), pp. 95–106.

UNPUBLISHED THESIS

Jeanes, G.P., 'Signs of God's Promise: Thomas Cranmer's Sacramental Theology and Baptismal Liturgy', unpublished doctoral thesis, University of Wales, Lampeter, 1998.

INDEX